# Millicent
# Fenwick

# Millicent Fenwick

## Her Way

*Amy Schapiro*

*Foreword by*
*Thomas H. Kean*

**Rutgers University Press**
New Brunswick, New Jersey, and London

**Library of Congress Cataloging-in-Publication Data**

Schapiro, Amy, 1970–
    Millicent Fenwick: her way / Amy Schapiro; foreword by Thomas H. Kean.
      p.   cm.
    ISBN 0-8135-3231-0 (cloth : alk. paper).
    1. Fenwick, Millicent. 2. Legislators—United States—biography. 3. Women
legislators—United States—Biography. 4. United States Congress. House—
Biography.   I. Title.
    E840.8.F46 S33 2003
    328.73'092—dc21

                                    2002012130

British Cataloging-in-Publication data for this book is available from the British
Library.

Excerpt from "Choruses from 'The Rock'" in *Collected Poems 1909–1962* by T. S.
Eliot, copyright © 1936 by Harcourt, Inc., copyright © 1964, 1963 by T. S. Eliot;
reprinted by permission of the publisher.

Manufactured in the United States of America

5/2003

*For Esta-Ann and Jack*

# Contents

# *Foreword*

You couldn't invent Millicent Fenwick. Lacey Davenport doesn't come close. She was unique. The best writers of fiction might have struggled to make her believable, but they would have failed.

She was an aristocrat of the kind Katharine Hepburn used to play in movies like *The Philadelphia Story*. Yet she had a particular affinity for the downtrodden, the poor, and the underprivileged. A liberal in her approach to most issues, she maintained a lifelong devotion to the Republican Party. Largely self-educated yet erudite, Millicent made her pipe a trademark. Although she ran for national office for the first time in her mid-sixties, it took only two years for her to become one of the best-known and -loved members of the United States Congress.

She was a national phenomenon and yet until now very little has been written about her, and nobody has pierced the veil that Millicent drew around her personal life. Because she was Millicent and because the press was in awe, she easily avoided questions she didn't want to answer. In an age of disclosure, I once heard a reporter ask, "Mrs. Fenwick, where does your money come from?" "The land, the land," she replied. There was no follow-up. She never answered questions about her failed marriage or even her family.

She was smart politically and not above a trick or two to achieve her ends. Once, when we were debating, she finished her comments and sat down. I rose to reply. About three minutes in, I had the sense nobody in the audience was paying attention. I looked over at Millicent. She had taken out her pipe and was slowly filling it with tobacco. The entire audience was watching, waiting to see if she was actually going to light it. They weren't paying attention to anything I was saying. Millicent won that debate.

She was the only really ambitious seventy-year-old I've ever met.

She loved serving in office, and whether in the state assembly or the United States Congress, she never ceased marveling that she had actually been chosen to represent the people. In legislative bodies she remained a maverick, but at home in Somerset County, she never went against the wishes of the county chairmen. And as much as she became a citizen of the world, she was never so much at peace as among her neighbors in Bernardsville. Beloved by many, she had few close friends.

Above all things, she hated hypocrisy and those who abused the public trust. Stubborn to a fault, she never betrayed her ideals or paid much attention to the polls. In the end, that was probably why she lost her last election, but the example she set and the way she conducted her life continue to stand as a model for all those who might want to pursue public life.

*Thomas H. Kean,*
*president of Drew University,*
*governor of New Jersey (1982–1990)*

# Preface

Millicent Fenwick's life spanned the twentieth century. In some ways her life mirrored the times, yet in other ways she was a woman ahead of her times—a pioneer. She continually challenged the status quo and succeeded. She rarely set goals for herself, nor did she visualize any barriers. She strolled along life's path, not knowing what her next step would be or where it might lead. Once Millicent made a decision she could not be derailed. She was a strong-willed, opinionated, independent woman who embodied charm, wit, and sophistication.

When Millicent Vernon Hammond was born in New York City on February 25, 1910, women did not have the right to vote, and would not for another ten years. If someone had told Millicent as a young woman that she would be elected to national office, she would have dismissed such a suggestion.

It was her passion to fight injustice that thrust her forward. Millicent always pointed to Hitler's terrorizing reign as the reason she became involved in politics. She was outraged at the possibility of government being the catalyst for social injustice. One can hardly argue with that point. But, as her son pointed out, it is likely that her passion for rectifying injustice can be traced to two additional factors: the injustices she confronted in her childhood household and the sense of noblesse oblige (a term she deplored) that characterized her upbringing.

For much of her eighty-two years Millicent commanded attention for her charisma, quick wit, impeccable English, and striking good looks. The press deemed her first congressional victory, in 1974, a "geriatric triumph."[1] Walter Cronkite dubbed her the "Conscience of Congress";[2] Henry Kissinger called her his "tormenter";[3] and Garry Trudeau immortalized her through the creation of his *Doonesbury* character Lacey Davenport, who often mimicked Fenwick's staunch stands on social issues and addressed everyone as "dear," just as Millicent did.

Millicent had the unique ability to transfer a sense of immediacy to her causes. Her knowledge and candidness appealed to the press and public alike. Several people interviewed for this book often referred to her mesmerizing effect on individuals and audiences. She had the power to convey her message in every medium, from one-on-one conversations and speeches to the radio and television airwaves.

Millicent stood tall, nearly six feet, trim, and she carried herself in an authoritative manner. She usually wore silk dresses or tailored designer suits and pulled her long silver hair off her face. Pearls almost always complemented her outfit. Her presentation seemed perfect and only improved when she opened her narrow mouth. She spoke an aristocratic dialect of English. Not quite the queen's tongue, but not colloquially American either. Her words dripped out slowly but firmly, captivating all within listening range. She had a certain mystique. Some were delighted by her, others scorned her. But few really knew her.

This book is the first attempt to unmask the life of Millicent Fenwick. For much of her life she hid her shortcomings from all but a relative few. With the invaluable cooperation of her son and numerous others, Millicent Fenwick's story is finally being told. Sadly, her son, Hugh Fenwick, did not live to see the publication of this book. Shortly before the manuscript was submitted to the publisher, I learned he had stage four lung cancer. Two months later, at the age of sixty-five, he passed away on March 16, 2002. Although he is no longer with us, I take comfort in the fact that he read, and liked, this manuscript.

*Note on nomenclature:* In the earlier chapters of this book, Millicent Hammond Fenwick is referred to simply as Millicent. She did not become a Fenwick until 1932, when she married Hugh McLeod Fenwick. So as not to confuse her husband with her son, Hugh Hammond Fenwick, I refer to the latter in the text as Hugo, which is the name his mother, relatives, and family friends used. Millicent's husband is referred to as Hugh. In this instance, last names are not used, so the reader will not be confused about which Fenwick is being referred to. Once Millicent becomes politically active and an elected official, she is referred to as Fenwick. In reality, few people called her by her first name. Most called her Mrs. Fenwick.

# Acknowledgments

Although writing is a solitary process, many people provided support along the way. I want to begin by thanking my college professor and thesis adviser, Charles McLaughlin, who started me down the path that led to this book. He encouraged his students to choose a research topic that "captivates you enough to write a book about it." I found that subject in Millicent Fenwick. Although I never met her, at the time I began my research she was still taking phone calls from strangers like me and responding to mail even though she was no longer a public servant. Her death shortly after my graduation caught me off guard and compelled me to drive from Washington, D.C., to New Jersey to attend her funeral. That day was the first time I met her son, Hugh (Hugo) Hammond Fenwick; it was also, though I didn't know it at the time, the beginning of this book. I went from being an unknown mourner to an invited guest at her home. Like so many others, Millicent Fenwick had touched my life too—little did I know how much.

Everyone I interviewed contributed to the shape of this book, and although their names are too numerous to mention here in the acknowledgments, I encourage readers to scan the interview list in the bibliography. In particular, I want to thank Hollis McLoughlin, one of the first people I interviewed, who generously gave his time and knowledge.

The most helpful person I spoke to was Hugo Fenwick. His willingness to talk for hours on end about his mother embodied every writer's dream. I am also grateful for his inclination to grant me the exclusive authorization rights to his mother's personal papers. That material, along with his cooperation and candor, made this book possible, as did the hospitality he and his wife, Joyce, showed me as I perused their attic. I cannot thank them enough for their support.

Thanks should also go to Bruce Martin, who granted me use of a research office at the Library of Congress. Without access to the library's vast resources and a quiet place to write, this book would still be a work in progress.

Writing a book leads to a greater appreciation of library staff, and I wish to acknowledge the many desk attendants and librarians in the Library of Congress's Adams Building, as well as Marion Kennedy and the other volunteers who staff the local history reading room at the Bernardsville Public Library. Thanks for your assistance.

In Superior, Wisconsin, I met librarian Teddie Meronek, whose insatiable interest in this book and vast knowledge of Superior and of the Hammond family's role in the early development of the city were invaluable. My only regret is that there was not more space for me to delve into that side of this story.

In Middleburg, Virginia, Cindy Fenton welcomed me to the Foxcroft campus and provided me with Millicent Fenwick's academic records. The Foxcroft material gave me a clearer sense of Millicent during her formative years.

To my friends, thank you for your support while I whittled away on this project, and in particular to the Crowley sisters, Jocelyn and Monica, and Rosemary DeMenno for their friendship over the years and willingness to read early drafts of this book. Thank you also to my mother, Esta-Ann; father, Jack; and brother, Steve. Their individual contributions aided me immensely.

To fellow writers Michael Carroll and Stephanie Griest: it was nice to have an outlet to share the discoveries and disappointments that one encounters during the writing process.

And I cannot forget Beth and Ed Murphy, Laura and Mitch Weiss, and Mara Rubin, who provided me with food and shelter during my trips to New York, and Stacy Soley, who did the same for my research trips to New England.

Erika Luedig in Rome helped me contact current and former members of the United Nations Food and Agricultural Organization. In Washington, Greg Harness at the U.S. Senate Library helped me find many useful sources.

My sincere thanks to the Gerald R. Ford Foundation for providing me with a research grant to travel to Ann Arbor, Michigan, and use the pristine Gerald R. Ford Library, one of the most efficient institutions I have had the pleasure of working in. Geir Gunderson and the rest of the staff's intimate knowledge of the collections led to the discovery of many vital documents, as did the declassification of material in preparation for my visit.

At Rutgers University there are many people to thank. First, Professor David Guston, for introducing me to Marlie Wasserman, director of

Rutgers University Press. To Marlie, for taking a chance on me and to Willa Speiser for her editorial prowess. At the Eagleton Institute of Politics, I want to thank Ruth Mandel and Kathy Kleeman, who shared their knowledge and files and managed to find a revealing thirty-year-old transcript of a state legislators' conference. Others who shared their personal files with me included Ray Bateman, Bill Canis, Jacqueline Levine, Susan Powers Lodge, Erin Ross and Jim Ross, and Sidney Frissell Stafford. I found the most useful source of information in the public domain in the Millicent Fenwick Papers housed in the Special Collections and University Archives at Rutgers University's Alexander Library, named for Millicent's cousin and close friend, Archibald Alexander.

This book would not have been possible without my parents' encouragement. Their faith in me was unwavering. They not only read early drafts, but my mother also did some last-minute research for me in New Jersey.

A special thanks to my colleagues at the Office of Community Oriented Policing Services, U.S. Department of Justice, and, in particular, to Veh Bezdikian, Dave Buchanan, Pam Cammarata, and Vonda Matthews, for their interest in and support of this project.

# Millicent
# Fenwick

# 1

## A Gilded

## Past

These men [the Stevenses] were the pioneers and founders who have made this country what it is. . . . No one who cannot go back as I can to the time when there were no railways, no ocean steamers, no telegraphs, no telephones, no armored navies, when the great West was yet unsettled, when this great empire was a wilderness,—cannot recall the primitive condition of things, and did not see it, can realize what the Stevens family had done for America.

—Abram S. Hewitt, former mayor of New York, remarks to the Stevens Institute of Technology alumni, 1897

On January 28, 1975, the Sheraton Park Hotel in Washington, D.C., swarmed with politicians, diplomats, and the press. They gathered for a dinner, sponsored by the Washington Press Club,* at which the newly elected congressional class of 1974 was introduced. This year was of particular interest because these new representatives had been voted into office as a result of the public backlash from the scandalous Watergate affair. Change was in the air. Never before had there been such a high turnover in Congress. The American people had spoken. They wanted new blood in the nation's capital, and they got it.

Six first-term members of Congress, including newly elected Senators John Glenn (D-Ohio) and Gary Hart (D-Colorado), were selected to address the thousand people at the event. Four of the six speakers were Democrats, two were Republicans, and only one was a woman.

As the guests were enjoying their meal, a tall, slender woman with long silver hair pulled back in a bun eased behind the podium. Her outfit

* The Washington Press Club merged with the National Press Club in 1985.

was well-tailored, like the woman herself. She stood with poise and began to speak.

At first only a few listened with interest, but it was not long before all eyes fixated on this woman. Many in attendance were unfamiliar with the freshman congresswoman standing before them. They did not expect much, but it did not take them long to learn that this sixty-four-year-old grandmother, Millicent Fenwick, was someone they would not soon forget.

As Fenwick spoke, her voice resonated with confidence, sincerity, and determination. She had the type of voice that could captivate any audience. Many have compared her voice to that of Katharine Hepburn. Both spoke slowly, enunciating every word. Rep. James Collins (R-Texas), one of Millicent's congressional colleagues, once told her that she was the most outstanding character he had ever known in Congress and that he was enthralled with her oratorical skills. "You will probably be remembered most for your command of the Queen's English," he told Millicent. "There is no one that can equal your vocabulary, pronunciation, and clear-cut presentation when you speak. You are the number-one voice of English in America." As it turned out, Collins was only partially right. Fenwick was known for her speaking prowess, but she is best remembered for many of her distinctive traits—such as smoking a pipe or her frugal nature, despite being a millionaire. But many also remember her determination to rid the world of injustice.

At the Washington Press Club dinner, Millicent shared one of her favorite anecdotes with the crowd. In a patrician manner, she carefully recounted one of her male colleague's objections to the Equal Rights Amendment when it was being debated in the New Jersey assembly in which she served. "He said he liked to think of women as kissable, cuddly, and smelling good." Without missing a beat Millicent responded in her aristocratic voice, "That's the way I feel about men. I only hope for your sake that you haven't been disappointed as often as I have."[1] When Millicent first uttered those words she was a junior member of the assembly, but she clearly had no qualms about speaking her mind, something her congressional colleagues would soon learn.

The rest of Millicent's remarks that evening were peppered with tales about her first few days as a member of Congress. She did not shy away from the fact that her Republican Party had just suffered a landslide loss in the November elections. Instead she capitalized on it. "As a Republican," Millicent said, she found the House of Representatives restful, since "we [Republicans] are very few and we know each other. We don't struggle for committee chairmanships. We never get knocked out, because we're not in."[2] Her sense of humor made Millicent an instant hit. Among the people whom she met that evening was Sen. George

McGovern (D-South Dakota). After hearing Millicent speak, the former Democratic presidential nominee introduced himself. "We spoke for a while," said McGovern, "and I came to a conclusion right then and there that she [Millicent] would be of special value to Congress—a Republican, but one with broad and humane views that would make her attractive to Republicans and Democrats."[3] After that night everyone knew who Representative Fenwick was. And they quickly learned that she was much more than the pipe-smoking grandmother she had been portrayed as. Her wit and feistiness charmed all and were to be reckoned with down the road.

———

Millicent commanded attention throughout her adult life. She was notable for her striking good looks and an overwhelming sense of compassion. She stood nearly six feet tall, was as lean as could be, and carried herself regally. Her figure helped her out of financial difficulties in the 1930s, when she landed work as a fashion model for *Harper's Bazaar* and *Vogue.*

On the surface Millicent led a fairy-tale life, but beneath the façade was a woman in pain. She dealt with her suffering in private, and as her life became more public she cleverly sidestepped questions that would unleash her sorrows. Millicent was not one to reflect openly. She lived to be eighty-two years old, yet in that time she had few confidantes. Her childhood was layered with personal injustices that later motivated her to champion causes of the less fortunate but also limited her ability to nurture her children and grandchildren.

Millicent's parents, Mary and Ogden Hammond, came from families entrenched in American history. Mary Hammond's maiden name was Mary Picton Stevens. She was a descendant of a host of men named John Stevens, whose achievements include the founding of Hoboken and of the Stevens Institute of Technology in Hoboken, as well as pioneering steam travel.[4] Ogden Hammond was the son of a Civil War general who helped develop Superior, Wisconsin.

Ogden was a tall, debonair fellow with a distinctive mustache, piercing brown eyes, and dark hair slicked back, replaced in time by a receding hairline. His wife resembled a porcelain doll. She had smooth, creamy skin, flowing brown hair, and a waist so slim it looked as if one could wrap the palms of one's hands around it. Mary and Ogden were introduced by one of Ogden's friends from Yale who lived in Bernardsville. When the couple married on April 8, 1907, Ogden was thirty-eight years old and Mary was just shy of her twenty-second birthday. On February 25, 1910, six weeks before their third anniversary, Mary and Ogden celebrated the birth of their second child, Millicent Vernon Hammond.

The first John Stevens (Millicent's great-great-great-grandfater) left

England in 1699, at the age of seventeen, to become an indentured servant to Barna Cosans in New York. Cosans was crown attorney, clerk of the royal council, registrar, and examiner in Chancery, which kept both Cosans and Stevens busy.[5] Stevens fulfilled his seven-year obligation to Cosans before moving across the Hudson River to New Jersey. His 1714 marriage to Ann Campbell produced nine children and gave rise to the Stevens historical legacy.

The Campbells, of Scottish descent, had been in New Jersey for years. Ann's father, John Campbell, owned a vast amount of land, which translated into wealth and political power. John Stevens soon embarked on a business partnership with his father-in-law; they acted as agents for land and speculated for property on their own behalf.

When John Campbell died, his daughter and son-in-law inherited nearly two thousand acres.[6] In colonial days landownership was directly linked to voting privileges. John Stevens became consumed with improving transportation—a cause his descendants also advocated and implemented—as a result of the difficulties he had in reaching his landholdings throughout the New Jersey area.

His son, also named John Stevens, became the patriarch of future generations of Stevens men who contributed to the development of steam travel both on land and sea. Because of the respect this Stevens commanded, he was known as "the Honourable [sic] John Stevens."[7] His recognition of overseas commerce as a vital element in America's growth was the catalyst for his small mercantile shipping fleet, which generated another source of wealth for the Stevens family.[8] Although the Honourable John started his career as a sea captain, he became active in local government as a result of his inherited property and the privileges associated with landownership. Because of his standing in the community he was called upon to help negotiate an Indian treaty in 1758, and he later was involved in settling the long dispute over the precise location of the New York–New Jersey border. Like his father, he was interested in transportation and served as a New Jersey road commissioner in 1765, paving the way for stagecoach travel and an early system of toll roads. Perhaps his most distinguished accomplishment came as a member of the Continental Congress when, as president of the state convention, he ratified the Constitution of the United States of America on behalf of New Jersey on December 11, 1787. New Jersey was the third state to do so.

During the Revolutionary War, the Honourable John experienced firsthand how difficult it was to traverse the landscape. As treasurer for the Jersey Colony, he traveled on horseback, weighed down by coffers containing hundreds of pounds of gold and silver coins needed to pay members of the Continental Congress and George Washington's troops. The Honourable John soon turned over this important task to his son,

Colonel John Stevens, who fulfilled the treasurer's duties from 1776 to 1783. Colonel John was affectionately referred to as the trusted "Treasurer on Horseback."[9]

Colonel John's parents were the Honourable John Stevens and Elizabeth Alexander Stevens. She was the daughter of James and Mary Spratt Alexander. It was rumored that Mary Spratt's parents, Jack and Maria De Peyster Spratt, inspired the rhyme "Jack Spratt would eat no fat, his wife would eat no lean, and so between them both, you see, they wiped the platter clean."

Colonel John did more than keep the troops paid. After the war, he revolutionized the worlds of commerce and transportation as a pioneer in steam engines, steamships, and railroad locomotives. Through these accomplishments, the erstwhile "Treasurer on Horseback" became more widely known as the "father of the American railway."[10] In 1815, Colonel John successfully lobbied the New Jersey legislature to grant him the first railroad charter in America, the purpose of which was to erect a railway between Trenton and New Brunswick. Spending his own money, Stevens in 1825 constructed the first steam-powered American locomotive and a circular track on his Hoboken property. Five years later his sons Robert and Edwin became president and treasurer of the Camden and Amboy Railroad, which had a monopoly on travel between Philadelphia and New York. In 1838, Colonel John died at the age of eighty-nine. "Like most inventors," wrote Ellsworth S. Grant in *American National Biography*, "John Stevens conceived imaginative yet practical ideas that were never carried out in his lifetime—an armored navy, a bridge across the Hudson, a vehicular tunnel under the Hudson, and an elevated railway system for New York."[11] Today, evidence of Colonel John's ingenuity can be seen at the Smithsonian Institution in Washington, D.C., where the oldest surviving American steam engine and boiler, which he built in 1804, are on display.

------------

Living up to the high standards and accomplishments of the Stevens family was an unspoken burden inherited by descendants such as Millicent Hammond Fenwick. Although Millicent's mother, a Stevens, died when Millicent was five years old, she had an intimate knowledge of her Stevens ancestors' numerous achievements. Her Stevens relatives told her tales about the family's dealings with prominent figures in their day—including George Washington, who in 1760 was a Stevens neighbor when they lived at 7 Broadway opposite Bowling Green in New York City, where the Stevens spent their winters; and Thomas Jefferson whose copy of Colonel John Stevens's 1787 pamphlet, *Observations on Government, including some Animadversions on Mr. Adams's Defence of the Constitutions of Government of the United States of America, and*

*Mr. De Lolme's Constitution of England,* now resides at the Library of Congress. This book is part of the collection that the United States bought from Thomas Jefferson to rebuild the library's stacks after the British burned the original holdings in 1814.

Colonel John's library rivaled Jefferson's in its vast array of subjects. Both men had a passion for horticulture, and Colonel John sought books from around the world to enhance his collections and ultimately a Hoboken beautification project and vegetable gardens. *Leading American Inventors,* published in 1912, noted, "In the home of this man [Colonel John Stevens] questions as wide as America were discussed day by day. . . . He was, moreover, a man of ample fortune, so that the talents of his children had generous and timely tilth, bringing to their best estate a fiber at once refined and strong."[12]

Colonel John's interests extended beyond the realm of property and politics. His efforts to achieve steam travel, and the fierce competition that steam travel sparked, resulted in the passage of the first United States patent law in 1790. He, along with three of his sons, designed, built, and operated the first seagoing steamship in the world, the *Phoenix,* which made its landmark voyage in 1809 from New York to Philadelphia. Before their feat, many doubted that a steamboat could make such a voyage and said, "They would as soon volunteer for that as for an expedition to the moon."[13]

Edwin A. Stevens, the Colonel's son, became the family business-man. He had a monopoly on transportation between Philadelphia and New York City—railroads, ferryboats, stagecoaches, and steamboats. "Holding a monopoly over one of the most heavily traveled routes in the country, the Camden and Amboy [railroad] became fabulously wealthy. Every railroad from the South and the West seeking to transport freight or passengers to New York City either had to pay duties and use the Camden and Amboy (plus the Stevens ferry line across the Hudson River) or else take a more circuitous route across New York State. Stevens's railroad was able to pay a 12 percent dividend every year, even during recessions that bankrupted other railroads."[14]

Another son of Colonel John was Robert Livingston Stevens, also an inventor, and the one who navigated the *Phoenix* on its first ocean voyage. He shared his father's passion for steam travel and engaged in several experiments related to steam engines. Through a collaboration with his father, he established the world's first steam ferry system; it ran between New York and Hoboken.[15] Also active in the family's railroad endeavors, Robert served as the president and chief engineer of the Camden and Amboy Railroad. He designed the T-shaped rail, which became the standard section on all American railroads, the hook-headed spike, and the iron tongue (now the fish plate), as well as the fastenings used to complete a rail joint.[16]

Prior to the family's success in its transportation endeavors, Colonel Stevens's wealth stemmed from his landholdings. In 1784, he purchased 689 acres of land called the "Isle of Hoboc" for $90,000 at an auction.[17] The title of the land dated to 1630, when three Indian chiefs sold the land to Michael Pauw.[18] Over the years, the property changed hands several times until 1663, when Governor Peter Stuyvesant granted the land to Nicholas Varlet. When Varlet died, the property was inherited by his wife, Anna Stuyvesant Bayard, the widow of Samuel Bayard and the sister of Peter Stuyvesant. The property remained in the Bayard family for more than a century until one of Bayard's descendants, William Bayard, a colonel in the British army during the Revolutionary War, fled to Canada and the state of New Jersey claimed his property, which it auctioned. Bayard was so distraught about the loss of his land that he became known as Weeping Willie.[19]

Weeping Willie's land, bought and developed by Colonel John, became Hoboken, New Jersey. Hoboken is generally associated with Frank Sinatra and Elysian Fields, where the first baseball game was played in 1846, but many years earlier, Hoboken was the center of the Stevens family. They owned Hoboken, including Elysian Fields, in every sense of the word, and incorporated the property into the Hoboken Land and Improvement Company (HLIC) in 1838, following the death of Colonel John. A century later, Millicent lived off income generated from the HLIC. The Hoboken land was valuable because it sat on the Hudson River directly across from New York City, which was just beginning to emerge as a financial metropolis.

Colonel John Stevens married Rachel Cox, the daughter of another prominent colonel in George Washington's army. Rachel and Colonel John had thirteen children. Their first child, John Cox Stevens, born in 1785, laid his claim to the Stevens family legacy by winning the first America's Cup sailing race in 1851. The race was named after his winning boat, *America*.

His brother, Edwin Augustus Stevens, also contributed to the Stevens legacy. When Edwin died in 1868 the Stevens family was the wealthiest family in America.[20] In his will, Edwin bequeathed nearly three-quarters of a million dollars to establish the Stevens Institute of Technology (SIT) in Hoboken. He envisioned an educational institution where students were trained for the innovations of the nineteenth century, primarily the railroad and steel industries. Prior to the establishment of SIT, universities were driven by the humanities, not by industrial endeavors. The Stevens family was acutely aware of the lack of skilled individuals to help them implement their inventive ideas, and SIT was created, in part, to fill this void.[21] Ironically, Edwin's wife, Martha Bayard Dod, was a descendant of Weeping Willie Bayard, the original owner of the land the Stevens family purchased and the present site of SIT.

The accomplishments of the Stevens family are still felt not only through SIT but also through the development of the T-shaped rail and hook-headed spike used on railroad tracks today and through the establishment of the prestigious New York Yacht Club, which was founded by John Cox Stevens.

Hoboken represented the nucleus of the family, and Villa Stevens was its castle. Villa Stevens was situated on the bank of the Hudson River, offering a spectacular view of Manhattan. The home was built by Colonel John in 1787. It was a magnificent edifice until it was consumed by flames in 1850. Its grandeur was surpassed only by that of its successor, Castle Point. The name originated from Colonel John's name for the land, "The Point of Castile."

When the house was rebuilt, the Stevens family put its ingenuity to work, and Colonel John's sons, Robert Livingston Stevens and Edwin Augustus Stevens, designed the new structure. They built a two-story brick house flanked by a tower that stood an additional two stories high. The brothers built walls two feet thick and coated them with stucco. There were thirty-one rooms, a chapel, and, in the center of the home, a grand rotunda with a stained-glass skylight. The floors were inlaid parquet, made of oak and multicolored woods arranged in geometric designs. The arched doorways were made of black walnut and had carvings etched above them. The home contained many family treasures, including generations of Stevens portraits, Chippendale cabinets, antique silver candelabras, Persian rugs, and fine glassware. Some of these cherished possessions and family portraits later adorned the walls of Millicent's home.

The elegance of Castle Point was admired by many, and its essence was captured in the *New York Times* magazine in 1897: "Perched on a high bluff and surrounded by an immense park of beautiful trees, between which can be seen sparkling the waters of the Hudson, stands Castle Point, the spacious mansion and estate of the Stevens family at Hoboken, New Jersey. No more attractive spot can be found near New York than this place, as it possesses many natural beauties. The site is an ideal one, as from its elevation it affords an extensive view of the majestic Hudson River. The park itself, composed of primeval oaks, luxuriant maples, and almost every other known species of tree peculiar to this locality, is a charming place in which to dream away the Summer afternoon. Added to these advantages is the mansion itself, which is built in the feudal Gothic style, and is large, roomy, and comfortable. It is filled from cellar to roof with rare old tapestry, family portraits, statues, objects of vertu [*sic*] of every conceivable shape and size, quaint antique furniture, and books in endless number."[22]

It was only natural that Mary Picton Stevens married Ogden Hammond in Hoboken. The ceremony, held at Trinity Church, was followed by a lavish reception at Castle Point. Mary's wedding was the last of many celebrated there. In 1911, Edwin Augustus Stevens's son, Edwin A. Stevens Jr., bequeathed Castle Point and an additional twenty-two acres of property to SIT, ending a family tradition of elegant parties and weddings hosted there.

For decades Castle Point remained the centerpiece of the SIT campus until 1959, when the administration razed it to build a modern structure. Five years earlier the alumni and the family had spent $100,000 renovating the home, complete with Stevens family heirlooms and a new roof. The school's rash decision to tear down Castle Point, after so much money had recently been invested in its preservation, caused a rift between the school and the Stevens descendants. Millicent and other family members voiced their distress over the school's decision to demolish the family home and stated that "they would have nothing to do with SIT."[23] And for a decade they did not.

It took ten years and the arrival of a new SIT employee, Richard Widdicombe, director of the school's library, to bridge the gap between the family and the school. As a result of Widdicombe's diplomatic demeanor and outreach to the Stevens descendants, a renewed relationship was established. Eventually, Millicent's anger cooled and she took an interest in the school, serving on its board of trustees for years, although in her will she left nothing to the school. Widdicombe observed that this was another example of her quirky personality and behavior.[24] Perhaps it was her retribution for the school's tearing down her family's beloved estate.

———

After Mary and Ogden were married they spent several months honeymooning in Europe before settling down in Superior, Wisconsin, which had been Ogden's home for the last fifteen years. His father, General John Henry Hammond, is remembered as "the father of Superior." His efforts helped transform the swampland at the southern base of Lake Superior into Superior, the thriving sister city of Duluth, Minnesota. Among his many claims to fame was his service in the Civil War, in which he served as General William Tecumseh Sherman's chief of staff and rose to the rank of general himself. He "was as brave as a lion—physically, mentally and morally—and was uncompromisingly honest," said his son John.[25]

Ogden Haggerty Hammond, born in Louisville, Kentucky, on October 13, 1869, was the second of six children born to General John Henry Hammond and Sophia Vernon Wolfe. Sophia was the daughter of Mary Vernon and Nathaniel Wolfe, a former attorney general for the state of Kentucky. Vernon, Millicent's middle name, came from her paternal great-grandmother Mary Vernon.

Although Ogden was born in Kentucky, his father traveled often—indulging his entrepreneurial nature. When Ogden was four years old, the Hammonds moved to Chicago, where his father had the misfortune of being a bank president during the Panic of 1873. In 1876, after Hammond's bank, and many others, folded, President Hayes appointed General Hammond the Inspector of Indian Agencies.

General Hammond's tenure in that position commanded newspaper headlines in the 1950s when his granddaughter discovered the missing Lewis and Clark papers inside his desk, which was stored in her St. Paul attic. A legal battle over ownership of the papers ensued between the federal government and the family. The family overcame its underdog status as the case wove its way through the court system. Eventually the case landed before the Supreme Court, where the family prevailed and maintained ownership of the papers, which it promptly sold. An anonymous buyer donated the papers to Yale University to complete that school's Lewis and Clark collection.

The most plausible conclusion about General Hammond's possession of those papers was traced to his tenure with the Indian Agency. During that time, the agency closed several regional offices, including one where William Clark, of the Lewis and Clark expedition, worked.

———

When Ogden and his younger brother, John, were boys, the General, as everyone called him including his wife, often took them to Superior on scouting trips, leaving Mrs. Hammond and her four daughters at home in St. Paul. They lived in the Forepaugh-Hammond mansion, now an elegant restaurant. Among the Hammonds' neighbors were a former governor and a judge.

In Superior, the General was a local hero. He contributed to Superior's success, plotting the early land allotments, building the first office building as well as many other edifices, and bringing major railways to the Great Lake region to capitalize on the natural harbor at the tip of Lake Superior. His success afforded him the opportunity to send his sons to the acclaimed Phillips Exeter Academy in New Hampshire and later to Yale University.

During Ogden's freshman year at Yale, in the spring of 1890, Ogden and John received a telegram from their father urging them to come home because he was gravely ill. Shortly thereafter, General Hammond died in the Forepaugh-Hammond House. The news of his death shook the Superior community, then numbering forty thousand. A special Pullman car transported dozens of Superior citizens to the funeral in St. Paul.[26]

A couple of years after his father died, Ogden graduated from Yale and moved to Superior, where his mother was living. Ogden entrenched himself in all aspects of Superior life. Within a few years he started an insurance business with his friend Phil Stratton. Their firm, Stratton & Hammond, handled general insurance, rentals, leases, and loans. Their business was likely buoyed by the numerous holdings the Hammond estate managed after the General died. At the time of his death, the General owned property valued at more than half a million dollars.[27]

Ogden, at the age of twenty-eight, earned the respect of his peers and wielded influence in the insurance field. Like his father, Ogden was active in civic affairs. He was a first lieutenant in the National Guard and was twice elected alderman from Superior's sixth ward. Both father and sons have streets named after them—Ogden Avenue, Hammond Avenue, and John Avenue—thanks to the General's early influence in plotting the west end of Superior. Hammond Avenue remains one of the town's main thoroughfares and is home to the Superior City Hall.

Ogden and Mary lived in Superior for a year before moving to the East Coast in 1908. Ogden purchased a town house on Manhattan's Upper East Side and an estate in Bernardsville, New Jersey, a small affluent township located in the majestic hills of New Jersey, forty miles west of New York City. The house and the land on which it stood had been in the Stevens family before and now became the Hammond family's homestead.

By the turn of the twentieth century Bernardsville had been discovered by the business and social elite. For them, Bernardsville was a summer refuge from New York City. Families of wealth and prestige populated the area; these included the Pfizer family, founders of the pharmaceutical empire; the Roeblings, known for designing and building the Brooklyn Bridge; the Dryden family, founders of Prudential Insurance Company; the Mars family, founders of the Mars candy company; and the politically, socially, and financially established Pyne, Stevens, Alexander, Brady, Livingston, Talmage, Ellsworth, Schley, and Wittpenn families. Many of the families were "financiers, who made their money out of the industrial growth, the railroads, the banking needs, the growth of the stock market, the development of minerals, timber, utilities, which attended the national growth and expansion of the latter 1800s."[28]

They discovered the beauty of the Somerset Hills, coupled with healthy pastures for their cattle. Many estates boasted horses, cows, chickens, and acres of vegetable gardens.

Bernardsville and its surrounding townships of Mendham, Bedminster, Pluckemin, Lamington, Gladstone, Peapack, and Far Hills, were referred to as the mountain colonies. The rolling Somerset Hills to which the term referred were far from being mountains, but the towns embodied affluence.

The early landowners built massive homes for a seasonal escape. Maintaining the property often required a dozen or more staff, but cost was not a concern. Some families had old money, others reaped the rewards of the industrial age. They gave lavish parties, played golf, rode horses, drove cars (before automobiles were a staple of daily life), participated in foxhunts, and flocked to elite country clubs.

The women showcased the latest fashions and adorned themselves with jewels. The men were privy to the latest technological advances long before the rest of the country could afford such luxury items as automobiles, telephones, electricity, and movie projectors. An influx of new money—corporate CEOs, Wall Street moguls, and bank executives—sought pristine property in Bernardsville. Each home was bigger than the next. Neighbors were a concept, not a vision. Decades later the serenity and privacy of the area remained intact and attracted Jacqueline Kennedy Onassis; two former U.S. Treasury secretaries—C. Douglas Dillon, who served during the Kennedy administration and later became chairman of New York's Metropolitan Museum of Art, and Nicholas Brady, who served during the first Bush presidency; Cyrus Vance, former U.S. secretary of state; Charles Scribner, president of Scribner & Sons publishing company; Henry Luce, founder of *Time* and *Life* magazines; Mike Tyson, boxing champion; Malcolm Forbes, publishing tycoon; and the king of Morocco.

It was in this world of wealth that Millicent was born and raised. Bernardsville was more than Millicent's hometown. It was her haven. She reveled in the lush open landscape that gave occasional glimpses of vast estates. Throughout her life, Bernardsville would be a safe harbor for her, and later for her son.

The Hammonds, like their peers, divided their time between their New York City town house and their Bernardsville home, a fifty-two-room brown-shingled mansion that looked more like a resort hotel than a house.[29] The family casually referred to it as their summer cottage. The estate was set on thirty-five acres that had been purchased by Millicent's great-uncle Ned (Edwin Augustus Stevens Jr.). Uncle Ned built the house in the late 1880s.[30] Inside it had everything from a boot room, sewing room, and pressing room, to a school room. Outside, a two-tiered porch wrapped around the upper and lower levels of the house.

A year after Mary and Ogden Hammond married they acquired the estate from Mr. Ellsworth, who had bought it from Uncle Ned. Ogden wasted no time in building a pool and adding a five-room wing to the house, bringing the number of rooms from the original forty-seven to the fifty-two that Millicent remembered. The Hammonds moved into the house just in time for the arrival of their first child, Mary, in 1908. Mary, two years older than Millicent, would become Millicent's closest confidante. As they grew older Mary was described as beautiful, Millicent as striking. Both girls were tall and lean. On occasion they were mistaken for twins.

A third child, Ogden Jr. (Oggie), born in 1912, rounded out the Hammond family. Millicent was two and a half when Oggie was born. After his birth Mary and Millicent were brought to the palatial St. Regis Hotel in New York City, where Oggie had been born, to see their baby brother for the first time. The girls were more impressed with the hotel than with Oggie. While he did not initially appear cute to his older sisters, he too grew into a handsome child and adult.

The three siblings had a formal upbringing that emphasized etiquette and diction. Their parents adhered to the old-fashioned philosophy that children should be seen but not heard. The Hammonds employed a staff of more than two dozen at the height of the summer season to maintain the Bernardsville estate and care for their children. The staff ranged from laundresses and chefs to tutors and nannies. Together they ran the household and outnumbered the family members. The Hammonds had a butler to answer the door, a footman to cater to Ogden's needs, two chefs to feed the family, a nanny to tend to the children, a tutor to teach them French, two laundresses to do the family's wash, and two upstairs maids and three downstairs maids to clean the family quarters, dining room, library, and parlor.

Outdoor staff included as many as four chauffeurs and nine gardeners/groundskeepers to do the yard work and cultivate the vegetable gardens. Three groundskeepers lived on the property and another six were day workers. The latter were seasonal employees because the Hammonds usually closed their Bernardsville home during the winter months, when they lived in Manhattan. When the weather warmed up, they returned to the New Jersey countryside. "In those days, nobody thought it very important if you missed a little bit of school," said Millicent, "so when the family wanted to move to Bernardsville, we'd leave New York. As long as Bernardsville stayed warm and we didn't have to heat the house— it took a ton of coal a day, which meant a man just standing there pushing in the coal and pulling out the ashes—we would stay in the country."[31]

Of the more than fifty rooms in the house, thirteen were for staff. Some staff members lived in the house, some above the stables, and a privileged few resided in one of the cottages on the property. One such couple was the Kocsises, who worked for the Hammond family for decades. Charlie Kocsis tended to the vegetable gardens and flowerbeds, and his wife, Katherine, tended to their home on the Hammond property and to the Kocsises' seven children. The Kocsises were Hungarian immigrants who met in New Jersey and were married in a Bernardsville church a year after the Hammonds were married. In 1910, the same year

Millicent was born, Charlie Kocsis started working for the Hammonds. Mrs. Kocsis had an open-door policy of which the Hammond children took full advantage. They loved her cooking and often sought her home-cooked meals, which she happily shared.[32]

Ogden's work on the East Coast reflected his earlier years in Superior. In New York, he started out as an insurance broker and expanded his business to include real estate. He was president of the Broadway Improvement Company, which had property holdings in Superior; president of the Hoboken Terminal Railway Company; and vice-president of the Hoboken Land and Improvement Company, a Stevens family business.

Ogden quickly acclimated to East Coast life and entered local politics. From 1912 to 1914 he served on the Bernards[ville] Borough Council. Within two years he was the committee chairman and a local political power. His political ambitions reached beyond the boundaries of Bernardsville and extended to the state Republican Party. In 1915, he was elected to a one-year term in the New Jersey assembly and was re-elected the following year. Ogden and Mary were visible on the political and social circuits, admired for their amicable personalities and genuine desire to help others—embodying their philanthropic backgrounds.

In Superior, General Hammond had built several buildings and helped plot much of the land, as Colonel John Stevens had done in Hoboken. Years later Ogden donated land for the main public library[33] and, in 1912, became instrumental in Superior's efforts to dedicate a park memorializing his father. He contributed funds to the project and attended the dedication ceremonies.[34] The Hammond Park is still enjoyed by residents today.

What Hammond and Stevens both realized early on was the potential of both towns. Hoboken and Superior became industrial centers, and during wartime both had bustling ports that were critical to America's war effort. Hoboken was known as the port of embarkation for soldiers headed to Europe during World Wars I and II, and Superior was a shipping hub for iron ore, coal, and other needed resources.

Another interesting parallel between the two families was their vested interest in railroads. General Hammond went to Superior with an extensive railway background. He had been president of the Manitoba and Southwestern Railway and helped organize the Eastern Railway of Minnesota, serving as its first president. His expertise proved instrumental to railroad expansion in the Great Lake region. Just as the Stevenses had been influential in developing the Camden and Amboy Railroad in New Jersey, Hammond was influential in acquiring the Duluth, South Shore, and Atlantic Railway to serve the Superior region. Hammond did not just speak of Superior's potential, he contributed to it, just as the Stevenses contributed to their region. The Stevens family was not only instrumental in bringing railroads to New Jersey; their inventiveness also contributed to the development of the locomotive, as it had steamships. They used their land to build a railroad track to experiment and perfect the locomotive.

Both Ogden and Mary were descendants of families who had been in America since colonial days. Mary's ancestors were English, and Ogden's were Huguenots. The similarities between the families are compelling. Colonel John Stevens developed Hoboken, and, in his day, transformed it into a popular escape for the masses living across the Hudson in New York City. The Stevens family investment in the city is still felt today through the Stevens Institute of Technology, as well as by the City Hall and public schools that occupy land donated by the Stevenses with the intent that the property be utilized for public purposes or revert back to the family.[35]

Millicent grew up with this historic and philanthropic heritage as a backdrop. Through hard work her ancestors accumulated massive wealth, but rather than spend their fortune frivolously they poured their funds into their local communities, setting an example for their children. Richard Widdicombe put it best when he said, "The Stevens family was not ostentatious and receded into the quiet recesses of America"[36] despite its historic efforts to improve modern life and transportation.

# 2

## Battle

## Cry

The cause of the sinking of the *Lusitania* was the illegal act of the Imperial German Government, acting through its instrument, the submarine commander, and violating a cherished and humane role observed, until this war, by even the bitterest antagonists.
—Judge Julius Mayer, United States District Court

Ironically, it was Mary Stevens Hammond's steadfast determination and philanthropic desire to aid victims of World War I that altered Millicent's future forever. In the spring of 1915, the Hammonds were preparing for a trans-Atlantic journey. War was raging overseas and Mary was anxious to help. She decided to embark on a humanitarian mission to help the Red Cross establish a hospital in France for the victims of the Great War. The United States was not yet in the war, and Mary, like much of the country, did not feel danger was imminent.

The British were embroiled in a naval race with the Germans that had begun with the crowning of Kaiser Friedrich Wilhelm Viktor Albert in 1888. By 1914, after more than twenty-five years of this tug-of-war, the British formally declared war against Germany. The British blockaded the North Sea, prompting the Germans to counter with their invisible killers, their U-boats, or submarines. Although the British had three times as many submarines as the Germans had, the German U-boats were better equipped, with stronger engines and greater range. Germany thought if it broke the blockade, it would win the war. Initially, when a German U-boat saw an enemy ship, it surfaced, fired a warning shot, and then boarded the ship to inspect the cargo. The crew was allowed to escape in lifeboats before the vessel was torpedoed.

By early 1915, with the land war dragging, the Germans changed their policy and began to sink ships without warning. The policy was not well known to their adversaries. It was in this hostile environment that the Hammonds planned to sail on the *Lusitania*, a premier luxury liner.

Rumors about the threat of German submarines started to circulate in the days leading up to the *Lusitania*'s departure from New York. But Mary was undeterred. She did not know that passengers such as Alfred Gwynne Vanderbilt, the thirty-seven-year-old millionaire and great-grandson of Commodore Vanderbilt, and Charles Frohman, the leading Broadway theatrical manager and producer, received anonymous notes warning them not to sail on the *Lusitania*. Neither heeded the warnings.

Days before Mary was supposed to embark on her journey she received a more personal warning from her Aunt Elsie. Aunt Elsie was a friend of Count Johann von Bernstorff, the German ambassador to the United States. Von Bernstorff had confided in Aunt Elsie and emphatically told her, "Do not let anyone you know get on the *Lusitania*." Aunt Elsie did not know why, nor did she want to. She did know that von Bernstorff meant what he said and that she had to warn the Hammonds. Rushing to Bernardsville, she shared the news with Mary. Leaning against a fireplace, Mary listened patiently as Aunt Elsie pleaded with her not to sail on the *Lusitania*.[1] Like the *Titanic* before it, the *Lusitania* was thought to be unsinkable.

Its speed, size (it was 790 feet), and magnificent accommodations gave the *Lusitania* its reputation as "a floating palace with all the luxuries of home." It was equipped with electricity, elevators, cabin telephones, and air-conditioning. The *Lusitania* boasted more modern conveniences than many hotels of its day. Electric controls were installed for steering, closing the watertight compartments, detecting fire, and controlling lifeboat davits for launching.

The thought that anything catastrophic could happen to the *Lusitania* seemed preposterous to Mary. When Aunt Elsie finished pleading her case, Mary laughed off her warning and declared, "I'm sailing on the *Lusitania*."[2] Ogden and his brother stayed up well into the night desperately trying to change Mary's mind, but to no avail. She was adamant about volunteering her services in Europe, and nothing could stop her. Mary was stubborn and determined, traits her daughter Millicent inherited. Although it meant leaving three young children at home, Mary was steadfast in her decision to sail on the *Lusitania*.

In the course of their conversation, Ogden's brother turned to Mary and asked, "Do you have a will?" She replied, "No, I haven't." To appease her worried brother-in-law, a lawyer, she said, "Why don't you draw one up for me and come aboard the *Lusitania* before she sails and

I'll sign it."[3] He obliged. On May 1, 1915, Mary signed a will that created a trust for each of her children and her unborn grandchildren. These trusts were set up with money Mary had inherited from her parents and from the Hoboken Land and Improvement Company.

Mary's father, John Stevens, had died when she was ten years old. He bled to death during an operation to remove a goiter. A few years later, his dashing wife, Mary Marshall McGuire, died, leaving their teen-age daughter, Mary Picton Stevens (Millicent's mother), parentless and a millionaire at the age of nineteen. Just as her parents had provided financially for her, she saw to it that her children would be provided for in the event of her death.

It is difficult to understand why Mary was so committed to traveling abroad despite the warnings. She did not seem concerned about the possibility of leaving her children to be raised without knowing their mother. Having lost her parents at an early age, it is surprising Mary was not more sensitive to the possibility of parental loss.

Clearly, it was Mary, not her husband, who had the final say about the trip. Ogden ignored his intuition and reluctantly gave in to his wife's wishes, not wanting her to make the trip alone. The Hammonds' voyage was to be the *Lusitania*'s 101st round-trip trans-Atlantic passage. It had safely crossed the Atlantic Ocean two hundred times; many people saw no reason to believe that this trip would be any different. But signs to the contrary had been surfacing for some time.

The Hammonds, along with more than 1,900 other passengers, set sail from New York City's Pier 54. Ogden's brother, John, was among the throngs of people who showed up for the 10 A.M. departure. While most reveled in the fanfare, John came with the grim purpose of getting Mary's signature on the will he had drawn up for her. She obliged, said her good-byes, and returned to the festivities.

Since the *Lusitania*'s first voyage in 1907, crowds had come to watch its departure. It was hailed as the largest movable object built by man. The *Lusitania* typically needed 5,000 tons of coal for its journey; 65,000 gallons of water per minute to keep the engines cool; and 250 miles of cable to supply electricity to everything from clocks and lamps to motors for cooking, dough-mixing, ice-cream freezing, and boot cleaning.[4] The ship represented the finest life had to offer.

The Hammonds and approximately 285 other passengers had booked first-class accommodations. These privileged passengers, like those on the *Titanic* just a few years earlier, were exposed to a world of elegance that other passengers heard about but did not experience. The two-level dining room where the Hammonds ate had a thirty-foot-tall domed arch. Corinthian columns and palm trees added to the splendid surroundings and led many to compare it to the Palace of Versailles.[5]

There was an equally grand lounge and music room where first-class passengers lingered and enjoyed conversation, cards, and cognac. The room boasted mahogany paneling, marble fireplaces, and plaster cherubs. The first-class cabins featured a large plush bedroom, sitting room, and bathroom. Some suites had their own dining room and pantry in case the passengers wished to dine in private.[6]

By the time the *Lusitania* set sail, the German embassy had caused quite a stir among journalists, who were quick to spot in several New York newspapers an advertisement paid for by the German embassy warning passengers not to sail on the *Lusitania* because "a state of war exists between Germany and her allies and Great Britain and her allies . . . and travellers sailing in the war zone . . . do so at their own risk."[7] This advertisement had been cleverly placed by Count von Bernstorff, Aunt Elsie's friend, on the same page as Cunard's notice of the *Lusitania*'s schedule. It was meant for the same audience.

The text of the advertisement was so startling the *New York Times* featured an article on page three about it, but the Cunard Line was skeptical about its origins, finding it difficult to believe it had been submitted by the German embassy, despite confirmations. Charles Sumner, a Cunard Line representative, dismissed the advertisement. "There's no risk to anyone, I can assure you, gentlemen. Everybody's safe on this crossing."[8]

What no one yet knew was that the U.S. tanker *Gulflight* had been torpedoed without warning the morning the *Lusitania* sailed, by a U-boat in the English Channel. Three Americans died. Despite the media frenzy evoked by the advertisement, many passengers were unaware of its existence. They had boarded the ship early in anticipation their departure, which was postponed for two hours. When the vessel finally pulled away from the pier shortly before 12:30 P.M. a fanfare erupted on board. The ship emitted three forceful blasts of her deep brass horn, drowning out the ship's band on deck. On the other side of the deck a choir was singing "The Star-Spangled Banner." People were waving and throwing confetti, and cameras were rolling, capturing the festive scene for posterity.[9] As the ship sailed down the Hudson River it passed Mary Hammond's childhood home, Castle Point at Hoboken.

The first six days of the voyage were relaxing and pleasant. The day before the ship was supposed to arrive at Liverpool, England, the Hammonds were enjoying afternoon tea in the ship's first-class lounge on what seemed to be another ordinary day at sea. The morning fog had lifted and the sun shone; as they approached the Irish coast, they could see land in the distance.

When the *Lusitania* was eleven miles south of the Old Head of Kinsale on Ireland's southern coast, the couple, still in the lounge, felt a vibration. To Ogden it "felt like a blow from a great hammer striking the ship. It seemed to be well forward on the starboard side."[10] Ogden immediately went on deck to see what had happened. He summoned one of the ship's officers and inquired about the shaking. Staff Captain Anderson reassured him that everything was fine and advised him to return to the lounge. He did. Ogden later condemned Anderson for "advising him not to be alarmed," adding, "I think the staff captain was to blame for giving this advice."[11] Had Anderson been straightforward with Ogden, the Hammonds could have better prepared for what lay ahead. The passengers and crew on the other side of the ship already knew. Some had seen a white streak barreling through the water. Terror paralyzed them, for they knew it was a torpedo.

Shortly after Ogden and Mary felt the initial jolt, there was another. Within moments the ship listed sharply to the starboard side. What neither the Hammonds nor the captain of the ship, William Turner, realized was that in the two and a half months since the Germans had issued their proclamation, ninety-one ships had been sunk by German mines or submarines—more than twenty of these having been torpedoed in the seven days since the *Lusitania* set sail from New York.[12] Not even Captain Turner was aware of the destruction. He was only aware of the threat.

Captain Turner received radio warnings from the British Admiralty about submarine activity off the southern coast of Ireland. He acknowledged the messages, doubled the number of men on watch duty, and had the lifeboats swung over the sides. But he did not implement the zigzag method suggested to thwart a submarine attack. He plowed forward at full speed, making his vessel an easy target because her course remained constant. The captain was anxious to reach English shores. He was confident in his ability; after all, he worked for E. H. Cunard, whose motto was, "We never lost a life."[13]

In an instant that motto changed forever. At 2:10 P.M. on May 7, 1915, Captain Schwieger and his U–20 submarine attacked the *Lusitania*. Captain Schwieger had patiently waited for this moment as his crew tracked the great ship's progress. The target was now in perfect range. They fired their last torpedo. The day before, Schwieger's crew had sunk two ships, the *Candidate* and the *Centurion*. In both cases, torpedoes were also fired without warning. Remarkably, neither incident produced casualties.[14]

That was not the case this time. The torpedo sliced into the *Lusitania*'s starboard side below the bridge, striking the boiler room and triggering an explosion that was initially thought to be a second torpedo. The ship never had a chance. Within eighteen minutes she disappeared into the sea.

Initially, an eerie calm hovered on deck as people scurried about searching for loved ones and digesting what happened. Gradually, the passengers became more anxious as they realized the severity of the situation. People clamored for life vests and for seats in lifeboats. Unlike the *Titanic*, which lacked a sufficient number of lifeboats for its passengers, the *Lusitania* was well equipped, in part due to the *Titanic*'s misfortunes. An investigation into the *Titanic*'s sinking identified a shortage of lifeboats as a reason for the high number of casualties, prompting regulations mandating ships to provide enough lifeboats for their passengers.

The *Lusitania* had forty-eight lifeboats. The sheer magnitude of the torpedo forced some lifeboats into the water on impact. Because of the ship's severe list the portside boats were swung so far inward that if released, they would rip against the ship, and on the starboard side the lifeboats were hanging so far outward that launching attempts were a challenge.

Adding to the problem was a lack of knowledge about emergency procedures. The staff had practiced some emergency exercises, but the passengers had not. Many did not even know how to wear their life jackets correctly, if they were lucky enough to have a life jacket. The life vests were kept in the cabins, and most passengers did not have one when the *Lusitania* was hit. Because the electricity had gone out, passengers had to crawl through darkness and water to reach their rooms, and thus their life vests. No life jackets were available on deck.

One passenger, Oliver Bernard, "had spent one to two years at sea in his youth and he knew how diligently emergency procedures were practiced on other ships. But aboard the *Lusitania* Bernard noticed that the drill always involved the same two boats, one on the starboard side, and one on the port side. At a signal crewmen clambered aboard the lifeboat, secured their life jackets, then got out again. They made no attempt to lower the boats, which seemed strange to Bernard. In his experience this was the riskiest part of all, and it required considerable discipline and practice to pay out the lines while maintaining control of the heavy boats as they descended, creaking and groaning, toward the water. Rough seas or strong winds made the job a nightmare in which crushed fingers and broken bones were commonplace. Could it be that the captain considered these hands so skilled that they needed no practice? Watching the boat crew Bernard doubted it. He questioned whether they could have handled this job in perfect conditions let alone anything remotely resembling heavy weather."[15] When other passengers had expressed similar concerns to Turner earlier in the voyage, he allayed their fears by reassuring them that a submarine could not compete with the sheer speed of the *Lusitania*.

The crew remained calm during the pandemonium, helping to ease the situation and preventing an even more chaotic nightmare. Crew members did their best to aid passengers, placing women and children in lifeboats as quickly as possible.

Because life jackets were not available on deck, Ogden wanted to return to his cabin to get some. "But, my wife refused to let me leave her," said Ogden. "We therefore walked towards the stern of the ship on the port side. . . . The [last] boat was only half full, about thirty-five passengers, men and women being equally divided."[16]

Ogden later recounted to a reporter what happened next, and the account appeared in the *New York Times* with the headline, "Ogden H. Hammond Struggled in Vain to Prevent Upsetting." "London, May 9— Ogden H. Hammond of New York, said:

"Some steward started to lower a boat and I put my wife and the other women in sight in and got in myself. A man at the bow let a rope slip through his hands while the man at stern paid out slowly.

"The situation was terrible. We were dropping to a perpendicular, and I caught a rope and tried to stop the boat from falling. My hands were torn to shreds, but the boat fell, and all in it were thrown in the water, a dense, struggling mass.

"I went down and down, with thirty people on top of me. I thought I never could come back and must have been partly unconscious, for I can only remember getting almost to the surface, sinking back again, and doing this three or four times. Then I was hauled into some boat, but no one else from the boat that fell was ever seen again."[17]

Everyone in Ogden and Mary's lifeboat plummeted sixty feet into the frigid water below, which was already littered with passengers. Cries for help permeated the air as people bobbed in the water and gasped for air. Passengers grabbed debris for survival. Some found chairs, kegs, and other pieces of wreckage to help them stay afloat. Ogden was lucky. "When I got my breath back," Ogden said, "I floated on an oar back out into the channel, and from there I watched the *Lusitania* go down, probably three-quarters of a mile away from me. . . . The *Lusitania* went down bow first, falling over on the starboard side, and I could see the decks almost at right angles, and just as she disappeared I heard this explosion."[18] Ogden was in the water for two and half hours before he was rescued by a lifeboat and transferred to a small trawler with 150 other passengers. A steamer named the *Flying Fish* retrieved the passengers from the trawler and brought them to land more than eight hours after the *Lusitania* sank. Ogden Hammond never saw his wife again.[19]

Many lifeboat passengers met a fate similar to the one that befell Mary Hammond. After the torpedo struck, the *Lusitania*'s sharp list steadily increased. The ship itself was still charging forward at full speed. It never slowed down, probably because of mechanical failure. The angle and speed of the ship and, reportedly, rotten lines and rusty gear, combined with Captain Turner's orders not to launch the lifeboats because of the dangerous list, made the situation hopeless for most passengers. Schwieger and his crew had successfully torpedoed a ship with nearly 2,000 innocent people on board. The German submarine was not only responsible for Mary Hammond's death, but also for the deaths of nearly 1,200 others, including 128 Americans and passengers from more than 20 other countries.

The sinking of the *Lusitania* dominated newspaper headlines and conversations. The world expressed shock at the callousness of the Germans, whose actions disrupted lives around the globe. This was the second sinking in three years of a ship proudly considered to be unsinkable. The *Lusitania* tragedy rekindled the horror of the *Titanic,* which hit an iceberg and sank in 1912. Surprisingly, the *Lusitania* crew and passengers had considerably less time to save themselves than those on the *Titanic.* The *Titanic* lingered above water for more than two hours before it slipped below the surface. The *Lusitania* floated for a mere eighteen minutes before the ship, heralded as "the Queen of the Seas," became part of the sea.

Once Ogden was rescued he was brought to Queenstown, Ireland. The *Lusitania* tragedy transformed the town into a makeshift morgue. Bodies were strewn everywhere. Survivors walked around in a daze looking at body after body trying to see if they recognized missing family or friends. Corpses were hard to identify because many were bloated or mutilated by birds and fish. About 140 unidentified victims were buried in mass graves at Queenstown. For months, bodies continued to wash ashore. They resembled skeletons more than people, and few could be identified beyond gender. Nine hundred passengers were never found.

As Ogden searched for Mary he prayed for news about her. At one point he was given a glimmer of hope. He was told a Mrs. Hammond was in a local hospital, and he rushed to her side. But it was not his Mrs. Hammond. A Canadian couple on board had shared his last name. That Mrs. Hammond survived, but her husband perished.

Ogden's emotional pain was matched by his physical pain. During the lifeboat's rapid descent Ogden had torn the skin off his hands as he tried to arrest the boat's plunge. It wasn't until he arrived in Dublin that he learned he had a broken rib and a neck injury. He spent three weeks recuperating in a Dublin hospital. Mary, like so many others, was never found. She died nine days before her thirtieth birthday. News of her death appeared in the *New York Times:* "Fifty New Yorkers Lost in First Cabin: Mrs. Hammond Separated from Husband and Drowned When Lifeboat Upset."

"Mrs. Ogden H. Hammond of 30 East Seventieth Street and Bernardsville, N.J., is thought to have been lost. She sailed with her husband, who is Secretary of the Standard Plungers Elevator Company, the Bernardsville National Bank and of several other institutions, and when the *Lusitania* was struck both of them, according to a cablegram from Mr. Hammond to his family, succeeded in getting into a lifeboat. But the boat capsized, the cablegram said, and Mr. Hammond was unable to reach his wife in the water. He was finally picked up and landed in Queenstown, but he was unable to find any trace of his wife. Mrs. Hammond's three children are at home in Bernardsville. Mrs. Hammond was a member of the Colony Club."[20]

Mary Picton Stevens Hammond did not live to see her children grow up or to see her middle child, Millicent, become a successful politician and popular public figure. Yet Mary's devotion to community service and volunteerism were characteristics her daughter embodied with enthusiasm.

On a global level the sinking of the *Lusitania* marked a diplomatic crossroads for American relations with the German Empire. So sensitive was the matter that it took President Wilson nearly a week to respond to Germany's blatant disregard for civilian life. The press portrayed the attack as premeditated murder, an act of the devil, a moral crisis, and a massacre. Closer to the core of the devastating event, mobs rioted and looted German-owned businesses in Queenstown. Many people the world over could not digest the reality and coldheartedness of Germany's actions, and they anxiously awaited America's response.

It came on May 13, 1915, when President Woodrow Wilson sent a message to the German government denouncing the sinking of the *Lusitania* and demanding disavowal, indemnity, and assurance that the crime would not be repeated. President Wilson had previously announced that Germany would be held to "a strict accountability." Berlin defied him by publishing an insulting counterwarning in American newspapers. American national pride suffered a humiliating blow.[21] As a result of the sinking of the *Lusitania,* many in the president's cabinet thought war was inevitable, but the American people did not. They wanted Wilson to condemn the attack through diplomatic channels without engaging in war. A week earlier American involvement in the war abroad had been a concept not contemplated by the American public. The torpedoing of the *Lusitania* changed that.

Two weeks went by before Wilson received an official response from Germany, arguing (falsely) that the *Lusitania* had carried weapons and was itself armed. Dudley Field Malone, the Collector of the Port of New York, later testified, "The *Lusitania* was inspected before sailing, as is customary. No guns were found, mounted or unmounted, and the vessel sailed without any armament. No merchant ship would be allowed to arm in this port and leave the harbor."[22]

In February 1917, the United States severed diplomatic relations with Germany. Count von Bernstorff, Aunt Elsie's friend, was handed his passport and sent back to Germany. On August 6, 1917, the United States declared war on Germany.

Despite the passage of more than two years, the *Lusitania* remained a factor in the decision to declare war. From the moment it sank, the words "Remember the *Lusitania*" were uttered as a battle cry for America's entry into the Great War. History, both during Wilson's life and after, criticized him for not issuing a declaration of war immediately after the Germans attacked the British ship carrying so many Americans and other civilians. Although the declaration of war came two years after the tragedy, the torpedoing was the catalyst that placed the thought of war in the minds of the administration and the American public.

# 3

## *A Blended*

## *Family*

What families have in common the world around is that they are the place where people learn who they are and how to be that way.

—Jean Illsley Clarke

The cataclysmic events of May 7, 1915, forever changed the lives not only of the wartorn world but also of the Hammond family. Millicent was only five years old when her mother died, too young to understand the circumstances surrounding her mother's death but old enough to understood that her "mummy," as she called her, was not coming home.

Throughout Millicent's life she avoided personal subjects such as her mother's death and her failed marriage. Both topics weighed heavy on her heart and mind until her final days. She dealt with them by offering long-winded animated responses that offered little depth into her true feelings. Millicent often told her children, grandchildren, colleagues, and reporters the same anecdote about her mother. "When my mother died I came home and my aunt told me the dreadful news. Immediately Mary [her seven-year-old sister] started crying and, rather, than bursting into tears myself, I reacted by calling Mary a crybaby."[1] Clearly Millicent did not understand the gravity of her mother's death, but her older sister did. Millicent never offered any reflection on the sense of loss she might have felt then or in later years when she better comprehended her mother's death.

The closest she came to acknowledging the pain she might have experienced came late in life, when she shared with her son, Hugo, how much her aloof response as a child to her mother's death troubled her as an adult.[2] Unlike many others who suffered the loss of a mother at an early age—Eleanor Roosevelt and Lady Bird Johnson, for example—Millicent never dwelled on her loss or framed it as a life-changing event. Such a loss usually plays an integral role in defining an individual. If it did for Millicent, she never reflected on its impact other than her childhood reaction. However, the lack of a nurturing mother affected her own children. As Millicent's son-in-law said, "She was very hard on them [her children]. She thought life was unfair and thus she had to raise them to be tough to protect them from the world. She didn't give Mary [her daughter] the love and encouragement she needed. Both children broke under the pressure."[3]

Although Millicent was popularly known as the pipe-smoking grandmother, she embodied few of the nurturing traits popularly associated with grandmothers. Millicent greeted her grandchildren with the latest *New York Times* headlines. It is ironic that this caring woman who opened her heart to the world had trouble doing the same with her own kin. Perhaps the answer lies in what happened after her mother died.

After Ogden returned home to Bernardsville, family and friends soon learned that his wife's death was a subject never to be discussed in the Hammond household or with him. As his children grew older they never confronted the reasons behind their mother's death. They compartmentalized it and moved on. They did not question their mother's decision to board the ship despite warnings not to do so, nor did they discuss any feelings of abandonment. Because it was a topic their father did not discuss, it became a topic they did not discuss.

Their daily routine remained essentially unchanged immediately following their mother's death. They played with local children and interacted with their nannies, tutors, and other household help. The children quickly learned life goes on. To ensure their lives were disrupted as little as possible, Ogden's youngest sister, Peggy, moved in and helped out, and his sister-in-law, Emily, also provided assistance.

Because Millicent was so young when her mother died, their relationship never fully blossomed. Millicent grew up with fleeting memories of her mother. Her parents were the epitome of style and grandeur. Millicent fondly remembered their love of the automobile, a relatively new phenomenon in the early twentieth century, and her mother getting ready to "go for a spin." There was a certain sporting mentality associated with cars, whose use was viewed more as a leisure activity than a mode of transportation. Automobiles were a toy for those who could afford them. Ogden Hammond could. He bought a Packard in 1910, the year Millicent was born. Ogden and Mary often went for Sunday drives, waving to their children as they left.

Millicent's childhood was as innocent and carefree as one could imagine. Bernardsville was her oasis. She was raised there and would marry there, raise her children there, and die there. She always beamed with joy at the mere mention of her childhood and never paused when asked to discuss it. She captured her youth with fondness in an article entitled "In the Days When Summers Seemed Endless":

"Washington—Summer is a time for memory, and I remember with peculiar vividness the summer of 1912 when my brother Ogden was born in the St. Regis Hotel in New York. My sister Mary and I went in to see him, but we were more impressed by the hotel, the first we had seen, than by the baby, a pale little gray-faced creature with black eyes like prunes.

"We would spend the whole summer in the country. Life in Bernardsville, N.J., seemed so secure, so ordered, so endless. We went out, except in the hottest summer days, dressed in khaki bloomers and middies, brown stockings and sneakers. Underneath we wore under-drawers and 'waists'—white cotton bodices with yellow horn buttons and garters advertised by Buster Brown and his dog, Tige.

"The sensation of the summer of 1913 was our Packard car, a flat platform, with two black leather armchairs in front and a stool behind, with a brass rail around the platform's edges. It was painted yellow on the armchair backs and around the stool's black cushion. There were black leather mudguards, an upright windshield and a brass lantern on each side. On weekend afternoons Mother and Daddy often went for what was called a spin. Cars were for sport—for church and for the train one took horses, because on steep hills cars often had to go backwards to make the gasoline reach the engine. They were not reliable.

"Mother would put on a big hat covered with a long veil with an isinglass panel for vision's sake. Then came the linen duster and white gloves. Daddy wore goggles and a cap with a visor. We children saw them off every time. There was a hint of danger in the expedition—a sporting chance of failure, at least.

"During this summer, I had a pet chicken and a lost family photo-graph shows us together—a fat child with drawers perpetually falling down. I had a donkey, too, which in the autumn of 1914 was part of my first big disappointment. The foxhounds were meeting at our house and my older sister, on her little sidesaddle, was to take part, with Dennis Cribben, the groom, leading her pony on a rein. I wanted to join in and got the donkey all ready, but we weren't allowed to. We just had to stay there and watch everybody ride off. It was a terrible day.

"Also that year, a clay-pigeon shoot at the end of the lawn taught me a lesson in the manners expected of a child in 1914. One participant was an older friend of the family, a man everyone called Ben. He was Benjamin Nichols, the grandfather-in-law of Cyrus R. Vance. After he had made a clean sweep of the clay pigeons, I in my excitement called 'Hurrah, Ben!' I was promptly marched up the hill to the downstairs bathroom by my mother, who washed my mouth out with soap. Children learned formal respect in those ways.

"As we grew older we stayed at home and played, making up games, climbing trees, playing touch football with the boys from across the road. No one thought of transporting children to and fro, no one rushed around to get lessons. It was up to us to spend the morning out-of-doors doing something healthy until the bell rang for washup and lunch. One day was like the next with only occasional but wonderful surprises, such as when we had movies in the darkened attic hall—'The Exploits of Elaine' and 'The Perils of Pauline.' All our touch football group came for such amazing entertainment.

"There was no air-conditioning, of course, but electricity gave us electric fans. Sometimes a big block of ice was put in front of a fan—ice from the icehouse, which was stocked in winter with ice cut from the lake two miles away. Sawdust kept it all summer long, melting slowly but useful for making ice cream, too. The big icebox, in a room off the kitchen, opened at the back so the ice could be put in from out-of-doors. Downstairs there were a flower room, a boot room and two laundry rooms where big oval copper basins were used to boil the clothes on the same stove that was used to heat the pressing irons. In the summer the heat was terrible.

"A trip to New York meant a ferry ride and people stayed home and played the piano for entertainment.

"Life was not easy in those days but for children it was slow and sure. The lines were clear. We knew what to expect and what was expected from us. We did not see many strangers. The voices we heard were few and the faces we saw did not seem to change. Life had a familiar and reassuring rhythm. We did not compare ourselves to others. There was no sense of competition. We just accepted things.

"These were the early summers—1917 was the last. After that we went away to the seashore for July and August, and somehow it was all different. We could read the papers—or at least the headlines. We knew there was a war. The endless season, the long slow days, never came back again, not for us, and perhaps for no children anymore."[4]

The article appeared in the center of the *New York Times* op-ed page with a photograph of Millicent sitting on her father's lap when she was a toddler. Ironically, the op-ed piece above hers was entitled "Forward with Japan," written by Cyrus R. Vance, the former secretary of state, whose grandfather-in-law Millicent alluded to in her article.

As an adult Millicent resembled her beautiful mother, but as a child she felt like an ugly duckling. She remembered herself as a "messy fat child."[5] It is hard to imagine the slender five-foot, ten-inch figure of her adulthood as a plump child. When it came to appearance, Millicent was a typically self-conscious young girl, and she was surrounded by people who sported fashionable clothes, accessories, and hairstyles. As Millicent got older, the chubby child became a slender adolescent and she never had to worry about her weight again.

————

The Hammonds' social circle included such prominent families as the Vanderbilts, Stevenses, Whitneys, Alexanders, and Pynes, all of whom were known for their successful business ventures, wealth, and philanthropy.

After Mary's death, Ogden mourned alone and became engrossed in his work. In his wife's memory Ogden presented a house, the Mary Stevens Hammond Home, to the United Aid Society. The purpose of the house was to help homeless and needy children in Hoboken, her home-town, something Mary would have viewed with pride.

Millicent grasped at any trace of her mother. Among the best links she found were the family's two laundresses. They had both worked for the Stevens family at Castle Point and often shared stories about her mother. The laundresses' memories of Mary kept her alive for her daugh-ter. As Millicent listened to them reminisce she kept her eyes focused on the big copper vats where the laundry was washed. A fire burned around the clock, even in sweltering summer weather, so the clothes could be cleaned in boiling water. After the laundresses washed the clothes in the vats they laid them outside on a drying green near the back door.

For two years following Mary's death the people in Millicent's life and household routine remained constant. That changed quite suddenly. In December 1917, Percy Pyne and his wife, Maud Howland Pyne, Hammond family friends, announced the engagement of Maud's sister-in-law, Marguerite McClure Howland, to Ogden Hammond. The an-nouncement was made at the Pynes' Park Avenue home during a wedding reception for their daughter, Mary Pyne, who had married Lieutenant Oliver Dwight Filley, one of the first American pilots to fly against the Germans during World War I. Mary Pyne, although seventeen years older than Millicent, would become one of her closest friends in adulthood.

Later that month at the Howland home on West Forty-ninth Street, now part of the site of Rockefeller Plaza, Ogden married Marguerite McClure Howland. Her nickname was Daisy, but she insisted the Hammond children call her "Mother."

The marriage was prompted by suggestions that Ogden remarry so there would be a woman to oversee the household and the children. There was speculation that the marriage was Maud Pyne's idea. Daisy, like Ogden, was widowed. And since the death of her husband, Maud's brother, Daisy had lived with the Pynes. Rumor had it that marriage was the only way Maud could get Daisy out of her house.[6]

Like Mary Stevens, Daisy was a striking woman from a wealthy family. She too had a petite frame, but hers was offset by incandescent red hair. Daisy's father was David McClure, a prominent New York attorney with his own law firm. Daisy had one sister, Katherine, who was the black sheep of the family. Katherine did not share her sister's good looks and was raised to care for her parents. Daisy was the center of her parents' adoration and was groomed for marriage. Her first husband was a wealthy older man named Dulany Howland, twenty-three years her senior. He died in 1915 at the age of sixty-two from appendicitis. The couple had one son, McClure (Mac) Howland, born in 1906. He was two years older than the eldest Hammond child.

Daisy's life revolved around her son, Mac. Just as she had been spoiled growing up, Daisy, in turn, spoiled her son. When Daisy married Ogden she became Mary, Millicent, and Oggie's stepmother, but she never took much interest in them. She made no effort to care for or nurture the three motherless children. She became an authority figure, not a mother. Her son commanded all her attention. She smothered him with love and stifled the other three children.[7]

Ogden's friends initially thought having a stepmother to care for his children was a good idea, but it did not take Millicent long to realize this was not the case. Daisy, consumed with herself and her son, had no sense of humor and took everything literally. She worried about everything, especially Mac. At the age of seven Millicent gained not a mother but an adversary. Daisy and Millicent were strong-minded stubborn women who clashed from the beginning.

Disputes often emerged between Mac and the Hammond children, with Mac sometimes hitting Millicent.[8] Daisy rarely listened to her stepchildren's side of the story, because, to her, Mac was always right. The Hammond siblings were often forced to cater to Daisy's demands, particularly where Mac was involved. If Mac wanted to stay up until three in the morning, then all the children were forced to stay up. Needless to say a good deal of resentment developed toward Mac. He also earned a nickname: Mary, Millicent, and Oggie referred to Mac, whose given name was McClure, as Manure.

Millicent's childhood was deeply affected by her father's remarriage. Daisy had, in effect, cast a shadow over Millicent's life. She was not as happy as she had been. New boundaries were set based on Mac's desires. Millicent loathed conceding to Mac or Daisy. In the beginning, Millicent turned to her father for help, but Ogden would not intervene on her behalf and often deferred to Daisy's judgment. Millicent soon realized that seeking her father's help was a waste of time. Ogden never acknowledged the tension between Daisy and Mac and his children. He either was oblivious to it or had no desire to be involved in the rivalry. After witnessing the tragic death of his first wife, he had grown emotionally distant. His marriage to Daisy reinforced his withdrawal, leaving Daisy to handle family disputes. Millicent did not like her new situation. She was not an important part of her stepmother's life, nor would she ever be. Millicent developed a sense of independence and learned to rely on herself before others because she had no alternatives.

Millicent's rather formal, but fond, relationship with her father and silent dislike for her stepmother brought her closer to her sister, Mary. They were not only sisters, but best friends for life. It was with Mary that Millicent shared any resentments she felt toward her parents. Mary became Millicent's sole outlet for her feelings.

Millicent turned to books and poetry as a means of escape. She was an avid reader and particularly fond of the young adult Patty book series by Carolyn Wells, as popular then as Nancy Drew books were later. Millicent immersed herself in the books and their title character, a girl named Patty Fairfield. Patty was not too different from Millicent. Patty lived in a New Jersey suburb called Vernon (Millicent's middle name), her mother had died, and her father worked in New York, like Ogden. As Millicent got older, books remained a central part of her life. She often read under one of the many trees on the thirty-five-acre Bernardsville property. Millicent and Oggie took great pride in the fact that they had climbed every one of the trees.

Millicent and her siblings often explored the Bernardsville property and relied on each other for amusement. Most of their leisure time was spent at home or at their neighbors, many of whom were Stevens cousins, or with children of the household help. Each morning the children were sent out to play. They created endless games such as "Still Pond, No More Moving," which was a mystery to everyone but them. As Millicent aged she proudly reflected on the imagination children of her generation had. They entertained themselves until they heard the familiar bell the servants rang to signal lunch time. The children would storm inside, wash up, eat lunch, and run outside to play again until the dinner bell chimed.

The Hammond children frequently played tennis on the family's grass court in front of their house. Mac often joined them; to their dismay, but by now Mary, Millicent, and Oggie had learned to tolerate the injustices imposed by Daisy. They managed simple pleasures—namely, revenge against Mac. When he wanted to play tennis with them, Millicent and her siblings would go into the woods and rub the handle of his racquet with poison ivy. This sly tactic kept Mac out of commission and off the court.[9]

Movies were another favorite family pastime. Once a month Ogden hosted a movie party for relatives, neighbors, and family friends. Everyone climbed the steep stairs leading up to the attic where films were shown in a dark passage. They were amused by such silent movie classics as The *Perils of Pauline* and The *Exploits of Elaine,* both featuring Pearl White, who became known as the "American Leading Lady," and later as "Queen of the Silent Serials." The films Ogden showed provided many nights of entertainment for the Hammond clan.

Despite the tensions and disappointments that followed her father's remarriage, Millicent grew up in a privileged and protected environment. She was accustomed to, and surrounded by, the best, from material objects, such as automobiles and movies, to prominent society figures and exclusive clubs. Ogden was a member of many such clubs including the Knickerbocker, Brook, Yale, Midday, Racquet, University, and St. Anthony clubs in New York; the Somerset Hills Country Club and Essex Fox Hounds Club in New Jersey; and the Newport Country Club in Rhode Island.[10]

Daisy's first priority, after Mac, was social status. She took great pride in the fact that her first husband's ancestors were among those who arrived at Plymouth, Massachusetts, in 1620. Daisy, a devout Irish-Catholic, felt snubbed by Protestant society. She spent considerable time and effort to gain what she considered her proper social position. Even though Mary Hammond was dead, Daisy felt animosity toward her, sensing that she was constantly being compared to the flawless first wife of Ogden Hammond. Mary had been loved by all. She had been full of charm, beauty, and warmth—the last a trait that Daisy lacked.

Millicent's father, on the other hand, was regarded by the community as a warmhearted gentleman. Even on the golf course, he was the center of attention. The caddies used to compete to carry Ogden's golf clubs. He was a personable man, well liked, well connected, and financially stable; he always provided the best for his family. All these characteristics, particularly his reputation and social status, appealed to Daisy, but even they were not enough to satisfy her. Years later, her son embarked on an intensive genealogy project connecting Ogden's roots to King Edward III of England who reigned in the fourteenth century, and, according to Mac's research, was a descendant of Charlemagne, Alfred the Great, and William the Conqueror.[11]

Daisy was preoccupied with being accepted by the most elite members of society, a goal that was attainable to her through Ogden's professional and personal status. Ogden's sister-in-law Emily Vanderbilt Sloane was the daughter of Emily Thorn Vanderbilt (a descendant of Cornelius Vanderbilt, the railroad tycoon) and William Douglas Sloane of the W. & J. Sloane furniture store on Fifth Avenue. For social reasons, Daisy decided the Hammonds would spend their summers in fashionable Newport, Rhode Island, in a rented summer home a few doors down from the

Vanderbilts' eighty-room mansion, The Breakers. Beginning in the summer of 1919, when Millicent was nine, her family abandoned New Jersey for Newport, disrupting Millicent's cherished tradition of summering
in Bernardsville.

Just as Ogden and Daisy settled into their marriage, the *Lusitania*
reappeared in their lives, this time in the form of a trial. Sixty-seven law
actions and suits were filed against the Cunard Steamship Company by
American passengers or survivors of victims. Cases were filed in Illinois, Massachusetts, and New York (where the majority of claims were
submitted). Under United States law the claims were consolidated into
one proceeding that limited Cunard's liability. The case was heard by
Judge Julius Mayer, a fifty-two-year-old Republican and former New York
attorney general, in the United States District Court, Southern District
of New York.

Two proceedings had already been conducted overseas. The first was
in Kinsale, Ireland, immediately after the ship sank. A few victims were
taken there, justifying a hearing with a jury of local residents. Days after
the *Lusitania* sank, Captain Turner testified. The jury absolved him of
any responsibility, placing the blame on Germany.

A more formal proceeding took place in the Wreck Commissioners
Court in London. The case was heard from June 15 to July 1, 1915, shortly
after the incident, to determine the circumstances of the *Lusitania*'s
demise. Lord Mersey, an expert on maritime law, presided over the hearings and found that Turner "exercised his judgement for the best. It was
the judgement of a skilled and experienced man, and although others
might have acted differently and perhaps more successfully, he ought
not, in my opinion, to be blamed. The whole blame for the cruel destruction of life in this vast catastrophe must rest solely with those who plotted and with those who committed the crime."[12] And so it was that the
Cunard Steamship Company, the Royal Navy, and Captain Turner were
absolved of any negligence, and all blame was placed on the German
government. Any other decision, regardless of evidence, would have been
difficult in wartorn England and would have hindered the forthcoming
liability suits.

Both Lord Mersey and Judge Mayer had heard *Titanic* cases in their
courts. It was perhaps based on the latter's ruling that the Cunard officials decided to entrust their fate to Judge Mayer rather than a jury. In
the *Titanic* case Judge Mayer ruled that the recklessly speeding White
Star liner was guiltless.[13]

Many of the claimants in the *Lusitania* liability case "contended
that the Cunard Company was responsible because the speed of the ship
had been reduced without notice, because ports were left open, because
collapsible boats were not loose, because the crew did not distribute life

belts, because the German Embassy in the United States had given public warning; because the Company did not direct the master of the ship to depart from the usual course, and failed to instruct him to make landfalls after dark, to cross the danger zone in the dark at the highest speed, and to zigzag. They further claimed that the navigation of the ship was negligent; that the master disobeyed Admiralty instructions; that the Company had failed to provide a competent master and crew, and that after the torpedoing ports were left open and boats were negligently handled."[14]

By the time the trial got under way on April 17, 1918, the United States was officially at war with Germany, heightening interest in the case. It took three weeks to hear from nearly one hundred witnesses, including passengers, crew members, and Cunard officials.

Ogden Hammond was one of the first witnesses. He filed a claim on behalf of himself and his children, and during his testimony he stated that he saw no life belts on the deck during the voyage and witnessed no boat drills.[15] Nor did passengers receive instructions about lifeboat proceedings, or which lifeboat they were assigned to in case of an emergency. Survivors painted a shocking scene where one lifeboat after another was unsuccessfully launched, tossing passengers to their death. Others mentioned victims who drowned because they put on their life jackets incorrectly. Some wore them inside out, upside down, or too loose.

The *Lusitania* could handle a capacity of 3,000 people and was well equipped for the 1,959 traveling on its fateful journey. There were 3,187 life vests on board, with 2,605 seats available in the 48 life boats. Yet these precautionary measures were not enough to avoid the massive loss of life—1,198 people. At the trial, victims were still coping with the sights and sounds of people struggling for survival, not to mention the lives of loved ones lost.

On August 23, 1918, a full year after America entered the First World War, Judge Mayer rendered his decision. In his Opinion of the Court he absolved Turner and the Cunard Line of not suspecting that the Germans would "authorize or permit so shocking a breach of international law as to sink without warning an unarmed passenger ship."[16] The judge also determined that neither Captain Turner nor Cunard was negligent and thus they were not responsible for damages. The claimants could seek reparations from the real culprit, when the Kaiser's Germany was defeated, for "one of the most indefensible acts of modern times."[17]

It was not until 1925, ten years after Mary perished at sea, that a Mixed Claims Commission assessed Germany more than $2.5 million, payable to victims and their heirs. As a victim of the *Lusitania*, Ogden was awarded $17,970. Each of the children borne by Mary Hammond, Mary, Millicent, and Ogden H. Hammond Jr., was awarded $5,000 to compensate for her death. An additional $31,143 was allocated to Mary's estate.[18] All told, the Hammond family received nearly $65,000 in 1925, a considerable sum, but by no means a replacement for the loss the family sustained.

The money Ogden and the children received from the Mixed Claims Commission was in addition to the trust funds Mary had established in her will. At the time of her death she was worth more than one million dollars.[19] The trusts included income and principal. Mary Hammond's unborn grandchildren owned the principal, making the funds transferable without taxes later in life. Half of the income generated from the principal went to Ogden, and the other half was to be equally divided among the three children when they came of age at twenty-one. Ogden successfully petitioned the court to receive some of that income to offset the cost of child care. The remaining funds were reinvested.[20]

# 4

## Building

## Character

I have a dream that one day, my children will not be judged by the color of their skin, but by the content of their character.

— Martin Luther King Jr.

When Millicent lost her mother she was barely of school age, but she had already begun her education at the age of four in the local Bernardsville school system. Every day Millicent and Mary were taken by horse and carriage to a nuns' school in town. Dennis Cribben, the coachman, and their governess accompanied the girls to and from school. Millicent remembered learning how to count by frolicking down the school's staircase, "We would start on the landing and go down the stairs counting 'one, two, three' and so forth."[1]

After their mother died the Hammond girls were sent to the Froebel League, an innovative private elementary school. The sisters were sent to the Froebel League at the recommendation of their Aunt Emily, who oversaw their needs between Mary's death and Ogden's marriage to Daisy. Aunt Emily sent her own son there as well. Oggie was too young to attend school.

After they had spent a few years at the Froebel League, Daisy sent the girls to Miss Nightingale's, a small school in New York City. Millicent was among the first girls to attend the school when it opened in 1920. The school was only a block from where Aunt Emily and Uncle John Hammond lived on East Ninety-first Street in an eight-story mansion built for them by Emily's family, the Vanderbilts. A few years later the school name was changed to the Nightingale-Bamford School, incorporating the names of the first and second headmistresses. Both women emphasized high academic standards as well as personal and moral development, a tradition the school continues to uphold.

The Nightingale-Bamford School is where Millicent's interest in history was first sparked. Her teacher, Miss Perkins, made history come alive. "She told us all sorts of [stories]—she was the one who started my interest in history," said Millicent. "She told us about how Joanna the Mad of Spain adored her husband, and when he died, she wouldn't let him be buried. [She] carried him from convent to convent all over Spain."[2] Decades later Millicent could ramble on about "Joanna the Mad" and other historical anecdotes she learned from Miss Perkins. History remained Millicent's favorite, and best, subject. She was enthralled by past events, but not yet by past politics.

Because of teachers like Miss Perkins, Millicent easily made the transition to her new school and was academically engaged in the classroom. During a summer vacation from the Nightingale School, Millicent encountered an even broader learning environment that fueled her curiosity.

Traditionally, the family spent their summers in Newport, Rhode Island, after Daisy and Ogden married. But in 1922, when Millicent was twelve, Daisy indulged Ogden's desire to travel to Europe with the children. On the trip Millicent and Oggie reveled in their new surroundings—the sites, people, history, language, culture, and even the currency. Ogden took great pride in their interest. In a letter to his mother he wrote: "I must say our trip has been a grand success so far—the children will certainly show the effects of what they have seen and heard—strange to say Millicent and Ogden have been the keenest sights ever. McClure and Mary take everything as a matter of course and show less interest."[3]

After the trip to Europe and three years at Miss Nightingale's School, Daisy sent Millicent and Mary to Foxcroft, an exclusive girls' boarding school located in the heart of Virginia horse country. Foxcroft's reputation was centered more on training girls in proper etiquette than in educational endeavors.

Foxcroft marked the first time that Millicent, now thirteen, had lived away from home. The change was liberating: she was free to express herself without worrying about retribution for her thoughts or behavior. Foxcroft symbolized a pivotal point in Millicent's life. It was there she solidified her character, her intellect, and her principles.

Just as Eleanor Roosevelt went to boarding school and discovered a mentor in her headmistress, Madame Souvestre, so did Millicent. Foxcroft's founder and headmistress, Charlotte Haxall Noland, was a role model for Millicent during her formative years. Miss Charlotte's mantra, and school motto, was *Mens Sana in Corpore Sano*, "a sound mind in a sound body." She instilled this in her girls through all aspects of the school, from the classroom to extracurricular activities.

Character, however, was what Miss Charlotte emphasized above all else. "Though her primary objective in starting Foxcroft had been to create a school which girls would love and enjoy, she knew that her girls could not live by fun alone. She believed an important part of education was the formation of character, and that intellect and character should develop simultaneously."[4] She subtly incorporated character into every aspect of the school including its honor system, scholastic standards, and activities. It was the value and emphasis Miss Charlotte placed on character that had the strongest impact on young Millicent. At Foxcroft, Millicent's outgoing personality and character began to flourish as she grew into her own skin.

Miss Charlotte was full of wit, charm, intelligence, and an endless imagination. She could be stern, yet fun. She understood the importance of balancing hard work in the classroom with extracurricular competition. Her guidance, athletic ability, and ceaseless knowledge were traits her girls strove to emulate.

As a student, Noland had been bored and contemptuous. Her poor attitude led to truancy and suspensions. She believed school should and could be fun, but her teachers disagreed. Setting out to prove them wrong, Noland was consumed by the notion of starting her own school—one that was different from those she attended and dreaded.

Her first introduction to what running a school would be like came when she was twenty-five. With her family's support, Noland opened a summer camp at the family homestead in Virginia. Her camp offered children an opportunity to ride and groom horses, swim, and play tennis and croquet, all activities that became a staple of Foxcroft life. The camp thrived, and so did its campers, including Wallis Warfield Simpson, who became the Duchess of Windsor when King Edward VIII abdicated the British throne to marry her. One of the youngest campers was Noland's five-year-old cousin, the future Senator Stuart Symington (D-Missouri),[5] who served in the House of Representatives with Millicent before he was elected to the Senate.

In 1912, Noland purchased land for a school and named it Foxcroft, inspired by a house she had seen in England owned by a Major Foxcroft. Noland always associated his name with grandeur and decided it was the perfect name for her school. Two years later, in September 1914, Foxcroft opened its doors as a girls' boarding school in Middleburg, Virginia, fifty miles outside Washington, D.C. Noland acted as the headmistress, housekeeper, bookkeeper, trained nurse, and athletic and riding instructor; when time allowed, she taught biology and Bible classes.

Noland was a knowledgeable, organized, and determined woman in an era when women were raised to have families, not dreams outside the domestic realm. She spent her life conveying her vision, energy, passion, and morals to the hundreds of girls who attended Foxcroft and became part of her family.

Mary and Millicent arrived at Foxcroft with their governess after a train ride from New York City to Washington, D.C., where they then traveled by car to Middleburg—their new home. As they left the city behind and drove through the countryside they learned their surroundings were not all that different from their beloved New Jersey. There was a familiarity in the open pastures and trees beyond the car windows.

Foxcroft was set on 262 acres, with a few structures dotting the campus. There was an imposing brick building near the entrance, simply called the Brick House, where Miss Charlotte received the girls, served tea, and lived during the early years of the school. The girls lived and worked in the Porch House just beyond the Brick House. Nearby there were horse stables and a schoolhouse. Other Foxcroft buildings included the Orchard for third-year girls and the Spur and Spoon where visiting faculty and family stayed.

Most students slept at the Porch House or another building called the Wing. Many of the younger girls, including Millicent, slept at the Porch House, outside on the porch, two to a cubicle, bundled up to brave the cold nights in canvas sleeping bags. This created an instant camaraderie among the girls, but it took longer for them to adapt to their spartan living conditions. The porch lacked screens or glass windows to protect them from insects and the elements. During the winter Millicent often awoke in a snow-covered bed. She, like the others, learned to sleep with her bathrobe crumpled under the covers so it would not become soggy with snow.[6] The girls were relegated to the porch for practical purposes; there wasn't enough room inside for everyone. The experience was also intended to strengthen their character.

When Millicent attended Foxcroft, she recalled, "it had a reputation as being the most expensive boarding school in America, but you never would have known it. Miss Charlotte's whole emphasis was not heaven knows, on material things, not even on intellectual things. Miss Charlotte's point was character."[7] The most important lessons learned were from the example Miss Charlotte set for her pupils.

More than a headmistress, Miss Charlotte was also a friend. If a girl was glum, Miss Charlotte noticed. She encouraged the girls to seek her counsel rather than stew about their problems. She listened with an open heart and mind, unlike Daisy and Ogden. Miss Charlotte once caught a girl smoking outside. Rather than forbid her to smoke or banishing her from school, she told the girl to smoke in the Brick House—where Miss Charlotte lived. The girl never did. The thought of smoking there was enough to stop the girl from ever smoking again at Foxcroft.

Miss Charlotte's spirit permeated all aspects of Foxcroft, including the classroom. Many children and adults remember days when they were cooped up working indoors while the sweet smell of flowers seeped inside along with the sound of birds chirping. On days so sweet, Miss Charlotte rescued the girls from their studies to prance around outdoors. The headmistress knew how to let the girls have fun, whether they were running in the fields discovering lollipops placed on evergreen trees by Miss Charlotte or were swimming in a creek. On these frolicking afternoons, Foxcroft girls were hard to miss. They all wore matching uniforms, green coats and fawn-colored skirts made of broad-ribbed corduroy.[8]

Miss Charlotte was also a fine orator, and perhaps it was from her that Millicent picked up her engaging speaking technique. Miss Charlotte captivated the girls with her famous horror stories, imaginative tales, and Sunday night sermons. Her sermons quickly evolved into a ritual that left Millicent and the others mesmerized. The girls often gathered at the Brick House, sat on the floor, and listened eagerly to Miss Charlotte emphasize her strong convictions, morals, and principles. When she gave her Sunday sermons she usually wore a blue tea gown that accentuated her turquoise eyes and trim figure. As she spoke, her composure reflected her dignity and poise, setting an example her girls emulated.

On evenings when the girls had no activities or schoolwork they gathered at the Brick House for impromptu storytelling by Miss Charlotte. She created a nurturing environment. She never married or had children of her own, and the students became her family. She was proud to see future generations pass through Foxcroft during their teen years. Decades later, Millicent's daughter, Mary, and granddaughter, Sarah, were sent to Foxcroft.

When thirteen-year-old Millicent arrived at Foxcroft in 1923, just one girl was younger, and only by a month. At the time there were approximately sixty girls at the school, divided into two general groups: the younger girls and the older girls, several of whom were nineteen. Their first year at Foxcroft Millicent and Mary were grouped with the younger girls. The following year, Mary, sixteen, joined the older girls. Most school competitions had two categories, one for each group. During Mary's first year at Foxcroft she won second prize for Younger Girls' Short Story, and during the 1924–1925 school year she won the second Prize for Older Girls' Poetry for her poem entitled "Disillusionment."

Disillusionment

I lay on the shining sand,
Close to the ocean,
Lazily dreaming.
Pulled by its motion

I envied the seagull,
Far upward winging;

Black on the silver sky,
    Carelessly swinging.

Why should so small a thing
    Aspire to a height,
While God's own human
    Basks in the sunlight?

Then from his place on high,
    With swift downward motion,
Quick was his plummet dive
    Into the ocean.

Hunger inspired him,
    Stomach had caused his height;
He dined on a speckled carp—
    Reward for his flight.

I lay on the shining sand
    And watched my seagull
Dine on his speckled carp—
    Eat to his full.

Then I turned over,
    Watched with one eye
The seagull progressing
    Once more to the sky.[9]

While Mary received accolades for writing, Millicent took to the stage. Her passion for the theater prompted her to join the Foxcroft Dramatic Club. The Foxcroft girls often devised their own skits and performed them for their classmates. Some of their creativity was attributed to discoveries they made in the "costume closet" in the attic of the Brick House. It was often the source of much merriment and arguments.[10] Hardly a week went by without a performance.

In one play, *The Rehearsal*, the scene was set in Shakespearean England at the Globe Theatre. The plot revolved around a rehearsal for the production of *Macbeth* featuring Shakespeare himself (or in this case herself). Millicent took on the role of Shakespeare and dazzled the audience with her portrayal of the famous playwright.

Miss Charlotte established an air of openness combined with tradition. There were many friendly, but fierce, Fox-Hound sport competitions. Upon arriving at the school, each girl was designated either a Fox or a Hound and remained on the same team throughout her Foxcroft years. The school calendar was packed with plays, horse shows, 'coon hunts, and annual rituals such as the Halloween Chamber of Horrors, Thanksgiving Fox-Hound basketball game, cutting down a Christmas tree, Miss Charlotte's birthday party, and an overnight trip via horseback to Luray Caverns sixty miles away.

Horseback riding was one of Miss Charlotte's favorite pastimes and she expected it would be of her students too. Some girls arrived with their own horses, while others had never ridden. Horseback riding was a part of the Foxcroft curriculum, giving all girls an opportunity to either learn how to ride or to hone their riding skills. Millicent and Mary were familiar with horses but had not done much riding themselves. Millicent's riding ability improved while she was at Foxcroft, but not enough to participate in the local hunts.

Fox and 'coon hunting were embedded in the Middleburg way of life, so much so that the school calendar accommodated the hunt schedule. The girls had classes on Saturdays to ensure they would not interfere with the local Middleburg hunt. Instead they had Mondays, a slow hunting day, off. The girls who wanted to hunt did so on Mondays instead of Saturdays. Millicent often spent Mondays at a dentist's office in Washington having her teeth straightened.

At Foxcroft, a majority of the students involved themselves in one or two extracurricular activities. Millicent and Mary immersed themselves in many. Mary was a team captain, choir member, bell monitor, foxhound monitor, and cloakroom monitor. Millicent followed in her busy sister's footsteps. She was the Younger Girls' Editor of the school yearbook, *Tally-Ho!* as well as a member of the choir and dramatic club. She consistently received A's in medieval history and English history, with her grades in algebra, French, and Latin not far behind. It was not just her teachers who noticed Millicent's academic merit; in the 1925 yearbook, the girls speculated about their classmates' future. Of Millicent, it was written that in four years she would be living in Paris, and "as there was no Honor Roll in the school which Millicent attended in Paris, it was absolutely necessary for her to have one started. However, her nerves became so unstrung during the arrangements that her average dropped considerably and is now only 95 per cent."[11]

And of Mary, it was projected that in five years she, too, would be abroad: "Miss Slenderform, the great literary light, has just returned from a trip to Italy. She is said to have gained three pounds. This miracle is due to the fact that when traveling she forgot all her Italian except the word 'spaghetti.' She had some trouble as she could not say 'stop.' As a result she was pursued around Italy by endless orders of said spaghetti."[12]

Both predictions were eerily accurate. The sisters were tall, slender, and fond of spaghetti. They would later attend school abroad and develop a passion for Italy. Mary would marry an Italian count and Millicent would live in Italy when she became the U.S. ambassador to the United Nations Food and Agriculture Organization based in Rome.

At Foxcroft, Millicent thrived because she was free from the burdens and pressures of her family life. While the landscape did not mark a drastic change for her, the school atmosphere did. Although both her home and school environments were structured, Foxcroft's openness granted Millicent the freedom and independence to discover herself and pursue her interests without worrying about Daisy's approval. As a child Millicent was inquisitive, and at Foxcroft she was provided with a forum in which she could satisfy her intellectual curiosity.

Like her sister, Millicent dabbled in poetry. More than half a century after she left Foxcroft Millicent recited a poem she had written there:

> What is this chain that binds us,
>    We who are weary of breath?
> When there is no joy but in madness,
>    And there is no peace but in death.

"Terrible poetry, terrible idea, and terrible attitude toward life; ridiculous, forgivable perhaps only in a child of 14," Millicent said in her own defense.[13] But she remembered feeling a sense of a pride when she wrote those words.

When Millicent arrived at Foxcroft, she later admitted, she did not have a good attitude. Perhaps the greatest contribution Miss Charlotte and Foxcroft made to Millicent's life was shaping her character. "It was extraordinary how much Miss Charlotte taught without seeming to teach . . . good sportsmanship, good attitudes, oh, there was a lot of that. Did you or did you not have a good attitude? My attitude was not as good as my sister's. My sister had a wonderful attitude. And that meant, not being moody or thinking about yourself or concerned with making trouble."[14] Foxcroft gave Millicent a renewed sense of hope, intellectual stimulation, and a mentor.

In later years when Millicent was asked about her wealth and education, she often replied, "If you want to know what kind of person I am, I think that the least important thing is how much you've got, and the next least important thing is how much you know. The thing that really counts is what's your character."[15]

# 5

## *Ambassador's*

## *Daughter*

The people know their King [Alfonso XIII], he has come among them, has talked with them as one human being to another, has shown himself interested in them, not only as his subjects, but as his people for whom he is responsible and for whom he is willing to sacrifice much.

—Evelyn Graham, *The Life Story of King Alfonso XIII*

Victorian principles dominated the Hammond household, and while the children gleefully played, Ogden was becoming entrenched in local and state politics. He plotted a course that Millicent unconsciously followed decades later, although when Millicent was a child, she was oblivious to the political power her father wielded.

When she was two years old, Ogden was elected to the Bernards Borough Council, on which he served from 1912 to 1914. In 1915 he was ready to expand his political horizons and run for a seat in the New Jersey State Assembly. Upon hearing the news one friend wrote, "The announcement that you have decided to become a candidate for 'Member of Assembly' will, I am sure be warmly received by all the citizens of this County who are desirous of placing in office men of clean character and business ability."[1]

In 1915, Ogden was elected to a one-year term in the lower house of the New Jersey legislature and was reelected the following year. He was a progressive and principled Republican who commanded respect. He lost a third bid for the assembly when he candidly spoke against a local option prohibiting light wines and beer, a major campaign issue. Although he lost, he was consoled by the fact that a majority of the borough council members elected were Republican.

In 1917, the year Ogden married Daisy, individuals in the Republican Party urged him to run for state senate. They thought he could win, but Ogden bowed out before entering the political contest because two others, a judge and a mayor, were considering a run for the senate seat in his district. Ogden wrote to a local political leader, "If I should enter the race also we would have a very bitter fight and I wish to prevent that."[2]

In political circles, conversation buzzed about Ogden, despite his decision not to enter the senatorial race. A letter to James Bathgate, another local community leader, said, "Hammond [is] too big a man for the assembly or senate, he [is] already spoken of for Congress. As chairman of the [GOP] county committee he will be kept before the public and come in contact with men who will be able to further his cause."[3]

One such man was Walter Edge, who served two terms as New Jersey governor. He was first elected to the governorship in 1917, during World War I, and was reelected more than a quarter-century later in 1943, during World War II. In between he served two terms in the United States Senate and represented the United States as ambassador to France. Edge was a Republican heavyweight, and one who had served in the New Jersey assembly and senate before holding national office.

Over the years Ogden and Edge formed a close friendship, and Edge appointed Ogden to a Prison Inquiry Commission chaired by Dwight Morrow, best known as the U.S. ambassador to Mexico from 1927 to 1930 and father of Anne Morrow Lindbergh. The purpose of the commission was to provide a history of the penal, reformatory, and correctional institutions of the state of New Jersey,[4] an important issue to the Stevens family, which was instrumental in the establishment of the Clinton Reformatory Prison for Women (since renamed the Edna Mahan Correctional Facility for Women). Generations of Stevens women, including Millicent and her daughter, Mary, dedicated their time and services to the prison.

By the 1920s Ogden had gained national recognition as a Republican delegate to the Presidential Nominating Convention, first in 1916, and then again in 1924 and 1932. Edge was one of his fellow New Jersey delegates in 1924 and 1932. Locally, Ogden was the Somerset County Republican Chairman, and in 1918 he was treasurer and an executive committee member of the New Jersey State Republican Committee. Even the Democrats took heed of Ogden's political prowess. President Woodrow Wilson, who had served as governor of New Jersey from 1910 to 1912, selected Ogden to chair a presidential committee formed in 1919 to reorganize the Foreign Service.

The young Millicent never saw the political side of her father. Yet in her adulthood she would unknowingly possess some of the same characteristics that endeared Ogden to his peers, chiefly his character, morals, principles, and personable nature.

————

On December 18, 1925, as Millicent and Mary prepared for their holiday break and bid adieu to their Foxcroft friends, the King of Spain sent word to Washington that he approved of Ogden, "as a suitable successor to Alexander Moore as the U.S. Ambassador to Spain."[5] Millicent's world was about to change once again. As she and her sister left Foxcroft for winter break they had no idea they would not be returning.

Ogden's affiliation with Edge helped garner him the ambassadorial post. Edge, in his position as senator, had been urging President Calvin Coolidge to nominate New Jerseyans, including Ogden, as presidential appointees. Edge told Coolidge that Ogden was an excellent candidate because he was "a prominent banker who was then treasurer of the state Republican Committee. He had been a member of the New Jersey legislature, he had a keen sense of public service, and he was in every way qualified for appointment to the diplomatic corps."[6]

Coolidge was familiar with Ogden and his loyalty to the GOP. During the 1924 presidential campaign, Ogden had headed Coolidge's election committee in New Jersey. (Coolidge was the incumbent, having ascended to the presidency after President Warren Harding suffered a fatal heart attack in the summer of 1923.) Coolidge believed in low taxes, business enterprise, and as little government intervention as possible. Ogden agreed with Coolidge's platform and was an ardent supporter. In the November election Coolidge was officially elected president. He defeated Democratic candidate John Davies and Progressive Party candidate Robert La Follette. The American people agreed with Coolidge that "the business of America was business," not government or politics. Coolidge's earnest belief in minimal government caused him to veto more legislation than he signed.

Coolidge and Ogden both believed in what came to be the cornerstone of Millicent's reasoning for being a Republican: "A good Republican is as sensitive to the suffering of others as anyone else, but a first reaction would be 'Let's get together and do something,' not 'The government must take charge of this.'"[7]

After Coolidge was elected, "it was known in exclusive circles that Mr. Hammond was highly esteemed by the president and that he would receive a foreign appointment when the opportunity came."[8] A year passed, and Ogden did not receive a presidential appointment, nor did any New Jerseyans—a fact that had not escaped the attention of New Jersey newspapers and political leaders.[9] Chief among them was Edge.

Earlier in the year Ogden's name had been mentioned as ambassador to Germany, but that went nowhere. One can only speculate that it was probably better for the country not to have a survivor of the *Lusitania*, torpedoed by the Germans, as a foreign diplomat there. By late 1925 rumors circulated again that Ogden was earmarked for an ambassadorship, and that he would have his choice between Argentina and Spain. This sparked the interest of his financial cronies. Soon Ogden, a bank president, was being courted by the J. P. Morgan Bank—one of the largest and most prestigious banking institutions in the country. They were anxious to establish stronger ties with Argentina and pressured Ogden to accept the ambassadorship to Argentina. In return, the Morgan Bank would make Ogden a partner. If he accepted, Ogden would never have to worry about finances. Although he was financially secure due to the inheritance from his first wife, a majority of that money was tied up in trusts for their children.

Despite the monetary benefits of a Morgan Bank partnership, Daisy did not want to move to Argentina. While the lucrative aspects of the deal enticed her, she was more interested in royalty, which Spain had and Argentina did not.[10] Ogden deferred to his wife's wishes, much as he had a decade earlier when Mary insisted on sailing on the *Lusitania*.

As speculation rose about Ogden's ensuing nomination, the local press tracked the story: "Hammond said last night at the Ambassador Hotel, where he is residing for the winter, that he 'would most certainly accept the post if the nomination is confirmed by the Senate.'"[11] Shortly after, Ogden's appointment became official. President Coolidge offered Ogden the ambassadorship, which he gladly accepted. A few days before Christmas, Ogden traveled to Washington for his Senate confirmation. While there, Ogden and Edge met with President Coolidge at the White House and with Secretary of State Frank Billings Kellogg, who, like Ogden, hailed from St. Paul.[12]

Once the appointment was announced, letters and telegrams offering Ogden congratulations poured in from friends, family members, business associates, and former classmates. Most likely at Daisy's insistence, Ogden hired the Walter Hyams & Co. Newspaper Clipping Service to track the coverage. The firm sent Ogden clippings about his appointment from a variety of newspapers, including the *New York Times* and the *Shanghai Times*.[13] One newspaper wrote, "[Hammond] is understood to be a man of considerable wealth and therefore capable of supporting the rather expensive post at Madrid. The appointment does not carry with it any grave responsibilities, although Madrid is considered one of the important listening posts of Europe. Ever since the days of Washington Irving it has been regarded as a most desirable assignment. During the residence of Mr. Moore it had a distinctly social flair."[14]

A Yale classmate wrote to Ogden, "Mr. Alexander P. Moore, your predecessor in Madrid, is a peculiar character, which you will undoubtedly learn after you have been in Spain long enough. Mr. Moore has been very successful as a newspaper man and in business generally but has [little] education or social refinement. He has a certain sense of humor which apparently 'went over' in Madrid, and delights in referring to Prime Minister [Miguel] Rivera as his friend Mike. Frankly speaking, I think that the United States will be much better off as well as Spain in the change of Ambassadors."[15]

Washington Irving, author of *Rip Van Winkle* and *The Legend of Sleepy Hollow*, was one of several distinguished men to precede Ogden as ambassador to Spain. Others included former U.S. attorney general Caleb Cushing, former Wisconsin governor Lucius Fairchild, and Abraham Lincoln's first vice-president, Hannibal Hamlin.

In Wisconsin, Ogden's ambassadorship was the topic of conversation and envy among his peers. His former business partner, Phil Stratton, was barraged with phone calls and well-wishes for Ogden. The *Chippewa Telegram*, a Wisconsin newspaper, wrote proudly of the news.

"In the appointment of Ogden H. Hammond, a former Wisconsin resident, as Ambassador to Spain, President Coolidge has exercised his keen judgement in selecting for this important foreign post a man of established business reputation as well as one possessed of a pleasing personality. . . . His activities in the civic affairs of Superior brought him a wide acquaintance which extended and still extends over the entire state of Wisconsin.

"Having laid the foundation for his political activities in this state, Mr. Hammond soon became a Republican power in New Jersey. After going to a number of national conventions as a Republican delegate, he was chosen by Coolidge to manage his presidential campaign in that state. . . . Wisconsin can well be proud of the President's selection of one of its successful citizens who has since gone afield to be honored with an influential trust in Europe. President Coolidge is to be commended for his selection and Mr. Hammond congratulated upon his newest success."[16]

By the time Foxcroft's winter term resumed in January, Millicent and Mary were preparing to move to Spain. Believing education was important for boys but not girls, Daisy withdrew her stepdaughters from Foxcroft. After two happy years at Foxcroft, Millicent's education ended abruptly. Had the girls returned it would have been Mary's final semester. Because she was close to graduating, Foxcroft awarded her a high school diploma, but did not give Millicent one. She had another year and a half to go. At fifteen, Millicent's formal education was over without her earning a high school diploma. Years later, Foxcroft awarded her an honorary degree. Meanwhile, while the family moved to Spain, Oggie and Mac remained at St. Paul's School in Concord, New Hampshire.

---

The Hammond family, minus the boys, sailed across the Atlantic Ocean and arrived in Madrid shortly before Millicent celebrated her sixteenth birthday. Excited about the new experiences ahead, Millicent paid little attention to politics or the fact that King Alfonso XIII was on the throne and General Miguel Primo de Rivera was prime minister and dictator. "We were so innocently unaware. I tell you, we were the most apolitical pair of girls that you could find anywhere," said Millicent. "Primo de Rivera was supposed to be a dictator, and that didn't even strike horror."[17] Three years earlier, Primo de Rivera had led a military revolt, with the support of the king, to take over the government and restore order in Spain and Morocco.

Initially, Millicent was oblivious to the impoverished living conditions of many Spaniards and to political turmoil in the country. During her first year in Spain some political skirmishes were quelled,[18] but Millicent was not acutely aware of them. Her attention was focused on adjusting to a new culture. Her parents easily became accustomed to socializing with royalty, diplomats, and other statesmen.

While Ogden and Daisy treasured their new life and status, Millicent was less enthusiastic. She was trying to adjust to a culture filled with rigid customs, stricter than those in the United States. In Spain, Millicent and Mary were afforded little freedom. The sisters were assigned a car and driver but were not allowed to travel in the car unless accompanied by a woman. Initially, the girls' longtime governess, who had been with the family since Millicent was seven years old, filled this role. But she left the family to work for E. W. Scripps, founder of the Scripps newspaper empire, and his family back in the United States. After the governess left, a maid acted as the mandatory female chaperone.

Spanish customs initially made it difficult for Millicent and Mary to enjoy their teenage lives. If they wanted to play golf with a man, the sisters needed a married woman present to adhere to the social norms. Their days of wandering the vast Bernardsville property or going for long walks on their own were over.

Gradually, Millicent learned to appreciate the formalities of the culture. Living in Spain "taught me not only self respect, but caution. The strictness was because women were considered a precious object. Men were fascinating and dynamite. And we (women) had to be protected from this dangerous element (men)," she said.[19]

Because there was no international school, Millicent and Mary were sent to a French convent in Madrid called the Convent des Soeurs de St. Jose de Cluny. The nuns, many of whom were recuperating from illnesses they had contracted in Madagascar, taught in French. The convent offered a striking contrast to Foxcroft, but Millicent adjusted. Although she attended the convent for only two months, she adored the nuns and speaking French, which she had learned as a child.[20] The nuns took great care in shaping the young minds sent to them. Their method of teaching was philosophical in nature. The nuns impressed upon Millicent the value of the individual. They taught her about existentialism and looking beyond social stereotypes to see what lay within each person, a lesson that became an underlying feature of her years in public life.

Millicent remembered one nun explaining, "When you go down the street and you see something that catches your eye, and you think maybe I would like to look at that, maybe it is a bargain, turn your eyes aside, and do this for the love of God, and every day you strengthen your soul."[21] The nuns emphasized that individuals had the power to resist the daily temptations of frivolous possessions. This heightened awareness of people, possessions, and power gave Millicent a renewed sense of self-worth. "[The nuns] gave you a whole feeling for life that I don't think we ever would have gotten anywhere else," said Millicent.[22]

The convent was headed by Ma Mère, the Mother Superior, "a very terrifying, dignified older woman of whom everyone stood in awe."[23] Formalities abounded at the convent, where the dozen students were taught to walk properly and curtsey in case they were presented to royalty. Once again, stairs provided a learning experience for Millicent. Just as she learned to count on stairs in elementary school, she learned how to walk down them properly at the convent. Ma Mère told Millicent and the rest of the girls, "You don't bob down stairs; you bend your knees at the top and you float down the stairs."[24] Millicent thought it was remarkable how pretty it was to see someone walk down the stairs, particularly the nuns in their long flowing habits.[25] Gliding down the stairs was in fact a useful skill for Millicent, who attended balls, galas, and other ceremonial and celebratory events with her parents while she was in Spain.

During the day she wore a school uniform—a crisp white shirt with a rounded collar that peeked out from underneath her dark jumper and tied at the hip. At night an extravagant wardrobe awaited. Millicent enjoyed the social circuit. She had the unique ability to converse and charm anyone with whom she spoke, including royalty.

She had a celebrated exchange with King George V, who was the English monarch from 1910 until his death in 1936. Millicent, then eighteen, was presented at court to the king along with several other girls. Millicent and Mary were sitting at a small table in the palace garden when the king, in poor health, greeted them. When he addressed Millicent she uttered something to him that made Mary twitch. Millicent never revealed what she said, but no mistake was made about the king's reaction. He laughed. Mary bewilderedly said to Millicent, "The king is supposed to be very sick and very weak, and you had him laughing." Millicent retorted, "Well, after all, the king is human, isn't he?"[26] After living abroad for more than two years she had clearly mastered her social skills.

Millicent had plenty of practice. She met Spain's Queen Victoria Eugenia and King Alfonso XIII; the Duke of Alba; the Duke of Kent; the Prince of Wales; La Nina de los Peines, a legendary flamenco dancer; and some of the best bullfighters in the country, who were celebrities in their own right. Millicent and Mary's names often appeared in newspaper articles citing "Las señoritas de Hammond" as guests at everything from palace events to aristocratic weddings.[27]

The Hammonds had many opportunities to socialize with King Alfonso XIII, a popular monarch loved by Spain's twenty-two million people. Hayden Talbot, a reporter, wrote that "King Alfonso knows his country and his people as perhaps no reigning monarch in all history ever knew them. And knowing, he uses his knowledge in such fashion as to be in fact, as well as in title, the dominant force in the administration of the affairs of his country."[28]

The king and his wife, the former English Princess of Battenberg, had four sons and two daughters. The six royal children were clustered around the same ages as the Hammond children. The heir to the throne was the same age as Mac; Don Jaime was the same age as Mary; Infanta Beatriz was a year older than Millicent; Infanta Maria Cristina was a year younger than Millicent; two more royal princes followed, with one the same age as Oggie. The princesses were heralded as the best-dressed in Europe, much as the Hammond sisters were heralded by the American press for their fashionable appearance.

The king's children and the Hammond children occasionally saw each other at formal social gatherings. For Millicent, the highlight of these events was when a man spoke to her. In Spain, interaction between the sexes was regimented and full of drama. "It was significant at a dance if someone said, 'Will you sit out?'" said Millicent. "That meant they were interested in you because they wanted to talk. It was practically a declaration—you were almost engaged. You see, everything was very heightened then. If someone pressed your hand, it was drama. There is no way of expressing the drama of life in those days, or explaining to a child of today what life was like then. It was all so romantic and interesting. Really, we've lost a lot, that's all I can say. Of course all this took place in a limited world. I was not interested in, and did not know anything about politics. I wrote a lot of poetry, learned a lot and wrote a lot.

That was more my bent. I would write in notebooks about nature or people or injustice."[29]

As a teen, Millicent expressed her inquisitiveness by her desire to read, write, and learn. While abroad she ordered dozens of books from the Smith Bookshop in Paris. "I had a Russian period, all the Russians, you know—Tolstoy, of course, Turgenev and Chekhov and all," said Millicent. "One phase after another—Russian phase, and French phase, and finally all-English phase, all Thackeray, all George Eliot, and my sister particularly, all Dickens. So it was that sort of haphazard education . . . that we worked out for ourselves."[30] Millicent also enjoyed Greek tragedies and poetry; Emily Dickinson was among her favorite poets. Millicent penned some poems in Bernardsville and continued to do so in Spain. Writing was an outlet for her, a tool she relied on throughout her life.

---

During the Christmas break, the Hammonds usually returned to New York to celebrate the holiday season with family and friends. They stayed in the penthouse suite at the Savoy Plaza Hotel. One night Bill Githens, a family friend, joined the Hammond siblings for dinner and an evening at the theater. Bill was the same age as Mac, and the two had played tennis together. It was on this particular evening that Bill met Millicent, Mary, and Peggy Starr, their first cousin. The three girls, dressed in designer gowns, were sitting on a big sofa in the middle of their spacious living room. Mac introduced everyone, and in the process he gently shoved Bill. Bill tumbled over Oggie, causing everyone to laugh nervously and easing the formalities of the introductions. Bill recovered quickly, jumped up, and joined the laughter, winning Millicent's praise in the process. "I like you," she said. "You know how to laugh at yourself."[31]

The group was set for a night on the town. Millicent wore a royal purple dress complemented by an antique necklace with a big rhinestone. She topped off her outfit with a gold tiara that belonged to her Aunt Hattie. Mary wore a golden dress woven with gold thread. She told Bill she thought her dress was "the first one ever made with gold thread. It was a special creation of Worth's of London, he told me so himself." Peggy wore an antique lace dress. "I bet that dress cost plenty, didn't it?" Bill asked. Peggy smiled, "Don't get the wrong idea. I am a model for Farquehar and Wheelock on 57th Street, and I am showing this creation off, hoping that somebody will like it."[32] And, somebody did. Bill and Peggy later married.

On what turned out to be Bill and Peggy's first date, this well-dressed group headed to the theater where they saw a comedy entitled *Blackbirds of 1928*. It was one of the first all-black shows on Broadway. During one scene, four characters were playing poker. One was cheating. He was hiding cards up his sleeve, and another poker player was beginning to notice. He slipped a large straightedge razor out of his sleeve. It was clear that mayhem was about to be unleashed. Then Bill glanced at Millicent, seated next to him. From their second row seats Millicent was making signs to one of the actors with her white-gloved hands. Bill asked her, "What are you doing?" She smiled and said, "I am trying to distract him."[33] She succeeded. The actor gave Millicent a big wink from the stage. Even at the theater Millicent did not suppress her prankster ways.

After the play, they went back to the Savoy Plaza. Shortly after they returned, Ambassador Hammond asked to speak to Bill. He led Bill into a private study off the living room. "Bill, I would like you to come back to Spain with us," said Ogden, "and you can be my private secretary for a year."[34]

Bill appreciated the offer but declined it. He told Ogden he had been awarded a teaching fellowship at the Harvard School of Business and was assured a job with a good company at the end of the year. Not satisfied Ogden said, "No. I want you to change your mind. It will broaden your outlook to have a year in Spain with me. You will be traveling on a diplomatic passport, and you will have all the advantages of being my private secretary. When you get back, you can go to the same company that made you the job offer, and I am sure you can get a much better salary after a year with me."[35] With a case like that, it was difficult for Bill to refuse Ogden's offer, so he accepted and joined the Hammond family in Spain in 1928.

Mac and Oggie didn't go to Spain until the school year was over. They spent their summers with the rest of the family in the chic resort town of San Sebastián on the northern coast of Spain. "During the months of August and September all who could afford it went to San Sebastián, and for eight weeks the capital was deserted; then at the beginning of October came the rush back, and by the end of the month Madrid was normal once more."[36] The affluent flocked to San Sebastián, following on the heels of the royal family. It was a chance to escape the variable climate of Madrid where a tropical summer heat descended on the city, in sharp contrast to the biting winds that swept down from the Sierras, making the capital city unmercifully cold during the winter months.

La Concha, a crescent-shaped beach sandwiched between two hills, provided a pristine setting for San Sebastián. On top of the first hill was Monte Igueldo, the king's palace. On the second hill was a five-hundred-year-old *palacio* where the Hammonds stayed. It offered majestic views of the beach below. San Sebastián's breathtaking scenery attracted people from around the globe. Visitors often saw the king and queen together, taking a swim, enjoying excursions in nearby towns, or relaxing on one of the royal yachts.

Daisy cherished the summers in San Sebastián and her reunion with Mac. He had had a difficult year at boarding school without her and was happy to return to his doting mother. Much of his time at St. Paul's had been spent in the infirmary as a result of stress and nerves. He was a lost soul without the guidance of his domineering mother.[37] Once reunited, Mac's health returned.

Millicent spent much of her summer on the beach. Social norms were no less stringent in San Sebastián than in Madrid, and most women wore a full-length terry cloth beach coat that draped around their ankles. Millicent's swimwear was not the norm. She wore a revealing sleeveless beach coat with a scooped neck and straight skirt that ended at her knees, not her ankles. Millicent was not shy, nor was she scared to take risks. The lifeguards did not have the same luxury. They had to wear the traditional long-sleeved bathing suits that came up to their throats and went down to their ankles. Their skin barely saw the light of day.[38]

Not only was Millicent a daring teen, she was also a practical joker. One of her favorite coups was a joke played on Bill. Mac, Oggie, Bill, Millicent, Mary, and some of their friends went swimming, and Bill was the last one out of the water, and the last person to reach the changing cabins. It was just enough time for Millicent to devise a plan that left poor Bill in his birthday suit. When Bill started changing, Mac and Oggie grabbed him and threw him outside stark naked. As Bill banged on the door, he heard Millicent laughing in the girls' cabin next door. She enjoyed seeing her plan come to fruition. None of the Hammonds came to Bill's aid. He was stranded outside, naked, until a beach attendant rescued him with a towel.

At dinner that night Bill asked, "Who thought of the practical joke?" Everyone chuckled and pointed to Millicent, who sheepishly said, "You don't mind, do you, Bill?"[39] Fortunately for her, Bill had a sense of humor.

Despite the merriment summer provided, Millicent was becoming more familiar with the country and cognizant of the poverty everywhere. Not far from the Hammonds' Madrid home, "there was a big wide street . . . called the Castellana, and the men were tending the bushes or repairing the cobbles. The mother and one or two of the children would come out at noon time with a can. This can had lunch for the men. It was a metal can with a cover that settled down into the mouth, and that was the plate to eat from. The women would then pour garbanzos, beans with a little meat, on the plate. And, that was the lunch routine for the men and women of Castellana."[40]

The nuns taught her to be more observant about her surroundings and the suffering of others. Many of the homes Millicent saw did not have electricity or running water. In Santillana del Mar, near the prehistoric Altamira caves, the town boasted medieval and Renaissance structures built between the fifteenth and seventeenth centuries. The local church stood near the sea and had a natural spring below it where the water was collected into three troughs. The first trough was for drinking, the second for rinsing, and the third for washing. The village women gathered at the troughs because they needed water. Collecting water was hard work, but the women exhibited a sense of community. This was not lost on Millicent, nor were the daily rigors of Spanish life in what was still primarily an agrarian society.

Other aspects of the society went unnoticed by Millicent and her sister. "In the '20s there had been no Hitler," said Millicent. "We didn't—I don't know how to describe it to you, we just didn't get the picture at all. Nobody spoke of censorship or anything like that. And we knew Primo de Rivera. His sons, there were two of them, I remember, often came to dances that we went to. We didn't know them well. Of course we went to the dances with Mummy and Daddy and came home with Mummy and Daddy."[41]

Millicent once had the opportunity to speak to Primo de Rivera. The dictator called Ogden in San Sebastián because he was anxious to finalize a deal in which the United States was going to set up a telephone system for Spain. Ogden's Spanish was not up to the task and he couldn't reach his staff, so he summoned Millicent, who spoke Spanish better than the rest of her family, including her ambassador father. The pair went to a little office in San Sebastián's city hall to speak with Primo de Rivera on the phone. Millicent translated the negotiations between her father and Primo de Rivera regarding the telephone company.[42] That was as close as she came to politics in those days. The subject of the conversation she translated for her father was the core of his speech to a group of American businessmen at a Waldorf-Astoria dinner in February 1927. "Madrid," he said, "had probably the best telephone service to be found anywhere. Spanish businessmen combined with American genius have given to Spain this latest and best in telephone service, a system which is the result of 50 years of American experience."[43]

Life as an ambassador's daughter had its advantages. Millicent was exposed to all aspects of the regional Spanish culture—architectural styles, languages, traditional costumes, dances, customs, and people. San Sebastián was the capital of Guipúzcoa, one of the four provinces of the Basque country in northern Spain. The family often explored the other three Basque provinces, Vizcaya, Álava, and Navarra, where they saw flamenco singing and dancing unique to the northern region.

One of Millicent's more memorable excursions was a pilgrimage to Lourdes, France, famed for its healing powers and not far from the Spanish border. The trip was chaperoned by nuns, priests, doctors, and nurses. As Millicent said, "I never liked hospital work or blood. I chose work in the dining room, washing dishes and serving, and my sister volunteered for the hospital. A lot of young men we knew were stretcher bearers." Millicent learned about Lourdes's mystical powers from a priest. "There have been numbers of people who have leapt from their beds, who never before were able to walk, but the Church says, 'No, that's no miracle,' because there is something in these nervous disorders that can produce physical effects which can be reversed by some tremendous surge of the spirit. So they don't count them as miracles. What they count as miracles is, and it's very interesting, a miracle occurs when a natural process is unaccountably accelerated. I remember an English priest who told me all about this. He had gone down as a doctor and had become a convert and stayed there because he was so overcome by one particular case . . . of a Belgian who had broken his leg very badly, multiple fractures—the bone was all pulverized. Something heavy had fallen on it and simply shattered the bone. And it didn't seem to be healing, and they took him to Lourdes. He was in continual pain. While he was on the stretcher, as the Blessed Sacrament passed with incense and candles in the procession—he called out 'I can walk, I can walk.' Well, of course they thought he was delirious. They tied him down to the stretcher. They brought him back again to the hospital. He was X-rayed [and] the bone was healed."[44]

On another trip, this one to Cadiz in southern Spain, the Hammonds sailed on the Guadalquivir River from Seville to the port of Huelva, near Cadiz. Among the passengers who made the voyage with them was Ogden and Daisy's friend Gertrude Whitney, founder of the Whitney Museum in New York. Mrs. Whitney was donating a statue of Christopher Columbus to be placed in Huelva, where Columbus and his three ships began their historic voyage.

"The ceremony at Huelva was very grand," said Millicent. "The Duke of Alba was there, and I think even Primo de Rivera. I have a picture of it still, a photograph taken. My sister and I in our best bib and tucker, an Augusta Bernards pale grey dress, with a print of white flowers with a little red design, and red wool coats, just the color of the red in the print, and hats that were woven of red and white straw, with a red and grey ribbon. I mean, all of it so Augusta Bernards [designer] of the 1920s. Then we had dances on the ship, wonderful taconcado, heel and toe, where the heels go in very sharp staccato, in time to the music."[45]

Millicent's social life required her to have an impressive wardrobe.

Her closet overflowed with the latest fashions and accessories. On one trip back to the United States in 1928, a photographer was waiting at the docks, and Millicent's picture appeared in the next day's newspaper:

"It is interesting to note that sister ensembles are quite the smart feature for big as well as little girls. Witness the accompanying photograph of Millicent and Mary Hammond, twin daughters of Mr. and Mrs. Ogden Hammond. Rough basket weave tweed fashions the top coats that are identical in style and distinctive points include kimono sleeves trimmed with self-stitching.

"The collars of nutria are cushion shaped and bear resemblance to Patov's skill. A novel treatment of the cuffs is revealed in the fact that the tweed is set over the nutria, producing the effect of a fur under sleeve.

"The accessories include soft felt hats boasting cleverly draped brims, large under-arm bags, chamois gloves, light stockings and kid oxfords.

"The Misses Hammond, whose father is U.S. Ambassador to Spain, are pictured with their Spanish police dog Victor. They returned yesterday with their parents on the *Leviathan* to spend the holidays in the United States."[46]

While she was abroad, Millicent had socialized with nobility and traveled to France, Morocco, and Scotland. On her way back to Spain from Scotland she and Mary stopped in London for a day. There they saw their first "talkie" movie. Millicent was so accustomed to the silent movies shown in their Bernardsville attic that she was ecstatic to see, and hear, *The Jazz Singer* with Al Jolson. By now, Millicent was eighteen and had secretly been smoking cigarettes for a couple of years, after sneaking her first puff in Bernardsville. "My sister and I used to climb the water tower with purloined cigarettes from the boxes in the sitting room. We thought we were so grown up," said Millicent. "I guess I was about 14; she was 16, and if I'd known then what you know, I never would have started. It's a terrible mistake."[47] What made Millicent's first sound movie more exciting was that she and Mary sat in the smoking section and enjoyed a cigarette while watching Al Jolson on the big screen. The sisters had so much fun they stayed and watched the movie a second time.[48]

Later in 1928 Herbert Hoover was elected president. As a matter of protocol, presidential appointees submit their resignations. Within a year Ogden turned in his credentials much to the dismay of the Hoover administration. Ogden was popular in Spain, and during his tenure, relations between the two countries had improved. As a token of appreciation, the Spanish Royal Court bestowed upon Ogden the Gold Cross of Isabella for his public service.

After three years, the Hammonds spent their final days in Spain soaking in the sun of San Sebastián before heading to Paris and ultimately the United States. They returned to New York days before the stock market crash in October 1929, and a few years before the blood and turmoil of the Spanish civil war.

When Ogden's ambassadorship began, America was enjoying a prosperous period. By the time he returned home, the country was entering a deep depression, and his middle child had fallen ill.

# 6

## *Love,*

## *Scandal,*

## *Marriage*

I don't think that there is a more honorable, more difficult, more terrific job than having a happy marriage. If you want to be happy on earth, get a good man and love him and make him love you.
—Millicent Fenwick

Millicent's last year in Spain was less enjoyable than her previous years there. That January she began experiencing a constant pang in her side. Diagnosed as a gallbladder problem, she was given morphine to ease the pain. When the pain persisted she received another prescription, but it did not help either. Millicent was in a wretched state. By the winter of 1929, side effects of the medicine caused her hair to start falling out, forming an inverted V-shaped patch of baldness in the middle of her forehead. Because she was believed to be suffering from a gallbladder problem the doctor told Millicent to lie on her right side for a few minutes every morning before getting up. She did as she was told and tried her best to cope with her illness.

When the Hammonds returned to the United States in the fall of 1929 they moved into the Ambassador Hotel in New York City. Their Bernardsville home, closed while they were overseas, was not yet ready for occupants. Within days of their return, Millicent had another gallbladder attack. The next morning a doctor stopped by the hotel to check on her. This time she received a different diagnosis. Her year of suffering was not due to gallbladder attacks but to appendicitis. She was rushed to a private hospital on Madison Avenue, and it was sheer luck that Millicent's blackened appendix did not burst. A friend of Ogden's from Yale removed her appendix for the hefty sum of $2,500.[1] "Poor Daddy," said Millicent. "He had come back from Washington to find all this disorder and disruption in the family, to say nothing of the stock market crash."[2] The Hammond family, thanks to the sheer size of its fortune, managed to escape the financial peril so many others suffered.

While the country was coming to terms with the financial crisis, Millicent was focused on getting better. As a result of the misdiagnosis, Millicent's appendix and surrounding area were badly infected, and she was quite ill. To recuperate, she was sent to Stockbridge, Massachusetts, the town Norman Rockwell later described as "the best of America, the best of New England." In Stockbridge, a quaint village in the Berkshire Hills, Millicent was a paying guest of Dr. and Mrs. Millett. Under their care she slowly regained enough strength to exercise and walk.[3]

Making the most of her time in Stockbridge, she discovered the renowned Austen Riggs Center, a psychiatric institute. The center sponsored lectures and occasionally opened them to the public. Millicent went to lectures with titles such as "What Is Memory?" and "What Do You Do About Sleep?" To many young people these may not have been titillating topics, but Millicent enjoyed them. Once again, she was able to satisfy her intellectual hunger.

In the spring, Millicent joined her family in Bernardsville. Although she had been fascinated and surrounded by fox hunts during her childhood and her years at Foxcroft, she had never participated. Her cousin, Mary Stevens Baird, was about to change that.

Mary, nine years older than Millicent, was her mother's first cousin. Both were Stevenses. Mary lived on an estate adjacent to Millicent's childhood home. Although the Hammonds owned horses, Millicent had limited access to them and was not permitted to ride alone because she lacked the requisite equestrian skills. Cousin Mary had a stable and reintroduced the Hammond sisters to the sport.

Millicent and Ma, as she sometimes called her sister, Mary, dressed in riding attire—long skirted tweed coats and jodhpurs—before they set out for the stables. The hunting schedule sanctioned four days a week for hunts. Although Millicent did not have a horse of her own, it was easy for her to borrow one from friends because she was a lightweight, weighing 120 pounds. Eventually she bought a thoroughbred mare she named Love Lea. Millicent decided that Love Lea was not an adequate name for a dashing hunter, so she nicknamed her horse Unca.

Foxhunting consumed more and more of Millicent's time. She was not only active on the New Jersey circuit but also in Virginia's fox-hunting territory, not far from Foxcroft. In Virginia, Millicent and Cousin Mary rode and socialized with Mary Rumsey, one of the founders of *Newsweek* and a sister of Averell Harriman; Archie Randolph, the master of the local hunting Piedmont Pack and cousin of Millicent's maternal grandmother; and Jock Whitney, philanthropist and businessman. "Fox-hunting was such a wild lovely thing to do," said Millicent. "I don't know why, it terribly appealed to me. Perhaps because we didn't often find a fox."[4]

Millicent enjoyed riding as a means of leisure. For travel she drove a car. One April evening, after midnight, she drove by the home of Reeve Schley, the vice-president of Chase National Bank in New York, mayor of Far Hills, and grandfather of Christine Todd Whitman, who would serve as governor of New Jersey from 1994 to 2001. The Schleys lived in Far Hills, an affluent town not far from Bernardsville. As Millicent approached, she saw flames shooting upward into the night sky. She ran toward the home to help.

William Johnson, a stableman for the family, had already noticed the fire, awakened the family, and called the fire department. Mr. and Mrs. Schley and their nineteen-year-old daughter, Eleanor (mother of Christine Todd Whitman), escaped from the burning home. Once outside they realized twelve-year-old John (Jackie) Prentice Schley was still inside. "Flames raging inside the house made it impossible for firemen to reach the boy's second floor bedroom by the stairway," reported a front-page story in the *New York Times*.[5] Another hour passed before firemen were able to enter the boy's room. It was too late. Jackie had died in the blaze. But, before the firemen had arrived on the scene, "an attempt to get into the home to rescue the boy while the fire was raging was made by Miss Millicent Hammond of New York, daughter of Ogden H. Hammond, former Ambassador to Spain, who has been visiting friends here, firemen said today. Miss Hammond's dress caught fire in the attempt and by ripping the dress off, she was saved from suffering burns."[6]

Despite the outcome, Millicent, then twenty-one, was praised for her courageous effort. That night, long before she became a public figure, by putting the welfare of another before her own, she demonstrated a characteristic with which she was closely associated during her long public service career. Only once did she mention the fire to her son. She never mentioned the events of that evening to Jackie's niece, Christine Todd Whitman, who in an interview said she was unaware of Millicent's reported attempts to rescue the boy.[7] Nor did Whitman know that Jackie's death had been front-page news in the *New York Times*. All she knew about the rescue attempts was that her mother reportedly crawled through the house to rescue him.

Later that year Millicent did not escape injury. Although she loved foxhunting, she was not a skilled rider. After thirteen falls, she had suffered one fractured leg and one concussion. Her stubbornness was the cause of her mishaps. "I fell off any time a horse refused. I couldn't believe the horses would refuse. I didn't have a very strong seat, so if he refused, I fell off, because I was headed over the fence and he wasn't."[8] When Millicent broke her leg, her accident made local headlines. Because the accident occurred in the autumn, Ogden and Daisy had already closed their Bernardsville home and retreated to Manhattan for the winter.

After Millicent broke her leg she stayed with her friend Rhoda Clark and Rhoda's husband John. Rhoda, older than Millicent, was one of her three closest friends in addition to her sister. The other two were Cousin Mary and Mary Pyne Cutting, a family friend. All were about ten years older than Millicent. Millicent was mature beyond her years and the company she kept reflected that. Her sister, the only one close to her in age, married that summer and moved to Italy, her husband's native country.

Ma's marriage to an Italian count was the talk of Bernardsville in the summer of 1931. The marriage attracted attention not only locally but also in Europe. Ma, the daughter of the former U.S. ambassador to Spain, as the newspapers were quick to point out, married Count Guerino Roberti, Ghino to his friends. Ghino, an Italian diplomat, was based in New York where he met Mary. He was the son of Count Piero Roberti, a prominent attorney in Rome.

At noon on August 8, 1931, Ghino and Ma exchanged their wedding vows at the Church of Our Lady of Perpetual Help in Bernardsville, with crowds gathered outside. Inside, the church was flooded with white summer flowers and the renowned Paulist Boys' Choir sang as guests arrived. During the mass, a papal blessing, sent by Pope Pius XI,[9] was bestowed on the young couple as Daisy beamed with pride.

Ma and Ghino had many guests and a large bridal party. Millicent, the maid of honor, was one of seven bridesmaids. Her brothers, Oggie and Mac, along with members of the Italian diplomatic corps, rounded out the wedding party. After the ceremony, guests converged on the Hammond estate for a brunch reception. The invitation list resembled a who's who of notable philanthropists, bankers, and politicians, including former New Jersey Governor Edward Stokes. Once the celebration was over the newlyweds went to Long Beach, Long Island, for a few days before sailing to Italy. Ma was now an ocean away from Millicent.

---

It was not long before Millicent was courted too. She was a fixture in the local Bernardsville circuit, as was her groom-to-be. Hugh Fenwick was hard to miss, always the center of attention. "He wasn't really good-looking," Millicent said, "but he was fascinating. Everyplace he turned up, he made it a party. There was something irreverent and very sensual about him."[10]

Hugh was a tall barrel-chested man. His wit, charm, and buoyant personality made him a perennial life of the party. He had a fondness for alcohol, adventure, and women and had a reputation for being a lady's man, despite the fact that he was married. His wife was the former Dorothy Ledyard, daughter of a well-known, wealthy stockbroker who happened to be president of the New York Stock Exchange and a Bernardsville resident. When Millicent and Hugh met, Dorothy was spending the summer in Bridgehampton.

Fenwick's roots were in Humboldt County, California, where his father, Frederick McLeod Fenwick, had inherited the family lumber business. Hugh's childhood, like Millicent's, was less than perfect. All he ever said about his mother, Agnes Duff Keese, was that she had a weakness for martinis and used to drink them out of a wastebasket.[11] His parents lived in San Francisco and later divorced. They often sent him to the family lumber ranch in Eureka, California. The ranch had been in the family since Hugh's great-grandfather bought it years earlier and revolutionized the timber industry in northern California by transporting lumber via the waterways rather than by mules.[12] Glen Timmons, manager of the Fenwick ranch, became a father figure to Hugh and someone he wanted to emulate. Timmons led a cowboy life; he liked to ride and shoot. Hugh split his youth between Timmons and his grandparents, who also lived in California. Shuttling between various public and private schools, he eventually graduated from Eureka High School in Eureka, California.

Following his high school graduation, Hugh was sent east to attend a collegiate prep school in New York City, where his father lived, and then was sent to the Germantown Academy in Pennsylvania. After a year at Germantown, Hugh went to Harvard where his extracurricular activities prevailed over his studies. This should not have been a surprise. His high school transcripts were filled with C's, D's and F's. But his father was adamant about Hugh attending Harvard, his own alma mater. In a telling letter to the dean during Hugh's first semester, his father wrote:

"Hugh does not like to study and he will have to be watched and not allowed to lay down on his work. If he does I will be willing to furnish him with help, provided I know of his delinquency before it is too late. Morally he is all right, except a disposition toward moral cowardice, when he gets into a jam. Most people with pleasant personalities have this weakness. He is inclined to dodge the issue when he should come clean. Have prodded him repeatedly but have made little progress. He seeks good company and, fortunately, has no bad habits, except that he is extravagant, which always leads to trouble. I feel he will never be a good student. He must depend on absorption to be benefited by a college education. My belief is that he would make a good salesman. He seems to have that turn of mind and an ability to make friends. He will work on anything in which he is interested. The problem is to find what interests him most. Perhaps Automobile Engineering."[13] Millicent would have done anything to be afforded the educational opportunities Hugh had, and he would have gladly traded the academic rigors forced upon him for her carefree education. The letter his father wrote foreshadowed much about his life.

Back in Bernardsville, Hugh was larger than life. He stood more than six feet tall, and often told tales as tall as he was. He easily befriended people. His outgoing personality and charm attracted the ladies more than his appearance did. His hair was receding and his weight fluctuated. Cousin Mary described Hugh as someone who "made a specialty of marrying ladies with money . . . he's coarse and he's funny. He has a lot of charm, ghastly as he is. Oh, he's full of charm. He can charm the birds off the trees."[14]

By the time Millicent met Hugh, he had been telling everyone that he was a graduate of Harvard in the class of 1928, and it was accepted as fact. But, as his father feared, Hugh never applied himself and faced expulsion for his failing marks. His father's intervention and Hugh's promises to apply himself bought him more time, which he used largely to socialize and to play on Harvard's football and polo teams. Finally, after a year of empty promises and probation, the dean sent a letter to his father, "I don't know how important you think it that he [Hugh] should make a really good record in his studies, but it seems to us, not only necessary that he should meet our minimum standard, but ridiculous, in view of his ability, that he should not do considerably better than that."[15]

In the spring of 1926, Hugh failed to take his midterm exams but was excused because of a head injury he had sustained in a car accident earlier that year. His academic shortcomings were attributed to his concussion and prompted his decision not to return the following year. It was a calculated and proactive move, however. For two years, Harvard had been reprimanding him about missed exams and failing grades. To return, Hugh would have to take, and pass, make-up exams. Knowing this, his father was still adamant about his son's return. In September 1926, the charade finally ended. Harvard informed his father that Hugh, still a freshman on probation, had not met the minimum requirements to remain enrolled. At last, after two years, Hugh was put out of his academic misery.

After Harvard, Hugh earned his wings at the U.S. Naval Air Station in Pensacola, Florida, and became a lieutenant in the flying section of the New Jersey National Guard. His career came to an abrupt end when he flew dangerously low over a Bernardsville apple orchard. Hugh, leading two planes, disappeared into a low patch of clouds. Before he knew it, the planes were much closer to the ground than he had expected. He pulled up, but the two planes behind him didn't have time to compensate for their low altitude and plunged to the earth below. Two men died. Although reprimanded for his irresponsible behavior, Hugh was not deterred from flying and used his passion for flight, a daring enterprise in the early 1930s, to impress Millicent with flybys and fun-filled rides. He borrowed a Curtiss Robin, high-winged plane with a fully enclosed cabin, to woo Millicent. The Curtiss Robin was a new air-craft, first built in 1928. It had a bucket seat in front for the pilot and a benchlike seat in the back for two passengers. Millicent thought flying was great fun and soon became an avid admirer of aviation, and of Hugh. Hugh piqued her interest in flight and inspired Millicent to take flying lessons.

But Millicent's ability to fly was no better than her ability to hunt foxes. "When you fall off a horse so often without hurting yourself, you soon learn that there's nothing much to it," said Millicent. "It was just like flying, you know. I tried to fly, be a pilot, and I flew one plane, a Wright J–5 Stearman, into the ground, landed it on its nose and damaged the propeller. I flew another time, landed the plane too high, and damaged the whole undercarriage. It was awful, very embarrassing. And finally I could not get anybody to give me any more lessons because of course they feared for the safe return of their planes."[16] After having four accidents and being banned by two airports, Millicent realized her depth perception was poor, and she reluctantly accepted that she would never amount to anything more than Hugh's passenger, not a pilot.[17]

Initially, Hugh and Millicent's courtship was kept quiet. After all, Hugh was married. But Millicent did not care. She was drawn to him. Friends sensed there was someone special in her life, but they did not know who he was. One society column alluded to someone in Bernardsville consuming much of Millicent's time and attention. Hugh's outgoing personality and quick wit pulled Millicent into his web. Her heart was trapped.

After keeping their affair secret for months, Millicent boldly decided to take the matter into her own hands. She went directly to Hugh's wife, a course of action even more drastic than going public. Millicent found Dorothy at home and bedridden with a 103-degree fever. Undeterred, Millicent walked into the bedroom, threw herself down on her knees at the edge of the bed, and said to Dorothy, "We must pray." Then she confessed her love for Hugh. When Millicent finished she desperately asked, "What should we do?"[18] Dorothy, already feverish, must have wondered if she was hallucinating. Before her eyes was Millicent Hammond in a quandary over her love for Dorothy's husband.

Millicent's efforts were not wasted. In 1931, after a mere three years of marriage and no children, Dorothy and Hugh Fenwick quietly divorced. Millicent had won. She got her man. Whether she could keep him was another matter entirely.

One can only imagine the gossip Millicent and Hugh's relationship generated. In the early 1930s, divorce was taboo and divorcées shunned. Societal norms were based on the teachings of the church—a Christian point of view, regardless of whether it was Protestant or Catholic. Bernardsville and New York social circles consisted of a strictly defined group of people. And in their midst was Millicent, a socialite, pawing over a married man. Whispers circulated, but it is doubtful that Millicent confided in anyone until she confronted Dorothy. Her closest confidante, her sister, was a world away.

Millicent's interest in first a married man, and then a divorced man, disgusted Daisy, a devout Catholic. The two women had always clashed, but this time Millicent shocked and embarrassed her stepmother. When Millicent announced her engagement to Hugh it was more than Daisy could bear. Making her disapproval known, she kicked Millicent out of the house, and Ogden, true to form, did nothing to stop her. Ogden, equally unhappy about his daughter's decision to marry Hugh, said, "He is no gentlemen."[19] It seemed that Hugh Fenwick was able to charm everyone but Millicent's parents.

After being thrown out of her parents' home, Millicent moved in with her Great-Aunt Carrie (Caroline Bayard Stevens Wittpenn), whose home was part of the Stevens Bernardsville compound on property adjacent to that of the Hammonds. On June 11, 1932, shortly after the move, Millicent and Hugh married. Once news of their marriage circulated, one society columnist wrote:

"That Millicent Hammond was being kept at Bernardsville by an attraction greater than hunger I said months ago. Unreasonable to suppose that a girl familiar with courts and embassies, Infantas and Grandees, preferred suburban New Jersey to cosmopolitan Manhattan. In addition there was Millicent's winter wardrobe. That was not selected for the delectation of dove parties. Those expensive gowns indicated that she did not expect to regularly dine en famille with a kinswoman chaperone. New York friends were sure that an adorer lurked in the background, but did not suspect that the favored one was Hugh McLeod Fenwick. Anybody knew, however, that Millicent would wed whom, when and where she pleased and that is precisely what she did."[20]

On her wedding day, Millicent wore a white satin V-neck wedding gown with long, fitted sleeves. Her cathedral veil of tulle was held in place by a wreath of orange blossoms, and she carried a bouquet of white orchids. Unlike her sister, Millicent was not married in the local Catholic church but on the terrace in the Hammond garden. Finding someone to perform a wedding ceremony for a divorced man was a challenge. Hugh turned to one of his aviation buddies, the Reverend Gill Robb Wilson, to perform the ceremony. Wilson was the first director of aviation in New Jersey, serving from 1930 to 1941, and the minister of the Fourth Presbyterian Church in Trenton. Millicent's marriage created a stir, but stopped short of being a scandal. Only Daisy ostracized her.

Millicent's wedding lacked the fanfare and grandeur that had surrounded Ma's nuptials. Because of the shame Daisy associated with the marriage, the occasion was a small affair camouflaged by the death of Daisy's brother, Arthur McClure. Typically, a larger wedding was expected for someone of Millicent's stature as the daughter of an ambassador who had been presented at the courts of Spain and Great Britain.

Because the wedding was small and Millicent's sister was not there, it is likely the arrangements were made hastily. In Ma's absence, Millicent chose her friend Rhoda Clark as her only attendant. Hugh asked Robert Livingston Stevens, Millicent's cousin, to be the best man. His ushers were Archibald Stevens Alexander, another cousin of Millicent's, and two of his friends.

Newspaper wedding announcements were quick to point out that this was Hugh's second marriage. They also highlighted his career and glory days at Harvard "where he won letters in football and polo. He played center on the varsity football team. He learned to fly at the United States Naval Air Station in Pensacola, Fla. . . . is president of Aviation Utilities of New Jersey [founded with funds from his wealthy first wife] and president of Fenwick & Co., insurance brokers, of Newark, N.J. He is a member of the Harvard Club of New York, the Racquet Club of Washington, the Aviation Country Club at Hicksville, Long Island, and is a leading polo player of New Jersey."[21]

Even before the ceremony, the marriage was off to a rocky start. Rhoda, Millicent's matron of honor, test-drove a new car the day of the wedding and was involved in a fatal accident. One man was killed and Rhoda sustained non-life-threatening injuries. Because she was hospitalized, Millicent asked Cousin Mary to stand in for Rhoda. Rhoda, like Millicent, was carefree, but it is doubtful Millicent would have behaved so recklessly on her friend's wedding day.

After the 5:30 P.M. ceremony things did not improve. Daisy was determined to sabotage the wedding. She had already ensured it would be a small event, limited to immediate family, but she took it one step further. Not wanting any painful reminders of the marriage, Daisy trailed the photographer and unplugged the lights every time he tried to snap a picture, making it impossible for photos to be taken inside. The only photographs left unscathed were taken outside in the natural sunlight, leaving Millicent with few photographs from her wedding day.

Even the honeymoon was marred. Soon after their wedding announcement appeared, the young couple made headlines again. The two planned to fly to San Francisco and then on to Alaska, but they didn't make it past Pennsylvania.

"Hugh Fenwick's flying honeymoon almost came to grief yesterday when he and his bride, the former Millicent Hammond of Bernardsville, ground-looped and turned over in their biplane at Norristown, Pa. Neither was injured, but the plane was badly damaged. . . . Witnesses said the plane had scarcely left the ground when its nose dropped, causing it to ground-loop and turn over. The plane is being repaired at the field, and when finished the couple will continue."[22]

To ease their disappointment about their foiled honeymoon plans, Rhoda Clark invited Millicent and Hugh to join her in Bermuda. The couple gladly accepted.

When Millicent and Hugh returned to New Jersey they rented a house set on several acres in Bedminster, ten miles from Ogden and Daisy. The newlyweds' home offered scenic views of the rolling hills of Somerset County. On the property, in the heart of New Jersey farm country, was a big red barn, water tower, windmill, and chicken coops. Although Millicent and Hugh lived in foxhunting country the expense of hunting was more than the young couple could bear, and Millicent's foxhunting days ended. Shortly after the two wed, Millicent learned that her family's business, the Hoboken Land and Improvement Company, was not going to pay any more dividends—the income on which they were living.[23] The Fenwicks stayed afloat thanks to the capital on her unspent inheritance, but Millicent was beginning to feel the effects of the Depression.

Both Millicent and Hugh were social by nature. Early in their marriage they hosted a local scavenger hunt that exhibited their sense of humor. Friends were given a list of things to collect like a strand of hair pulled from the tail of a white horse or to bring someone from the area that no one had seen before—a lot of people hitchhiked—and participants would nab these wanderers and bring them to the party. At the end, whoever collected the most items and brought them to the Fenwick's front lawn won a prize.

The Fenwicks spent a year at their rented residence before purchasing a house and 150 acres in Bernardsville, just a quarter-mile from where Millicent grew up. Their new home, paid for by Millicent's inheritance, dated back to pre-Revolutionary days. Originally it had four rooms, but by the time they bought it there had been many additions.

Millicent and Hugh built a chicken coop and planted vegetable gardens. Since Hugh was not a farmer, they hired men to tend their land, cattle, and chickens. Their excess milk and eggs were sold to local dairies.

With the farm staffed, Hugh commuted to Newark where he sold airplane parts.

To many who knew them, Hugh and Millicent were an odd match. While both were daring in their exploits, Millicent held honesty and truth above all else. Her husband, on the other hand, seemed ill-equipped to tell the truth. "Daddy was incapable of telling the truth even when it served no purpose. He changed his stories depending on who he was talking to. He could tell someone he went golfing yesterday with three women, and then twenty minutes later he would tell someone else he was out on the farm milking cows yesterday, and if you called him on it he would say something like I went golfing the day before. His lies were not consistent nor would he, or could he, keep track of which lie he had told whom,"[24] said their son, Hugo, years later.

Yet both had intellectual interests, were concerned about world affairs, and shared a passion for flying and riding. Millicent and Hugh were well-mannered, strict disciplinarians, and stubborn in their ways. Maureen, Hugh's daughter from a subsequent marriage (after his divorce from Millicent), remembered him as formidable. He always used to say, "You can forget anything in your life you ever learned, but never forget your manners."[25] Maureen remembered having to curtsy, shake hands, and be polite.

Hugh used to turn the dining room table into a forum in which he predetermined who would be in the hot seat. He would bring up embarrassing subjects, making guests uncomfortable. It was his way of testing people. He could be mean in pointing out other people's faults. Despite his mean streak, more people were familiar with his charming, witty side. Hugh could be a lot of fun; he could make others howl with laughter. While Millicent possessed his charming and witty characteristics, she rarely let down her serious guard.

---

Millicent's married life was rather modest. She frequently played solitaire, read, or knitted, often waiting for her husband to return home. She loved being near him. A week after her first child was born she wrote in her journal that it was not "an exciting winter but pleasant for me—feeling content in the present and hopeful for the future . . . watched Hugh cutting wood on the revolving saw blade, made an awful noise, shrieking as it cut the wood, sun was warm, and Hugh ruffled my hair as he passed by me."[26] She longed for his affection.

On Millicent's twenty-fourth birthday, February 25, 1934, she gave birth to their first child, a daughter, Mary Stevens Fenwick. As their family grew, Hugh's family shrank with the death of his father that same year. To commemorate his passing, Hugh did a low flyby in California.

He was not willing to stop taking risks in his plane despite the lessons of his past.

With the birth of their first child, Millicent hired a nanny for $75 a month, slowly using up her capital of $2,400 a year. Millicent paid the bills, but Hugh incurred more expenses than they could afford. Millicent drew the line at his private clubs and refused to pay his annual dues. Her inheritance, which she gained access to the year before she married, was derived primarily from the devalued family-owned Hoboken Land and Improvement Company.

Hugh often promised to be home by dinner but never made it. His words were worthless. Millicent never knew when, or if, he would be home. His womanizing ways had not changed, nor did his penchant for golf and country clubs. In the beginning Millicent let it slide. As time passed, she couldn't keep silent. But Hugh always had an answer.

Besides worrying about her husband's whereabouts, Millicent now had an infant to care for. Motherhood did not come naturally to Millicent. As a child she had been provided for, but not nurtured. Ogden's remarriage left Millicent and her siblings estranged children in their own home and left Millicent with no maternal instincts. She never knew what it was like to have a nurturing mother, nor did she know how to be one. After Mary's birth, the nanny Millicent hired worked six straight weeks before her first day off. Alone with the infant for the first time, Millicent screamed as she bathed her child. Mrs. Kocsis, the Hungarian woman whose husband worked for the Hammonds, ran to her aid. In the bathroom she found a panicked mother who feared she had almost drowned her firstborn.[27] Mrs. Kocsis, there to do the laundry, quickly gained control of the situation, and mother and daughter were fine.

When Mary was nearly three she gained a baby brother, Hugh Hammond Fenwick. Hugo to his family. His birth prompted a visit from Ghino and Ma, who came to see their newborn nephew, his mother, and his three-year-old sister. Millicent spent two weeks in the hospital and cherished visits from Ma and Hugh. If she was having a bad day, the mere arrival of her husband brightened her spirits, regardless of how long he stayed.[28]

By the time Hugo was born, signs of marital trouble were emerging. A few days after Millicent and the baby returned home, it was Hugh's birthday. Instead of spending it with his family he unexpectedly went to New York, much to Millicent's dismay. A week later it was Millicent's and Mary's birthday. Mary was turning three. To celebrate, Millicent, Mary, and Ma ate dinner in a Bernardsville restaurant and feasted on cake and ice cream for dessert. Hugh came home hours later.

A few weeks later, Millicent decided she needed to get away. She went on a whirlwind trip with her Great-Aunt Florence and Great-Uncle Arthur Whitney, on their private 270-foot yacht and left her five-week-old infant son and toddler daughter in the care of others. Hugh did not accompany her. For two months she traveled from port to port in Italy, Greece, and Yugoslavia, devouring the sights on shore and literary classics on deck. Among the works she read were *Antigone*, *Oedipus Rex*, *Plautus*, *Jane Eyre*, and *Romeo and Juliet*. Keeping a journal during the voyage, she always noted when she spoke to her husband. Sometimes the conversations were good, other times disappointing. The trip was not her first without her husband. Earlier in the marriage, Millicent had traveled to Italy and Greece with Rhoda. At the time the Fenwicks had not yet been married a year.

Within the first few years of marriage Hugh succumbed to his playboy ways. Millicent overlooked his sexual indiscretions but could not do the same with his countless lies. Truth was sacrosanct to her. When Millicent confided her marital woes and her difficulty living with a liar to her sister, Ma simply said, "You must learn that you can not have life on *your terms*."[29] In the end it was a combination of Millicent's stubbornness and Hugh's lies and liaisons that led to the demise of the marriage after six years. In 1938, as Europe was bracing for war, Hugh went to Europe to sell airplanes for Vultee Aircraft. He never returned.

Millicent's marriage remained a mystery to others throughout her life. She did little more than acknowledge its existence. When asked about her marriage she nonchalantly sidestepped the question by reminiscing about the farm she and her husband owned. She referred to the animals, but never to the man. Even to those in Millicent's inner circle the subject was forbidden. Growing up, her two children knew little about their parents' union, but they knew not to ask. Millicent never minced words about their father. She allowed them to form their own unbiased opinion, distinct from her own.

Millicent used to tell Hugo that everyone needs a safe harbor, and she felt her marriage should have been her safe harbor but wasn't. Bills should have been paid, Hugh should have come home on time. A safe harbor should embody some security and control, ingredients missing from the Fenwick marriage.[30]

In a rare moment, decades after the marriage collapsed, Millicent confided in Annette Lantos, wife of California Congressman Tom Lantos, that if she had to do it all over again, she "wished she made more of an effort in keeping her marriage. She talked about how charming her husband was and how much she loved him. She said she didn't so much mind his running around as much as the lies that bothered her."[31]

Millicent managed to survive her mother's death and her stepmother's reign, but surviving a broken heart was another matter. To release her pent-up angst she turned to writing. Her short stories revealed a woman scorned and vengeful:

"She had fallen madly in love with him at once the first time they met: and it was she rather than he who did the courting. In a thousand ways, some sub-conscious some half-admitted, she set out to marry him. The meetings she arranged she could only half-admit because of her pride; the assumptions of compliance and softness were entirely sub-conscious. They married quite soon—a year after meeting—and the evasions began two or three years later.

"At dinner parties she could hear him, boastful but gentle, talking to the women on either side. Her ear was so attuned to his voice that even when the table was very long she could pick out his words. The first shock was a small one '—and it was so wonderful to see you and Harry at the Stewarts' . . . ' Certainly innocent enough: Harry was the woman's husband. But at the Stewarts'! He had never told her he'd been there on a trip described to her as a desert of business in the heart of Baltimore. The rest of the evening—the dinner and the music and the endless goodbyes—was like a tightening vise. And when at last she could speak to him she longed for the comfort of a complete, heart-warming explanation. What she got was a vague stammer about it being unimportant, a rush of over-good-natured banter and reassurance.

"From then on the pursuit of certainty was her only goal. And soon she would have been almost satisfied with any clear answer. But she could never bring him to terms, never she felt—as though he were a hunted fox—bring him to ground. He would neither admit any lie, nor would he stop lying. Evasion was his tactic, hiding perhaps even from herself, rationalizing his infidelities. The failure of their marriage—The more she pressed for any hard fact, the more he fled from her and from all facts. Her self discipline concealed it from everyone else, but she knew that she was almost a mad woman.

"And then the crisis came. One summer night, hours after they had come home from dinner, she heard a car's motor starting in the garage. One quick look in his room proved that he was gone and running down the gravel in her thin satin mules and dressgown [*sic*], she started the chase in another car. Guessing the way he had gone, straining to see lights through the leaves, she [drove] along the country roads, with pale fields on each side. She did not know exactly what she planned and her foot was jerking so wildly that she had trouble keeping it on the accelerator. But when she saw the car, and verified the license plate she knew exactly what she would do—she would kill him, drive him into the ditch, smash into him with the car, face him [with] something he could not evade and kill him.

"As soon as she started to pass him, he speeded up. Then, finding he was being followed, he went still faster. It was a long chase but hopeless for him. Her car was faster and on a long straight piece of road she caught him. The moment had come. She drew even with him. The whole beautiful moonlit sky turned red in her eyes—dark red with brighter eyes— and she jerked the wheels of her car.

"Locked together, the cars rocked down the road and came to a stop against a telephone pole. She felt sick and emptied and tired. His car was wrecked but hers could still be driven and she sat speechless while he drove her home.

"The incident was never referred to again. He was so frightened at her violence that he didn't dare try her further for the time being and she was so shocked at the revelation of her capacity for violence that she could hardly think of anything else and carefully avoided looking for evidence. For the time being, there was an uneasy truce and it didn't last too long because he conveniently and quite respectably died of pneumonia.

"Mrs. Parkinson, was punctilious arranging the funeral, correct about her period of mourning, stricter than ever in her civic and charitable work. When she thought of the incident—and it was rarely as the years passed—she would always answer herself 'Yes—but if only he hadn't pretended it wasn't so.' She had learned very little."[32]

How far from the truth this story was is hard to know. When Millicent ran for Congress in 1974 she told a similar story to staffer Roger Bodman about a standoff with her husband in which they were both in their own cars facing each other in, he thought, their driveway. She never revealed the outcome.[33] Millicent had a temper, and nothing triggered it more than dishonesty. She could not even utter the words "affair" or "unfaithful," which certainly were at the root of her marital ills. Instead she chose the word "evasions."

"There are two theories on why Millie never remarried," said Hugh. "One theory is that she had such a miserable experience the first time, she didn't want to repeat it. The second theory, and the one I prefer, is that she could never find anyone as charming as me."[34]

# 7

## *The* Vogue

## *Years*

A woman, to make a success in the fashion world, should have one qualification above all others. She should have trained and distinguished taste.

—Edna Woolman Chase

As the Depression continued, Millicent found herself an unemployed single mother. She had a fixed income and a four-year-old daughter and one-year-old son to support. Hugh not only deserted his wife of six years and their young children, but unbeknownst to his wife he also left behind a mounting pile of debt. When he went to Europe, it caused alarm among individuals to whom he owed money. Thinking Hugh had skipped town, debt collectors inundated Millicent with his unpaid balances. Although caught off guard, Millicent didn't get a lawyer. "That never occurred to me," she said. "Maybe that helped too, because they realized that they were not going to be opposed or anything fancy." Setting aside money each week, Millicent slowly paid her husband's debts. Cousin Mary advised her to only pay the locals. "I told her she should pay the butcher, the baker, the candlestick maker, but not his New York debts—Giovanni and Club 21."[1]

Hugh's accumulated debts were "a terrible discovery," said Millicent. "[On] Friday nights this man called Bill Boyd who was a processor in Somerville used to bring another bill. And finally he said to me, 'You know I can hardly stand this, Mrs. Fenwick,' and I said, 'Well, neither can I.'" Ultimately, by allotting $10 a month for some debts, and $20 for others, she managed to pay Hugh's creditors. "It really didn't amount to so much—a couple of thousand dollars, but at the time it seemed so huge."[2] And indeed it was huge. The average annual income in 1938, the year Hugh left, was only $1,293.[3]

Prior to Hugh's departure, Millicent occasionally modeled and had been photographed by fashion photographer Cecil Beaton. Pictures of Millicent appeared in magazines such as *Harper's Bazaar* and *Vogue*. Her slender figure, tall stature, creamy skin, and natural radiance were easily captured on film. On at least one occasion Millicent shared mirror space with the illustrious Clare Boothe Luce, who modeled before her writing and political careers took shape.

All the while, Millicent continued to write. She had always thought she could be a writer and sometimes used the pseudonym Joan Cliquot. In her writing it was difficult to discern between fact and fiction because her prose seemed to draw upon her own experiences. In one story, about the tender relationship between a mother and daughter, she wrote:

"There was something touching in these belongings of her mother's— so long dead. Her early childhood was a vague dream through which the figure of her beautiful mother moved— always gentle, always lovely and with a clear low voice. She saw her in flashes like pictures: in the rose garden, bending over a yellow rose, laughing; in an open automobile in winter, wrapped in furs, with a dark Russian fur hat. She remembered the ease, the security of those days; they formed the strong rich background against which her mother stood out—the single, brilliant figure. . . . It had all ended shortly after her sixth birthday. What a nightmare those intervening years had been."[4]

Minnie Astor, wife of Vincent Astor, was one of the friends with whom Millicent shared her publishing dreams. She told Astor about her stories and her quest to find a literary agent. Agonizing over a typewriter, but not knowing how to type, Millicent tried to turn her handwritten prose into the typed text needed to submit to an agent. Like many other writers, Millicent learned about the difficulties and disappointments of trying to find an agent or a publisher. Although Millicent's work was eventually rejected, Minnie did not know this when she sat next to Condé Nast, renowned for his publishing ingenuity, at a Newport dinner party.

As Astor and Condé Nast chatted, he asked if she knew anyone "with dash and style who could write."[5] He was looking for someone to add to his *Vogue* staff. Astor told him about Millicent and facilitated a meeting between the two. She told Millicent to bring her short stories to him. Fortunately, Millicent had made a carbon copy of her typed text; the originals were still with the agent. During the interview Millicent was asked if she had sold any of her writing. "No," she said, "but my agent has three stories," which, of course, was true. What Millicent didn't know was that they were in the mail. The agent had rejected her material and offered the following critique:

"I think you are sort of in the halfway ground—not the greatest writer in the world, but by no means the worst. In fact, I'm rather inclined to think that you don't take yourself quite seriously enough about it. There are some passages in these stories which struck me as very nice indeed— the sort of emotional or lyrical or sensuous thing that goes for really fine writing. . . . When I first began about four years ago, there was nothing I would like better than to take on people with the first beginnings of talent like you, but the trouble is that I now have between fifteen and twenty of the poor devils on my hands and that makes things so hectic that I have to be very stern with myself about taking on more."[6]

Although this response deflated Millicent's writing aspirations, the timing could not have been better. *Vogue* liked her stories and she was hired. "So again the good Lord was kind, because if I had to say that the agent sent them [the stories] back, I might not have gotten the job," said Millicent.[7] She began her fourteen-year career at *Vogue* as a caption writer. She earned $40 a week, or $160 a month, adding to her $200 monthly income from her investments for a total monthly income of $360.

Before Millicent accepted the *Vogue* job she unabashedly laid out her terms of employment. She told her employer she "did not want anything to do with fashion or high society,"[8] the core of the magazine. She felt it was too snobbish and did not want to lean on family or friends, many of whom were featured in *Vogue*, and she feared they would be embarrassed into helping her. Regardless of Millicent's patronage concerns, her high-society friends and blue-blooded upbringing made her ripe for the position.

Prior to her good fortune with Condé Nast, Millicent had embarked on a job search. She set out on a sweltering summer day in Manhattan with one mission, to find work. The unbearable heat forced her to seek relief inside Bonwit Teller's air-conditioned environment. Often a customer at the upscale department store, Millicent decided to apply for a position. She was led to a non–air-conditioned cubbyhole by a "nice looking woman with saddle shoes and a bandana who looked like someone out of Vassar." The woman peppered Millicent with questions, "Date of birth? Mother's name? Father's name? College?" It was on this, the fourth question, that Millicent's prospect of employment began to fade. Millicent told the woman, "I'm sorry, I never went to college." The woman made a note of it, and then asked, "High school?" Millicent said, "Well, I did go for two years to a school in Virginia but I never graduated." The woman looked at Millicent, put down her pencil and reluctantly told Millicent she could not hire her without a high school diploma. Millicent, not one to easily give up, then asked, "Couldn't I sell stockings or be a runner [carrying important messages or items from one department to another]?" "No," the interviewer replied, "You are twenty-eight. You're too old."[9]

Dejected, Millicent went back outside, where she found herself once again in the bright sunlight and agonizing heat. All she could think was "My God, what am I going to do?"[10] The former society girl was at a crossroads. Most people would turn to family for help, but not Millicent. When asked why not, her response ranged from the naive, "Why it never occurred to me," to the steadfast, "Well I didn't want to." When writer Peggy Lamson questioned her further, asking if it were a matter of pride Millicent said, "No, I don't think so. You know, the funny thing is, it never occurred to me to say I'm *not* going to talk to the family about this. But on the other hand it never occurred to me to say I think I'll ask them. My own sister, my father, my cousins. I don't understand it. To this day I don't understand it. But I'm sure it was not done in any spirit of defiance."[11] Her reluctance to seek financial support was likely a combination of pride and denial. She did not want to admit, particularly to Daisy and Ogden, that her marriage was in shambles. The marriage had forged a wedge between herself and her parents. They maintained a cordial relationship, not an intimate one.

Millicent's experience at Bonwit Teller became a defining moment for her. By refusing to seek the simple solution of asking those around her for help, she realized for the first time the daily struggles common to many others. Never before had she needed to seek employment; she had always had the security of an income generated by her mother's trust fund. Millicent's job search was a vital lesson that broadened her awareness about the work force and molded the compassionate politician she became. On some level she understood what it felt like not to have the means necessary to feed, clothe, and shelter her family. Although by no means destitute, she identified with the burden of providing for a family combined with the lack of a stable source of income. As a result of her Bonwit Teller interview, and the importance placed on a high school diploma, Millicent said, "Perhaps that is why I now feel very sympathetic to those who are not given a chance. Many good people are turned down without the right credentials."[12]

In the end, Millicent was better suited for a job at *Vogue* than at Bonwit Teller. Although she disdained high society and fashion she realized she was a part of that world. In truth she probably knew *Vogue*'s subjects better than she did its readership. Its pages were filled with family friends such as the Astors and Vanderbilts. Feature stories were about topics Millicent experienced firsthand such as foxhunting and flying. In 1940, Millicent wrote an article entitled "They Fly," which featured American women pilots who flew for pleasure, profit, and charity.

About the same time that her article appeared in *Vogue*, Hugh attempted a reconciliation. It had been two years since he left the United States to sell airplanes in war-torn Europe. From London, his home base, he tried to persuade his estranged wife to join him. In response, Millicent asked for a divorce:

"Dear Hugh,

"I am finally writing the letter I know you have been expecting for some time. After a great deal of thought, considering both your position and mine, but above all, the children's, I have come to the conclusion that we had better get a divorce.

"I know that you will agree that your conduct, of which I am fully informed, had made such a decision inevitable. But I don't think it is necessary to go into the details here. It has convinced me that your often repeated remark, that you were not happy with me, was the truth. You will agree, too, I am sure, that I have really done everything I could to make our marriage a success, but I now feel that there is no longer any possibility of it. I hope so fervently that we can end it with dignity and reticence, for the sake of the children, who would, I think, suffer greatly from any other course.

"I think the general consensus of opinion today is that children are better off with their mother in the event of a divorce. Every recent decision that I know of has been decided that way. As to the financial end— I hope that you will be able to make some settlement on the children, so that they may have the doctors and the kind of schooling we both want them to have.

"Will you ask your lawyer here to get in touch with Colonel William J. Donovan, whom I have consulted in this matter. This has not been an easy decision to make. Do let me hear from you as soon as you can. Painful things are better over quickly."[13]

Hugh, not willing to fade into Millicent's past, wrote back:

"Dear Millicent—

"I received your letter of May 24th Wednesday morning. It was not posted until June 1st, which is perhaps somewhat the reason for the delay.

"From your letter, it is somewhat difficult for me to entirely understand your wishes, or, the answer that you wish me to make. This, perhaps, due to the fact, that, I don't believe you wrote it, and, as a consequence, it was impossible for me to get the real spirit or mood that you are in. Couple this to the fact that the last time I saw you was in November, and you will possibly understand my hesitancy in giving you a hasty answer which might cause us both future regrets.

"I cannot agree with the only two reasons you gave for your decision. Both are open to answer. To what 'conduct' do you refer? My conduct in Ankara during Christmas—Baghdad or Palestine in July—Helsinki during continual bombardments—Stockholm in January—Brussels during bombing, fires and an evacuation—a winter in the Balkans, a life

continually in and out of suitcases—heavy bombardment in Paris, where
bombs hit the Air Ministry while I was there, and I spent every night on
the stairs running up and down to and from shelters—travel being limited to a bit of space in the tail of a bomber—endless work which is night
or day, and often both? No one in their right mind would be in Europe, if
they could be in America since last August.

"I came over here to do a job, which no one, including myself, thought
would take so long, and I am not going to quit until it is finished. To
start with, it would be impossible to replace me, with a war on, and,
secondly, I can't let my Company down, after the way they played ball in
peace, just because there is a war. Hundreds have run, but I will not. It
has not all been a bed of roses, and under the conditions, a 'conduct'
remark such as you have made, falls on slightly unsympathetic ears. On
the same subject, it is stupid to say that you are 'fully informed', because
you are not—you have not seen anyone who has had sufficient knowledge to inform you fully of my conduct. Had you come over in June 1939
when I asked you by cable, or, in July when I asked you by telephone,
you could have observed my conduct—then you could say you were fully
cognizant. I was sorry then that you did not, and now, particularly wish
that you had. Your reference to my oft repeated remark that I was not
happy with you, makes little sense—in the same vein, I told you often
that you had flat feet—remarks were often made by us both that were
always forgotten the next morning, and were never meant when they
were said.

"I do agree entirely with your statement that you had done everything to make our marriage a success, but not, that there is no longer
any possibility of it, but, if the end is inevitable, you can be assured that
your fervent hope for dignity and reticence will be realized.

"My ideas on divorce, where children are involved, you know too
well; I experienced it, and the frightful memory is still poignant—you
had a miserable existence due to a step-parent. As a consequence, my
wish is to leave no stone unturned to change your mind, compromise in
any manner you may suggest, or, in short, do anything I can should your
decision not be final.

"Please do not consider the above as a refusal to your request, or a
stall for time. Short of your wishing to marry someone else, I can see no
reasons that could not be obviated, or, at least discussed—my mind is so
open and contains so strongly the wish to go on, that any suggestions or
demands on your part would receive a blanket acceptance by me.

"I have no Lawyer in New York as you know. Also, this is a rather
delicate matter to handle with one by cable, particularly a Lawyer I don't
know, and I cannot think of a friend in the Legal Profession off hand. I
have not written to Colonel Donovan, as you asked. This is in no way

intended as a slur to him—I have met him several times, and have the highest regard for him, but I would prefer to feel, before going that far, that I have done everything possible to change your mind.

"I have not sent you any money since March—mainly, due to pique caused by your silence. Cable me what you need, and I'll telegraph it to you.

"The war looks so grim. I left a deserted Paris Sunday afternoon that would have made you cry—I cannot see anything, short of a miracle, saving France; then England is for it—and that will be a fight."[14]

In his response, Hugh innocently questioned what 'conduct' his wife meant. Although she did not state specifics, his liaisons were well known. "He always had women," said one friend. "The last time I saw him he had a gold cigarette case with a map etched into the lid. A ruby marked every city where he had stayed with a girlfriend."[15]

In the end, Millicent could not dismiss Hugh's deceitfulness or adulterous behavior. Around him she was powerless and enamored. Not wanting to risk opening her wounds, she tried to bury them by ending her marriage. She feared Hugh's willingness to concede to any terms she offered would yield more empty promises. Through written correspondence, the Fenwick marriage met its cordial demise.

"Dear Hugh,

"Thank you very much for your letter. I am sorry, but I still feel as I did when I first wrote you that there is really no use in trying any longer to give our marriage even a pretense of reality.

"You must know that I am sincere in saying I am sorry but I am glad that you feel as I do about ending it with as much dignity as possible. Every acquaintance, and almost every stranger, coming here from England, has given me a broadside about you *&* at least I know that you are well. But there is no need for me to write angrily and with recrimination since you must know what I feel.

"As to the money you said you would send me, I have, as you say, received nothing since March. I would be very glad if you could send me all, or part, of the twelve hundred dollars, as both children, though now quite well, were ill a great part of the winter. Among other bills, there is a big one still owing Dr. Schloss, and very probably, tonsil operations to come this summer.

"Colonel Donovan will bring you this. I hope you will meet him and discuss this whole matter with him.

"Excuse this typewriting, I am using an antique in the Bernardsville News Office."[16]

Five years passed after their exchange of letters before the divorce was finalized in 1945. At the time, less than one percent of the female population living in New Jersey was divorced.[17]

A few years later, Millicent was strolling down a Manhattan street with Mary and Hugo when she bumped into Hugh, also living in New York. Although Millicent never tarnished her ex-husband's name in front of their children, Hugo had a distinct memory of witnessing this awkward encounter between his parents. "Daddy was well-dressed, and they were both uncomfortable . . . they talked at arm's length."[18]

As vice-president of Vultee Aircraft, Hugh caused quite a stir in 1942 with a visionary speech, sponsored by the *New York Times* and later published. In remarks entitled "The Challenge of Air to American Business Men," Hugh highlighted the potential for air transportation based on his experiences abroad.

"How many American business men have ever seen, heard, smelt, or felt what warplanes are now doing, day and night? That is a handicap Europeans do not have. They have seen, heard, smelt and felt aviation, the cruel, hard way. They have suffered as nations were overthrown with lightning speed. In terror, they have watched winged destroyers crumble their cities in flames. They have seen countries conquered by a new kind of battleship operating in the air ocean.

"How many American business men have ever had to hide underground from air attacks?—or have even seen one warplane take off for battle?—let alone hundreds—or thousands!

"Who, among us, has ever watched planes in a simple formation covering twenty to forty square miles?—or in a few minutes felt the earth beneath us tremble as their tons of lethal cargo were released upon objectives many miles away?

"This does not imply that the United States needs to be invaded in order to bring us abreast of Europeans in our air thoughts. But we must be realistic. . . . Millions of European business men have been forced to become air-conditioned as a result of the destructive power of airplanes. They will be ready, and quick, therefore, to employ aircraft for *constructive* purposes after this war."[19]

Hugh clearly had macro visions for the future of air transportation, but not for his marriage, still at an impasse when he gave that speech.

––––––

When Millicent and Hugh separated in 1938, Mary and Hugo were too young to remember their father's presence in the household. Hugh sent money but rarely visited. Hugo only saw his father on a handful of occasions, many of which were in his teen years or after. He, however, had a better relationship with his father than either his mother or sister did. Mary and Hugh never had much of a relationship, although he did fulfill his fatherly duty of walking his daughter down the aisle on her wedding day.

In 1954, Hugh married for a third and final time. He wed Barbara West, a wealthy widow with four children. Together they lived in Aiken,

South Carolina, and had a daughter, Maureen, reportedly named after Lady Maureen Stanley, one of Hugh's former mistresses. His wartime paramour was the wife of Oliver Stanley, the British secretary of state for war. Hugh, still married to Millicent, had returned to the United States, apparently after Stanley learned of the affair and effectively had Hugh thrown out of England.[20]

Unlike Hugh's first two marriages, the third endured. Millicent, on the other hand, was wary of relationships and never remarried. "I once worried about why I wasn't getting remarried, you know, would it damage the children and so forth," Millicent said. "So I went to a psychologist and I asked him, 'What's the matter with me? Why won't I remarry?' He said, 'Well, you've had a rough experience, and you don't want to repeat it.' I realized perfectly well that I have some kind of strong bias [against] any form of deception."[21] Work became her only indulgence.

Early in Millicent's *Vogue* career she was assigned her first interview—with actress Mary Martin. Martin was embarking on a Broadway and film career and in 1938 appeared in her first Broadway production, Cole Porter's *Leave It to Me*. Millicent remembered the interview vividly, "I was terrified," said Millicent, "because I had never interviewed anybody. I told her that this was my first interview and that if I asked rude questions I'd hope she would forgive me. She said, 'Don't worry, my dear, I've never been interviewed before.' The two of us were very amateur."[22] Martin later became known for her performances as Nellie Forbush in *South Pacific* and in the title role in *Peter Pan*. (Her son, Larry Hagman, followed her acting pursuits and was immortalized as J. R. Ewing on the *Dallas* television series.)

Two years before Millicent joined *Vogue*, the magazine merged with another Condé Nast publication, *Vanity Fair*. While *Vogue* was known for its elegance and trendsetting women's fashions, *Vanity Fair* focused on men's fashions, sports, arts, and literature. *Vogue* incorporated *Vanity Fair*'s arts pages and feature articles and reaped the benefits of its staff, many of whom moved over to *Vogue* after the merger. One of its legendary editors was Frank Crowninshield, uncle of the *Washington Post*'s now-retired editor-in-chief Ben Bradlee. Crowny, as his friends called him, was well traveled and well respected as an art connoisseur. He remained in the Condé Nast organization and often contributed features about the art world or social scene. He had a penchant for parties and was admired by all, including Millicent, for his humor and charming nature.

Crowny was not the only legendary figure at *Vogue*. Among the people who passed through *Vogue*'s doors early in their careers were Dorothy Rothschild, better known for her biting wit as writer Dorothy Parker, and playwright Clare Boothe Brokaw, who later married *Time* and *Life* magazine publisher Henry Luce. While Millicent was working at *Vogue*, Clare Boothe Luce, a Republican, was elected to the House of Representatives by the people of Connecticut. By 1948, Luce had secured a reputation for her oratorical prowess, prompting the GOP to tap her as the keynote speaker at the Republican National Convention in which she nominated Thomas Dewey for president.

Millicent enjoyed working with Condé Nast, the prestigious publisher; Edna Woolman Chase, *Vogue*'s revered editor from 1915 to 1952, who came to the organization in 1895—three years after *Vogue* was founded; Alex Liberman, the art director; and Allene Talmey who, like Crowny, came to *Vogue* with the *Vanity Fair* merger.

Talmey had originally been hired by Condé Nast in November 1935 as managing editor of *Vanity Fair*. Within six months, *Vanity Fair* merged with *Vogue*, and Talmey soon made a name for herself there. When Millicent started at the magazine, Talmey became her boss and mentor. Millicent gradually went from writing captions to writing articles. She successfully steered away from gossip and fashion and focused her attention on charitable events.

Millicent established a good rapport with Talmey, as she did with the eminent editor-in-chief, Edna Chase, who Millicent admired for her principled work ethic and political beliefs. Both women were lifelong Republicans. Chase, like Millicent, had a distinguished air. She had cropped wavy gray hair, usually wore pearls, and possessed a matronly appeal. She was a petite woman thirty-seven years older than Millicent. "Mrs. Chase was as strong as iron," said Millicent. "She was a woman of principle, you see, and I got on wonderfully well with her. I made it a practice that every woman of society we photographed would be identified with her charitable work so that this became a matter of character and good taste. At *Vogue* you were dealing with people of some principle, and that was a wonderful thing. It was a good place to work."[23]

To many, the bespectacled Condé Nast seemed like a sophisticated but distant individual, hosting elaborate parties at his twenty-room Park Avenue penthouse. His bashes were big-budget productions that attracted individuals often featured in the pages of his magazines. Besides *Vogue*, he published *House & Garden*, *Glamour*, and *The Pattern Book*. His magazines came to life at his parties, where high-profile guests conversed about the arts, theater, decoration, sports, fashion, finance, and politics. He was one of the first important hosts to mix people from these different worlds into a social salad. Many of Nast's guests found him formidable or artificial, not realizing he was acutely shy. But they all reveled in the impeccable and lavish taste that permeated the penthouse, often the site for *Vogue* fashion shoots. Staff also benefited from Nast's hospitality. He occasionally entertained small groups of employees at his home, in contrast to the 350 guests he accommodated at his grander affairs. Although the staff evenings were business oriented, an informal social atmosphere prevailed. People were at ease and felt they knew the boss as a friend.[24]

Chase and Nast made *Vogue* the formidable society and fashion magazine it became. They were dedicated to their work and had an insurmountable passion for it. Together Condé Nast and Edna Chase created a congenial and energetic work environment. They had a talented staff whose creative juices flowed through the organization and created an energetic work environment. *Vogue* became Millicent's extended family much as it was for Nast and Chase, both of whom also had their own respective families to go home to.

Although Millicent generated income to support her family, she was conservative with her spending. Each month she allocated part of her check to pay Hugh's debts. Millicent's efforts to balance the household expenses and her husband's debts gave rise to her lifelong frugality. Years later she recalled her struggle "as a wonderful experience. It really was. I was very careful with money. I never took a taxi. For lunch I used to have frankfurters and sauerkraut, stewed plums and coffee—that cost 80 cents in the cafeteria, and with 20 cents tip, you could count on $5 a week for lunch."[25]

Millicent tried to instill the value of money in her children. "We were raised to be economical and to do a great many things for ourselves long before women's lib became fashionable. Mummy herself used to save by picking up designer clothes after the *Vogue* models had finished with them," remembered her daughter Mary.[26]

---

A year after starting at *Vogue,* Millicent was given a unique assignment that was testimony to the management's trust and confidence in her. She was sent to South America with famed fashion photographer Toni Frissell to take the pulse of life and fashion in Argentina, Brazil, Chile, and Peru. Later, Toni Frissell was the official photographer at the wedding of her friend Jacqueline Bouvier to John F. Kennedy. Toni, like Millicent, was an attractive, tall, and slender brunette. She, too, was hired by Nast and started out as a caption writer.

"This was quickly recognized to be a mistake (Toni could not spell, for one thing), so she was encouraged instead to take society snapshots at the parties and events of the season, an occupation for which she was much better suited, since she had excellent connections and went everywhere. Frissell soon became interested enough in photography to wish to be taken seriously, and began working on fashion shots as well as her social coverage. . . . In the late thirties Frissell's work took on a new significance. She had always been accustomed to taking her snapshots outdoors—on the ski slope, on the beach, on horseback. These action shots were, by the end of the decade, replacing formal studio fashion photographs in every magazine in the country. Frissell, quite unconsciously, was spearheading a revolution."[27]

In 1939, Fenwick and Frissell traveled fifteen thousand miles in a Sikorsky amphibian plane, weighed down with Toni's camera equipment and Millicent's extensive wardrobe. Millicent packed everything from evening gowns to an entire trunk of shoes for the forty-day journey to seventeen South American cities.[28]

Despite her ample supply of clothes she never seemed to be properly dressed. Toni remembered one instance when "Millicent, failing to have sneakers, blistered her feet on the hot rocks and in walking back to the house stepped on a burning cigarette. Good Ole Millicent. She was always equipped with the wrong apparatus. No hat in the hot sun, high heels and picture hats in the Andes. But in spite of this she was a demon for work."[29]

Toni and Millicent were an odd pair. Toni was spontaneous, Millicent methodical. While Toni rapidly snapped pictures Millicent desperately tried to jot down the name of each person. To do this Millicent devised a complicated numbering system. "This often proved to be a nightmare," said Toni. "I take my pictures very quickly to catch a definite moment and I am not the soul of patience when kept waiting. One can see we were not getting on beautifully. To keep up with herself [Millicent] often spent hours at night typing. The only available place was the bathroom, perched on the toilet, typewriter on her lap, because I would complain about being kept awake. I must have been a disagreeable companion."[30]

Throughout South America, Millicent and Toni were courted by the society they were there to report on. An upcoming issue of *Vogue* was planned to feature the landscape and people of South America that the duo met. To facilitate meetings, Millicent carried a letter from Condé Nast addressed to the U.S. ambassadors. He urged the ambassadors to assist Toni and Millicent in any way possible.

Tensions were high. Germany had invaded Poland shortly before Millicent and Toni embarked on their trip. World War II was underway. From the outset Millicent made it clear to Toni that she should not photograph any pro-Nazi individuals or activity. Millicent was outraged by Hitler's tyranny and didn't want to promote anyone remotely associated with him.

After days of traveling, Millicent and Toni landed on the Amazon River in Brazil to officially begin their South American sojourn. Millicent recalled the Amazon as "this tremendous river, pouring out top soil into the Atlantic. You could see how it bleeds the land way out to sea, this enormous flood, 100 miles wide at the mouth."[31]

After stops in a few more cities, the pair arrived in Rio de Janeiro. By this point the women had a keen sense of the immense size of the country. From the air Millicent felt as if she were "flying over an enormous broccoli, a huge broccoli, except that every now and then the broccoli has sort of a mauvish blush, and that's the Jacaranda tree—that lovely tree which has mauve flowers. But it [Brazil] is immense."[32]

In Rio, Millicent and Toni interviewed the legendary composer/ musician Heitor Villa-Lobos at his plantation, which was surrounded by a wrought-iron fence. The pair were met at the gate, and Millicent recalled "one of those strange sugarloaf mountains in the backyard. It had a spring on it, and a garden walk and big lilies in the ponds, that one could stand on."[33] When they went into the house, Villa-Lobos played the piano while they sat in gilt wooden chairs with red seats. As the beautiful music played, a trail of cockroaches descended from a nearby wall and scampered across the floor in front of them and up another wall. Nobody flinched.

Millicent was responsible for the $1,500 allocated for their trip. Even though this trip was financed by the magazine she was as frugal with the funds as if it was her own hard-earned cash. Occasionally, Toni would politely ask Millicent for money for a martini. Each time she was rebuffed. "No, no, that's on you," Millicent sternly told her. "No martinis on Condé Nast."[34] Years later Lew Wurzburg, a director of *Vogue*, said, "You know Millicent, I must tell you, the first time I ever heard your name mentioned, it came up at one of the directors' meetings. Someone told the group, 'Listen, we've got a real kook who went off in charge of Toni Frissell (who herself was quite a character) on a South American tour. We gave her $1,500 for an expense account and she brought back $900. What kind of a crazy woman is that?'"

"You know, I was so careful, because it seemed to me a sacred trust," Millicent told Lew. "It was their money, you know."

"That was the first time I ever heard of you," said Lew. "I asked, 'What's her name? and was told 'Millicent Fenwick. She's a real character.'"[35]

Millicent and Toni's mission was to photograph people who were noted in the world of South American art and society. In Rio, Millicent was certain their assignment was destined for disaster. While Toni rested Millicent visited Jefferson Caffrey, the U.S. ambassador to Brazil. She handed him Condé Nast's letter. He read it, looked at her, and said, "Mrs. Fenwick, I'm delighted to see you, but I'm sure you understand, it's perfectly impossible for me as ambassador to ask any of these ladies or gentlemen or people of any kind in Brazil to involve themselves with a commercial enterprise such as *Vogue*." How stuffy, Millicent thought. Then she began to worry, "My God. I'm a failure. What am I going to do now, take Toni home?"[36]

Millicent slumped into a chair in the embassy waiting room and pondered her future. "This is it. This is the end of my working life," she thought. "The first real assignment on which I'm editor, and I've failed." Millicent was close to tears when a familiar figure approached her and said, "For God's sake, Millicent, what are you doing here?"[37] It was Nony Griggs, an acquaintance of Millicent's who worked at the embassy. Millicent explained her fruitless encounter with the ambassador, her mission to photograph prominent people, and the fact that she didn't know a soul in Brazil.

When she had finished, Nony reassured her. He told her that she did know someone who could help, his wife, Margaret. "What's more," he continued, "I'll bet there are dozens of Brazilian ladies longing to be photographed."[38] Nony was right.

As Millicent's trip progressed, she realized she no longer needed Condé Nast's letter. She trotted from one country to another, meeting women referred to her by people she and Toni had interviewed and photographed. Margaret Griggs helped start the chain reaction. Along the way Millicent became an informal courier, carrying letters from one friend to another. These contacts yielded mountains of material for *Vogue*'s third Americana issue. The articles reflected the flavor of the vibrant cultures that permeated South America. Profiles ranged from bull breeders to leading hostesses and their palatial homes. The articles captured scenery, fashion, food, drinks, fiestas, sambas, and rumbas. Enough material was gathered to generate stories throughout the year.

For the most part, Millicent and Toni indulged in the pulsating society life they were covering. Constantly courted, they accepted invitations for dinners, dances, and receptions. But, in Chile things took a different turn. Touring a hospital in Santiago, the nation's capital, Millicent made a poignant discovery—one that had a lasting impact on her political beliefs.

As she walked through the hospital corridors she was stunned by the deplorable conditions and care patients received. Women occupied one-third of the beds. What was most shocking was why. They were dying. Dying not from disease, but from self-inflicted wounds. These women were losing their battle for life because they had tried to prevent another soul from entering their cruel and meager world. The women wanted to terminate their pregnancies because they did not have the means to provide for another mouth to feed, clothe, or shelter. Abortions were illegal in the Roman Catholic country, leaving these women few choices. Their desperation and the drastic measures it had led to were obvious. Speaking with these women and witnessing their suffering prompted Millicent to adopt a lifelong stance in favor of legalized abortions worldwide.

While Millicent traversed South America, her children remained in Bernardsville. They were cared for by a nanny they referred to as "Mademoiselle" and by Agnes Engblum—Aggie—their Swedish cook. Because Millicent was a single working mother, she employed Mademoiselle and Aggie to ease her household responsibilities. Millicent commanded a strict household and set high standards for herself and her children. Mary's and Hugo's responsibilities seemed endless, failure and blame inevitable.[39] There was no room to deviate. They followed the course their mother set, from private schools to French lessons at home taught by Mademoiselle.

In addition to the nanny and the cook, Millicent also employed Mrs. Kocsis to do the laundry and other chores and Elmer, who cut the lawn, cultivated the vegetable garden, and was an all-around groundskeeper and handyman. He stayed with the family until 1942, around the same time Millicent sold her cattle, hay, and chickens. By then she knew Hugh was not coming back. She also knew that the men he hired to help with the farm generated more problems than productivity. One man was accused of replacing eggs with packing paper in the egg cartons. Without Hugh to sort through these headaches, it was not worth it for Millicent to maintain the farm and its associated costs.

One means Millicent had to escape from her daunting family and work responsibilities was her never-ending quest for knowledge. Her first attempt to further her education was after she recovered from appendicitis, when her family spent the winters in Manhattan at 18 East Eighty-second Street. Their multilevel town home was just half a block from the Metropolitan Museum of Art. Millicent wanted to take some courses at the Met. "But," she remembered, "it was thought to be intellectual arrogance on my part to wish for more education so that fell through."[40] Her next opportunity came while she was married, when she took a philosophy course at Columbia University. She enjoyed the subject but was unimpressed by the professor.

Several years later she learned that the renowned British philosopher Lord Bertrand Russell was going to be teaching at the New School for Social Research, and she signed up for his class. She went to the first lecture with her supervisor, feature editor Allene Talmey. Although Talmey expressed interest, she did not enroll. So Millicent convinced her friend Rhoda Clark to take the class with her. The two women faithfully attended Lord Russell's Thursday evening classes.

"I was fascinated by this extraordinarily interesting man," Millicent recalled. So much so that she said to Rhoda, "'You know, we ought to see if he wouldn't like to have dinner with us beforehand. He's so amusing.' So we waited until everybody had finished their questions, piling up on stage after the lecture was over and Rhoda said, 'You're going to have to do it, I wouldn't dare.' So I said, 'Mr. Russell,' of course that was my first mistake, because he was *Lord* Russell, and although a Socialist, very much liked to have that remembered—'We have a rather different sort of question to ask you. Would you like to have dinner with us before next Thursday's meeting?'"

"So he looked at Rhoda, who was very beautiful, and said, 'Why, yes, I think I would.'

"So we used to dine every Thursday night, and eventually he became really quite a friend, and he used to stay with Rhoda when he came to New York. She had a flat at Sutton Place. The three of us would dine every Thursday night before these wonderful lectures."[41]

At the time Lord Russell was approaching seventy and married to his third wife. Millicent occasionally entertained Lord Russell, his wife, and their young son, Conrad, at her Bernardsville home. Conrad, as Millicent recalled, "was a perfectly terrible little boy who was really quite out of control, and not at all like most English children."[42]

Millicent reveled in debating the controversial Lord Russell, author of *Principia Mathematica*. But their friendship faltered when Millicent recognized his anti-American sentiments. "He found something unruly, unorganized, undisciplined about America that he didn't like."[43] His class in 1941 marked the last trace of Millicent's formal education.

––––––––

Because Mademoiselle and Aggie cared for the children, Millicent was able to spend Monday, Tuesday, and Thursday nights in Manhattan, where she shared a ground-floor apartment with a friend so she would not have to commute daily to Bernardsville. Millicent began this practice during World War II when rationing limited her to four gallons of gas a week. Her son remembered that she didn't take an extra gas ration during the war because she felt it was wasteful. To conserve fuel she let her 1941 Plymouth coast downhill from her driveway to the commuter train station. The only problem was the bump at the Episcopal church. Her kids got out and pushed.[44]

Although Ogden and Daisy lived nearby in Bernardsville they did not help Millicent or her children, nor did Millicent ask them to. Each day Mary and Hugo trekked a mile to the school bus stop. Often Ogden, president of the First National Bank in Jersey City, passed them in his chauffeured car, but rarely did he offer his grandchildren a ride. Ogden's household overflowed with staff and vehicles, but the wealth of his resources did not extend to the Fenwick household.[45]

––––––––

During World War II, Millicent became the self-appointed editor of war news for *Vogue.* "I not only photographed and wrote about women working in war factories," said Millicent, "I saw that we had all the proper information about the bombing in England. I was a member of the Committee to Defend America by Aiding the Allies, and I'd get a lot of information from them."[46] In 1940, Millicent took her beliefs to the street. She gave a speech on behalf of the Committee to Defend America by Aiding the Allies at an anti-Nazi rally in Yorkville, a predominantly German neighborhood on the Upper East Side of Manhattan. Millicent told the crowd that the United States should not wait until the Nazis were at its door, that America should involve itself now.[47] Afterward she was beckoned to a side street, and "before I knew it I'd been knocked down," said Millicent. "I was lying in the gutter, being kicked in the back, and was rescued by a soldier who came along and freed me from the crowd and [he] dragged me into a bar."[48] This encounter, however, did not dissuade her from advocating her beliefs. She continually voiced her opposition to Hitler's tyrannical rule.

Like many Americans, Millicent supported the war effort by purchasing war bonds. Although she lived on a tight budget she felt she couldn't ask her coworkers to participate in the war bond program if she did not. Years later, war bonds helped pay for her daughter's wedding.

Surprisingly, the magazine saw its circulation peak during the strained war years. As the world endured the adverse effects of war, some speculated on the possible demise of *Vogue* as a result of people's inability to maintain the luxurious lifestyle it portrayed. Responding to such criticism Edna Chase staunchly defended her magazine. "We dare hope that we have so successfully presented the arts of painting, writing, dressing, and gracious living, which are among the causes for which this war is waged," she wrote "that *Vogue* has become . . . to the world at large, the leader of the great fashion industries, as well as the symbol of the fashionable woman herself. There are, today, thousands of manufacturers, designers, and merchants who depend upon the knowledge, the taste, and the integrity of *Vogue* for correct information and guidance in businesses that are dependent upon the element of fashion."[49]

In the early years of the war, *Vogue* struggled to maintain its quality. Many European fashion houses were raided by the Germans, who confiscated their designs, leaving them nothing to send to the United States. During this period, when *Vogue* was starving for fashion content, a couple of French-speaking Swiss gentlemen showed up at the New York office asking to speak with Mrs. Chase. Because she did not speak French, she beckoned Millicent to her large corner office.

Millicent dutifully translated as these two men offered to sell Mrs. Chase original designer drawings. It was the lucky break *Vogue* needed. Chase's eyes lit up and she said, "Oh, that's absolutely splendid. Have you got them with you?"

"Oui, oui," replied the Swiss men.

"Well, how do we arrange payment? Isn't Mainbocher [the designer] still in Paris?" Chase asked as Millicent translated.

"Yes."

"Well, you are suggesting that the payment should be arranged to you in Switzerland?"

"Yes," the men once again replied.

"Well," Chase said, "how is he going to get the payment? Are you going to keep it there in a sequestered account?"

"Oh, no, we will turn it over to him."

Chase began to stiffen as she asked, "What do you mean?"

The Swiss replied "Well, of course we have to send the money to Monsieur Mainbocher in Paris."

"Oh," Chase answered. "And the Germans there?" Perplexed, she continued, "I would rather print *Vogue* with empty pages, blank pages from cover to cover, than have one dime wind up in the Nazis' hands." Millicent was ecstatic as she translated Chase's words into French.[50]

The Swiss were not quite so thrilled by Chase's strong stand. They left.

Chase's handling of the situation endeared her to Millicent. Despite the magazine's desperate need for the designs, Chase adhered to her principles by rejecting what the Swiss men had to offer.

As war editor, Millicent, too, established and maintained high standards. She was responsible for feature stories and profiles. She set down a guiding principle, reflecting her upbringing, that *Vogue* "would not photograph any society woman without telling what good work she was doing, to show that we valued such work. In other words, this is not just Mrs. John Jacob Astor, period. This is Mrs. John Jacob Astor who is the head of the Women's Branch of the Hospital . . . or whatever."[51] Nast accepted Millicent's insistence that personality captions include the person's war work, but he did not escape her wrath entirely. Millicent took him to task in late 1940 for allowing himself to be photographed with René de Chambrun, the Vichy French ambassador to the United States. According to Millicent, "Condé was totally open to these suggestions and quickly changed his attitude to the collaborationists. It just had not occurred to him."[52]

As Millicent's responsibilities at *Vogue* expanded, she tired of shuttling between her Manhattan apartment and her children in Bernardsville. In the fall of 1945 she moved to New York with her children and Aggie, their faithful cook. Aggie prepared the meals for the family and tended to the children, now eight and eleven. She made it possible for Millicent to juggle her job and her family. By now both children were attending private schools. Hugo was sent to the Buckley School on East Seventy-third Street between Park and Lexington, and Mary attended

Brearley Private Day School on East Eighty-third Street, overlooking the East River.

Millicent's untraditional household, which included Aggie but no father for her children, lived on the top two floors of a three-story town house on the corner of East Sixty-ninth Street and Lexington Avenue. On the lower level there was a living room, dining room, and kitchen, and on the top floor they each had a small bedroom overlooking a garden maintained by the first-floor residents.

For Millicent, the new living arrangement was a nice change. She was now able to spend more time with her children. Her Manhattan home was much closer to *Vogue*'s offices in the Graybar Building on Lexington Avenue at Forty-second Street. Occasionally she brought her children to work with her. Hugo remembered these trips and that "she wore black suits and had large black floppy hats and smoked Chesterfields at the speed of light."[53]

At the office things were going well. Millicent enjoyed working for Nast and Chase, and they appreciated and respected her opinion. During the war Condé Nast asked Millicent to critique his publication *House & Garden*. After reviewing the magazine Millicent candidly reported, "I don't think it's properly directed. It seems to me that if there were no more head gardeners or estates, there wouldn't be any audience. It's just not for the public at all. It's fine in the way of the Latin names of things they might want to order from abroad, but it is not useful or interesting otherwise."[54]

With a critique like that Nast offered Millicent the job as editor of the magazine, much to her horror. "There was a very nice woman who was editor and I had no intention of taking her job."[55] Millicent was happy with her own. By now she had an office to herself and covered topics like food, nutrition, and how to spend money and get the most for it during wartime rationing. Millicent wrote articles telling readers how to make things like soup without fat, a rationed commodity. She created a perfect niche for herself, aided by her frugal nature.

By the end of the war, Millicent was an associate editor of *Vogue*, focusing primarily on household topics, dealing with rationing, and encouraging women to work in war factories. During the 1940s, *Vogue* suffered two devastating losses to its family. In the autumn of 1942 Condé Nast died from a heart condition. His impact on the fashion industry was not forgotten. "You may say that Condé Nast's was a trivial field compared to [Averill] Harriman's and [J. P.] Morgan's transformation of the United States with railroads," Millicent said. "But it was part of the same enthusiasm, verve and zest that developed this country."[56] Condé Nast's biographer, Caroline Seebohm, wrote, "By insisting on the best-quality paper and printing, Nast paved the way for the success of the art magazine; his publications proved that a connection between fashion and art was not only plausible but promotable."[57] Five years after Nast passed away, Frank Crowninshield, the magazine's esteemed in-house savant, art critic, and comic relief, lost his battle with cancer.

During Millicent's *Vogue* years she fought her own medical battles. At the age of thirty-five she had her gallbladder removed; later she had a hysterectomy, skin cancer, and a mastectomy. Her bout with breast cancer was a silent battle. She dealt with it privately and rarely referred to it other than to acknowledge having had a mastectomy in 1949. It would be another twenty-five years before Betty Rollin published her groundbreaking memoir, *First, You Cry,* about her struggle with breast cancer. In the 1970s, "breast cancer—any kind of cancer," Rollin remembered, "was not something you told people you had. Some people didn't even tell their own children."[58] When Millicent dealt with the deadly disease her children, twelve and fifteen, were unaware of her medical condition until Cousin Mary informed them.

A couple of decades later, in the midst of Millicent's first congressional election, First Lady Betty Ford was diagnosed with breast cancer and had a mastectomy. Her bout with breast cancer raised national awareness. As Mrs. Ford wrote in her memoirs, "Lying in the hospital, thinking of all those women going for cancer checkups because of me, I'd come to recognize more clearly the power of the woman in the White House. Not my power, but the power of the position, a power which could be used to help."[59] Even then, Millicent did not share her personal experiences with the same disease. To her, cancer was a private, not a public, matter.

---

When Millicent declined the job of editor of *House & Garden* she was given another proposition. She was told her household columns did not merit an individual department and she needed to branch out. "If you don't want to go be editor of *House & Garden,* you've got to write a book of etiquette."[60] Millicent was tapped for the task because of her strong moral convictions. "Oh, my goodness, what a horrible thing to do," Millicent thought, "but it's better than taking that woman's job. I won't do that."[61]

Reluctantly, Millicent resigned herself to accepting the etiquette assignment. She thought it would take a few months, but it took four long, miserable years. For a working mother this project had its benefits. It provided Millicent more time to spend with her children, because she worked at home, now back in Bernardsville. Occasionally, staff from *Vogue* came to the New Jersey countryside to help Millicent plow through her less-than-desirable assignment. She felt "etiquette itself is a trifling unimportant subject as compared to the moral and ethical values it was supposed to—and in some instances did—embody."[62]

"It seemed to me snobbish and a source of great unhappiness for people," said Millicent. "And what I tried to do was to tell them [*Vogue* management] that if we were all perfect in our ways, in our hearts, toward others, we really wouldn't need such a book, except that it's handy to know where people are accustomed to finding the fork, which side of the plate, and what kind of fork is apt to be most useful for what sort of food."[63] But that's what *Vogue* readers wanted to know. The book, said Millicent, "was done entirely in response to people's letters to *Vogue*, so I knew they were concerned about it."[64]

Although Millicent had assistance, the mammoth task of producing *Vogue's Book of Etiquette* rested with her. She was the primary author and researcher. Meticulous about her research, Millicent quizzed the butler of her friend Sophie Schley about the most intricate details.[65] Emily Post's etiquette book was already on the market, but Millicent didn't dare consult it. She feared it would compromise her own work.[66]

Four tedious years later *Vogue's Book of Etiquette* was finished. The 648-page tome covered a wide array of subjects, from how to treat beggars to planning weddings and writing thank-you notes. When Simon and Schuster published it in 1948, one bookstore reported that Soviet officials ordered four hundred copies the week it came out.[67] That sale was an indication of what was to come. The book, referred to as the etiquette bible, went on to become a best-seller, with sales reaching the million-copy mark. Its success was aided by excerpts that had been appearing in the magazine for months along with full-page ads citing the book as "an indispensable addition to every family library." For a while Millicent received royalties for the book, completely unexpected since she had been paid to write it as part of her job.

The final product reflected Millicent's strong organizational and writing skills as well as her perseverance to make the best of what she considered a loathsome task. Throughout her life she emphasized that the book "did not then reflect [her] opinion as to what is important in life and it does not now. . . . My own belief [is] that if one is reasonably intelligent, perfectly straightforward, perfectly kind and loving and self-respectful one doesn't need any book of etiquette at all. But millions of people buy books of etiquette, not as an acknowledgment that they lack these qualities, but because they are intelligent enough to know that customs vary and one can make people more comfortable by learning what they may expect."[68]

Although it was not her ideal project, Millicent did come away from the book with a valuable lesson. "It taught me self discipline, which is of inestimable value. To learn to do what you don't want to do when it's got to be done—that's one of the most useful lessons a human being can learn."[69]

The book opened with Millicent's introduction discussing the importance of etiquette in daily life. She made these observations:

- Etiquette is an important subject because it is concerned with human beings and their relations to one another.
- Etiquette is based on tradition, and yet it can change. Its ramifications are trivialities, but its roots are in great principles.
- A system, or a set of rules, is vital for anything in which human beings are involved.
- The practical beauty of etiquette is that it is precise, detailed and widely accepted.
- The greatest value of etiquette . . . is its value to the individual.[70]

Her reflections about etiquette can be applied to the realm of government and politics. In the preceding examples, the word "etiquette" could easily be replaced by "democratic government" and the context would still apply. It is interesting to see how, in 1948, Millicent's thoughts on etiquette represented her firm principles. Whether Millicent discussed etiquette or politics, her concern for the individual and sense of right and wrong were apparent. She found comfort by framing etiquette within the context that "you put the convenience or feelings of others above your own."[71]

Although she disliked writing about etiquette, she enjoyed the promotional book tour that followed. It gave her an opportunity to hone her speaking skills and to travel across the United States. She had already seen most of Europe and part of South America, but much of her own country was unknown territory to her. "She was astounded by the versatility of the American landscape, the American mind and the boundless variety of the customs."[72]

Initially, the book tour concept "absolutely terrified" her.[73] As she traveled from Buffalo to Hamilton, New York, and on through Illinois and Akron, Ohio, she began to feel more at ease on the lecture circuit, and by the time she addressed a crowd of thirteen thousand people in St. Paul she was comfortable in her new role.

On the book tour Millicent crisscrossed the country by train. Her promoters deemed air travel unreliable. Millicent didn't mind. She simply enjoyed soaking up her surroundings. From the frozen Mississippi River to the first tiny sprouts of lilies-of-the-valley, and the black soil of Iowa's Crittenden Belt, Millicent loved it all.[74]

Wherever Millicent went she drew a crowd. In Dallas she spoke at the Neiman Marcus department store. Draped in a pale green Italian silk dress with a jacket and a matching white hat with pale green and black ribbon woven through it, Millicent was stunned to see the other women dressed in formal evening attire and sporting orchids on their dresses for a three o'clock book talk. Her outfit did not detract from her discussion; she was a hit. This crowd absorbed everything she said about etiquette, while Millicent absorbed the Texas milieu. The Lone Star State proved to illustrate yet another aspect of American culture far removed from her familiar East Coast lifestyle. The vast land and long distances between Texas towns, as well as the oil wells that dotted the state, were in stark contrast to the small townships of New Jersey.

The book tour marked the end of Millicent's full-time career at *Vogue* after ten years with the company. Chase, not willing to lose a valuable asset, convinced Millicent to remain on the payroll for a few more years as a contributing editor.

———

The same year that *Vogue's Book of Etiquette* was published, Ogden sold the family's Bernardsville mansion to Cousin Mary Stevens Baird. Already owning one mansion, Cousin Mary certainly did not need another, but the two properties bordered each other and she preferred to keep Ogden's in the family—Ogden's first wife had been her first cousin. A couple of years after Cousin Mary bought the estate she told Millicent, "I don't need another fifty-room house. Don't you want it? I will give you a good price."[75] She did. Millicent bought 14.52 acres—a fraction of the land her father sold to Cousin Mary—her childhood home, two cottages, and a swimming pool, all on the property, for the sum of ten dollars. Cousin Mary retained ownership of the rest of the property and reserved the right to buy the property back from Millicent if she ever wanted to sell.[76]

As much as Millicent revered her girlhood home she knew she did not need such a vast estate, nor could she afford to maintain or heat it. With that in mind she boldly demolished much of the original house. "I had practically three-quarters of the original house taken down. It was put together with square nails and oak timbers, and it literally screamed when the wreckers tore it apart; they told me that always happens with that kind of wood and those kind of nails,"[77] said Millicent.

Preserving a more recent library wing, she converted it into a charming, reasonably sized, French provincial home. She filled the house with furniture from the attic, favorite antiques, and Stevens family heirlooms. Downstairs she created a cozy parlor with portraits of her ancestors adorning the canary-colored walls. A dining room paneled in dark wood, and an adjacent kitchen and servant's quarters, were on the lower level. Upstairs were four bedrooms—including Millicent's childhood room, three bathrooms, and a steep stairwell that led to a full-size attic. A dumbwaiter transported food from the lower level to the upper-level residence.

After Millicent bought the family estate from Cousin Mary she sold her Bernardsville home and the 10 acres it was on as well as 100 of the 150 farm acres she and Hugh had purchased during their marriage. During the renovations, which were paid for by the sale of her land, Millicent lived in one of the cottages on Cousin Mary's property. By this time both children were in boarding school. Hugo was at St. Paul's in Concord, New Hampshire, and Mary attended Millicent's beloved Foxcroft.

Two years after settling into her refurbished house, Millicent's inherited assets improved substantially. After fourteen years at *Vogue* she could afford to leave her job, and she did. That same year, 1952, Edna Chase stepped down from her editor-in-chief throne, after nearly four decades, to become chair of *Vogue*'s board of directors. For Millicent, what began as a desperately needed job writing captions evolved into a career as an associate editor and author. Envisioning her new life to be that of a country gentlewoman, Millicent planned to spend her days in Bernardsville reading, writing, gardening, and doing needlepoint. She was ready to adopt a more relaxed lifestyle, or so she thought.

# 8

## Retreating

## to the

## Country

The world turns and the world changes,
But one thing does not change,
In all my years, one thing does not change.
However you disguise it, this thing does not change:
The perpetual struggle of Good and Evil.

—T. S. Eliot

As Millicent settled into retirement, she became engrossed in local issues. It wasn't the first time. Back in 1938, before her children were of school age, Millicent had been elected to the Bernards Board of Education.[1] Her six years on the school board were not without irony. In 1916, Millicent's father wrote a letter to John McGuinness, a local political operative. "I have been thinking for some time," wrote Ogden, "that it would be a good plan for Bernardsville to have a woman on the school board. Do you approve of this, and do you think that the people could unite on some representative woman?"[2] McGuinness deemed the issue "too complex" to discuss via written correspondence. Ogden's letter netted few results, but sixteen years later, in 1932, his idea became a reality when two women were elected to the board of education. Millicent was not the first.

Millicent's gravitation toward public service stemmed not only from her background but from within herself. Adolf Hitler's blatant disregard for civil and political rights awakened Millicent's inner sense of justice. Hints of her feelings were evident at *Vogue* where she instituted a blanket policy to ban anyone affiliated with the Nazi Party from appearing in the magazine.

Millicent had difficulty comprehending how Germany, one of the most literate countries in the world, elected Hitler. "It was like a bad dream. With the depression still having its effects here in the United States, nobody knew what was going to happen. The world was in a state of flux. There across the Atlantic was this madman. You couldn't help but be interested in politics," she observed later.[3] "I got interested in politics on account of Hitler and I didn't know what to do, exactly, to express it. I joined the National Conference of Christians and Jews. [It has since changed its name to the National Conference for Community and Justice.] It seemed to me that would be at least a gesture. And I went to meetings in New York. Mr. Roger Strauss . . . used to hold meetings in this beautiful house. We weren't many. At one of these meetings, there was a wonderfully interesting old gentleman called Judge Joseph M. Proskauer."[4] Judge Proskauer, appointed to the New York Supreme Court by Governor Al Smith, was active in civic reform and Jewish philanthropic work. Proskauer, like Millicent, was passionate about his beliefs and moved easily in various religious circles. Proskauer was most proud of his lobbying for the historic change in Roman Catholic doctrine at Vatican Council II (1962–1965), which removed blame from the Jews for the death of Christ. This effort reflected the many close associations that Proskauer had developed with Catholic leaders.[5] It was leaders such as Proskauer whom Millicent learned from as she embarked on social justice.

Hitler's power led Millicent not only to the National Conference of Christians and Jews—a nonprofit organization focused on reducing bias, bigotry, and racism in America—with which she remained active for the next half-century, but also to a distrust of government. She identified her skepticism as the reason why she became a Republican. She believed, "a good Republican is as sensitive to the suffering of others as anyone else, but a first reaction will be 'Let's get together and do something,' not 'The government must take charge of this.'"[6]

Later in life, when asked why she was a Republican, Millicent wrote: "I can tell you exactly why I am a Republican. When I was a young woman, Hitler was elected (by over 80 percent of the vote, as I remember) in one of the most literate countries of the world, by a people preeminent in music, science and many other fields. And the government of that country proceeded to exercise the most cruel injustices against many of its people. Some who had fought for Germany in the First World War were treated like criminals, or worse, only because of their race or religion. It struck me as a hideous perversion of what government is meant to be— an institution designed to bring a just society.

"Since then, I have never really trusted government and it is because I don't trust government that I am a Republican. Most of my family were—and are—Democrats, particularly in the older generation, and I have noticed that this trust, or lack of trust, is what divides us. . . . When there is no way of organizing relief apart from government, Republicans are as quick as Democrats to turn to government for help, as can be proved by the impetus Republicans and Republican administrations have given to government programs. But the general trend of Republican thinking (it cannot perhaps be called a philosophy or ideology) is to move toward private, volunteer, or religious action as a first step.

"A good Democrat, on the other hand, takes solid satisfaction in setting up a good big government: a new department in Washington, perhaps, with a secretary and deputy assistant secretaries, regional directors and deputy directors, and all the offices, outreach agencies, statisticians and employees that a good big program, in their view, really deserves.

"Good Democrats don't mind mandatory laws, regulations, and ordinances, nor do they object, as a rule, to measures that prohibit citizens to do certain things. Good Republicans tend to ask 'Why?' Is the situation such that we must order people around like that?

"It's a different point of view and I believe it is the basic difference between a Republican and a Democrat. And it goes further, of course, into the question of the individual versus the whole of society. Republicans believe that the strength of the individual initiative and motivation will produce ever-widening choices and greater freedom; they try to encourage opportunities for choice. Democrats are more concerned that government should organize in such a way as to make individual choice—with all its chances for mistake and failure—less important. A Republican speaks of 'Freedom to . . . '; a Democrat of 'Freedom from . . . ' I'm a Republican."[7]

Although Millicent's father was a prominent New Jersey Republican, her Stevens relatives were ardent Democrats living in a Republican enclave. Millicent consciously chose her party affiliation based on political beliefs, not heritage. She was fiscally conservative and socially liberal.

Rejecting the notion that her political activism was anything other than her negative reaction to Hitler, she denied a link between her passion for justice and her privileged background. To Millicent, the concept of noblesse oblige implied a class structure in America, a structure whose existence she dismissed. She believed everyone should give back to society, as her Hammond and Stevens ancestors had done through their philanthropic endeavors.

Her son offered another viewpoint about her path to politics. "She always took the easy way out and said 'Hitler' because no one could disagree with her . . . but it went deeper," said Hugo. "Her drive came from our family legacy. She used the word injustice and I think it stems from the injustices of Daisy. If family can impart daily injustices, and her father could not do anything about it, then think how the government can misuse their power and the injustices that could result."[8]

Signs of Millicent's Republican activism were evident during her early years at *Vogue.* In 1940, she was an avid supporter of Wendell Willkie, a Republican businessman who challenged Franklin Delano Roosevelt for the presidency. One of Willkie's prominent female supporters was Clare Boothe Luce. It was Luce's speech before twenty-two thousand people at a Willkie rally in Madison Square Garden that established her as a national political figure whose influence endured long after Willkie died in 1944.[9]

"The trouble with Mr. Roosevelt was a certain deviousness. . . . He wanted to be popular, more than anything, I think. I was very much in favor of Wendell Willkie . . . as a candidate in the Republican Party, and [I] worked hard, 'We Want Willkie' and all that. I was working for *Vogue* then and they allowed me to have the day off to go to the convention in Philadelphia. I was so excited," remembered Millicent, "that I fainted, when Minnesota gave him the proper number of delegates and he was going to be the candidate.

"I had a bet with my friend Rhoda Clark, who adored Mr. Roosevelt, and thought he was almost perfect. I said, 'You wait and see. Mr. Willkie is going to come out for Selective Service [draft] before Mr. Roosevelt does. Roosevelt's not going to risk his popularity in an election year, but we've got a candidate with courage and principle [Willkie], and we've got to have a Selective Service, with the world in this state and he's going to come out before the President—you mark my words.'

"I bet $20. It is the only time I've ever bet money on a political race—and I won. I won, because Mr. Willkie did come out and say, 'We're going to have to have Selective Service,' and then Mr. Roosevelt was able to say it, although he went on saying, in Boston, 'I promise you that no American boy is going to be sent overseas,' at the same time he was telling the allies that as soon as he could manage it, they would be helped."[10]

Although Millicent did not care for FDR she found strength in Eleanor Roosevelt's words and actions. "Mr. Roosevelt never impressed me the way she did, because she was the first person that I could say, God, she really means it."[11] This notion became Millicent's self-imposed litmus test of others—whether their behavior emulated their words. Cognizant of her litmus test, Millicent made sure her actions mirrored her words. Her public and private personae were the same. The principles she advocated, she adhered to. The verbal commitments she made, she kept. Both characteristics set her apart from political colleagues as she eased into public service.

"Mr. Roosevelt did wonderful and extraordinary things in all sorts of legislative ways, but he left the desegregation of our Armed Forces to Mr. Truman and he left the desegregation of the Washington restaurants and facilities to Mr. Eisenhower. I mean he [FDR] wanted to get re-elected and wanted to get the important things done that he had a vision about, but she [Eleanor] was talking about human rights and human justice, and that's what I cared about, the business of government is justice, and she seemed to feel that and really mean it and it was an affront to her that some of our fellow citizens didn't have an equal chance and equal opportunity.

"I really inherited from her, perhaps, a feeling that you cannot look at people in groups, that there is nothing more damaging than to say all blanks are blank. . . . I think we have three things in this country that are sacred: our Constitution; the principle of an independent judiciary; and a free press. And if we haven't got the free press that is there to chide and warn and criticize and praise, we have got to defend it."[12]

---

A few years after Millicent discovered the National Conference of Christians and Jews she became engaged in civil rights. Her first cousin, John Hammond, a member of the National Association for the Advancement of Colored People (NAACP), told her about a case of blatant racial discrimination involving a black man, serving in the navy, who tried to help his mother get her radio fixed at a local store in Tennessee. His mother kept getting pushed aside for a steady stream of white patrons. When her son protested, he was incarcerated. Hammond established the Committee for Justice in Columbia, Tennessee, to collect money for the man's defense.

"Well, this is terrible," Millicent said to John. "I've never heard anything like it."[13]

And so Millicent sent what she could afford. "Probably $10 at that time, I was pretty hard up still. But in any case, that alerted me, and I began to notice similar injustices."[14] Millicent decided to join the NAACP and later, when she could afford to, became a life member. Not one to be merely a member, Millicent served as a volunteer chairman of the NAACP Legal Defense and Education Fund's annual fund-raising efforts in New Jersey. Realizing that people respond to people, not causes, Millicent introduced potential contributors to the organization.

John Hammond, whose father had the foresight to draw up the will Millicent's mother signed on board the *Lusitania,* was a legendary jazz talent scout and producer. He is credited with discovering Billie Holiday,

Count Basie, Benny Goodman, and, years later, folk legend Bob Dylan and rock legend Bruce Springsteen. Hammond dedicated his life to discovering, promoting, and producing some of the greatest names in jazz. And like his Hammond ancestors, he was active in promoting social justice and philanthropy. He was involved in the integration of New York clubs such as Café Society in Greenwich Village, where an eclectic crowd gathered to hear the latest jazz talents.

On one occasion Millicent accompanied Benny Goodman, married to Alice Hammond, Millicent's first cousin and sister of John, to a Billie Holiday concert. "She [Holiday] came out—dazed, drugged, with long white gloves to hide the needle marks on her arms. She could hardly remember the lyrics—and what there was, was degenerated, abused, sophisticated in the worst sense. Could she ever have been what Ella Fitzgerald is? Even when she was young—in the touching photographs of her in the Metropolitan exhibit 'Harlem on My Mind'—I am sure there was something wild and frail—as different from Ella Fitzgerald as Baudelaire was from Shakespeare."[15] Not long after this performance Holiday succumbed to drug and alcohol abuse in 1959, at the age of forty-four. Her career had been launched by John Hammond, who discovered her sultry voice in Harlem. She was still a teenager when he convinced Goodman to record a song with her.

———

The year Millicent left *Vogue* was the same year her elder child, Mary, left home to attend Radcliffe College. Mary resembled her father. She was not blessed with her mother's slender physique but rather had a broader frame. Although she did not inherit her mother's figure, she possessed her mother's intellect. Despite this, or maybe because of it, mother and daughter often clashed.

Hugo, on the other hand, resembled his mother's side of the family. He was emerging into a tall and handsome young man. Where Mary was an introvert, Hugo was the extrovert. He was outgoing and social, Mary somewhat reserved. The siblings were not particularly close. They attended boarding school during their formative years and saw each other mostly on holidays. Mary was sent to Foxcroft but did not take refuge there as her mother did. Hugo attended St. Paul's in New Hampshire where his roommate, John Todd, was the brother of future New Jersey Governor Christine Todd Whitman.

After her children left home, Millicent diligently wrote them and they dutifully responded. After graduating from Foxcroft, Mary went on to Radcliffe, where she met Ken Reckford, a Harvard student. The two soon fell in love and wanted to marry. Mother and daughter initially quarreled over the matter. Millicent thought her daughter too young to marry and disapproved of Mary's plans to drop out of school at the age of twenty. Millicent was anxious for her daughter to take advantage of the opportunity she never had—to earn a college degree. Mary, just as stubborn as her mother, prevailed. Soon Millicent was entrenched in the role of the doting mother planning every detail of her daughter's wedding, no doubt with the help of *Vogue's Book of Etiquette* and its extensive section on weddings.

Mary and Ken were married by Father John Torney at Bernardsville's Church of Our Lady of Perpetual Help, the same church where Ma and Ghino had been married. Mary and Ken's ceremony was delayed slightly while the guests awaited the arrival of the bride's father. Hugh fulfilled his fatherly duty, albeit late, by walking his daughter down the aisle. Afterward, invited guests went to Millicent's house for the reception. Years later, Hugh told his son Hugo that it had been made clear to him that he was unwelcome at the reception.[16] Respecting the wishes of his daughter and his ex-wife, Hugh quietly slipped away after the ceremony. He never saw Millicent in person again.[17] Although he was not at the reception, Hugh could see pictures of his daughter's wedding featured in *Vogue* magazine.

Shortly after their wedding, Mary and Ken headed to Italy, where Ken accepted a graduate fellowship on his way to becoming a classics professor at the University of North Carolina at Chapel Hill. The pair were well matched, sharing an intellectual hunger. Mary, like her mother, possessed "the rare integrity of someone who said what she thought."[18]

With Mary married, Hugo now in the military, and Hugh's debts repaid, Millicent had more time to herself. Her retirement visions of retreating to the country and gardening, reading, and knitting soon gave way to her natural urge to aid people. The Visiting Nurse Association of Somerset Hills, founded in 1904, tapped her to be a board member. A few years later the Somerset County Legal Aid Society sought her guidance. She became its first female president and the first non-lawyer to hold that post.

She also took up the cause of prison reform, long championed by the Stevens family. Millicent's great-aunt Caroline (Tantine) Wittpenn was instrumental in the establishment of New Jersey's first female prison, the Reformatory for Women in Clinton, and had donated the land on which the prison was built, as well as a chapel where an altar had been erected in 1915 in memory of Millicent's mother. Two of the cottages at the reformatory were named after Stevens family members. The premise of the Clinton facility was not incarceration, but rehabilitation. There were no walls around its land or bars at the windows. The focus was to counsel the women and improve their skills so they could be productive members of society.

Before Great-Aunt Tantine suffered a fatal heart attack at the age of seventy-three, she passed on her passion for prison reform to two of her grandnieces, Mary Stevens Baird and Millicent, who in turn passed on the cause to her children. Millicent's daughter, Mary, worked at the reformatory one summer before she married. At the time, Cousin Mary was chairman of the reformatory's board of managers and had the power to grant parole. Mary Fenwick was given the task of reading and censoring the prisoners' mail. Her fondness for her work was evident in the many letters she wrote Ken during their courtship. She demonstrated a characteristic mix of objectivity and sympathy. Deeply affected by her work, years later she became a member of the board of visitors to the Hillsborough prison in North Carolina.[19]

Mary's work emulated that of her grandfather, Ogden, who served as vice-chairman of the New Jersey State Board of Charities and Corrections, and during his stint in the New Jersey assembly he served on the Prison Inquiry Commission, which "investigate[d] the conditions of the penal, reformatory and correctional institutions of this State [New Jersey], and also into what is known as the 'State use system' and the employment of prisoners on roads, prison farms or in other capacities."[20]

It wasn't long before Millicent was also deeply involved in prison reform. She served on the board of directors of the Dwight Morrow Association of Corrections, now the New Jersey Association on Corrections. Serving with her were Harry Wilmerding, a family friend; Mary Stevens Baird; and Mrs. Archibald S. (Nina) Alexander Jr., who married a Stevens descendant. The Morrow Association educated the public about problems in the corrections field, engaged in research, consulted experts, and emphasized the need for prisoner rehabilitation.

The prison reform movement meshed well with Millicent's philosophical thought process. "Incarceration is the legal aspect of prisoners," said Millicent's son, "whereas, rehabilitation is the human aspect, and when you treat inmates with this in mind the result can be remarkable."[21] Millicent became president of the Society for Prison Reform and president of the Dwight Morrow Association.

---

While Millicent was becoming anchored in various community service endeavors she suffered the loss of her father two weeks after his eighty-seventh birthday. Ironically, his friend Walter Edge, former New Jersey governor and U.S. senator and the catalyst for Ogden's ambassadorship, died the same day, October 29, 1956.

With Ogden's death came more money. When his first wife died he had received half of her estate, with the other half divided among their three children. Up until Ogden's death Millicent received interest on one-third of one-half of the estate. After her father's death her income doubled because each child received one-third of the entire estate.

Ogden left instructions with Daisy that he wanted to be buried in St. Paul with his father at the Oakland Cemetery. His only other wish was that his daughters each receive a portrait of him and that Oggie receive all of his personal jewelry and masculine objects with the Hammond crest or the initials, "OHH."

Two years after Millicent lost her father she had another death to grieve. Her sister had cancer. Ma's wealth afforded her the opportunity to receive cutting-edge treatment in New York, and she tried everything possible to conquer the disease. In those days external radiation was not available. Instead, radiation pellets were inserted inside the patient and strategically placed around the cancer to help prevent its further growth.[22] The treatment failed, and the radiation pellets inflicted internal burns. Millicent flew to Italy to be by her sister's side until the end. Ma's doctors in Rome alleged she died as a result of too much radiation, and not from the cancer, adding a more painful twist to her death. Ma's final breath came two days before Millicent's forty-eighth birthday. Grief overwhelmed her. She had not only lost the person she was closest to but also felt as though she had lost her whole childhood.[23] Distance had not diminished the sisters' bond.

After Ma's death Millicent stayed in Rome to help Ghino settle her sister's affairs and adjust to life alone—the couple had no children. Before Millicent returned home Ghino gave Millicent two of Ma's large, chain-link gold bracelets. As an Italian diplomat, Ghino had been deported, with Ma, from Mexico when Mussolini aligned himself with Hitler and declared war on France. In their haste to leave the country Ma converted her liquid assets to gold and bought the bracelets.[24] One of the bracelets had a medallion of Our Lady of Guadalupe dangling from it. Millicent rarely went anywhere without the heavy bracelets, which dwarfed her dainty arm. The bracelets were a constant reminder of Ma and became a Millicent trademark.

For the rest of Millicent's life she remained close to Ma's husband, Ghino, the last link to her sister. That link was preserved through weekly telephone calls, which continued even after Ghino remarried a few years later. Millicent was fond of his new spouse and the trio often spent time together whenever Millicent made her way to Italy, a country of which she never tired.

With the loss of her sister, Millicent's income from her mother's trust once again grew as it was now shared by two siblings instead of three. To distract herself from her loss, Millicent focused more than ever on philanthropy and politics. By 1958, recognition from her philanthropic work catapulted her into the political realm. Someone (she later said she didn't remember who) suggested she run for a vacant seat on the Bernardsville Borough Council. She did, and she won, becoming the first woman to serve on the nine-member council. Her election came forty-five years after her father served on the same council from 1912 to 1914. The *Bernardsville News* summed up Millicent's tenure on the Bernardsville Council as "a combination of idealist and tough-minded practitioner."[25]

One of the first projects she tackled was building a township swimming pool. Mayor Ed Faulkner appointed Millicent to the Bernardsville Recreation Commission, where she was well positioned to advocate for a public pool. Having the luxury of a pool in her backyard, built in 1914, Millicent thought the children of Bernardsville should enjoy the same luxury. She believed in fairness and equity and saw the pool as a means to achieving this. Swimming would no longer be for those who could afford a pool, but for everyone. However, she did not want to use taxpayers dollars to achieve her goal, "because when we do we just tax older people right out of their homes."[26]

To get the pool built, Millicent needed to raise nearly $100,000. "It promised to be a little bit tricky. But the first step was to go to all the clergymen in town, [and ask], 'What would you think of a swimming pool and have you any suggestions?'" She strategically set out to seek the support of Father John Torney, one of the community's most influential members. Although she was not a member of his church, Father Torney knew Millicent. He said of her, "She really respected the Ten Commandments, particularly love of God and love thy neighbor."[27]

Millicent convincingly explained the pool project to Father Torney, who immediately saw the value of increasing the recreational opportunities for local youth and gladly offered his support and two suggestions. He wanted to ensure that the pool, when open, was supervised and that it would be closed on Sunday mornings so the children could attend church. Millicent eagerly agreed. Once she secured Father Torney's blessing she was able to gain support from the other local clergy and their congregations.

With the clergy behind her, Millicent sought donations from the town's wealthy residents. One of the first people she tapped was one of Father Torney's parishioners and her friend, Charles Engelhard, a business tycoon specializing in industry and precious metals. It was his wife, Jane Engelhard, who had introduced Millicent to Father Torney.

Charles asked Millicent, "How much do you need?"

"I hadn't really worked it out, but it just popped out, and I said $50,000," said Millicent.

"Oh," he said, "that's all right, you can have that."[28]

Delighted, Millicent continued her fund-raising crusade. The children held bake sales, the women sponsored fashion shows, and community members opened their checkbooks. Millicent herself gave generously, but quietly, to the fund. All told they raised $94,000. The money—combined with masons, plumbers, and electricians who donated their services—was enough to build an L-shaped pool without using tax dollars. Of course, the pool needed water to be complete. For this Millicent sought out her father's former colleague, John McGuinness, who had been a political fixture in town for half a century. "He was our health officer, and absolutely incorruptible," Millicent said.

"I went to him and said, 'We're going to need water. Tell us how to operate.'"[29]

He advised her to dig a well so the pool would not be dependent on the water company. "That was really better because we're independent. We were down in a wonderful hollow, very high water table area. It was very lucky. After the pool, we built a little clubhouse. At first we couldn't afford much, but there was never a penny of tax money in it. We had wonderful volunteers."[30] And at every meeting Millicent recognized volunteers who donated their time, money, or labor to help Millicent's dream of a township pool materialize.[31] The pool was one of Millicent's earliest and proudest accomplishments. It foreshadowed her ability to unite individuals toward a common goal.

With her roots grounded in local politics, her interests expanded to the state and national levels. By 1955, she was a Republican state committeewoman. She recruited volunteers, mobilized canvassing efforts, and coordinated the local municipality chairmen throughout the state. In 1956, she worked for President Eisenhower's reelection committee and helped raise $80,000.

By 1961, Millicent was the vice-chairman of the Republican State Committee and served as the head of the women's party organization within New Jersey. She planned programs to build Republican women's organizations and helped the State Federation and Young Republicans. She also served as a liaison between the state committee and the county vice-chairmen to ensure that voting precincts were sufficiently staffed for canvassing, registration, and getting out the vote for all elections.[32]

One of Millicent's earliest experiences on the campaign trail was with Clifford Case. He, like Millicent, was a New Jersey Republican whose political career began at the local level. He served on the Rahway Common Council, then was elected to the New Jersey assembly before moving on to the U.S. House of Representatives, in which he served from 1945 to 1953. The following year he launched a campaign for the U.S. Senate. Case, a graduate of Columbia University's law school, embraced the same causes Millicent held dear—human rights and equality.

Another quality that Millicent admired was Case's willingness to speak his mind. Case vocally opposed Senator Joseph McCarthy and pledged to vote against allowing him to continue chairing the Committee on Government Operations. At the time, only one Republican senator voiced the same view. As a result of Case's strong anti-McCarthy stance, experts said it would be a miracle if Case won, but that didn't stop him. He campaigned harder. When his liberal tendencies prompted people to question his party affiliation Case said, "I refuse to give the Democrats exclusive rights to all liberal and humanitarian programs."[33]

Case's beliefs enticed Millicent to volunteer during his first senatorial campaign, in 1954, and the lessons she learned in the process aided her as she rose through the state party ranks in the years that followed. Case won and six years later, when he was up for reelection, Millicent was again involved. This time she took on a more active role, serving as co-chair of the Citizens for Senator Case Committee. She coordinated volunteer efforts and telephone committees and hosted coffees and teas for workers, who in turn did the same for the people in their neighborhoods.

Millicent also planned large events, confirmed speakers, placed flyers on cars, hung posters in supermarkets and factories, canvassed door-to-door, and helped make decorative corsages with a "Citizens for Senator Case" ribbon. She was often tapped to give stump speeches on behalf of the senator. Even in 1960, her oratorical skills earned her lavish praise and fan mail. "Had you heard the expressions of admiration of your speech, personality, appearance, knowledge of public affairs, diction, and voice you would be blushing for some time!" wrote an English teacher after hearing her speak at a local high school.[34]

One woman wrote Millicent "that if you are running for any office—all of us [in the audience] would be inspired to work for you. As for myself you sold yourself to me a few years ago—but I was happy that all my friends feel your sincerity as I have. I wish you would run for office some day. Every woman would back you."[35] Millicent thoughtfully responded to each letter. To one potential voter she wrote, "It has been a great experience to work in politics. The goal for all of us of course, is to further what we believe best for the country, but the heartwarming part is to work together with others and letters such as yours mean so much."[36] It is no wonder many people in the audiences she addressed urged citizen Fenwick to become candidate Fenwick.

Case won another six years in Washington, where he was revered by his colleagues and gained a reputation for the courage with which he championed his convictions and the integrity that characterized his service. Whether the topic was ethics in government, the war in Vietnam, or racial justice, Case was willing to speak out and lead. He was one of the bipartisan floor managers of the landmark Civil Rights Act of 1964.[37] Over the years Case garnered a reputation for his independence and liberalism, traits Millicent also embodied.

"Case was a rather unusual Republican," said Thomas Kean, a Case volunteer who later became governor of New Jersey. "The people who supplied the muscle for his campaign were generally organized labor who had a great affinity for him. And so the Republicans who worked at his headquarters were very few and far between. I used to work there and so did Millicent." Even then Millicent was a workaholic. "She would do anything for Clifford Case because she thought he was an extraordinarily good public servant," said Kean. "I think because there was integrity. I mean he was involved in things like civil rights, he supported environmental causes, and so [did] she. I think she always had a penchant for the underdog and I think Case did too. She saw in him something she really liked in a public servant . . . integrity and decency."[38]

When Case was up for reelection in 1966 and 1972, Millicent was there. She worked out of the Case headquarters and didn't mind her shabby surroundings. Rhoda Lieberman (now Rhoda Denholtz), another Case volunteer, remembered Millicent "as very much her own person. She worked long hours, drove her own car, smoked a pipe, and constantly snacked on raisins."[39] The two women had desks facing each other and were responsible for maintaining quarterly financial reports; providing information on Case's record; coordinating the county chairmen; and providing leaflets, bumper stickers, biographical information, and photographs to volunteers throughout the state.

While Millicent and Case were known for their honesty and integrity, a conversation Millicent had during the campaign seems to reveal a woman who also wanted people to know she had a devilish streak. But no one will ever be sure why she shared this story.

One day while working in their crowded Newark office space Millicent asked Stephanie, a secretary, "Have you ever stolen anything?"

Stephanie said, "No."

Then Millicent asked Rhoda the same question. Rhoda said, "Yes, I once stole a paper flower from a five and dime."

Then Rhoda asked Millicent, "Have you ever stolen anything?"

Millicent said, "Oh, yes. I stole a painting from the Louvre."

Intrigued, Rhoda probed Millicent further and learned the painting was a reproduction, most likely from the museum shop. Millicent never explained her behavior, nor did she clarify when she had done it. Millicent gave Rhoda the impression that she stole just "because." This conversation made quite an impression on Rhoda and Stephanie as they tried to picture this refined woman stealing a painting. It took them both by surprise and neither knew quite what to believe.[40]

That year, in 1966, Case won a third term by half a million votes, followed by another landslide in 1972 when he defeated former Congressman Paul Krebs, who had lost his House seat to redistricting and decided to run for Senate.[41]

Millicent's activism extended beyond party politics and gained her statewide recognition as a civil rights leader. In 1958, she had been appointed to the New Jersey Committee of the U.S. Commission on Civil Rights. The committee held hearings related to racial discrimination and equality. Millicent spent fourteen years as vice-chairman. The chairman was someone Millicent came to respect and admire, Rabbi Gershon B. Chertoff of Elizabeth, New Jersey. Chertoff, with a doctoral degree in philosophy and anthropology from Columbia University, headed Temple B'nai Israel. "He was not a lawyer, but he was interested in the law and doing the right thing," said his son, Michael, who served as the United States Attorney in New Jersey from 1990 to 1994 and in 2001 was nominated to serve as assistant attorney general of the U.S. Department of Justice, where he heads the Criminal Division.[42] Like Millicent, Rabbi Chertoff was "erudite, intellectual and well respected," said Michael Chertoff.[43]

A mutual respect and friendship developed between Millicent and the rabbi, both motivated by a strong sense of justice. Every Sunday morning Millicent called Rabbi Chertoff to brief him on the past week's work. Often discouraged, Millicent told him, "Oh, Rabbi, the harder we work, the worse it seems to get."

"Millicent," he said, "there's something you have to learn," and then he recited in Hebrew a passage from the Talmud, before providing the English translation. "We will never arrive at the solution, but we are never absolved from the responsibility of trying."[44]

"Isn't that beautiful," Millicent thought. "The responsibility of trying—you cannot get away from it. That falls on you, that obligation, and success is not the measure of the human being. Effort is. What are you trying to do? How hard are you trying to do it? That's what measures a human being. Not success. Success is a byproduct."[45]

Millicent never forgot what Rabbi Chertoff said. She echoed his words to schoolchildren and set an example by striving to live up to that standard of trying. She was constantly troubleshooting in all areas of her life, whether as mother, community member, or elected official.

Rabbi Chertoff gave Millicent a book entitled *The Ethics of the Talmud: Sayings of the Fathers*. On the title page Rabbi Chertoff inscribed, "For Millicent Fenwick, Our guiding principle (page 62, no. 21), Gershon B. Chertoff." His words, lessons, and integrity brought Millicent much comfort over the years.

During her tenure on the commission she served as co-chair of the Newark subcommittee with Herbert Tate, a former member of the Newark Board of Education. Among the issues they studied was housing discrimination. To learn more about the problem, the commission held hearings in which public housing tenants testified about the deplorable living conditions, alleged racial discrimination, and rent strikes. Millicent was very sympathetic to the people who testified, and their problems. She visited public housing complexes, attended community meetings, and participated in minority rallies in an effort to gain a better understanding of the problems and potential solutions.

She became vested in the issues and approached them the best way she knew how—through personal involvement. When one woman testified before the commission about her failed attempts to get a repairman to come to her home to fix her broken washing machine, Millicent took the matter into her own hands. She called the company. When she asked them about the problem, they didn't deny it. Instead, they told Millicent their repairmen refused to go to the woman's neighborhood, even in daylight. They were scared. Challenged, Millicent solved the problem. A repairman agreed to go to the apartment after Millicent arranged for a police escort.[46]

In 1963, Governor Richard Hughes, a Democrat, appointed Millicent along with two other prominent Republicans, Bernard Shanley and Webster Todd, father of Christine Todd Whitman, to his Committee on Equal Employment Opportunity. At the time Millicent was a visible Republican as vice-chair of the New Jersey Republican State Committee. Her passion for the issues brought respect from both parties, which was evident when she proposed to the governor a Bipartisan Conference on Equal Opportunity as a forum for New Jersey political leaders to address civil rights in the state, and in particular, education, housing, and employment. Governor Hughes agreed.

In a speech before the Bipartisan Conference, which she co-chaired, Millicent said, "We are faced with a great issue which has been called Civil Rights, but in a larger sense, its true name is justice: Justice to our fellow citizens, faithfulness to the principles of our constitutional law, and to the soul and spirit of the idealism in which our nation was conceived and to which it is dedicated . . . but side by side these high ideals, we have allowed a system to develop which is in too many ways quite contrary to their spirit. We have proclaimed justice and taught our children to love justice, and the system we have tolerated has not been just. . . . A widespread feeling of injustice, a sense of outrage against a system that leaves men apparently helpless, is what produces crises such as this. . . . We have called this Conference to study the system and its inequalities and to take action to make it more just. The force behind the fires of discord that are raging in so many cities is a simple and terrible one: the suffering of our fellow citizens . . . we must, with prudence and good will, achieve a social system in which no human being is left out. We know the way: Do justice, love mercy, and walk humbly with thy God."[47]

"There were many skeptics and few believers who thought the issue [civil rights] could be removed from partisan politics," reported one newspaper, "But it apparently has been. . . . From the conference came a pledge from several major industries to their continued opposition to discrimination in hiring, and a number of craft unions agreed to merit tests for entrance into apprentice programs."[48]

The success of the Bipartisan Conference and Millicent's powerful words before an audience that included the governor led to her appointment as chairman of the Governor's Conference on Job Opportunities for African Americans in New Jersey. As chairman, Millicent was able to leverage corporate support from Ford Motor Company and General Motors. Both companies donated automotive equipment for vocational education. Every position Millicent held garnered her more support as her peers heard the magic in her words and saw the action behind them. She rarely was idle.

———

By the end of the year Millicent was ready for a temporary escape from her exhausting schedule, so she embarked on an overseas adventure with Jane and Charles Engelhard—regulars on *Forbes* magazine's list of wealthiest Americans. Dubbed the "Platinum King," Charles, an ardent Democrat, garnered his vast wealth through the precious-metals industry. He and Jane lived at Cragwood, their Georgian-style home set on 150 acres in Far Hills, near Bernardsville. The pair were globe trotters with homes around the world, including one in South Africa, the cradle of the Engelhard Minerals & Chemicals Corporation. In 1963, they set off in their private transoceanic jetliner, with a dozen friends, including Millicent, on a month-long whirlwind trip that would take them from Zurich to Beirut, Teheran, New Delhi, Bombay, and Johannesburg.

In between sightseeing, massages, and tea, the group consumed champagne, caviar, and other delicacies. "I have decided that this whole trip is going to be indulge-yourself week," Millicent wrote Cousin Mary, "After all there will *never* be anything like it in my life again. I don't care whether or not I have the *right* clothes; I'm going to talk to the people who amuse me, *not* the one that's left out or shy, unless it's a question of decent guest duty, of which I plan to do the absolute decent minimum. And it is lovely and cozy to feel that you approve of this change of pace—or is it that we are accomplices?! Anyway, that's the spirit in which on this cold, sunny Saturday I start off."[49]

The Engelhard contingent, which included Mr. and Mrs. Alfred Gwynne Vanderbilt, received VIP treatment everywhere. They dined at embassies, met with diplomats, and received private tours of collections such as the Persian crown jewels. "There is no way to describe them," wrote Millicent, "gold, diamonds, rubies, emeralds, turquoises—but gold and diamonds and emeralds most of all."[50]

Jewels were not the high point of the trip for Millicent. For her, the peak experience was meeting Indira Gandhi, who was draped in a purple and white sari. After a conversation with Mrs. Gandhi, who later became prime minister of India, serving from 1966 to 1977, Millicent rushed to her hotel and wrote Cousin Mary. "She made these points," wrote Millicent. "It is hard to keep India united—what with all the divisive factors of language, race and caste—and many things that are questioned have to be done to keep the delicate structure on balance." Then Indira Gandhi told her, "Second, those who govern should be judged as pro or anti-Communist not by what they say but by the results of their actions. What do their actions lead to versus the question to ask." Millicent agreed. "Third, the Indian masses must be made to feel that the government is determined to better their conditions. . . . The people must feel that there is not only hope for future improvement but that there is present action to remedy their ills." Fourth, "Industrialization is producing some benefits and many social difficulties. The communal family system—which was a form of private social security—is breaking up and there is nothing to take its place. People are at sea, having lost the old ways and values and being without any new ones that are clear and fixed." And finally the fifth point: "The whole world is in need of idealism or a cause— India, for example, is suffering from the loss of the cause which the struggle for independence gave the people."[51]

Wherever Millicent went she sought, and found, something to satisfy her intellectual appetite. Millicent summed up her observations of Indira Gandhi by writing, "She struck me as an extremely active and determined woman, with a good sense of humor, a little self-centered and willful—very energetic —not deeply thoughtful, very attractive and good-looking."[52]

It also was during this lavish trip that President John F. Kennedy was assassinated. Millicent absorbed the news through the eyes of a foreign nation. She was in Jaipur, south of New Delhi. Immediately her thoughts revolved around home, the national political current, the nominating conventions the following year, and civil rights. "There are so many things and to be traipsing around the world doing *nothing* seems absolutely *mad*," she wrote Cousin Mary. And then, as a postscript, she added, "I don't quite know why I feel so badly—I neither liked nor respected him but to have our President murdered—and his assassin murdered—it is shameful and he was so young—so pre-eminently full of life—so brilliant in many ways."[53]

The trip was winding down when the news broke and Millicent, alone, continued on to Rome to see Ghino and other friends, as planned. When she returned to the United States, the issue of civil rights was looming large in her mind.

# 9

## Outhouse

## Millie

What lies behind us and what lies before us are tiny matters compared to what lies within us.

—Ralph Waldo Emerson

In a racially segregated America, Millicent Fenwick regularly crossed unspoken color barriers and dedicated herself to achieving equality for all. Civil rights was her chosen field, fighting injustice the core of her being. She took solace in the words of the Declaration of Independence: "We hold these truths to be self-evident, that all men are created equal, that they are endowed by their Creator with certain unalienable Rights, that among these are Life, Liberty, and the pursuit of Happiness."

Fenwick's tenure as vice-chairman of the New Jersey Committee of the U.S. Commission on Civil Rights, established by Congress in 1957 and authorized by the Civil Rights Acts of 1957, 1960, and 1964, heightened her awareness of racial issues. She and the other committee members served without compensation and were tasked with identifying local civil rights issues and informing the public about federal laws and programs.

Fenwick spent many days and nights reading about alleged civil rights violations. She and Herbert Tate, a lawyer and black activist, co-chaired the Newark subcommittee. They sponsored meetings in which low-income tenants testified about substandard living conditions and racial discrimination in Newark's Central Ward. The meetings revealed a host of problems ranging from poor maintenance, inadequate locks, unlit hallways, and irregular elevator service to overcrowded schools, unqualified teachers, and strained tenant-management relations. Police were scarce, so many residents took it upon themselves to carry weapons for protection. As one woman said, "I would rather for the police to catch me with it [a knife] than for the hoodlums."[1]

A cadre of people with varied backgrounds listened to the testimony. Members of the Newark subcommittee included a telephone company official, a union official, a college professor, city registrar, a rabbi (Chertoff), a lawyer (Tate), and Fenwick, who was referred to as "a magazine editor long active in civil rights and politics."[2]

Fenwick was no stranger to the inner city, where many of the civil rights battles were being waged. "When we started working in Newark—with its proportionately high black population—there was only one black employee in any Newark bank who wasn't a janitor or something. Only one black teller. The telephone company was more or less the same. The people coming upon the civil rights movement now say there's been no improvement," said Millicent. "They just don't know what it was like at the beginning."[3]

Through political circles she befriended Mary Burch, a slim, attractive black woman. Burch was as outgoing and involved in the community as Fenwick. Burch served on the board of governors of the Women's State Republican Club and was the first African American appointed to the parole board at the Clinton Reformatory.[4] A former teacher, she and her husband, Dr. Reynolds Burch, moved to Newark from Philadelphia in 1946. Three years later, Mary Burch combined her philanthropic instincts and nurturing tendencies to form the Leaguers, a Newark-based nonprofit organization. For three decades the Burches primarily funded the organization themselves. "That's what community service is supposed to be about—putting your energy and resources behind what you believe," said Burch.[5]

Encouraging cultural and educational development for black youth, predominantly from Newark, the Leaguers provided opportunities through job training, etiquette classes, mentoring programs, and tutoring. Among the young people helped by the organization were singer Dionne Warwick, former U.S. Energy Secretary Hazel O'Leary, and Democratic Congressman Donald Payne. In the 1960s, while Fenwick was a board member, Donald Payne's brother, New Jersey Assemblyman Bill Payne, served as chairman of the board of the Leaguers. "She always had a corncob pipe, not fancy, but she smoked on it throughout our meetings," said Payne. "Millicent was invincible. She came across as having a lot of wisdom . . . and she always talked about how to improve and expand the Leaguers."[6]

A couple of evenings a week Fenwick would volunteer at the Leaguers. Emphasizing literary and learning endeavors, the organization used education as a means to deter youth from crime and drugs. Mary Burch cultivated the young people's socialization skills to help them forge careers and to promote economic and social mobility. "She [Burch] was like the iron fist in the silk glove—tough love," said Bill Payne.

The centerpiece of the Leaguers' year was their annual Cotillion at which the girls and boys danced and practiced their etiquette skills and social graces—which Mary Burch viewed as important stepping stones in their paths to success. At the 1968 Cotillion, Fenwick was recognized as the "Citizen of the Year." In bestowing this honor Burch said the award was being presented for Fenwick's "distinguished service to humanity, [and] her dedicated devotion to the cause of equal opportunity for all."[7] Over the years Fenwick introduced Burch to the philanthropic world, taught her how to establish and sustain a charity, and set up endowments, which Burch later did at Essex County College and Kean College. When the Leaguers needed money to repair a leaky roof, Fenwick introduced Burch to one of the Astors over lunch at the Waldorf-Astoria. Several weeks later a check arrived from Mrs. Astor. It was enough to replace the roof.[8]

The Leaguers also provided college scholarships to young leaders. In 1952 future Congressman Donald Payne, was president of the Leaguers and received a scholarship from the organization so he could attend Seton Hall University. "Mrs. Burch was a visionary who implemented programs for young people decades before the federal government ever thought of them," said Representative Payne. "She got us assistance for school long before college grants and loans became possible. . . . She taught us that just because we were black and poor it had nothing to do with our dignity and respect."[9]

Former Newark Mayor Kenneth Gibson, the first black mayor elected in a major northeastern city, recalled that by the 1960s "Millicent was already legendary. She was involved in the Urban League of Essex County, helped with community groups and got funding for them. She was also a strong supporter of the NAACP and involved with a fair housing group. The public did not know her, the leaders knew her," said Gibson. "She was a philanthropist . . . involved in helping grassroots organizations receive funding. Some of the funding came from her, some came from foundations she led people to."[10]

Newark in the 1960s was volatile, like many other cities. Racial problems were mounting, and although the civil rights committee was unmasking some issues, its efforts were not enough to stem the tide of unrest. Locally, African Americans lost faith in their Caucasian elected officials, three of whom were under indictment in Newark in the spring of 1970—including then Mayor Hugh Addonizio—for extortion. The political turmoil set the stage for Ken Gibson, a young black engineer, to be elected mayor of Newark in 1970. Many didn't realize that four years earlier he had been one of three mayoral candidates but was largely dismissed because he entered the race only six weeks before the election. One person who took him seriously in 1966 was Millicent Fenwick. Despite differing party allegiances, Fenwick held a fund-raiser for Gibson at her Bernardsville home. Although he lost that year, his strong showing surprised many and helped pave the way for his victory in 1970.

In the interim, Newark was paralyzed by political corruption, slumlords, and crime. In what had once been a thriving city, deteriorating conditions led to white flight and an influx of black migrants from the South. Housing was limited, and deplorable. To make matters worse, "a proposal to demolish several blocks of Central Ward housing to create a campus for the embryo New Jersey College of Medicine and Dentistry . . . led to mounting anger over the inept handling of a site for the College." Neglected during the decision-making process was the community directly impacted, causing a divide between the residents and the local and state officials who were negotiating the deal without citizen input.[11]

It was in this contentious environment that Fenwick regularly visited the city. On at least one occasion, on her way to the Leaguers, she was stopped by a Newark police officer. He said, "Ma'am, what are you doing here?"

"I'm heading down a few blocks," she told him.

The officer warned, "It's not safe."[12]

Fenwick acknowledged his words and continued on her way.

It wasn't long before the city's tension erupted into a full-scale riot. As New Jersey historian John Cunningham put it, Newark "seethed with resentment and hatred—against the police, against blatant political skullduggery in City Hall and against slumlords and out-of-town storekeepers who gouged the ghetto residents at every turn. This was 1967, the summer of black discontent in every city throughout the nation. The hope of President Lyndon B. Johnson and the Democratic-controlled Congress to revitalize urban areas . . . had been sidetracked in the massive, costly outpouring of arms and manpower to wage the hopeless war in the jungles of distant Viet Nam."[13]

One of the underlying causes for the violence in Newark dated to the mid-1960s, and the plans to build the New Jersey College of Medicine and Dentistry, which, as a result of legislation signed in 1981, became part of the University of Medicine and Dentistry of New Jersey (UMDNJ), which today includes eight schools on five campuses. Building the medical school in Newark led to the involuntary relocation of thousands of residents whose homes were demolished to make room for new buildings. A housing crunch ensued, creating the foundation for adversarial relations between the community and elected officials.[14]

Adequate plans were not implemented to relocate the residents, already living in poor conditions, who lived on land targeted for the development of the medical school.

Strained relations between the police and the public were painfully visible in Newark's Central Ward. Police abuse of force was accepted as the norm. In 1966, the Newark subcommittee that Fenwick co-chaired submitted its findings to the U.S. Commission on Civil Rights. The document said, "One of the most serious and potentially the most explosive issue in Newark is police-community relations. Every civil rights leader and intergroup relations specialist agrees that if trouble breaks out it will be sparked by an incident involving 'the use of excessive force' by the police."[15]

On July 12, 1967, the committee's findings became all too real. A simple traffic stop provided the spark that ignited the city. Two white police officers pulled over John W. Smith, a black cabdriver, for swerving past their moving vehicle. Smith argued that the police car was parked. When the officers learned his license had been revoked, they roughed him up and threw him in the back of the squad car. A rumor spread that the cabdriver had been beaten to death. Many who witnessed his arrest believed he was dead.

A few hundred people congregated outside the police station to protest Smith's arrest. The protest led to a four-day riot that began with looting, vandalism, and two dozen arrests on the first night. Across the river, the New York media were quick to jump on the story and headed to Newark the next day. That evening throngs of black citizens postured for reporters and photographers and were characterized as young and jubilant rather than angry.[16] Once again looting occurred, but by midnight city and police officials thought the situation was contained. A few hours later, before dawn on July 14, police reported sporadic shooting, and soon chaos reigned. An unorganized police force was unmasked. Police officers had no city maps, no riot gear, and no concept of where the problem areas were. The mostly white state police and National Guard were called in and eventually sealed off fourteen square miles, but not before twenty-six people were killed—some by young National Guardsmen who feared reports and sounds of snipers. Hundreds of residents were trapped in their apartments. Sometimes, peering out a window might induce gunfire; forty-one-year-old Eloise Spellman did just that. Her innocent action resulted in a bullet fatally piercing her neck as her children helplessly watched her die. In less than three days the state police and National Guard fired fifteen thousand rounds of ammunition.[17]

Only two of the twenty-six victims were killed prior to the arrival of the National Guard. What began as an innocuous traffic stop on a hot summer evening ended four days later in chaos and death. But, John W.

Smith, the cabdriver, was not among the dead. He survived the head and rib injuries sustained during his arrest and detainment. The city was not so lucky. More than 1,000 stores were destroyed, 1,500 people wounded, and 1,600 arrested.[18]

"I was not surprised by the Newark riots in 1967 because I had been in Newark, listening to the people there, hearing their complaints about the courts and the police," said Fenwick. "When the riots finally came and 26 people were dead, I was not taken by surprise. It was a terrible thing. . . . A sense of injustice was the root cause of these riots. If you listen to the people you can feel the rising sense of injustice, the warning of a storm to come."[19]

Although Fenwick listened to the people and was not caught off guard by the destruction of the city by a restless public and ill-prepared law enforcement, she alone could not stop the violence. But she understood it, later noting, "I have come to believe that one thing people cannot bear is a sense of injustice. Poverty, cold, even hunger, are more bearable than injustice. If you feel that the deck's stacked against you—that the very organs of the state which are supposed to be protecting you are against you, that your taxes are not giving you equal protection—if it's all loaded against you, it's unbearable."[20]

She remained active in the Newark community after the riots left the city haunted by burned buildings, debris, and other reminders of the violence. Newark's troubles, while not unique, highlighted the problems of a population jammed into the city's twenty-five square miles. Soon Fenwick was involved in one of the root causes of the violence, the construction of the medical school. Not only did this Newark project force thousands of people to relocate, it deprived skilled minority workers of the opportunity to benefit from the construction. The unions' thinly veiled argument for not using these workers was that as long as there were unemployed union members the unions could not expand their ranks. Their other argument, equally transparent, was that there were not enough skilled minority workers to train for the construction jobs. "When people are relocated involuntarily," said civil rights activist Gus Heningburg, "they go the shortest distance they can go to find another house, so in effect, those people are going to be sitting on the perimeter of this tract of land, and watch white construction workers come in here from somewhere else and make a lot of money building . . . where their house used to be."[21] The ironworkers union, like the other building-trades unions, refused to admit minorities.

The U.S. Department of Labor held hearings to determine if there was a pattern of discrimination, and in particular, if there were violations of the Civil Rights Act, which stipulated that opportunities be provided for minorities to work on federally or state-funded projects. The medical school fell into this category, and a formal plan was to be established to address the problem.

Fenwick entered the federal courthouse in Newark and waited her turn to testify. Seated in the same row was Heningburg, a young civil rights activist and president of the Greater Newark Urban Coalition. He, too, was there to testify.

Although the pair had never met, Heningburg was familiar with Millicent Fenwick's name. As he listened to her testimony he was struck by how similar her remarks were to his. "The lawyer for one of the unions, the ironworkers I believe, got up to the microphone and with heated emotion, basically called her and me 'bleeding heart liberals,' 'racists in reverse,' I mean he went off," said Heningburg. "And there must have been seventy-five people in there. He picked the two of us out to direct his venom towards. And, it struck me that if this is the way that industry is going to react to us, maybe we should get to know each other."[22] Sharing a common purpose—equality, Fenwick and Heningburg forged a working relationship.

The first day they met, Heningburg remembered, "I couldn't help feeling sorry for Millicent. Here she was, this wealthy white woman from the suburbs who had to endure a public tongue-lashing. [The union lawyer] talked worse about her than he did me because you know I'm black, and he makes the assumption I'm supposed to do this kind of stuff," said Heningburg. "So when he started on the two of us, she was much more the target than I was. He was passionate. He was very much overweight and you could almost see the blood rising in his neck muscles. I mean he was going a little bit berserk." As for Fenwick, she just sat there. "She didn't react at all. If he was expecting something from her, or if he was expecting her to get up and argue with him, he was disappointed. She had said her piece. She was finished. She didn't have to deal with him. I sort of reacted the same way. I figured maybe whatever that lady [Fenwick] down there was doing was the best thing to do. I said, don't let this guy get under your skin, don't let him make you get up and say something that you may regret. But, I would say that easily 60 percent of his hostility and anger was directed at her, not me."[23]

Her unexpected presence in the courtroom—no one knew her, not the civil rights activists, community leaders, or union members—had a profound impact. Here was an obviously wealthy white patrician from the suburbs who seemed personally motivated to advocate on their behalf. "She wasn't looking for visibility," said Heningburg. "Being known in Newark wouldn't get her elected because she wasn't elected from Newark in the state legislature or congress."[24] It was her inner passion for justice that compelled her. Through her work with the Civil Rights Commission, she was aware that of the more than four thousand apprentices registered with unions in New Jersey, only fourteen were not white.[25]

"There are 1,130 union electricians," said Heningburg, "only 18 of them are blacks or Spanish. Out of 2,000 plumbers, pipefitters, and steamfitters, there are only 8 of whom are black or Spanish." Fenwick testified that she personally escorted blacks or Puerto Ricans to apprenticeship programs only to see them rejected. "The combination of the passive employer and the union jealously guarding its privileges is a deadly one," said Fenwick.[26]

In addition to the labor hearings, which did result in the implementation of a plan to address the blatant discrimination, Gus Heningburg, Governor Hughes, and Ralph Dungan, New Jersey's chancellor of higher education, who oversaw the medical school, teamed up to halt the $35 million in federal funding for the construction project until the discriminatory policies were abolished. Their efforts netted results, and they succeeded in delaying disbursement of the funds. As a result, a training program was set up at the construction site, fostering a healthy partnership with the medical school.

While the construction battle was waged, the private sector invested in the city. Two weeks after the riots, the Prudential Insurance Company, headquartered in Newark, announced that it was underwriting a multimillion-dollar project that included a hotel, office building, and shopping plaza to be built near Penn Station. Another company that contributed to the revitalization effort was the Engelhard Corporation, owned by Fenwick's friend Charles Engelhard. His Newark-based business provided an interest-free loan and legal services to the New Community Corporation, a group of local activists who sought to improve the quality of life by building and renovating housing units.

———

By 1969, Fenwick was restless. She had been active in the Republican Party for decades but decided she "wasn't pushy enough. I was too hesitant to promote myself, and in politics if you don't no one else does."[27] Tired of following "the typical female pattern" of community activism and volunteering, she wanted more. "I always wanted things in the most foolish overmodest, hesitant way," she said. "I finally learned that when a man wants more he says, 'Listen George, I want a bit of the action.' Well, we've been taught: 'You have to wait to be invited to the dance.'"[28]

Two years earlier she waited for that invitation, but it did not come. As she sat at a table listening to names being discussed for state assembly seats she silently hoped to hear her own name mentioned. It wasn't. In 1969, she wasn't about to make the same mistake. When Webster (Danny) Todd Jr., announced two months before the November election, and after the primary, that he would not seek another term as a state assemblyman—he accepted an appointed position, with higher pay, at the U.S. Department of Transportation—Fenwick let county Republican leader Lewis (Luke) Gray know she was interested.

With the blessings of Somerset County Chairman Gray and Somerset County State Senator Ray Bateman, Fenwick was named the Republican candidate for the Eighth Assembly District. By this time Fenwick was the grandmother of eight: her daughter had five children, her son three. Fenwick said, "I took up pipe-smoking when my seventh grandchild [Hugh Wyatt Fenwick, born in 1966] was born and I thought I had reached the age when my conduct would not scandalize society."[29] Before starting to smoke a pipe, Fenwick was a serial cigarette smoker, consuming a pack a day. She often puffed on long, dainty cigarettes, using a cigarette holder and never putting the cigarette in her mouth. She switched from cigarettes to pipes after the doctor advised her, for health reasons, to stop smoking cigarettes. She took him literally, and the pipe became her new vice.

With the full backing of Luke, for whom nothing happened in Somerset County without his approval, and the rest of the party, Fenwick won her race. One of the first people to write her a letter of congratulations was Rabbi Chertoff. "It should not be necessary for me to say that the congratulations are not being extended to you, but to the voters of your Assembly District who have shown the wit and wisdom to elect you as their representative . . . they have caught your spirit and recognized not only your enthusiasm and ability and independence, but that quality from which all this stems: your moral integrity."[30]

Fenwick and Republican Josephine Margetts from New Vernon in neighboring Morris County were the only women in the New Jersey assembly. "The two were an interesting contrast. Millicent instantly attracted attention. She created focus. The public and press loved her," said Bateman. "Interestingly enough, Margetts was rather low-key, but was able to accomplish a lot. She sponsored most of the significant environmental legislation long before it was popular to do so. Margetts was an effective inside legislator and Fenwick was an effective outside legislator. Fenwick had the ability to focus an argument in a legislative session. Whereas Margetts was not as good on the floor, but she also was an effective legislator."[31]

Fenwick wasted no time settling into the assembly and proposing legislation. The first bill she introduced was a measure to outlaw discrimination on the basis of gender or marital status. Under the New Jersey civil rights statute people could not be discriminated against based on race, creed, color, national origin, ancestry, or age. Gender had been an obvious omission. Working women, in particular, benefited when the measure passed. At the time, employment discrimination against women was a complaint commonly received by the state division of civil rights. "Just to insure that Mrs. Fenwick is not being discriminated against herself," wrote one local paper, "the title of her bill identifies her as 'assemblyman,' the same title held by male members."[32]

Because of Fenwick's interest in promoting minority businesses, she divested herself of stock in the minority-owned Evanbo Construction Company. She said, "I'm going to get out of this because I want to push the state to give opportunity to minority businesses and I can't do it if I own stock in one."[33] Buying the stock had exemplified Fenwick's active support for what she advocated, as did her method of disbursing it—she donated the stock to a nonprofit organization.

Fenwick's first term as a state legislator was effective. She sponsored four bills and co-sponsored fifteen more that became law. Her success was due in part to what some considered a photographic memory. Her uncanny ability to rattle off statistics muted opponents' arguments. She, however, attributed her effectiveness to the "courtesy, indulgence, and kindness of the leadership."[34]

One victory that was particularly sweet for Fenwick was a bill that leveled the playing field between men and women in the work force. The bill repealed a law that limited women to work no more than ten hours a day or fifty-four hours a week and forbade them from working between midnight and seven in the morning unless they were nurses. Because these restrictions kept women from working the same hours as men they also kept them from earning the same overtime wages. The existing law was particularly vulnerable because of Title VII of the Civil Rights Act of 1964, which prohibited employment discrimination based on gender. An avid supporter of equal rights for women, Fenwick eloquently lobbied in favor of the repeal several times before it finally passed the assembly. "What women insist on, not plead for, is the right to work when and where they please . . . it is a liberation in the truest sense that women can do what they want with their lives," she said.[35] One assemblyman who disagreed with the repeal was Republican Ken Wilson. He asked Fenwick whether she had ever worked in a factory and added that he had not received any letters from female factory workers who supported the bill.

Fenwick shot back, "It is as absurd for Mr. Wilson to say I cannot talk about women working in factories because I never worked in one as it would be for me to say that he cannot talk about women because he is not a woman."[36] Her comment was greeted by applause and laughter from her colleagues and an entertained public watching from the visitors' gallery.

Another cause Fenwick embraced was protecting abused children. As chairman of the Joint Legislative Committee on Child Abuse and

Child Welfare, she pushed for an overhaul of state programs and facilities for children caught in the system. After holding several hearings in which doctors, prosecutors, law enforcement officers, and social workers testified, Fenwick wrote a report documenting the shortcomings inherent in the state system. The report revealed that the system was lax about providing protection and care for abused children.[37]

The findings also alerted lawmakers to a glaring problem—the underreporting of child abuse, and subsequently the need to educate lawyers, doctors, teachers, and police officers about the signs of abuse. Fenwick sought to enhance and enforce legislation that defined the rights of parents and children. By May 1971, she had succeeded: the assembly voted 66–0 in favor of tough legislation to protect children from injury and abuse.[38] Throughout her years in the statehouse she became the voice of the children, whether advocating the establishment of a child-protection unit or making sure school-age children in public care received an education.

Migrant farm workers also received the attention of Assemblywoman Fenwick. She introduced legislation that made it mandatory to provide drinking water and toilet facilities to seasonal farm workers. Fenwick also sponsored another bill that required farm employees, often paid on a piece-rate basis, to be paid for each day worked at the minimum hourly wage per hour worked. Both bills became law. In co-sponsoring the latter, Fenwick was trying to rectify the injustices of the piece-rate payment system: "My bill provided that they [the workers] had to get the larger, whichever was the larger sum," said Fenwick.[39] Her advocacy on behalf of better facilities for migrant workers, particularly the availability of toilets, earned her the nickname "Outhouse Millie." "It was awfully funny," she said. "I was introduced once in the [heavily agricultural] southern part of the state, as Mrs. Fenwick, and the Chairman, or the Sub-chairman, interrupted, and said, 'Well, maybe in the northern part of New Jersey she's known as Mrs. Fenwick. Down here she's 'Outhouse Millie.' I thought that was lovely, on account of the portable sanitation."[40]

In 1971, Fenwick and Josephine Margetts were both reelected; they were joined by a third assemblywoman, Ann Klein, a Democrat from Morris County who was the president of the New Jersey League of Women Voters. The three women served with seventy-seven men in the state assembly. The state senate had one woman among its forty members. Out of the 120-member bicameral legislative body, only 4 were women.

Although the Democrats enjoyed a one-person majority in the assembly, Tom Kean, a young Republican, was elected speaker of the assembly. Hudson County Democrat David Friedland and two others struck a deal with Kean to make him speaker because there was a split in the Democratic Party. In return, Friedland, whose chances of being nominated speaker by his own party were dwindling, secured influential leadership posts as well as assurances of increased aid for his district. Outraged by this backdoor tactic, the assembly, with forty Democrats, thirty-nine Republicans, and one independent, was off to a contentious start. Later that year, the New Jersey Supreme Court found Friedland guilty of unethical conduct in an unrelated matter that dealt with extortion charges against an alleged loan shark.

Locally, the Bernardsville Democratic Committee was furious with Fenwick, but not with Jack Ewing—the other Somerset County assemblyman—both of whom voted for Kean. "As one of the 39 [Republican] representatives elected in November, I voted for Kean who is without question one of the finest public figures in New Jersey," said Fenwick. "I think he is universally acknowledged as not only able but a person of highest integrity. I certainly wish that there had been 41 Republican votes that would have put him in the speaker's chair."[41]

Prior to the Kean-Friedland deal, two factions of the Democratic Party made a pact not to talk to the Republicans. Obviously, Friedland broke the pact, but Fenwick didn't learn that until after the vote. "If I had known about this agreement," she said, "I would have insisted that we talk to Woodson's side, which is the majority of Democrats."[42]

Adhering to her principles, Fenwick was a stickler for rules. After her 1971 reelection she returned a campaign contribution because although the check was dated before the election, she received it after. "By law, checks must be deposited within 24 hours of receipt and not later than five days before election day," wrote Fenwick to the donor. "My understanding is that no contribution which arrives later can legally be deposited."[43] The likelihood of anyone investigating her campaign finances was slim, but, Fenwick in good conscience could not accept the check.

Fenwick's second term in the state assembly was more contentious than the first. Democratic bitterness over Kean's ascension to the position of speaker initially plagued the legislative body. But despite the mood, much was accomplished. Two months into her second term, women achieved a symbolic victory in the statehouse when Republican leader Richard W. De Korte (R-Bergen) initiated and passed a bill to take down "Ladies' Gallery" and "Men's Gallery" signs that hung above double doors leading to the visitors' gallery. Although the rule designating that women sit on the right side of the gallery and men on the left had long since been abolished, the signs had remained. Fenwick watched as custodian Arnold Constantani climbed a ladder and removed the signs of a previous era. De Korte recommended the signs be sent to the state museum. But being a woman in the state legislature was not easy. "There were obvious problems—no proper ladies' room, we had to set aside a space for the women," said Kean. "She, I think, did very well because of her individuality."[44]

Elected women officials were still a rare breed. "Women holding positions in the legislature were so unusual that they were under more pressure to perform," said Bateman. "And, as a result they worked much harder than most of the men because they had to make up for not being one of the boys."[45]

Of approximately 7,700 state legislators nationwide in 1972, 344 were women—making up 2 percent of state senates and 4 percent of state assemblies. Women fared better in the 1972 November election, with 424 women serving in state legislatures, representing a 19 percent increase.[46] Tactics varied from candidate to candidate. Some women camouflaged their gender by using their first initial and excluding photos from campaign literature. Others flaunted it. One woman used pink stationery for correspondence and campaign material. Fenwick herself thought gender helped her secure the coveted Republican slot in her first assembly election. "Several people wanted the job, and I think leadership in the party, in the county, felt if we give it to Millicent it won't make all these other men mad, because instead of picking from among the men who wanted it they thought, there is Millicent; and I had really worked so hard in Case's campaigns and with various gubernatorial campaigns, and with civil rights."[47] It is hard to determine how much credence this notion should be given; Fenwick's name was the one most often cited by the press as the likely choice of the Somerset County Republican leadership. In fact, Luke Gray said that Fenwick was the unanimous choice, and no one else was nominated.

Believing that there was a difference between male and female colleagues at the time, Fenwick said, "The world of politics, even a toehold on power, is new to us [women]. It is intoxicating. I have talked to girls in Douglass College [Rutgers University] at home and you can see them lighting up at the idea that they can go to law school and become senators! You can't get a boy to light up about that, because he takes it for granted. . . . We are like the Founding Fathers of our nation, seeing a whole new world, a world we can re-make."[48] Embracing her pioneering role, Fenwick continued to advocate on behalf of civil rights, prisoners' rights, child welfare, and equality—the same injustices she fought against as a citizen.

Despite the political turmoil that opened the legislative season, the assembly was able to unite to pass what some considered revolutionary laws because of their widespread impact, including the first state aid extended to private colleges and no-fault auto insurance.

What received equal attention was New Jersey's ratification of the Equal Rights Amendment (ERA), becoming the thirteenth state to do so.

**Figure 1.** Millicent Fenwick's childhood home in Bernardsville, New Jersey. In 1950 she demolished all but the library wing on the right and turned it into a French provincial home because she could not afford to heat and maintain the original fifty-plus rooms. *Courtesy of Hugh Hammond Fenwick.*

**Figure 2.** Millicent's mother, Mary Picton Stevens Hammond, holding her young daughters Millicent (*left*) and Mary (*right*). (Date unknown.) She did not see her children grow up because she died when the *Lusitania* was sunk in 1915. *Courtesy of Hugh Hammond Fenwick.*

**Figure 3.** Millicent thought of herself as a "messy and fat child." Her love of reading was evident at an early age. (Date unknown.) *Courtesy of Hugh Hammond Fenwick.*

**Figure 4.** The Hammond family poses for a picture during Ogden Hammond's ambassadorship in Spain (1926–1929). Seated are Daisy (Millicent's stepmother), and father, Ogden. Standing behind them are Millicent (*left*); stepbrother, McClure; sister, Mary; and brother, Oggie. *Courtesy of Hugh Hammond Fenwick.*

Figure 5. Millicent, Ogden, and Mary Hammond on Easter Sunday 1930. *Courtesy of Hugh Hammond Fenwick.*

Figure 6. Millicent and Hugh Fenwick on their wedding day in June 1932. *Courtesy of Hugh Hammond Fenwick.*

Figure 7. On assignment in South America for *Vogue,* Millicent boards a plane in Buenos Aires in 1938. During that trip, she and photographer Toni Frissell traveled to Argentina, Brazil, Chile, and Peru. Photograph by Toni Frissell, courtesy of the Library of Congress.

**Figure 8.** Fenwick at work in the New Jersey State Assembly where she served from 1970 to 1973 before the governor appointed her director of consumer affairs. *Courtesy of Hugh Hammond Fenwick.*

**Figure 9.** Three weeks before Fenwick's first congressional election she met with President Gerald Ford to discuss the effect of inflation on the consumer. After the meeting, the president endorsed her candidacy. (October 1974.) *Courtesy of the Special Collections and University Archives, Rutgers University.*

**Figure 10.** Vintage Fenwick reading New Jersey newspaper. (Date unknown.) *Courtesy of the Special Collections and University Archives, Rutgers University.*

DAVENPORT.
As indispensable
as sensible
shoes.

PAID FOR
BY HER
CHUMS

*G B Trudeau*

**Figure 11.** Garry Trudeau's *Doonesbury* character Congresswoman Lacey Davenport shared many of the traits for which Representative Millicent Fenwick was known. *Doonebury © 1986 by G. B. Trudeau. Reprinted with permission from the Universal Press Syndicate. All rights reserved.*

**Figure 12.** Standing in front of Fenwick—the only female representative in a congressional delegation to the Soviet Union led by House Speaker Carl Albert—is Soviet General Secretary Leonid Brezhnev. (August 1975.) This trip sparked Fenwick's legislation to establish the U.S. Helsinki Commission. *Courtesy of the Special Collections and University Archives, Rutgers University.*

**Figure 13.** In the Oval Office, Vice-President George H. W. Bush shakes Fenwick's hand as President Ronald Reagan looks on, August 17, 1982. *Courtesy of the Special Collections and University Archives, Rutgers University.*

**Figure 14.** President Ronald Reagan hits the campaign trail at the Flemington (N.J.) Fairgrounds in support of Fenwick's bid for the Senate, September 1982. Governor Thomas Kean (l.) and Millicent Fenwick (r.) applaud the president's endorsement of her. *Courtesy of the Special Collections and University Archives, Rutgers University.*

**Figure 15.** Millicent Fenwick surrounded by her congressional staff. (June 1982.) *Courtesy of the Special Collections and University Archives, Rutgers University.*

**Figure 16.** At the end of a four-day field visit to Ghana, the village of Gomoa Ojobi hosts a good-bye ceremony for Ambassador Fenwick. (February 1985.) *Courtesy of Hugh Hammond Fenwick.*

**Figure 17.** A doting Millicent looks adoring at her first great-grandchild, Spencer Reckford, born in 1989. *Courtesy of Sam Reckford.*

**Figure 18.** At the unveiling of the Millicent Fenwick Statue in Bernardsville, Mayor Hugh Fenwick, Millicent's son, shows Governor Christine Todd Whitman the outline of a pipe, symbolic of Millicent's pipe-smoking habit. (October 1995.) *Photograph by Robert Boye, courtesy of Helen Walton.*

After Fenwick made remarks in favor of the ERA, she said, "One of my colleagues rose and with real anguish—you could see he was touching very close to something that was very important to him—and said: 'I just don't like this amendment. I've always thought of women as kissable and cuddly, and smelling good.' It was the kind of thing you don't really believe," she continued. "The only answer, of course, was: 'That's the way I've always felt about men. I only hope for your sake you haven't been disappointed as often as I have."[49] Her wit kept colleagues on their toes. And her charisma, character, and hard work captured the attention not only of the legislative body but also of the media and the public. However, Fenwick's witty retort was not reported at the time, because she never verbalized those words. In a 1972 transcript from the Conference on Women State Legislators, Fenwick said, "I was really tempted to say, 'Well, that is just the way I feel about men—and I hope you haven't been disappointed as often as I have!' I think my electorate back home, that has always branded me as the Bella Abzug [the rebellious New York congresswoman] of Somerset County, would not like that riposte."[50] It wasn't until later that this exchange became well known when Fenwick often recounted the tale.

Another issue contested in the assembly in the summer of 1972 was Governor William Cahill's proposed state income tax. Fenwick was one of nine Republicans who supported the legislation despite its unpopularity in her district. She brought her eldest grandson, thirteen-year-old Joe Reckford, to Trenton to hear the debate. He watched as the assembly voted 52 to 23 against the bill.[51] "On the car ride back to Bernardsville she was very quiet," said Joe. "And finally she said, 'I just lost the election. I think it was that vote.' She absolutely adored the legislature and sacrificed it. It was the only time I saw her vulnerable. . . . She was for the income tax because she thought it was more fair. She gave me a lesson in the car," said Joe. "She explained that property tax penalized people whose incomes were lower, but their property values had increased. Thus taxing based on income, not property, made more sense."[52]

As Fenwick's second term drew to a close, Assemblyman De Korte wrote, "The Republicans in the Assembly have remained an effective and productive group, not withstanding our individual differences, and notwithstanding the extraordinary odds against our accomplishing anything."[53] When Kean needed her vote she obliged. "I never asked her to violate her principles—[legislation] that would have been against civil rights or the environment or some of the [other] things she cared about," said Kean. "But when there was a question she might have voted against and I said 'Millicent, we really need you,' she was always willing to go the extra mile."[54]

In addition to supporting her party, in her second term she sponsored nine bills that became law and co-sponsored an additional sixteen. Besides her efforts to protect abused children, she sought to protect prisoner rights. "I keep reminding people that the prisoner has no one to speak for him. Unless he resorts to violence, there's no way for him to gain attention. And that's wrong, because everyone has the right to decent, humane treatment."[55] She arranged for inmates to testify before the assembly about their living conditions and sponsored legislation returning voting rights to prisoners who fulfilled their sentence and completed parole. Believing in rehabilitation and forgiveness, Fenwick said the bill "is based on the principle that anyone who has paid his dues to the society he has offended is no longer a second-class citizen."[56]

Over the years Fenwick familiarized herself with New Jersey's correctional facilities and prisoner population. She regularly visited inmates, advocated on their behalf, and provided them with Bibles—and sometimes even money—once they were released. The money was technically a loan, not a gift. She never expected to be reimbursed, but sometimes she was.[57] Her efforts were not wasted. "It has been 14 years since your support won my Expedited Clemency and release from prison," wrote Robert Pierre. "Of course, there is no way to ever repay such a gift. However, I thought the knowledge that I have not betrayed the trust that you had in me (I was released from parole more than 8 years ago because of good behavior) would be gratifying. . . . While so many others talked about prisons and the people in them in an abstract sense you took action and created a profound change in the direction of one life."[58]

Fenwick's final achievement as a state legislator was the passage of the landmark Flood Plains Act of 1972, which she sponsored in the assembly and Bateman sponsored in the senate. The legislation aimed to reduce flood-related devastation by giving the state "Department of Environmental Protection the authority to share in the regulation of development in flood prone areas of the state."[59] New Jersey was at the forefront of the issue and one of the first states to enact legislation recognizing the importance of regulating the use and development of flood-prone areas to protect landowners from potential flood damage while also preserving wetlands and their function in the ecosystem.

At the signing ceremony on December 14, 1972, the governor paid tribute to Senate President Ray Bateman and Assemblywoman Millicent Fenwick, the primary architects behind the bill. "If it weren't for Millicent—her enthusiasm and persuasiveness in the Assembly," said Governor Cahill, "we would not have this before us for signing." Then the governor leaned over and gave Fenwick a peck on the cheek and a souvenir pen. In her remarks she paid homage to Somerset County for being blessed with citizens concerned with conservation and the environment.[60]

Two weeks earlier the governor had made what was considered a surprise announcement when he appointed Fenwick director of the New Jersey Division of Consumer Affairs—a sub-cabinet post requiring senate confirmation. The announcement was made, fittingly, at a meeting of the Talent Bank for Women, a project introduced to bring more women into state government. The governor, whom some chastised for not having many women in high-level posts, heralded Fenwick's appointment as "the beginning of more women in top positions of state government."[61] As chairman of the assembly's Subcommittee on Consumer Affairs, Fenwick was the natural choice for the job. And, although she was qualified, rumors circulated that the appointment was Cahill's way of removing a rabble-rouser from the assembly.

Upon Fenwick's resignation from the state legislature, the assembly passed a resolution praising her work. One assemblyman sent her a dozen long-stemmed roses, while another sent a new pipe. Fenwick recalled her legislative experience as a "wonderful, messy, contentious, magnificent spectacle of representative government at work [which] is absolutely irresistible, and that's where it takes place—in the Assembly. Really, it's a wonderful experience."[62]

When Fenwick accepted the $26,500-a-year consumer affairs post and was confirmed by the state senate, she became the most highly paid and highest-ranking woman in the Cahill administration. Her predecessor, lawyer Charles J. Irwin, said, "My mission from the governor was to get the division established and rolling and I've done that. There's plenty still be be done, but I'm a head knocker, not an administrator."[63]

Fenwick started her new job around the same time Ralph Nader was spearheading his consumer movement. While many people were captivated by Nader's efforts, Fenwick was not. "I think someone like Ralph Nader is more concerned with hating large corporations than with helping the consumer," she said. "I don't think that is constructive to society."[64]

Fenwick eagerly assumed the reins of her new position, approaching her new office with considerable creativity. She was adamant about incorporating the public into the government process and ensuring that consumers paid fair prices in the marketplace. Fairness was a theme that resonated during her tenure. Instead of protecting her own pocketbook she was minding the nickels and dimes of the public. Her prevailing philosophy combined a sense of justice with cost consciousness.

"Maybe the men who do the appointing think women have the temperament for consumer affairs," she said. "Men are used to dealing with thousand-dollar expense accounts. It is a woman who decides whether to buy a leg of lamb instead of chicken, there's no way to write it off. I think for that reason women are more prudent with their dollars and are good choices for a consumer advocate post."[65] At this time, Bess Myerson was serving as an effective consumer chief in New York City by publicizing the consumer office and its purpose. Fenwick hoped to do the same. "It exists for their [the public's] protection and it must be responsive to their needs," said Fenwick. "People today so often feel helpless, like nobody cares. I want them to know that this office cares."[66]

When the governor appointed Fenwick, he hoped more women would "take their place beside her." He said, "If we can get more women like her [Fenwick] to serve this government, this state truly will be a better place for everybody to live."[67]

During Irwin's tenure he had revamped the old Consumer Protection Agency and created a more responsive entity. Under his leadership individuals and organizations who deceived consumers were prosecuted. Fenwick continued Irwin's mission. During her tenure New Jersey settled its first class-action suit related to a consumer fraud scheme. Her dedication to consumers foreshadowed her congressional career, as did her interaction with the public—characterized by handwritten responses and personal phone calls to concerned citizens. "The Office of Consumer Affairs hopes to give some comfort where the law doesn't quite cover," said Fenwick. "This division will somehow restore the confidence in government and respond to the people who pay for it all."[68]

On Fenwick's first day on the job as head of an agency with 350 employees, she opened the mail herself and read a letter from a consumer who had not received a set of steak knives she ordered. "So [Fenwick], on her first day, called the company to inquire about its whereabouts. . . . Here was this woman who looked like an aristocrat, but was for the people," said reporter Barbara Kukla.[69]

Also interested in office efficiency, Fenwick instituted sign-in sheets. "I tried to make it a matter of honor to be the first in and the last out, but I found that the entire Office of Consumer Protection [one division within the agency] was signing in with ditto marks and out with ditto marks. They all apparently arrived in a phalanx, in some super-elevator that could deliver a hundred people in one gulp, and absorb them in one gulp."[70]

After four months of this charade, Fenwick broached the subject with her staff. "You know, I'm very puzzled," she said. "I don't know how all of you sign in at 9 o'clock precisely and leave at 4:30 precisely. Doesn't Mrs. Alvarez ever want to talk to you until 4:45 about the icebox that doesn't work and the baby coming home from the hospital? Maybe you don't belong here. Maybe you ought to be in the Bureau of Motor Vehicles—sending out licenses. Something less urgent."[71]

Fenwick believed education was vital to helping consumers get the most for their money. "There must be a certain native prudence on the part of the consumer."[72] Consumer concepts were introduced in adult education classes and public schools. Price comparison was incorporated into math classes; understanding contracts and leases became part of English classes; and nutritional information was taught in science class.

Implementing and enforcing numerous regulations to protect the consumer became a mainstay of Fenwick's administration. In one instance car dealers were required to post the suggested retail price so consumers could compare advertised prices with listed prices. Other provisions of the auto-sale law mandated truth in advertising—car dealers needed to substantiate their claims about lowest prices, durability, and quality of the vehicle.

No complaint was too small for Fenwick. She listened to consumers share their woes about everything from deceptive sales pitches to not enough nuts in a candy bar. The agency dealt with complaints by going directly to the source, the sellers of goods and services. When necessary, one of the deputy attorney generals would take up the fight in court. Whether advocating for civil rights or fair prices, Fenwick utilized the resources available to her to protect the individual.

# 10

## A Geriatric

## Triumph

In the long run, we shape our lives, and we shape ourselves.
—Eleanor Roosevelt

For twenty-two years, Peter Frelinghuysen repre-
sented Bernardsville and the rest of the Fifth District of New Jersey in
the House of Representatives. The Frelinghuysen family has been a political powerhouse since colonial days and remains so today. They arrived in New Jersey in 1720, almost as far back as Millicent Fenwick's
Stevens ancestors. Over the past two centuries six Frelinghuysens have
served in Congress, beginning with Frederick Frelinghuysen, who was a
member of the Continental Congress and was later elected to the U.S.
Senate in 1793. He served with the Honorable John Stevens, Fenwick's
great-great-great-grandfather, as a member of the New Jersey convention that ratified the federal Constitution in 1787. Frederick Frelinghuysen's great nephew, Frederick Theodore Frelinghuysen, served in
the U.S. Senate in the mid-1800s but is best remembered as Henry Clay's
running mate in the 1844 presidential election, in which James Polk,
not Clay, was elected president. Peter Frelinghuysen's son, Rodney—
great-great-grandson of Frederick Theodore—is the latest Frelinghuysen
to serve. He was first elected to the House in 1994 and represented his
district as the country entered the twenty-first century.

The Frelinghuysens, active Republicans on the state and national
level, have been described as the "aristocracy of New Jersey."[1] It is only
fitting that another patrician, Millicent Fenwick, would find her fate
entwined with the Frelinghuysens.

Early in 1974, Peter Frelinghuysen announced that after eleven terms
in office he was not seeking reelection. For the past fifty years, New

Jersey's Fifth District had been represented by only two men—the other being Charles Eaton, son of industrialist Cyrus Eaton—making the news of change, and a successor, significant.

The press wasted no time throwing names into the ring. A March 10, 1974, *New York Times* article mentioned eight people as candidates, including State Assemblyman Tom Kean, who later became governor, and former Assemblywoman Millicent Fenwick. In Peggy Lamson's book *In the Vanguard: Six American Women in Public Life,* the author captured a story often told by Fenwick about her decision to run for Congress. "One day in the early spring of 1974, as [Fenwick] tells it," wrote Lamson, "a newspaper man named John Davies of *The Camden News* who was a particular friend said to her, 'Watch my column tomorrow.' What she saw was startling. Peter Frelinghuysen . . . was not going to seek reelection, the column said, and now everyone was talking about Millicent Fenwick as his successor."[2]

Fenwick firmly believed the idea of her candidacy was originated by Davies, despite earlier articles that had suggested the same thing. Davies, an award-winning journalist, covered the state house as bureau chief for the Gannett newspaper chain. In reality, no Davies column had suggested she run for office, nor was there a paper called the *Camden News*. Davies's articles appeared in the *Camden Courier-Post* and the *Courier News*. As Davies said, "I admired Millicent. She always gave credit to others, but in this case it was misplaced. . . . Perhaps she did not want to look too aggressive by going after the congressional seat . . . and she didn't know if Kean would run." Davies said newspapermen should be objective and that "as a newspaperman I would never tell anyone to run for Congress as she suggests."[3] Indeed, Davies was one of the most respected and trusted reporters in Trenton. He covered the statehouse under five governors: Alfred Driscoll, Robert Meyner, Richard Hughes, William Cahill, and Brendan Byrne. During an era when few women held public office, it is possible Fenwick was reluctant to admit her political ambitions and thus credited someone else with the idea.

Fenwick was a natural candidate for the open seat. She had statewide name recognition, thanks in part to her stint as director of consumer affairs, and she was actively involved in local and state politics. The other formidable contender was Tom Kean, assembly minority leader. Both Kean and Fenwick were party moderates with progressive records on tax reform, the environment, and other major issues. "Because they admire[d] each other, one would be expected to withdraw in favor of the other." Initially, Fenwick told reporters she had "not decided what to do about her own candidacy and possibly would not [decide] until after Mr. Kean's decision." She went on to say, "We'd be blessed with such a representative as Tom Kean."[4] While Fenwick would support Kean, Somerset

Republican leaders believed she "would be difficult to dislodge in favor of anyone else if she made up her mind to run," because of her name recognition and local popularity.[5]

By the end of March, as the April 23 filing deadline for the primary neared, there were lots of contenders, but no one had declared. Everyone was waiting to see what the front-runner, Kean, was going to do. On March 26, a month before the filing deadline, Kean announced his candidacy. Like Frelinghuysen, Kean came from a politically connected family. His father, Robert Kean, had served in Congress for twenty years, and his grandfather, Hamilton Fish Kean, served one term in the United States Senate. As Kean said in his autobiography, "Politics in our family has always been a sort of disease of the blood . . . the Roosevelts, Stuyvesants, Fishes, Livingstons, and Winthrops—are all cousins of the Keans."[6]

Based on Fenwick's favorable remarks about Kean, it was expected that she would bow out of the race and support him. Instead she decided to resign from her state post as director of consumer affairs and run for Congress. Leaving her consumer affairs job was not a risky move, because there was speculation that the recently elected Governor Brendan Byrne would replace her with one of his Democratic colleagues.

Fenwick made her decision after a telephone conversation with Kean. He was hoping his call would sideline her candidacy, but it did the opposite. As Fenwick remembered the conversation, she felt that Kean, "expected me to step back as I've done so often before. After all I was 64 at the time and he was 38. And in his voice I could hear that he really expected me to say, 'Well, if you want to run, I won't.' And, there was something about that expectation that got under my skin. If he'd said, 'Millicent, I hate to oppose you, but are you really set on it?' I think I would have said no. And my life would have been entirely different. But something about the way he put it got my back up. Maybe the ERA, which I had of course supported but at the time more or less taken for granted, had affected me more than I realized. I don't know. But I just decided to go ahead."[7]

Within two weeks of Kean's announcement, Fenwick was embroiled in a congenial but close primary fight. "Against the specter of Watergate, there are those who will wonder why I, as a lifelong Republican, choose to run—particularly in a contested primary election," Fenwick said. "The truth is that I welcome a primary for several important reasons. First, it will give the voters a choice, and choice is one of the larger parts of freedom. Secondly, it will serve the public notice that there are many Republicans who, however they are saddened by what their party has been going through, will not run away from it at a time of its greatest need. Competition for the Republican nomination will demonstrate dramatically that there are still many of us who are proud of the great traditions of the Republican Party and the contributions it has made to the history of our country."[8]

The candidates had less than two months to bolster their campaigns before the June 4 primary. The Fifth District seat was traditionally Republican, and it was important to the GOP to maintain it, particularly as the Watergate scandal unfolded. New Jersey had fifteen seats in the House—eight were held by Democrats, seven by Republicans.

During the primary election the country was besieged by the Watergate scandal, a corrupt Republican White House, an energy crisis, an inflationary economy, and the Vietnam War. Congress, and particularly the Democrats, advocated campaign finance reform in light of the Watergate scandal and Nixon's Committee to Re-Elect the President (CREEP). The public's trust in politicians eroded. It was going to be a tough year for Republicans, but Kean and Fenwick were up to the challenge.

Both candidates were lifelong residents of New Jersey. Kean lived in Livingston, at the edge of the district. Encompassing forty-two towns, the Fifth District stretched from the wealthy enclaves of Princeton in Mercer County (near Trenton) up north through foxhunting country in Somerset and Morris counties and then to several affluent suburbs. Somerset County, with twenty-one towns in the district, accounted for 40 percent of the area, including Fenwick's hometown of Bernardsville. The rest of the district included fourteen towns in Morris County, three in Mercer County, and two each in Middlesex County and Essex County. This district was among the wealthiest not only in the state but in the nation.

Since Tom Kean lived in the fringe of the district in Essex County and Millicent Fenwick lived in the heart of it in Somerset County, Republican leaders supported Fenwick. Although both were viable candidates with similar stances, the Republicans thought they could secure more votes with a candidate embedded in the district. In fact, it was local party leader Luke Gray, the heart and soul of the Somerset County GOP, who encouraged Fenwick to run. He ran a tight operation and firmly believed a Somerset person should gain the House seat since the entire county was in the Fifth District.

Gray was a well-respected, disciplined, and powerful party leader. Despite this, Fenwick was initially considered a slight underdog to the much younger Kean. Fenwick countered age-related concerns by pointing out that businessman-turned-public servant W. Averell Harriman, then eighty-two, and NATO Ambassador David K. E. Bruce, then seventy-six, were considerably older than she was, and they were still going strong. Bruce had held a record six major ambassadorial assignments under six presidents and was appointed ambassador to NATO in September 1974.

Arguments about Fenwick's age focused on how long it would take her to gain seniority in the House of Representatives and whether she had the staying power to be reelected time and again to become a ranking member.

Age became an issue because it was one of the few differences between these two moderate Republicans. "It was hard to run against each other when we had co-sponsored many bills," said Kean.[9] Both were well known from the New Jersey assembly and had good name recognition, similar policy positions, and voting records. Millicent Fenwick received additional exposure because of her position as the consumer affairs director, while Tom Kean had additional name recognition based on his leadership in the assembly and his father's and grandfather's congressional service. A Kean-sponsored poll showed that Millicent Fenwick's name recognition was three times higher than his in the contested congressional district.

Although Fenwick secured the Somerset County support, Kean received the support of the Morris County Republican Party. Of the two counties, Somerset had a more powerful party organization. As the June 4 primary approached it was clear the contest between Kean and Fenwick would be among the closest in the state, if not in the nation. Thanks to the support of the county GOP, Fenwick went from being a slight underdog to being the odds-on favorite. She felt her age would not hinder her electability and that voters were more inclined to trust a woman with a strong background in consumerism than a traditional politician like Tom Kean.[10]

As expected, the primary contest was too close to call quickly. A low voter turnout made each vote critical. The initial tally indicated that Fenwick had won the race by 86 votes out of 25,000 cast, or one-third of 1 percent. Kean ordered a recount that showed an even closer margin of victory. The recount declared Fenwick the victor by a mere 76 votes.[11] Instead of heading to Washington, D.C., Tom Kean's political path took him to Drumthwacket, the governor's mansion in Princeton, in 1981. He served two terms as governor of New Jersey before becoming president of Drew University, in Madison, New Jersey, in 1990. Kean conceded that "it was a very lucky thing [I lost] because I didn't want to run that time [he had been talked into it]. So things worked out for the best."[12]

After the primary victory, Fenwick geared up for the general election. In the summer, Roger Bodman, a recent college graduate and Bernardsville resident, joined her campaign. His father was active in the Bernardsville community, serving as chairman of the planning board and active in the Bernardsville Swimming Pool Association. Roger, a political science major, started out as a volunteer and then became Fenwick's paid driver and confidant.

Roger accompanied Fenwick to campaign events throughout the district. He was not only her driver but also her traveling aide and right-hand man. His days began early, around six, when he drove from his Bernardsville home to hers, just a couple miles up the road. From the road, visitors were greeted by the wide base of Fenwick's gravel driveway and a stone wall with a plaque simply stating the address. Roger turned left and drove slowly along the winding gravel driveway, until, after a quarter of a mile, the pale yellow French provincial home came into view, and the gray gravel gave way to neutral-colored pebbles. Roger would pull around to the front portico and Fenwick would plant herself in the front passenger seat. Her days were spent passing out literature, attending street fairs, greeting morning and evening commuters at train stations, and giving speeches. Fenwick didn't start out distributing information on the platform, however. Instead, against the advice of campaign manager Jack Ewing, she rode the train. "I tried to tell her," said Ewing. "I said, 'Millicent you are going through the first car, then at the next station, you've gone through the first car towards the back of the train . . . and you don't want to interrupt people reading the paper, or sleeping.' I said, 'You stand on the platform because they are waiting for the train and they have a few minutes.' But no, she was going to ride [the] train. She did that just once."[13]

Fenwick's ability to charm the public was evident during her stump speeches. "Integrity means far more than simply honesty," she told crowds besieged by news of Watergate. "Money is not the only temptation—the desire for power is more often the trap officials fall into. Intellectual honesty is just as important. When differences of opinion arise, the public must be able to know that an elected representative is honestly trying to do the right as God gives me to know the right. The mutual trust and respect that comes from this understanding is the cement—the bond—that holds representative government together and makes it work."[14]

Fenwick was a tireless campaigner, often staying on the campaign trail until midnight. She needed someone young like Roger to keep up with her. "She was an enormous bundle of energy, incredible for a woman of her age," said Bodman. "She worked me to death, I'll tell you that. . . . It was fifteen- to eighteen-hour days normally, particularly as fall rolled around."[15]

By this point Fenwick's staff included Hollis McLoughlin, a Princeton graduate; Dave Demerest, who later became communications director in President George H. W. Bush's administration; Assemblyman Jack Ewing, campaign manager; Harry O. H. Frelinghuysen, finance chairman; and Julius Mastro, an unofficial advisor. Her campaign committee was made up of a list of notable Republicans from the five counties in the Fifth District. Kean represented Essex County; outgoing Congressman Frelinghuysen, Morris County; State Senator Bateman, Somerset County; Dunellen Mayor Lawrence Anzovino, Middlesex County; and former Princeton Mayor Henry Patterson, Mercer County. They provided Fenwick with a strong base, as did the countless volunteers Fenwick made a point of visiting regularly.

Her campaign headquarters were located in Somerville at 41 North Bridge Street, also the site of the Somerset County Republican Headquarters. It was the same building where Fenwick had had her district office when she served in the assembly. "I loved working with her on the campaign," said Assemblyman Ewing. "She was a very strong individual. We hired somebody to do her releases, and there wasn't a release that she didn't rewrite all the time."[16]

Each day Jack Ewing, her campaign manager, gave Roger a campaign schedule. Personal appearances were at the core of the campaign, and the strategy suited Fenwick well. She easily connected with people and was able to project an authentic sense of compassion and determination. On more than one occasion she put her fluency in foreign languages to use. At the Raritan Street Fair and Parade, which attracted a large Italian American audience, Fenwick addressed the crowd in Italian. After one speech an elderly woman walked up to her, and before the woman uttered a word, Fenwick started conversing with her in Italian. The woman was overjoyed, and the two discussed, in Italian, the woman's problem with social security.

It was important for Fenwick to be highly visible in person, because television did not yet play a large role in campaigning. None of the candidates in the Fifth District aired television commercials because the New York media market was the most expensive in the country, and the costs were too high in a crowded market for local candidates to benefit. Fenwick's outreach was primarily through direct mailings and, occasionally, print or radio advertisements. She sold herself on a three-tiered platform: as a working woman (citing her *Vogue* experience), civic leader, and politician/civil servant.

In the general election Fenwick had three opponents. Her most formidable challenger was Democrat Frederick Bohen, a thirty-seven-year-old television news and public affairs director at a public broadcasting station in New York. Although he worked in New York, he lived in Princeton with his wife and three daughters. Bohen had defeated former Congressman Paul Krebs for the Democratic nomination, having gained name recognition two years earlier when he unsuccessfully challenged Frelinghuysen for the congressional seat. (Two years earlier Krebs had lost his bid to unseat Senator Clifford Case.)

Another contender was fifty-two-year-old John Giammarco from

Middlesex. He headed a small taxicab corporation and was the candidate of the American Independence Party, headed by Alabama Governor George Wallace. Giammarco had run unsuccessfully for office twice before, losing a state senate race in 1971 and a bid for county freeholder in 1970. The fourth candidate was forty-eight-year-old Leonard Newton, director and vice-president of a market research firm. He ran as an independent under the label of "New Leadership."

Although there were four people running, it was really a two-person race between Bohen and Fenwick. Bohen gained name recognition two years earlier when he unsuccessfully challenged Frelinghuysen for his congressional seat. During the campaign Bohen and Fenwick debated several times; among the issues was her age. Fenwick's speaking skills and confidence soon quelled any questions voters might have had about age interfering with her ability to do the job, and Bohen began to realize what he was up against. On one occasion, her younger opponent looked exhausted and Fenwick, energetic as ever, chided him, "I'd be glad to stay and talk as late as you like." When asked to confirm this remark, Fenwick did, adding, "Wasn't that nasty of me."[17] In 1974, that was as nasty as her campaign got.

Julius Mastro was an integral part of the campaign. He was essentially the political mastermind behind the scenes and a fixture in New Jersey politics. A shoe shop owner, he was elected to Bernardsville's borough council and served as council president and police commissioner. Mastro monitored voting patterns and provided constant feedback and advice to the Fenwick campaign. He became a valuable friend to many New Jersey politicians, including Governors Tom Kean and Christine Todd Whitman. Mastro had a reputation as a political genius; he helped Fenwick get elected to the New Jersey assembly, and he did the same for her congressional campaign.

Fenwick ran her campaign based on her experience and issues. She championed causes such as civil rights, consumer rights, public housing, and campaign finance reform. She was adamant about limiting campaign contributions from individuals to one hundred dollars. She refused to accept a check from businesses or lobbying groups, and her practice of refusing corporate money, which she had established in her assembly days, helped highlight her personal integrity.

Bohen could not contest Fenwick's legislative experience, so he tried to make age and wealth an issue. He distributed campaign material and advertisements that showed a wrinkled Fenwick. The photograph was of poor quality, very grainy, and obscured her elegance. He also was quick to highlight her financial status as a multimillionaire. Fenwick handled these charges by refusing to apologize for either her age or her wealth. Against the advice of her trustee, she released her financial records, which stated her net worth as $5,112,638.40, primarily from the trust fund her mother had created in 1915. The trustee, Democrat Archie Alexander, a cousin and close friend, felt that since, technically, most of the money was held in trust by her children, the amount of her fortune was misleading. Fenwick disagreed. She thought it would be dishonest to hold back such information. In the end her fortune made headlines in the *Trenton Evening Times,* which began its story listing her net worth but also included her 1973 federal income tax payment of more than $61,000 on an income of $150,000, of which $29,000 was her consumer affairs salary. Fenwick shrugged off the flurry of interest in her personal finances. "My own feeling is the hell with it. If people are going to get excited, I'm sorry. I give away what I think I should. I try to handle the whole thing wisely and have some sense of responsibility about it all."[18]

Interestingly, while age and money were raised as issues, gender was not. Although there were not many women holding political office in 1974, some women were visible in public life and had been for years. New Jersey voters first sent a female representative, Mary Teresa Norton, to Congress in 1925. Norton was the first Democratic woman elected to the House and the first woman to be elected from an East Coast state. She served from 1925 until 1951, when, at the age of seventy-five, she chose not to run for a fourteenth term. Over the years she had become chair of the Committee on Labor, where she played an important role in the passage of New Deal legislation during President Franklin Roosevelt's administration. Like Fenwick, Norton fought for legislation supporting equal rights for women in the work force and improved work conditions for laborers. Following on Norton's heels was New Jersey's next congresswoman, Florence Dwyer, elected in 1956 from Elizabeth and parts of Essex and Union Counties. A Republican, Dwyer's liberal views easily won her reelection until her retirement in 1972. Like Fenwick, Dwyer often crossed party lines when it came time to vote, particularly on issues related to housing. There were many similarities between the two women. Both had served in the state assembly, both were consumer advocates, and both despised federal waste. While serving on the Government Affairs Committee, Dwyer became the ranking Republican and fought to eliminate pork-barrel projects buried in legislation. "It's a common failing, I suppose, to take all you can get, but it's a failing people in public office should try to resist," said Dwyer.[19] And in 1974, in the Thirteenth District in the northwestern part of the state, Helen Meyner, a Democrat and wife of former New Jersey Governor Robert Meyner, was running against incumbent Joseph Maraziti.

When Fenwick ran for office in 1974, the Democrats controlled the House, 248 seats to 187 seats, and they were hoping to widen that margin because of the public's distaste for the events leading up to the Watergate scandal. Across the country Republicans were facing heavily contested Congressional races. In a relatively unusual move for a Republican, Fenwick denounced President Nixon. For this, she received a spot on his infamous enemies list. Fenwick's comments made life harder for Bohen, who was trying to do what Democrats around the country were doing, tying the corrupt Republican White House and the nation's economic decline to their local Republican opponents.

The campaign also gave many, including Bohen, a sense that Millicent was not a staunch Republican because she opposed President Ford's September 1974 pardon of Richard Nixon. Bohen later reflected that "when she [Fenwick] came out against the pardon as strongly as she did, I think that put the election on ice."[20] Another disadvantage for Bohen was that regardless of Fenwick's individual views, she was generally perceived as a loyal New Jersey Republican in a district dominated by GOP residents.

Despite the flurry of interest in politics that the Watergate affair had generated, historical lack of interest in off-year elections, first seen during the primaries, continued during the general election campaign, largely because Nixon had resigned in August—three months before the election, and President Ford had subsequently pardoned him. It was difficult for most candidates to get attention and campaign contributions, but not for Millicent Fenwick. She grabbed the attention of voters and attracted donors. She was surprised to learn how many people remembered her stances and achievements on consumer issues of importance to them. And although she opposed Political Action Committee (PAC) money, she had a well-oiled campaign thanks to her private wealth and the financial backing of the Republican Party. By mid-October Fenwick had reportedly collected $98,000 and spent $92,000. Other campaigns were having trouble raising funds, and spending was down in virtually every district. One New Jersey Democratic incumbent raised only $10,000 during the same period in which Fenwick had raised nearly ten times that amount. Fenwick's fund raising success was attributed to her political power, and the affluent residents of her district. Despite the success of her fundraising efforts, keeping campaign costs down was of utmost importance to her. She conceded that she would have to spend some of her own money to be elected, but not a dime more than necessary.

Fenwick owned a decrepit gray Chevrolet Chevelle, which Roger Bodman described as a "chintzy, plain-Jane car complete with dents." She sat in the passenger seat, and, while Bodman drove, she smoked her pipe, read briefings, scanned the *New York Times* or *Wall Street Journal*, and listened to the news on WCBS radio. Once she even remained in the car, smoking her pipe and reading the newspaper, as Bodman, in a suit, hoisted the car up to change a flat tire. Eventually, Fenwick conceded that her car needed to be replaced and asked Bodman to drive her to the local Chevy dealership in his car. He did. Without getting out of the car, Fenwick, from the passenger seat, told the salesman to get her another car like the old one, no frills. The one detail she emphasized was that her personal hood ornament, a fox (in honor of her terrier, Foxy), was to be transferred and securely attached to the hood of the new car. When the new Chevy arrived it was opulent by Fenwick's standards. "Oh my dear boy," she said to Roger, "this will not do. People will think I am ostentatious." The new car had floor carpets, which she did not need; velour seats, which she did not want; fancy hubcaps and whitewall tires, both unnecessary. So she exchanged it for a simpler model. The car dealership had to special-order a plain model for Millicent that had rubber mats, vinyl seats, plain hubcaps, and blackwall tires. It probably cost more to special-order a plain car than the basic Chevy originally delivered would have cost. The one luxury she afforded herself was air-conditioning. She loved her air-conditioner and would always ask Roger to turn on the *delicious* air-conditioner.[21] Brakes, on the other hand, not a luxury, were treated as one by Fenwick. She was notorious in town for her unconventional driving habits. Reluctant to use her brakes for fear of unnecessarily wearing them down, her fast-paced car was a familiar sight as it sped down the hilly roads of Bernardsville.[22]

As election day approached, Fenwick received the endorsement of the *New York Times*. "We endorsed Frederick M. Bohen, Democrat, two years ago, when he ran against Representative Peter Frelinghuysen, now retiring. While we still think well of Mr. Bohen, we are even more impressed with his Republican opponent, Mrs. Millicent Fenwick. With both legislative and administrative experience in government, she has made an outstanding record. Either candidate would make a good Representative but our preference is for Mrs. Fenwick."[23]

Bohen struggled to earn votes. Years later he conceded "that in 1974 I would have beaten any ordinary garden-variety Republican. But Fenwick was . . . a tireless expert campaigner, an excellent and witty speaker, very quick with one-line rejoinders. Her integrity was, of course, unquestionable. She had an almost uncanny ability to turn complicated questions into simple easily understood formulations that catch the popular fancy. And she quickly demonstrated her capacity for independence, her willingness to make up her own mind."[24]

By October, Republicans in New Jersey and around the nation were worried about a voter backlash. Watergate and the pardon still loomed over the nation and voters wanted a change on Capitol Hill. New Jersey GOP leaders were primarily concerned about retaining their seven congressional seats in the fairly moderate state. The one contest that was of little worry was the Fifth District, a Republican stronghold.

On election day, November 5, 1974, the GOP's fears came true. New Jersey Republicans suffered their worst election defeat in recent history, losing four of their seven congressional seats to Democratic opponents.[25] Voters braved the rainy weather to cast their votes against Republicans. The Democratic Party now controlled twelve of New Jersey's fifteen seats in the House. One of the three seats the Republicans retained was the Fifth District, where Millicent Fenwick defeated Fred Bohen by 16,500 votes out of nearly 149,000 cast. Her victory, while solid, was not a runaway. Bohen received approximately 44 percent of the vote to her 55 percent.

Matt Rinaldo and Edwin Forsythe, both of whom had also publicly distanced themselves from Nixon, retained the other two Republican seats. Of the three, however, Fenwick was the only one to go on the attack against the former president.

Fenwick's victory at the age of sixty-four was hailed by the press as a geriatric triumph. More significantly, she was credited with helping the two incumbent GOP Somerset County freeholders in their narrow victory over their Democratic challengers. Frank R. Nero, the lone Democrat on the Somerset Freeholder Board, said the GOP freeholders "rode to victory on the coattails" of Mrs. Fenwick's plurality in the heavily Republican county.[26] Two years later Nero experienced firsthand Fenwick's power when he ran against her for Congress. She defeated him by a two-to-one margin.

Millicent Fenwick's first congressional win was testament to her vitality as a campaigner and her magnetic personality, wit, charm, and passion about social issues. What made her victory surprising was that she was a Republican woman elected in the year Watergate stole the headlines and Democrats swept election after election. Only seventeen Republican freshmen were elected to the House. Fenwick was one of six freshmen women elected to the House in 1974, including fellow New Jerseyan Helen Meyner. These six women joined the twelve female incumbents. Four other women who had previously served had not sought reelection, so the election represented a slim gain of two women in the House. There were no women in the Senate. Despite this, because of the record number of eighteen women in the House, and the fact that more women ran for political office than ever before, including state and local races, 1974 was dubbed "the year of the breakthrough for women" by Frances Farenthold, chairman of the National Women's Political Caucus.[27]

In January 1975, Fenwick traveled to Washington, D.C., where she was sworn into office by the Democratic House Speaker Carl Albert from Oklahoma. She was indeed the oldest member of the freshman class of

'94, as they called themselves, to reflect their first year in office as members of the 94th Congress. Age aside, Fenwick was in good company. Other freshmen members of the class of '94 included Democratic Senators John Glenn, Patrick Leahy, and Gary Hart. Other newcomers were Representative Henry Hyde (R-Illinois), best known as the House Judiciary chairman who oversaw President Clinton's impeachment, and Representatives Max Baucus (D-Montana), Christopher Dodd (D-Connecticut), Charles Grassley (R-Iowa), Tom Harkin (D-Iowa), James Jeffords (R-Vermont), Paul Simon (D-Illinois), Paul Tsongas (D-Massachusetts), and Timothy Wirth (D-Colorado), all of whom went on to serve in the U.S. Senate. Out of this distinguished dozen only three were Republicans, and one of those, Jeffords, switched his party affiliation to Independent in 2001, allowing the Democrats to regain control of the Senate.

The Democrats gained 43 seats in the House, increasing their majority to two-thirds, with 291 members against the Republicans' 143 members. This marked a substantial shift in ideology, because not only did the Democrats gain dozens of seats, but the freshmen Republicans elected were more moderate than many of their predecessors. Eight incumbents were beaten in primaries, and the high turnover rate was attributed to the Watergate scandal and the retirement of forty-four House members, including Frelinghuysen. The vacancies opened up more seats than at any time in at least a quarter-century, paving the way for freshmen, like Fenwick, to infiltrate the political system rapidly.

Years later, Fenwick's faithful assistant, Roger Bodman, remembered accompanying her on one of her early trips to Washington, D.C., after the election. As the two walked, Fenwick paused and reflected in awe of the whole experience. She stared at the Capitol, amazed that the People sent her here to represent them. "She was in the business for all the right reasons and none of the wrong ones—power, prestige, and money," recalled Bodman.[28]

# 11

## The

## Conscience

## of Congress

The business of government is justice.
—President Woodrow Wilson

Millicent Fenwick arrived in Washington amid the fanfare of her victory as a sixty-four-year-old pipe-smoking grandmother. Resigned to the fact that she had been pigeonholed by the media, she pleaded to be referred to as the equally appropriate "hard-working congresswoman."

Fenwick wasted no time in making her mark in Washington. Her panache, pipe, age, gender, diction, candidness, and assertiveness soon set her apart from her male colleagues. Many members of Congress received their first introduction to Fenwick at the annual Washington Press Club dinner. She was one of six freshmen who received top billing from their unusually large class of 104 new members, representing a nearly 20 percent turnover; there were 92 new members of the House and 12 new members of the Senate.[1]

Dazzling the audience, Fenwick was touted as a new star. The next day the *Washington Star-News* reported, "A Republican—and a woman at that—was the funniest speaker at last night's Washington Press Club dinner honoring the returning Congress. The triumph of freshman Rep. Millicent Fenwick of New Jersey was the more noteworthy since women and Republicans both are somewhat endangered species in Congress. . . . Mrs. Fenwick confided she started off badly the first day by arriving 'in my best outfit, including a little fur hat,' only to be told that 'the hats are appropriate as a mark of respect in the house of God [and] are absolutely out of line in the House of Representatives.'"[2]

The thousand people in attendance at the dinner paled in comparison to the many thousands she had addressed decades earlier during her *Vogue* book tour. Over the decades she had honed her speaking skills and no longer worried about what to say or wear. Neatly tailored designer suits, many acquired during her *Vogue* years, still lined her closet and fit her slender form. It was said that her suits endured because she did not dry clean them but instead aired them out of doors.[3]

A strand of pearls draped her narrow neck, sometimes wrapping around two, three, even four times. Large pearl earrings adorned her ears, and her left wrist was weighed down by her sister's gold chain-link bracelets. The small corncob pipe, while not always visible, was never far—usually on her desk or in her hand or purse if not in her mouth. Some quietly feared that one day ashes from her pipe would spark a fire in her bag. Also in her bag was a blend of Dutch amphora tobacco. While her pipe-smoking habit was well publicized she desperately tried to keep her pipe out of the camera's way. Being photographed with the pipe would only perpetuate her bad habit and set a poor example for others. Cognizant of being caught in the public eye she did not want children to see her pictured with a pipe or emulate her nicotine addiction.

When Fenwick moved into the tight quarters assigned to her in the Longworth House Office Building, she had assembled a young and relatively inexperienced staff. She sought bright people with an inner drive, ideally from her district. Among her two most esteemed employees were two Ivy Leaguers, Hollis McLoughlin and Larry Rosenshein, whom staffers referred to as Golden Boy #1 and Golden Boy #2, respectively.

Hollis, a Princeton University graduate, began working on the Fenwick campaign in the summer, after her primary victory. Initially, no one from the campaign was hired because Millicent was advised to hire people who knew the Hill and not the "kids" who had worked on her campaign. Within a few weeks she disregarded that advice and hired twenty-four-year-old Hollis because, as he said, "Of course, people on the Hill always think they know best, but after a few weeks I was hired because I knew where routes 24 and 287 were, and the issues of the campaign."[4] Hired as a file clerk for $8,000 a year, he quickly gained Millicent's confidence and was promoted on a trial basis to legislative assistant with the understanding that if it didn't work out because he was so young, he would return to his original position. That turned out not to be necessary.

Immediately following the election, Lou Vetter was Fenwick's administrative assistant, and when twenty-year-old Larry Rosenshein, a Dartmouth College student, came looking for an internship, Vetter offered him a full-time job. Larry, from Bound Brook in New Jersey's Fifth District, already had Hill experience. As a high school student at Exeter Academy he had participated in the school's Washington Internship Program and worked for Bronx Democrat Jack Bingham. Putting off plans to drive cross-country, Larry went to work for Millicent. Larry hadn't worked on the campaign, and the fact that he was a college student had not gone unnoticed by the rest of the staff. A year and a half later, still working full-time, Larry received his degree from Dartmouth after taking evening classes at Georgetown University.

Three months into Fenwick's term, Vetter left and Hollis was running the show. He had Fenwick's complete trust. In an effort to staff the office, he hired John Schmidt, a twenty-two-year-old from the Princeton area who had volunteered on the campaign. Meanwhile back in New Jersey Roger Bodman, another campaign worker and recent college graduate, headed her district offices in Somerville and Morristown. Bodman's political career began as Fenwick's district office manager—representing her at meetings, accompanying her to events, and working with the Washington office—before he became a cabinet member in Governor Kean's administration. He later went on to be one of the top lobbyists in New Jersey.

---

As a freshman member of Congress, Fenwick openly expressed discontent with her committee assignments and with the House leadership. She had naively thought that because she was elected to Representative Peter Frelinghuysen's seat she would replace him as a ranking minority member, on the House Foreign Affairs Committee. Instead, she found herself on the Banking, Currency and Housing Committee, often referred to as "Beirut" as an indication of its undesirability, and on the Small Business Committee. That was her first introduction to the power structure that dominated Capitol Hill. Fenwick disliked the Banking Committee and latched on to the Small Business Committee. At least, she thought, that committee would give her the opportunity to concentrate on the plight of individuals.

While Fenwick found issues of interest on the Small Business Committee, she had a more challenging time with the Banking Committee. In the evenings, she often read through regulations and other banking material so she could at least be informed, if not interested, about pressing matters. All the while she lobbied for an appointment to a committee where her true passion, human rights, resided. Meanwhile, fellow freshman Helen Meyner received a coveted slot from the Democratic majority to the International Relations Committee, which had been called the House Foreign Affairs Committee a year earlier when Frelinghuysen was the ranking Republican.

Meyner's election to Congress marked her first elected office, but not her introduction to politics, since she was a distant relative of Adlai Stevenson as well as the wife of Robert Meyner, New Jersey's governor from 1954 to 1962. When Helen first ran for Congress in 1972, she had little personal experience in politics and lost. Two years later her victory was aided by the Watergate scandal. She defeated Judiciary Committee member Joseph Maraziti of whom it was written in *The Almanac of American Politics*, "Maraziti might have remained, in fact would certainly have remained, an obscure backbencher were it not for the fact that he sat on the Judiciary Committee which decided to impeach Richard Nixon. Maraziti . . . was the oldish junior Republican [sixty-two years old], whose tongue-tied oratory always left him satisfied with the President's innocence. Named by *New Times* magazine as one of the ten dumbest members of Congress, Maraziti did precious little to dispel that reputation."[5]

Fortunately for New Jersey, and the country, another member of the state delegation, Democrat Peter Rodino Jr., served on the Judiciary Committee. A Newark native, Rodino was chairman of the House Judiciary Committee, and his handling of Nixon's impeachment hearings elevated his reputation. Although he staunchly believed Nixon should be removed from office, Rodino presided over the hearings in a fair and ethical manner that received praise from both sides of the aisle and respect from the nation.

---

Because there were only eighteen women in the House of Representatives, the female legislators stood out. "Millicent came to Congress about the same time that we women felt we should have some type of organization whether it was informal or not," remembered Democrat Representative Lindy Boggs of Louisiana. "We would meet for lunch . . . and help with committee work, research, and so on. It was the beginning of the women's caucus which is now a lively sixty-nine members."[6] Notable Democratic colleagues included House Majority Leader Hale Boggs's widow, Lindy Boggs, who was well-versed on the Hill; the feisty New Yorker Bella Abzug, with whom the media begged to compare Millicent even before she was elected to Congress; two other New Yorkers, Shirley Chisholm and Elizabeth Holtzman; the energetic Patsy Mink; the politically astute Gladys Noon Spellman; the outspoken Pat Schroeder; the widows of George Collins and John Sullivan; Tennessean Marilyn Lloyd; Kansan Martha Keys; the eloquent and politically savvy Barbara Jordan; Yvonne Brathwaite Burke, the first member of Congress to give birth while in office; and Helen Meyner. Fenwick's three Republican peers were attorney Peggy Heckler, who later became ambassador to Ireland, and conservatives Marjorie Holt and Virginia Smith.

"By 1975, with more pressure coming to bear from outside women's groups, we finally were able to start the bipartisan Congressional Women's Caucus, under the chairmanship of Liz Holtzman and Peggy Heckler," said Pat Schroeder.[7] To help fund and staff the caucus, the women allocated a percentage of their staff funds and pooled it together. They also established the nonprofit Women's Research Institute to study issues of importance to the Congressional Women's Caucus. To raise money Millicent Fenwick and Lindy Boggs were sent to New York to tap into their philanthropic contacts. After that trip Boggs came away with a greater admiration for Fenwick's tenacity. "I was crazy about her," said Boggs. "Millicent had a very interesting life and she turned around every situation into a forward-looking situation—that was significant, that was interesting—and she didn't let adversity get her down."[8]

Although not a driving force of the Women's Caucus, Fenwick readily stepped up to the plate when it came to abortion issues and the Equal Rights Amendment, but she "didn't grasp equity issues," said Schroeder. When discussing pensions for widows, Schroeder felt Fenwick's perspective was a bit skewed. "Since her sister was married to a foreign service officer, and her sister wouldn't take the money, it was hard for her to understand the women who don't have money."[9]

Because of Fenwick's so-called equity gap and distaste for government intervention, women's organizations did not embrace her, nor did she embrace them. She argued that "if there's a need for them [women's organizations], then they really aren't women's issues at all but rather civil rights or citizenship issues."[10] Nor did Millicent adopt the political correct term "congressperson"; instead she preferred to be referred to as a Republican representative.

---

Millicent lived two blocks from her office in the Longworth Building. She rented a narrow, two-story brownstone on South Capitol Street and often referred to it as her "shack," much to the dismay of her landlord, Pierre S. Du Pont, then the governor of Delaware. The decor of her Washington home was modest. A sofa, two overstuffed chairs, and a large stool created a simple living room setting. A small throw rug covered the hardwood floor. She often worked at a small table in the living room. Her literary favorites were housed in two nearby bookcases. Off the living room in the dining room stood a medium-size table that could seat six people, but rarely did. Millicent often ate alone. Her traditional dinner fare was a bowl of spaghetti with a little butter and a glass of wine. Her grandson, Joe Reckford, spent six weeks with his grandmother one summer while he interned for another member of Congress, and he remembered that she "would carry a box of store-bought spaghetti and a fresh loaf of bread from New Jersey to Washington. One box got her through the week."[11]

After a long day Millicent retired upstairs to her stark bedroom. It contained the basics—a bed, nightstand, straight-back chair, and small table. The only extra items were an overstuffed chair and a small television. A second bedroom was even barer. It had a bed, a small bookcase, a table, and a lamp—sufficient accommodation for a grandchild, Cousin Mary, or any other guest.

Millicent didn't spend much time in her bleak abode. Most of her waking moments were spent at her Longworth office or on the House floor. Often the first to arrive at the office, before seven in the morning, she picked up the bundles of mail piled outside the door and carried them in. Settling behind her desk, she carefully untied the twine and wound it into a ball—preventing unnecessary waste. Her drawers were filled with twine balls meant for recycling. Her staff didn't have the heart to tell her that there was no use for the small twine strands that she saved and they threw away.

Each day Fenwick plucked through the heaps of mail and separated the handwritten letters from the typed correspondence. Handwritten mail was a priority because, she believed, it was from real people. Fenwick opened, read, and responded to as many letters as she could. The sheer volume of mail she handled was quickly evident to an unsuspecting staff, who fielded calls flooding in from constituents who had received one of Millicent's handwritten responses. The staff, having no control over Fenwick or knowledge of the content of these letters, was helpless. They explained the problem to her and presented a solution—making carbon copies of her handwritten notes. These copies were affectionately referred to as pinky letters. The pinkies were then filed and available to staff as needed. Fenwick had always been an avid letter writer. Her handwriting crusade, which dated back to her campaign days with Senator Case and continued through her Consumer Affairs tenure, had evolved as part of her daily routine decades earlier when she faithfully wrote her children, friends, family, and Ghino, the husband of her late sister.

Fenwick carried a red satchel filled with constituent letters to the House floor, where she sat and composed her handwritten responses. She sometimes perched there for ten or twelve hours, listening to speeches and writing letters. She carefully reviewed each letter regardless of whether the person was from New Jersey or Idaho. Writing thousands of letters, Representative Fenwick became revered by the public for her personal touch, which she viewed as a gesture of thanks for voting her into office.

Personally prioritizing constituent mail, an atypical task for members of Congress, attracted widespread attention, as did the amount of time she spent on the House floor. The public loved Millicent's individual approach, but her congressional peers regarded it as another aspect of her eccentric nature. They didn't realize there was method to her idiosyncrasies.

Fenwick's letter writing kept her connected to her constituents, and her prolonged time on the floor was more calculated than her peers gave her credit for. In 1980, when Representative Marge Roukema joined the New Jersey congressional delegation, Millicent Fenwick dispensed this advice. "In those days," Roukema recalled, "we had significant debates on the floor. In recent years the debate forms have been more perfunctory, but in those days there were genuine debates and she advised me. 'Marge,' she said, 'you need to sit on the floor to get to know your colleagues. Get to know them, not only in committee, but on the floor when debates are going on. It is then you can learn to judge whose opinions you can trust, and whose opinions you must be skeptical of. Be able to evaluate them.'"

"That was wonderful advice," said Roukema. "The first year or so I spent a lot of time on the floor listening to the debates . . . and got a sense of things. Not only the issues but a sense of the evaluation of the people that were presenting things and who was being superficial and political and who was being substantive and incisive. It was excellent advice. Of course, she was always there. Third row on the aisle."[12]

Taking seriously her congressional duties and the voters' trust in her to represent them, Fenwick rarely missed a vote. If Congress was in session, she was there. "[Some] people in Congress felt she did not pay enough attention to a narrow agenda . . . and considered her time on the House floor to be a waste [because] she should have been working in committee and behind the scenes," said Hollis. "Now that is somewhat unfair because she never missed a committee meeting. I think if she could be faulted it was because she did not narrow her agenda. . . . One of her strengths was that she was interested in all aspects of public policy and her effectiveness was her independence and willingness to speak out on a whole range of issues regardless of whether or not she had a say on that committee."[13]

As soon as Congress recessed for the week, Fenwick could be found on the next train to New Jersey, where she spent her time giving speeches, holding town hall sessions, and meeting with constituents. Often the local grocery store provided an ad hoc forum in which constituents took advantage of Fenwick's willingness to listen. Like clockwork, every Sunday, Fenwick boarded the 4:17 P.M. Metroliner from Trenton back to Washington to pursue the interests of her constituents.

To keep up with the demands of her job and the ever present media, Fenwick's staff typed appointments on yellow unlined index cards to help keep their boss organized. By early May 1975, Fenwick generated enough attention to land on the cover of *Parade* magazine. The article,

titled "Rep. Millicent Fenwick: A Star of the New Congress," characterized her as a "Republican version of Eleanor Roosevelt, though the taut
elegance of her looks and assertiveness of her manner are more reminis-
cent of Katharine Hepburn."[14] As a former magazine writer, Fenwick
gained "a respect for the press and an understanding of the needs of
reporters," observed Bernardsville reporter Sandy Stuart.[15] Fenwick
claimed to "never have been misquoted."[16] Her ease and candidness only
added to her media appeal. "She's a strange combination," wrote Judy
Bachrach in the *Washington Post*. "She reveals her wealth but won't
mention, for instance, what kind of cancer she recovered from 15 years
ago."[17]

--------

On Millicent's sixty-fifth birthday, she readied herself to board a
military aircraft for her first congressional trip. President Ford was sending a congressional delegation to Vietnam and Cambodia to review his
request to provide hundreds of millions of dollars more in supplemental
military aid to Southeast Asia as part of a three-year phase-out plan. He
hoped the trip would sway Congress to endorse his legislation.

Of the eight members on the trip, five Democrats and three Republicans, half were thought to support continued aid and the other half
were believed to be opposed to it. Fenwick was one of the more open-
minded members on the trip but was leaning against continued aid. Bella
Abzug, the New York Democrat, was the only other congresswoman.
For years the New Jersey media had compared Fenwick to Abzug. Both
were characters in their own right. While Millicent was known for her
pipe smoking, Bella was known for her ever-present hats. The pair was
an odd couple—Millicent refined, Bella rough. Despite their contrasting
styles their politics were not dissimilar. Both advocated abortion rights
and the Equal Rights Amendment. Their records were fairly similar despite their different party allegiances. In Fenwick's first year in Congress
she and Abzug voted together 61 percent of the time. The following year,
1976, that number increased to 77 percent while Fenwick voted with
her party less than half the time—only 44 percent.[18]

Becoming better acquainted in Vietnam, each earned the respect of
the other. Of Fenwick, Abzug said, "I always like style, and she has style.
We both have a sense of ourselves. We're both women of the world. I
have crossed many boundaries, and I am sure she has too."[19] Fenwick
also admired Abzug for the same reason she admired Eleanor Roosevelt—
she meant what she said. One *New York Times* writer characterized their
relationship as an "odd couple who seek out each other's company, try to
ease each other's paths and provide moral support, solace, humor and sympathy in what some feminists might call an expression of sisterhood."[20]

Upon arriving in Saigon the delegation met with the U.S. ambassador to the Republic of Vietnam, Graham Martin. From there the delegation was welcomed by South Vietnamese President Nguyen Van Thieu, who advocated the need for aid and candidly answered the delegation's questions. He also let them know they were free to travel and meet with anyone they pleased.

Splitting into groups, the delegation members pursued their own agendas. Fenwick, Abzug, and Democrat Don Fraser of Minnesota met with political prisoners, publishers, and opposition leaders, as well as with government officials regarding American soldiers still listed as missing in action. A visit to a political prisoner incensed Fenwick and incited a feud with Abzug. The Indochina Research Center, a United States–based organization, told them about a young medical student who was wrongly imprisoned and being tortured. Fenwick, Abzug, and Fraser made arrangements to make the tedious journey to investigate the allegations. What they found was a student, said Millicent, "who wouldn't admit he was a Communist so he was kept in lockup where he said himself he'd been perfectly well treated."[21] Upset about the wasted time and cost of the trip, Fenwick lashed out. She accused "the organization [Indochina Research Center] of being so pro-Communist that they simply had no sense or responsibility about telling the truth."[22] Those remarks sparked a screaming match between Fenwick and Abzug, who defended the Indochina Research Center. Fenwick shouted, "Listen here, Bella Abzug, I can scream just as loudly as you and I've got just as bad a temper." Once their heated exchange ended, Abzug tapped Fenwick on the elbow and said, "That was fun wasn't it?" thus, putting the whole episode behind them.[23]

In Cambodia, the delegation met with the U.S. ambassador there, John Dean, before spending time with Cambodian leader Lon Nol, who "offered to do anything that would result in a solution to the Cambodian war. Most people in attendance including myself understood this to mean that Lon Nol offered to resign if necessary," said Bob Wolthuis, special assistant to President Ford.[24]

At the conclusion of the trip President Thieu hosted a dinner for the delegation and delivered a speech in which he emphasized their freedom of movement to travel wherever they wished. He told the members of Congress, "I hope to destroy the myth carefully nurtured by the dissenters according to which the Republic of Viet-Nam is just another police state. Even though we are presently faced with aggression, you can see that there is much more freedom here than in many other countries living in peace and where national security is not at all threatened. Secondly, the evidence is here for all to see that, far from being the warmongers so often depicted in Communist literature, we are actually being attacked— and massively so—by North Vietnamese Communist Troops, in violation of every provision of the Paris Agreement of January 27, 1973. So it is evident to any impartial observer that the first thing to do in order to save the Paris Agreement is to stop the Communist aggression. Once the cease-fire is effectively implemented, all other provisions of the Agreement can be carried out. We are ready to do our part and we are disposed to resume the peace negotiations without any precondition," said Thieu.[25]

Upon the delegation's return Wolthuis wrote a memo to Max Friedersdorf, head of the White House Congressional Relations Office, in which he characterized Millicent as pensive. "I believe of all the people on the delegation she has wrestled harder with the problem than anyone else. She read everything she could get her hands on," wrote Wolthuis, "and while she spent a great deal of time with [Don] Fraser and [Bella] Abzug, she looked at both sides very carefully. I think a Presidential nudge may be helpful in her case based on the fact that she told one member of our party that when she was a little girl she learned that if a person made a commitment, that commitment should be kept."[26] Most likely Millicent contemplated the concluding remarks President Thieu made at the dinner in which he stated, "During the past two decades, the People of South Viet-Nam have been told time and again by five U.S. Presidents belonging to both parties of America—all of them supported by successive legislatures of the U.S.—that the United States is determined to provide them with adequate assistance as long as they are willing to resist Communist aggression to preserve their freedom. That solemn commitment had been renewed at the time of the signing of the Paris Agreement. This issue boils down to one simple question: is the commitment made by the U.S. to be any value? Is the word of the U.S. to be trusted?"[27]

A few days after their return, the congressional delegation went to the White House to brief President Gerald Ford, Secretary of State Henry Kissinger, and National Security Adviser Brent Scowcroft. Aid to Vietnam and aid to Cambodia were viewed and discussed by the delegation as separate matters. The general consensus was that the Foreign Affairs Committee would narrowly pass a limited aid package. The pros, cons, and limitations were candidly presented by members of the delegation. A majority seemed to view a phase-out aid package as feasible, but Abzug considered it unrealistic. Torn, Fenwick told the president, "If we can hold off until the rainy season, I would vote for ammunition. If we could get people out in the meantime—such as civil servants, teachers, refugees—I would vote for ammunition [to Cambodia]." As to Vietnam she was undecided and wary about Thieu's continued leadership and corruption problems. "If you asked who could replace Thieu, that is an unsettling question because there is no one. I find myself sharing [Rep. Paul] McCloskey and [Rep. Don] Fraser's view—that is we can't vote money without seeing a viable solution. We need a plan . . . I cannot go along with the idea of a phased-out aid program. I cannot see where it leads."

"If you have reservations about a phase-out would you stop [aid] period?" asked Ford.

"Not so," said Fenwick. "I will regret my vote no matter which way I vote."[28]

A couple of weeks after the White House meeting, she wrote an op-ed piece for the *New York Times*. It was entitled "Military Aid for Vietnam and Cambodia? No." After wrestling with the issue, she, like her constituents, felt the United States had given enough aid to the decades-long effort in Indochina. She thought continued aid would be misperceived as support for Marshal Lon Nol, the head of the Cambodian government, and on a more humanitarian note she was deeply affected by the dying children. "The children are so famished that they must be fed intravenously before their bodies can accept food. I have never seen or imagined such human suffering and the first thought that comes to mind is 'stop the killing.'" Where Vietnam was concerned she wrote, "I think we must face the fact that military aid sent from America will not succeed. It will only delay the development of the kind of stable situation—whatever form that takes—that will at least stop the horrible suffering of war."[29]

Public opinion mounted against providing further aid to Indochina, and the president's request of $300 million in aid to South Vietnam and $222 million for Cambodia floundered.

---

One day, in the autumn of her first congressional term, Millicent was overcome by dizziness. She attributed it to the stifling Washington humidity, but when the House doctor examined her he noticed a slow heartbeat and recommended she go to the Bethesda Naval Hospital. She did. After careful analysis, the doctors determined that Millicent needed a pacemaker to regulate her heartbeat.

Hollis was told to call two people—her daughter and Mary Baird—with very strict orders: her daughter was to call Hugo, then living in Italy, and neither of them was to come and see her. Not abiding by the patient's wishes, Mary Baird traveled with Archie Alexander to Washington. Knowing Millicent would be upset, they told her Archie had a meeting in Washington, which was true, although it was not until the following week. Hollis watched as Millicent chastised her two cousins for coming to see her. Quite a scene erupted as Mary and Millicent, two stubborn older women, yelled back and forth. Seeing that Millicent was back to her usual stubborn self, Archie took the next train back to New Jersey while Fenwick's staff tended to Mary Baird.

One day, while Millicent was supposed to be recuperating in the hospital, Hollis stopped by only to find her upright and busily answering each get-well card with a personal note. Scolding her, Hollis took the letters away. He explained that her staff would take care of it and ordered the Naval Hospital not to let Fenwick see any more mail. After that incident, he felt he had earned Mary Baird's complete trust.[30]

But even Hollis couldn't stop Millicent from returning to the House floor earlier than anticipated. The week after the surgery she was back. The heavy workload prompted her early return. She said she felt "just fine," despite "feeling as if I was hit by a small truck."[31]

She was candid about the procedure. Via her district newsletter, she informed constituents about the pacemaker operation and reassured them of her health. She had nothing to hide, made a swift recovery, and quickly returned to work and waged battles on behalf of her constituents.

Within a few months she went on her second congressional trip. The female members of Congress accepted an invitation from Chinese women officials to visit their country. As part of only the second congressional delegation to go to China since President Nixon's landmark visit, Millicent and several of her female colleagues were invited to bring a guest. Some, such as Helen Meyner, brought their spouses. Millicent, because of her pacemaker, brought a doctor.[32]

Helen's husband, Robert, the former governor of New Jersey, chatted with Fenwick and helped with her luggage. Thus, it came as a surprise to some members of the delegation to learn, upon their return, that Millicent had blasted Helen for bringing her husband on the trip at the expense of the taxpayer. Pat Schroeder, a member of the congressional delegation to China, said that incident "always said to me she is fascinating, go talk to her, but beware."[33]

Sixteen-year-old Joe Reckford also remembered his grandmother's trip to China. Aware that members of Congress could bring someone on the trip, Joe tried to convince his grandmother to take either him, his mother, or one of his siblings. "No," she sternly responded, "we are not invited to take somebody, we are invited to take spouses." "I knew she would say no," said Joe, "but the joke fell flat because she had no sense of humor . . . she felt it would have been an abuse of riding in a government plane." He conceded that she may have "protested if someone else took a friend or relative who was not a spouse. As she said, 'spouses were invited, not others.'"[34]

While the congressional delegation was in China, the country's premier, Chou En-lai, suffering from cancer, died at the age of seventy-eight. Chou En-lai, an adept politician, had ruled China since 1949 when the Communists assumed power. Flags were lowered to half-staff as radio stations continued to broadcast their regularly scheduled programming, something that would not have occurred a few years earlier. President

Ford released a statement hailing "Premier Chou En-lai as a remarkable leader who has left his imprint not only on modern China but also in the world scene. . . . We Americans will remember him especially for the role he played in building a new relationship between the People's Republic of China and the United States."[35]

As the congressional delegation—braving the bitter cold of January—traveled in Peking, Chengtu, Kewilin, and Shanghai, Millicent was struck by the warmth of the people. "I have never in all my travels, through India, Europe, and South America, I have never seen such friendly people," she said. "If you smiled at them, they would break into smiles, and the babies and teenagers would clap."[36] As congenial as the people were, Millicent still asked tough questions of her Chinese hosts. She prodded them about intellectual freedom, the criminal justice system, and their work ethic. "Maybe we were a little sharp sometimes, but you don't go 10,000 miles to show how charming you are."[37]

As the whirl of Watergate eased, Capitol Hill was rocked by another scandal in the spring of 1976. House leader Wayne Hays of Ohio, often referred to as the Mayor of Capitol Hill, took center stage in this scandal. Hays, a Democrat, was one of the most powerful and feared members of Congress. He chaired the Joint Committee on Printing; the Subcommittee on International Operations of the International Relations Committee; the House Administration Committee, which controlled payroll, telephones, and other vital necessities; and the Democratic National Congressional Committee (DNCC), which dispersed hundreds of thousands of dollars to congressional campaigns.

Many of Hays's peers dodged him. Opposing him often produced repercussions. Hays did not hesitate to threaten to stop payroll payments or disconnect phones, and he followed through on those threats. As chairman of the House Administration Committee he wielded the power to cut off vital resources. Despite his ominous reputation, Fenwick was not intimidated by him. When Hays proposed increasing congressional expense funds, something Fenwick deemed unnecessary, she called for a debate. In response, Hays reportedly bellowed, "If the Republicans think their expense allowance is too large, I can reduce it for them. I can strip them of their staffs." Fenwick, still a freshman with little political leverage, replied, "Mr. Chairman, I think we have heard something today for which we are all going to be sorry and ashamed."[38] With that, Fenwick scurried off the House floor to an anteroom where Bill Canis, one of her staffers, awaited. Flustered, she told Bill about her "critical exchange" with Hays. Bill listened in wonderment at his boss's willingness to take on the powerful Hays. "I don't care about offending such a powerful man," she said. "What he was advocating was wrong."[39] After cooling off Fenwick returned to the House floor and saw Hays emerge victorious. His provision passed, but he removed his remarks from the record. From that point forward Hays viewed Fenwick as a political adversary. "I've never heard any other man talk to another man as roughly as [Hays] did to me," Millicent recalled. "We got into some real fights."[40]

When the *Washington Post* revealed Hays's entanglement in a sex scandal, the mainstream media reported it in epic proportions. Within a week the story was plastered everywhere. It stemmed from allegations made by Elizabeth Ray, a committee secretary paid $14,000 a year (the median income at the time was $10,833),[41] to serve as Hays's mistress. Her famous quote, "I can't type. I can't file. I can't even answer the phone," did nothing to help Hays.[42] Ray's allegations triggered a Justice Department examination of criminal fraud based on her charges that she was on the public payroll for sexual, not secretarial, purposes. The investigations did not end there. *Newsweek* reported, "The House ethics committee voted unanimously to investigate Hays, one of the most powerful men in Congress. And Democrats on the Hill set out to topple him before he tarred his party and the House itself with a stain of guilt by association."[43]

A few weeks earlier the recently divorced sixty-four-year-old Hays had married the manager of his district office. She was half his age. It was in the aftermath of this second marriage that a scorned Ray revealed her two-year affair with Hays. He reluctantly admitted to the affair but insisted that Ray fulfilled her secretarial duties.

Many silently rejoiced at the compromising position in which the detested Hays found himself. Before the scandal erupted, few in Congress besides Fenwick were willing to oppose him. Now they were lining up. House Majority Leader Tip O'Neill urged Hays to relinquish his chairmanships, which he eventually did.

Fenwick's congressional peers gleefully watched as she passionately castigated Hays on the House floor for his behavior and breach of the public's trust and money. Unfortunately, her remarks have not survived because, according to *Congressional Record* rules "remarks or other materials that violate the rules of a house, such as derogatory statements about another member" can be expunged.[44] Age had given Fenwick a sense of security, and, unlike other members of Congress, she felt she had nothing to lose by doing what she did best, speaking her mind.

Curious why others were reluctant to challenge Hays, Fenwick asked a colleague, "Why does Hays command such influence? When he presents these terrible ideas, why does he always get 230 votes? Why?" The response was, "Well, he's got the goods on some of us, and goodies for the others." Millicent was horrified but understood. "He was the head of the House Admin. Committee. If he didn't sign your staff's checks, the staff wouldn't get paid," she said.[45]

Needless to say, not many members of Congress were upset that Hays's improprieties were made public. Capitalizing on the scandal, *Newsweek* showed a blonde bombshell resembling Ray on its cover. The leggy woman, scantily clad in a patriotic red, white, and blue bikini, was pictured leaping out of the Capitol dome as if it were a giant birthday cake. Despite the barrage of negative publicity in an election year, Hays won his primary. But two months before the general election, with a House ethics hearing pending, Hays finally resigned, bringing his nearly three-decade reign on the Hill to a woeful end.

The stain Hays's escapades left on Congress was mitigated to some extent by Fenwick's boldness in standing up to Hays, even before his political power was shattered. While some of her congressional colleagues viewed her as eccentric, they could not help but respect her adherence to her principles, which gave her the courage to challenge Hays.

In the scandal-ridden atmosphere of Washington, where Watergate, Vietnam, and sexual improprieties marred the public's faith in government, Fenwick's honesty and candor were not only refreshing but helped her do her job. Her work ethic, opposition to government waste, and advocacy for social justice prompted CBS news anchor Walter Cronkite to dub her the "Conscience of Congress" in the 1970s.[46]

# 12

## *Pursuing*

## *Human*

## *Rights*

There is no limit to what a man can do
Or where he can go
If he doesn't mind
Who takes the credit.

—Plaque on President Ronald Reagan's desk

Millicent Fenwick could not have better orchestrated her entrance into the congressional club. As she gained national attention, one of her lifelong passions, human rights, was building momentum on an international scale. After nearly three years of negotiations, the Conference on Security and Cooperation in Europe was about to unveil a document—the Helsinki Final Act (HFA)—that would help change the course of the cold war.

On July 30, 1975, world leaders from thirty-three European nations plus the United States and Canada convened in Helsinki, Finland. The origins of this historic meeting dated back to 1954 when the Soviets, in an effort to undermine the North Atlantic Treaty Organization (NATO), proposed a conference on European security and cooperation. Initially, the conference was aimed only at European countries and excluded the United States. The idea went nowhere until it was revived more than a decade later, in 1966, and again in 1969 when the Warsaw Pact countries, a loose association of nations dominated by the Soviet Union dur-

ing the cold war and also known as the Eastern bloc, met and reintroduced the prospects of a conference on European security. A couple of
months later Finland proposed a similar conference and later earned the
honor, as a neutral country, of hosting the conference.[1] Within a year
the Warsaw Pact agreed to remove the dissolution of NATO from its
agenda and to include the United States and Canada in prospective discussions about European security, symbolizing their desire to move
détente—Nixon's policy to improve relations with the USSR—forward.
From the late 1960s to the early 1970s, the Eastern alliance emphasized
a need to address European security while the West pushed for negotiations on mutual and balanced force reductions (MBFR).

In 1972, President Nixon embarked on a historic trip to Moscow,
marking the first time a United States president had visited the Soviet
Union. He met with Leonid Brezhnev, the Soviet general secretary, and
the two leaders agreed to link MBFR talks to European security. The
result was three years of cooperative endeavors between the East and the
West. An umbrella of détente was slowly spreading across Europe. By
the year's end, a Conference on Security and Cooperation in Europe
(CSCE) opened in Helsinki, and in early 1973 exploratory talks on MBFR
began in Vienna.

Although the CSCE process brought the United States and Soviet
Union together, neither the Nixon nor the Ford administration embraced
the multilateral process. The lack of enthusiasm for tying human rights
to the thawing relations with the East was linked to Henry Kissinger
who served as secretary of state and then national security adviser during the mid-1970s. He preferred bilateral negotiations between Washington and Moscow rather than dealing with another thirty-plus nations
assembled at the table. Kissinger's primary focus was to reduce arms and
troops, whereas the Soviet Union was focused on formal recognition of
its post–World War II borders and its sphere of influence in the Eastern
bloc nations.

As détente progressed and tensions eased abroad, political pressure
was building on the president. Mounting evidence related to the 1972
Watergate break-in of the Democratic National Committee was drain-
ing the administration. Eventually twenty people with ties to President
Nixon or his reelection campaign were indicted, and some were convicted as early as January 1973 for crimes related to the break-in or the
cover-up.

In an unrelated scandal, Vice-President Spiro Agnew was forced to
resign in October 1973 for accepting financial bribes for favors while
governor of Maryland. As a result, Nixon appointed House Minority
Leader Gerald Ford as vice-president. A year later Ford assumed the presidency when Nixon resigned as a result of Watergate. It was Ford who

would become America's representative in Helsinki for the culmination of the CSCE talks.

The CSCE process began in Helsinki with preparatory discussions lasting from November 1972 to June 1973. A few months later in Geneva formal talks began that led to the official establishment of the CSCE. Ambitions ran high. Participating in the CSCE discussions were all NATO and Warsaw Pact countries plus every neutral and small country in Europe including Liechtenstein and San Marino. Only Albania opted out of this impressive ensemble. It was hoped that the CSCE "would promote a greater sense of security by mitigating cold-war tensions and would eventually reduce—possibly remove—all barriers between the East and West."[2]

The United States, represented by Secretary of State William Rogers, was rather subdued. Rogers took his direction from Kissinger, who was skeptical about the entire endeavor. As a result, the democratic super-power remained placid during the two years of negotiations in Geneva. Although the United States did not assume a leadership role, the thirty-five participating nations effectively collaborated and prioritized their goals into three committees. The first covered European security and sovereignty issues; the second dealt with migrant labor, tourism, and economic, scientific, technical and environmental cooperation; and the third focused on humanitarian issues. Two years of ongoing deliberations, from September 1973 to July 1975, produced a draft document referred to as the Final Act which addressed the three original areas as baskets.

Drafting the Final Act was tedious. "As decisions could only be reached by consensus in closed discussions," wrote William Korey, a leading human rights scholar, "the debates were heated and intermi-nable and deadlocks not infrequent."[3] After nearly three years and the efforts of 375 diplomats, the Helsinki Final Act was born. Although its body consisted of three baskets, it was basket three, with its focus on human rights, that became the heart of the document. Although not legally binding, it marked the first time the Soviet Union signed an in-ternational document protecting human rights. The Soviets abstained from voting on the passage of the landmark United Nations Universal Declaration of Human Rights signed in 1948. Raymond Garthoff, a former diplomat and Brookings Institute scholar, wrote, "The Helsinki Final Act in 1975 had crowned with success a decade of efforts to consolidate the postwar order in Europe."[4]

By the time the CSCE nations gathered in Helsinki, Ford had been president for nearly a year following Nixon's resignation. Kissinger ac-companied Ford to Helsinki. Prior to their departure the press condemned the administration's participation in the Helsinki Accords. The *Wall Street Journal* ran a headline urging "Jerry Don't Go," and the *New York Times* concurred.

The Brezhnev regime embraced the HFA for its own purpose, and some members of the Western press interpreted the agreement as U.S. acknowledgment of the Brezhnev doctrine—used by the Soviets to justify their intervention in satellite countries such as Czechoslovakia. As a result, "public attitudes in the United States overwhelmingly focused upon the 'inviolability of borders' theme . . . evok[ing] negative images of another Yalta, another capitulation to Soviet imperialism . . . and a defeat for the west," wrote scholar William Korey. "It [was] startling to note," he continued, "that this view of Helsinki was similar to Moscow's perception. The USSR publicly placed virtually exclusive emphasis upon the 'inviolability of border' theme and totally minimized the extensive human rights elements of the Final Act."[5]

The administration's efforts to inform the public about the content of the Helsinki Final Act, as well as the years of negotiations that produced it, were overshadowed by misperceptions. "Some of the ethnic groups like the Baltic states had the misunderstanding that the language [of the Helsinki Final Act] drew specific lines that prevented them from getting their independence, which was totally untrue," said President Ford, "but they had been misled by individuals who did not agree with the Accord."[6]

One such individual was Alexander Solzhenitsyn. His first novel, *A Day in the Life of Ivan Denisovich*, rocked the literary world with his gripping portrayal of human suffering in a Stalin-era Siberian prison camp, reportedly based on his own experiences in a gulag. By 1975, Solzhenitsyn was living in exile in the West and adamantly opposed the Helsinki agreement. He was well-versed in the security aspects of the agreement, but not the human rights provisions. He wrongly viewed the Helsinki Accords as a betrayal of Eastern Europeans because he thought the Accords abandoned Latvia, Lithuania, and Estonia, which had been annexed by the Soviets in 1940.

Because Ford and Kissinger were uncertain about the process's final outcome they did not want to invite a scrutinizing public to voice unwanted criticism. The Jackson-Vanik amendment is a case in point. Co-sponsored by Senator Henry (Scoop) Jackson (D-Washington) and Representative Charles Vanik (D-Ohio), the amendment linked foreign policy to human rights by stipulating that if the Soviet Union eased its emigration policies, the United States would make concessions in its trade policy, and specifically sell the Soviets much needed grain. The amendment passed in 1974 and reflected a new public concern for human rights. The Ford administration wanted to avoid a repeat of the Jackson-Vanik amendment or any future legislation that conflated human rights with foreign policy, a practice Kissinger despised.

GOP support was sparse. California Governor Ronald Reagan, in preparation for his challenge against Ford for the 1976 Republican presidential nomination, echoed the media's sentiments: "I think all Americans should be against it [the Helsinki Final Act]."[7] Even Ford's staff was defensive. "They should have lauded the accord as a victory," Ford said, but, "instead they intimated that it was another Kissinger deal that was forced down the President's throat."[8]

Nonetheless, Ford and Kissinger moved forward. A day before they went overseas the president tried to allay skeptics' fears by meeting with Americans of Eastern European descent. Seated in the Cabinet Room of the White House Ford told the assembled group, "There are those who fear the Conference will put a seal of approval on the political divisions of Europe that has existed since the Soviet Union incorporated the Baltic nations and set new boundaries elsewhere in Europe by military action in World War II. These critics contend that participation by the United States in the Helsinki understanding amounts to tacit recognition of a status quo which favors the Soviet Union and perpetuates its control over countries allied with it. On the other extreme there are critics who say the meeting is a meaningless exercise because the Helsinki declarations are merely statement of principles and good intentions which are neither legally binding nor enforceable and cannot be depended upon. . . . If I seriously shared these reservations I would not be going, but I certainly understand the historical reasons for them and, especially, the anxiety of Americans whose ancestral homelands, families and friends have been and still are profoundly affected by East-West political developments in Europe."[9]

His comments were meant to ease the concerns of representatives from Ukrainian, Polish, Hungarian, Czechoslovakian, Latvian, Lithuanian, and Estonian groups. The last three Baltic states were particularly worried about the ramifications of the United States signing the Helsinki Final Act. They feared that by doing so the United States would formally recognize the Soviet annexation in 1940 of the Baltic nations, often referred to as the captive nations.

"I would like to make clear," President Ford told them, "that the United States official non-recognition of the Soviet incorporation of the Baltic states is not affected by the results of the CSCE." He emphasized, "We [the United States] have never recognized the Soviet incorporation of Lithuania, Latvia, and Estonia and we are not doing so at CSCE."[10]

Because of the unpopularity and misunderstanding of the Helsinki Accords at home, the administration downplayed the historic moment on August 1, 1975, when Ford gathered with thirty-four other heads of state to sign the Helsinki Final Act. The document was significant for several reasons. It did not ratify postwar frontier changes but rather confirmed that borders could not be changed through the use of force, a concept widely misunderstood in the United States. It also contained provisions for confidence-building measures in which countries would notify each other of military exercises, while establishing a uniform agreement in basket three advocating the "freer movement of peoples and ideas, . . . through family reunification, increased access to broadcast and printed information, and increased educational and cultural exchanges."[11] The fact that Warsaw Pact countries signed a document with the NATO alliance was momentous, as was the Soviet Union's written support of basket three and the fundamental freedoms it endorsed.

After the historic signing in Helsinki's regal Finlandi House, Ford patiently waited for his turn to speak. While listening to the other dignitaries, Ford was particularly struck by Brezhnev's remark: "We assume that all countries represented will implement the understandings reached. As regards the Soviet Union, it will act precisely in that manner."[12] Brezhnev was essentially endorsing the HFA and agreeing to abide by the human rights provisions.

When it was Ford's turn to speak the media kept a watchful eye. Although many reporters were critical of his trip, his speech received adulation. It was "probably Mr. Ford's most impressive speech," reported the *Los Angeles Times*. "Peace is not a piece of paper," said Ford, "but lasting peace is at least possible today because we have learned from the experience of the last thirty years that peace is a process requiring mutual restraint and practical arrangements. This conference is a part of that process—a challenge, not a conclusion. We face unresolved problems of military security in Europe; we face them with careful preparation, if we focus on concrete issues, if we maintain forward movement, we have the right to expect real progress."

Then Ford looked straight at Brezhnev and said, "To my country these principles are not clichés or empty phrases. We take this work and these words very seriously. We will spare no effort to ease tensions and to solve problems between us, but it is important that you realize the deep devotion of the American people and their government to human rights and fundamental freedoms and thus to the pledges that this conference has made regarding the freer movement of people, ideas, information. History will judge this conference not by the promises we make but by the promises we keep."[13]

Not everyone was as optimistic as Ford about the promises of the future. That evening the diplomats who labored to thrash out a document agreeable to the thirty-five philosophically different nations could not agree on what the impact would be. Some thought the Helsinki Final Act would be buried and forgotten, while others disagreed.[14] Neither of the two superpowers, despite their words, had high expectations of a long-term international outcome beyond the diplomatic gesture of signing the legally nonbinding document. Both administrations were in for a surprise.

_____

A week after the Helsinki Final Act was signed, Millicent Fenwick was part of a nineteen-member congressional delegation, led by House Speaker Carl Albert, to the Soviet Union, Romania, and Yugoslavia during the August congressional recess. Other members of the delegation included future House Speaker Thomas Foley (D-Washington); future chairman of the House Ways and Means Committee, Bill Archer (R-Texas); and future House Minority Leader Robert Michel (R-Illinois). Fenwick was the most junior member of Congress on the trip, but her peers could not rein her in. On the last day of the trip she met Leonid Brezhnev. Not one to miss an opportunity, she asked the Soviet leader to look into specific human rights cases. Her advocacy on behalf of Soviet dissidents left a lasting impression on Brezhnev. He viewed her as "obsessed."[15]

Earlier in the trip Fenwick had attended a reception at the American embassy in Moscow. There she met Christopher Wren, the _New York Times_ Moscow bureau chief. The two became engrossed in a conversation about Soviet dissidents. When Wren mentioned he was going to see Valentin Turchin, head of Amnesty International in Moscow, Millicent expressed a keen interest in tagging along. Wren extended an invitation and the next day they were off to southwest Moscow where Turchin lived.

Wren picked up Fenwick in his taxilike white Volga sedan. Its discreet appearance did not draw undue attention to them even though Wren made no secret of his meetings with dissidents. His purpose was to gather information about what was happening on the human rights front including who had been detained, released, or imprisoned by the KGB. The best way to obtain this information was to meet with dissidents, such as Turchin, in their apartments. The dissidents did not want to speak on the phone because it was usually bugged, nor could they go to the _New York Times_ bureau office because it was guarded by the KGB. Although neighbors informed the KGB of Wren's visits, his appearances were too sporadic to track.

As Wren drove his clanky white vehicle through the streets of Moscow he was amused by Millicent's constant smoking of her pipe, even in the car. "I never saw that before, a woman smoking a pipe," remembered Wren. "I didn't smoke, but I remember opening the windows as we drove, and later emptying the ashtrays."[16]

Fenwick was not the first dignitary Wren had taken on such an excursion. Occasionally, he took Westerners to meet dissidents because the embassy could not. Often politicians were uncomfortable during these visits, but Millicent was not. "She was very cool, level-headed—cool as a cucumber," said Wren. "Other politicians were nervous, but she was not nervous at all. She was very plain-spoken."[17]

Fenwick was enthralled by the experience. "It was like a spy movie," she recalled. "We moved from car to car before we got to the depressing little flat" where Turchin lived. "He was under pressure from the authorities because he had testified against Andrei Sakharov."[18] Turchin, Fenwick, and others, including scientist Yuri Orlov, discussed the prospect of cooperation between the West and the Soviet human rights movement on the basis of the humanitarian articles of the Helsinki Final Act.[19]

"You read about an automobile accident and you're shocked," Fenwick said. "But you come upon that accident and see the blood on the victims and hear their cries—how different it is. Well that's what it was like to go to Russia and hear the cries of all these desperate people."[20] As a result of Wren taking Fenwick to meet Turchin, dissidents streamed into Fenwick's hotel hoping to speak with this infamous sympathizer from the West. Many of the refusniks came to her despite the presence of Soviet surveillance. The surveillance actually enticed them because, as one dissident said, "The KGB has to know that you know we live, otherwise we'd just be numbers."[21]

The dissidents were well organized when they met with Fenwick. Yuri Orlov, a physicist, and two others presented the delegation with a document entitled "An Appeal to the United States Congressmen," which detailed the conditions of political prisoners in the USSR. It contained fifteen demands of prisoners, including the abolition of forced labor, torture, and restrictions on correspondence and packages received with printed matter.[22]

In Moscow a core group of dissidents led by Orlov formed the Moscow Helsinki Watch Group, the first of many such organizations that would take hold around the world. Orlov brought direction to the group by establishing a mechanism of informing the West about HFA violations within the Soviet Union. His efforts in May of 1976 coincided with a complementary crusade in the United States led by Fenwick, whom he had met briefly on her Soviet trip the previous year.

Fenwick had long since been referred to as the Republican Roosevelt, a comparison to Eleanor, not the real Republican Roosevelt—Teddy. Like the former First Lady, Millicent had a passion for social justice, equality, and democracy. After FDR's death, Eleanor Roosevelt immersed herself in the United Nations Commission on Human Rights, which she chaired. Mrs. Roosevelt, along with the other framers of the Universal Declaration of Human Rights, seized advantage of a narrow opportunity between the end of World War II and the Soviet blockade of Berlin to establish the Universal Declaration of Human Rights. The Declaration, although not legally binding, marked the first time human rights principles were explicitly defined.[23] When the Declaration emerged after a process similar to that experienced by the HFA framers, Mrs. Roosevelt observed that the UDHR would "lift human beings everywhere to a higher standard of life and to a greater enjoyment of freedom . . . in which to develop [their] full stature and through common effort to raise the level of human dignity.[24]

Human dignity and justice were Millicent's pillars. Her continuing efforts to further the rights of individuals were about to move into a new phase, just as Mrs. Roosevelt's life had done when she assumed responsibility for shaping and drafting the UDHR—her proudest accomplishment.[25]

———

In traditional Fenwick fashion, Millicent returned to the United States armed with personal sagas. One woman in particular, Lilia Roitburd, haunted her. As Lilia told the congresswoman her story, Millicent couldn't help noticing Lilia's ashen face and mental exhaustion. Lilia had traveled from Odessa to Moscow to tell about the plight of her husband, Lev.

Eleven months earlier the Roitburds' application for an exit visa to Israel had been denied. Lev, a mechanical engineer, was fired. The local paper printed a distorted portrayal of him as an "imperial puppet" and "carrier of secret information." When he tried to travel to Moscow to meet Democratic Senators Jacob Javits and Edward Kennedy, part of a senatorial delegation that preceded the House delegation, he was arrested at the Odessa airport and charged with striking a militia officer.[26]

Mr. Roitburd's papers were in order, but while trying to board the plane the police forcibly removed him, his wife, and their son, Sasha, from the boarding area. They grabbed Mr. Roitburd's hair and twisted his arms as he writhed in pain. His wife and son waited for nine hours before Mrs. Roitburd was told her husband would be detained for three days. A week later she was told a criminal case had been initiated against him for resisting authorities with use of force and that he faced imprisonment for a period of five years. When she met with Millicent a month later the family was still torn apart.[27]

As Lilia talked about her husband she reached into her purse and pulled out a photo. Fenwick gazed at the picture of a young and healthy Lilia with thick, bushy black hair and asked, "When was this picture taken?" She would have guessed five to ten years ago. Lilia told her, "Six months ago." Fenwick looked up at Lilia's tiny ravaged face, with her hair matted to her head, "and tears came to my eyes," Fenwick remembered. "I still have nightmares about it."[28] It was Lilia's desperation and sorrow, among that of so many others, that moved Fenwick to action.

Wasting no time upon her return to the United States, Fenwick introduced H.R. 9466 on September 9, 1975, to create the U.S. Commission on Security and Cooperation in Europe, better known as the Helsinki Commission. Her goal was to establish a congressional commission to monitor the compliance or violation by signatory countries of the third basket of the Helsinki Accords dealing with the rights of individuals, freedom of movement, and family reunification. The Commission would also observe and encourage economic cooperation and the exchange of ideas between the Eastern bloc and the Western world. The Commission itself would be responsible for periodically reporting to the House and Senate and responding to congressional requests.

"In my innocence," Fenwick recalled, "I thought of equal numbers of both parties, six senators, six members of the House, and a member of the Commerce, Defense, and State Departments [serving on the commission]."[29] She felt the inclusion of the executive branch representatives was vital, as those agencies, along with Congress, shared responsibility for implementing the Helsinki Accords.

Fenwick's idealistic notion of a bipartisan commission that paired members of the legislative and executive branches was not well received by the administration. Two days after her legislation was introduced the White House took notice. In a memo to Robert McCloskey, assistant secretary for congressional relations, Arthur Hartman wrote, "Since we do not feel such a device would be a practical or effective means for coordinating and guiding implementation efforts, we suggest that . . . a letter be sent to Congresswoman Fenwick."[30] Fenwick received a lengthy two-and-a-half-page letter explaining the administration's position. But she was not discouraged.

Both Kissinger and Scowcroft were irate at the suggestion of mixing representatives from the legislative and executive branches on one committee. They wanted to prevent Congress from meddling in their foreign policy arena. They feared an infusion of human rights policy would jeopardize the relationship between the United States and the Soviet Union and set unwanted precedent for future committees to follow the same vein. As Kissinger put it, "I want to avoid a precedent where the various departments could pursue personal vendettas completely outside the scope of Presidential authority and control."[31]

Because Fenwick's Helsinki Commission idea did not fade, Kissinger half-jokingly referred to her as his "tormenter."[32] In the early to mid-1970s, with the United States embroiled in both the Vietnam War and the cold war, Kissinger put concrete vital interests ahead of human rights. He was acutely aware of how fragile America's relationship with the Soviet Union was. His efforts were concentrated on the strategic arms limitation talks (SALT) and mutual and balanced force reductions (MBFR) talks. He articulated his views when he spoke to the Senate Foreign Relations Committee about détente: "Since the dawn of the nuclear age the world's fears of holocaust and its hopes for peace have turned on the relationship between the United States and the Soviet Union."[33] He advocated, and the Administration's foreign policy reflected, "a strong national defense while recognizing that in the nuclear age the relationship between military strength and politically usable power is the most complex in all history."[34] As Kissinger plotted strategic moves to maintain the nation's balance of power and self-interest, arms negotiations remained a clearer priority than human rights.

Ford, with Kissinger at the helm, adhered to the Nixon administration's policy of détente. But when relations with the East became strained Ford banned the word "détente" from his vocabulary, about the same time Fenwick was fighting to pass her proposed legislation.[35] Both Nixon and Kissinger, classic realists, refused to allow human rights a disproportionate role in their policymaking decisions. They embarked on a path of détente to modify Soviet external behavior—specifically to halt Soviet invasions and exportation of Communist ideas—not to dismantle the Soviet regime.

Thrown into this mix in which détente was a priority for strategic, not humanistic, reasons was Fenwick, an elderly freshman House member who plowed forward relentlessly to pass the Helsinki legislation on behalf of Lilia Roitburd and the other dissidents in Eastern Europe who were denied their freedom. Social justice was Fenwick's motivating factor. Desperately appealing to the House Committee on International Relations to hold a hearing on her proposed bill, Fenwick was rebuffed. The committee did not yet see the value in her idea but referred the matter to the subcommittee on International Political and Military Affairs chaired by Florida Democrat Dante Fascell. He, too, stalled the issue.

Discouraged, a determined Fenwick sought the guidance of her friend and fellow New Jersey Republican, Senator Clifford Case. Two months later Michael Kraft, Case's chief foreign policy aide, saw a window of opportunity for Case to introduce language creating a Commission on Security and Cooperation in Europe. "It was kind of funny," said Kraft. "There was a Russian-related resolution proposed by Senator Cranston that had to do with missiles on the agenda for markup. Since the Soviet Union was on the agenda, Case offered the Helsinki language amendment as part of the State Department authorization bill. . . . Once it passed the Senate it picked up momentum and went through the Senate without any hearings, some discussion, but not much." By then Fenwick had rallied more support from her peers but still could not persuade Fascell to hold a hearing on her proposed legislation. "Dante Fascell was not initially enthusiastic, but I don't think it was partisan," said Kraft. "Quite the contrary. It could have been a bit of inertia."[36]

In March, Fenwick took to the House floor to reintroduce her bill. Although progress was at a standstill, she had spent the previous six months securing seventy-three co-sponsors. "When the Commission is working we will have one central place where all the information about the human rights guaranteed in the accord can be gathered together," she told the Speaker of the House. In an effort not to exclude anyone she continued, "We will know what is happening to the Ukrainians, the Baltic peoples, the Jews and Anabaptists of Russia; to the Poles, Hungarians, Czechs, and Bulgarians; and in Romania, to the Germans, Hungarians, Baptists, Catholics, and Jews. We should know if there is hope for the people we met during the Speaker's trip to the Soviet Union and Romania last August. We should also know of the plight of the millions we never knew, or if there is nothing for them but the prison that refuses to let them go, that dismisses them from any employment as soon as a visa is requested and then jails them as parasites."[37]

While Fenwick was laboring to get her legislation passed, she was also busy advocating for the release of dissidents. On March 15, 1976, her office issued a press release announcing that Russian Victor Abdalov, married to an American student, had been released by the Soviets. Fenwick and a dozen other colleagues had contacted the State Department on his behalf a few months earlier. Praising the Soviet decision to release him, Fenwick said, "Permission for Mr. Abdalov [to leave Russia] follows the principles set forth in the U.N. Declaration of Human Rights and, more recently, the Helsinki Accords. I am working on a number of cases of this kind and I hope that Soviet action in this case represents a new direction in their emigration policy which will be extended to others for whom I have been requesting visas."[38]

By now Fenwick's idea had garnered support from the media. On the House floor she read an editorial that appeared in the *Washington Star*: "Non-binding international agreements—such as the declaration signed by the United States, the Soviet Union and 33 other nations at Helsinki last August—are significant only to the extent that they actually succeed in changing the behavior of the countries concerned. And since, in the case of the Soviet Union, such changes are unlikely to occur without a certain amount of discreet and continuing outside suasion, we welcome the idea of setting up a joint congressional commission to monitor the results of the Helsinki agreement, particularly in the area of human rights . . . introduced in the House by Rep. Millicent Fenwick of New Jersey and in the Senate by fellow Republican Clifford Case. . . . It is quite a simple mechanism for keeping Congress and the American people informed on an aspect of Soviet policy in which all the nations have a legitimate interest. It should provide the factual information to support—or dispel—the impression in the West that Soviet policies have not been significantly liberalized since the signing of the Helsinki declaration . . . itself a product of the east-west detente. The proposed congressional commission would be able to make a dispassionate judgement on how well—or how badly—that policy has paid off."[39]

Late in April, eight months after introduction, the bill cleared the Senate Foreign Relations Committee and was adopted by the Senate without opposition on May 5, primarily due to the efforts of Case, the ranking minority member on the Senate Foreign Relations Committee. "Immediately we had a House hearing," said Fenwick, "but by this time they [Democrats] had twisted it all around. There were four Democrats, and two Republicans from each House [to serve on the commission]."[40] This new configuration undermined Fenwick's intention of having a balanced commission with an equal number of representatives from both political parties.

Ironically, Fascell, the chairman who stalled the bill in committee, was responsible for the new composition of the commission. He was concerned that the three executive branch representatives would tilt the committee to a Republican majority. In a stroke of political maneuvering Fascell reengineered the committee to have four members from the majority party and two members from the minority party in each house. This calculation gave the Democrats a majority of eight members compared to seven Republicans—two senators, two congressmen, and three executive branch representatives. This diluted Fenwick's initial intention of having a bipartisan committee with an equal number of Democrats and Republicans from the House and Senate. "What difference does it make," Fenwick consoled herself, "as long as they are people who are interested in the subject?"[41]

After Case successfully pushed the Fenwick-Case bill through the Senate, the House International Relations Committee reported the bill with amendments. Three days later, with Senate passage and mounting support from interest groups such as the National Conference on Soviet Jewry—a coalition of 38 Jewish organizations—the House passed Fenwick's legislation to create the CSCE. There were 240 votes in favor of the bill, 95 opposed, and another 97 abstaining.[42]

Prior to the vote, and with ninety-six co-sponsors, Fenwick reflected on the conception of the legislation: "The [Moscow] trip made a lasting impression on most of us who realized, after talking for many hours with dissidents and Soviet citizens wanting to emigrate, that the hopes of these people had been pinned to the implementation of the Helsinki Accord which had been signed before our arrival." She reiterated the importance of the commission as a step in the right direction and one that would "indicate to the world that the United States will continue its dedication to human rights."[43]

On May 21, four days after the House vote, the Senate took final action and approved the House version of S. 2679. The House version authorized a fifteen-member commission and $350,000 as opposed to the Senate version which initially authorized an eleven-member commission and a $250,000 budget.[44]

After the Fenwick-Case bill passed Congress, it was sent to the White House where it lingered. Kissinger, who adamantly opposed the legislation, was not directly consulted about whether Ford should sign it or not. From Kissinger's perspective the legislation was anathema with respect to both the human rights thrust and legislative assertiveness in foreign affairs. He was not alone. White House and State Department staffers believed that the monitoring of the Helsinki Accords was an executive branch function.[45]

Despite internal opposition, Ford quietly signed the bill on June 3, 1976, in an unusually small private Oval Office ceremony that lasted five minutes. There was no fanfare, not even a press release. The only witnesses were Fenwick, Case, and Bill Canis—Millicent's legislative assistant who had aided her in the process of turning an idea into a law. Missing from this small contingent were the chairman of the Senate and House Committees on Foreign Relations. Mike Kraft, Case's top foreign policy staffer and a central figure behind the scenes, wasn't there either. Even though Kraft did not attend the signing he remembered, "It happened very quickly, short notice, with only one or two reporters. It was done as quietly as it could be."[46]

Present was Brent Scowcroft, who ensured that the signing ceremony would be a low-key event. "I recommend against a full public ceremony for the CSCE Commission Bill," he wrote in a White House memo, "on the basis that we have consistently opposed this legislation and because it represents another Congressional intrusion into Executive Branch functions."[47]

Kissinger also made his opposition clear. "The President," he told his top advisers, "signed the bill only because I had not been told what was happening. I would have fought it to the death." He assured them, "It never would have passed if I had known more about it."[48]

What Kissinger and others did not understand was the president's commitment to the Helsinki process. "Having signed the accord I felt it was absolutely essential to proceed with the review process. If we were going to implement the Helsinki Accords we were going to have to monitor it," said President Ford when asked why he signed the Fenwick-Case bill.[49]

When the President signed the bill—against the advice of his foreign policy advisers— many believed his decision was linked to the presidential race and the upcoming New Jersey primary five days later. Some thought Ford would benefit politically because the bill was sponsored by two popular New Jersey Republicans. They were right. When Philip Buchen, counsel to the president, inquired about why the bill was signed, he was given two reasons: "1. Make hay in New Jersey (Pictures taken with Sen. Case, Cong. Fenwick?); [and] 2. People felt in general if the president didn't sign it, he would be painted as anti-people (anti-prisoners)."[50]

Although the White House did nothing special to promote the signing, the *Newark Star-Ledger* carried the story and quoted Case and Fenwick as saying, "The commission is necessary both to reaffirm the United States' commitment to the promises made at Helsinki and to make violations of the agreement a matter of public record."[51]

Although Ford was expected to win the New Jersey primary, he left nothing to chance and visited the state two days before the primary. During a heavy downpour he told a crowd of ten thousand supporters, "If you want to win locally, you'd better get 67 delegates for Jerry Ford on Tuesday."[52] Drenched, Fenwick, also on the dais, appeared oblivious to the torrential rains. She did not have to worry about her own primary because she was uncontested. On primary day, Ford won the state of New Jersey and split the other two contests that day, ending the primary season.

With primaries over, pressure mounted on the GOP convention in Kansas City. Neither Ford nor Reagan had enough delegates to lock up the race. As the August convention approached, rumors swirled about vice-presidential prospects. A year before the June primaries Ford had endorsed Rockefeller, his vice-president, as his running mate. But as a result of campaign reform laws passed after Watergate, the RNC could only handle the presidential nominee's campaign—not the primaries. So, abiding by the law, Ford set up a separate committee to start raising funds for the primaries.

The new election laws also stipulated that Ford and Rockefeller had to run separate campaigns. Bo Callaway, Ford's campaign manager, held a press conference to explain the new procedure. "The Ford and Rockefeller campaigns are not one and the same," he said.[53] This was true. But Callaway got carried away and implied that Rockefeller was a political liability. A few weeks later Callaway fueled rumors by telling the press that the president might select a younger running mate. A furious Ford was not able to undo the damage. Three months later Rockefeller voluntarily withdrew his name from consideration, fearing he was now a hindrance to the ticket.

Weeks before the convention Reagan selected Pennsylvania Senator Richard Schweiker to be his running mate. Reagan was hoping to secure the votes of the dozens of Pennsylvania delegates for the nomination. His tactic backfired. Pennsylvania stood by Ford. In mid-August the convention kicked off, and Ford had still not selected a running mate.

While Ford's team was busy strategizing backstage, one of the party's newest national figures was tapped to receive the limelight onstage. Fenwick proudly took on this task. She, along with the rest of the New Jersey delegation, led by Case, supported Ford.

Fenwick, a member of the GOP Platform Committee, participated in a televised debate about the ERA. She went head-to-head against Phyllis Schlafly, the outspoken Stop ERA national chairwoman. At the time, the GOP platform incorporated a pro-ERA stance and an antiabortion position. Fenwick, a pro-choice Republican, who never forgot what she had witnessed on her South American *Vogue* trip, tried unsuccessfully to remove the platform committee's antiabortion plank. Meanwhile, Schlafly was trying to overturn the pro-ERA stance, but her efforts failed. The ERA remained in the GOP platform by a narrow margin, 51 to 47.[54]

"I think it is sad and a little comic that in a bicentennial year to be wondering about whether we ought to admit that 51%–52% of the citizens of America are really citizens," said Fenwick during the Schlafly debate. "When ERA started I thought oh sure, and I didn't take it too seriously, it seemed so natural. I thought it was an oversight, but now as a result of all the opposition so cleverly orchestrated by my companion here, I am getting quite severe about it. We need the ERA because it is a statement that women are citizens."

But as Schlafly pointed out, "The majority of voters in your state voted against the ERA. . . . They know women are citizens and do not need ERA which will do all sorts of mischievous things like ban mother-daughter banquets in school and subject women to the draft because ERA requires that we treat men and women equally."[55]

Fenwick had the first lady on her side. Betty Ford, who had also been asked to debate Schlafly but declined, wrote of Schlafly in her memoirs, "She contends that a women's place is the home, yet she's out touring all over the United States in order to bring women that message. I wonder how often she's home to greet *her* husband when he comes in for dinner."[56]

Fenwick, still a freshman, was the only New Jerseyan listed on the roster of convention speakers. On the second day, her moment arrived to address the delegates. She chose the nation's bicentennial as her topic and began her remarks by presenting the convention with a bicentennial memorial plaque from Somerset County. In doing so she received a booming applause as the band played "Everything's Coming Up Roses."[57]

Drawing upon the American bicentennial and the founding fathers, she told the crowd, "We must remember their high priorities and their great goals. We must emulate their courage and their wisdom." Continuing in her aristocratic drawl she highlighted modern-day problems in the cities and prisons, and told the crowd, "It takes compassion to deal with them—compassion and common sense."[58]

The next day Ford secured the nomination. He did so on the first ballot in a close contest against Reagan. The buzz quickly shifted to speculation about Ford's vice-presidential nominee. There was at least one person who thought Ford's choice should be Millicent Fenwick. Before a high-level meeting with Ford, Case said "he intend[ed] to recommend [to the president] the same vice-presidential names [he] has presented in the past, Sen. Edward Brooke of Massachusetts, Sen. Howard Baker of Tennessee, and Rep. Millicent Fenwick of New Jersey."[59] Instead of heeding Case's advice, Ford chose Senator Bob Dole.

---

A week after the Fenwick-Case bill was signed, House Speaker Carl Albert announced the appointment of four Democrats and two Republicans to the Commission on Security and Cooperation in Europe. Fascell, a twenty-year House veteran, was appointed chairman instead of the freshman from New Jersey. In addition to Fascell the three other Democrats selected were Sidney Yates and Paul Simon, both from Illinois; and Jonathan Bingham from New York. Millicent's Republican House peer on the committee was John Buchanan of Alabama.

"I guess I'm lucky to even be on the commission," a frustrated Fenwick remarked after Fascell reconfigured the composition of the commission. "In fact I've learned that it's easy to get things done here in the House as long as you're willing to let other people take the credit."[60]

Once Fascell saw that this legislation had staying power he latched onto future developments related to the Helsinki Commission. He had more political muscle than Fenwick to counter delaying tactics introduced by the administration. One such tactic challenged the constitutionality of the Commission, particularly its hybrid composition. The matter was referred to the Department of Justice, but the administration received no support. The Justice Department dismissed the concerns on grounds that the Commission was an intergovernmental agency with no legislative authority. It could hold hearings, issue reports, and make inquiries of other governmental agencies, but it had no direct role in the formulation of legislation.

The next battle for Fascell was the appointment of the three executive branch members to the Commission. By late summer conversations between the Commission and the administration only yielded empty promises.

The first step toward progress and compromise didn't occur until August 24, when Kissinger met with Chairman Fascell, Co-Chairman

Claiborne Pell (D-Rhode Island), Case, and Fenwick. Fenwick immediately went on the attack. She was upset with the State Department for reiterating the right of individuals to immigrate to the United States, but not to other countries of their choice. Kissinger's response underestimated the information citizens had behind the Iron Curtain. "Do you really think people in Eastern European countries and the USSR know that 35 countries signed the Final Act? I think many of them probably believe that the United States and USSR were the only signatories."[61]

After this exchange they moved to the pressing issue at hand, the appointment of executive branch staff to the Commission. "There are two problems here," said Kissinger. "Executive Branch relations with the Congress on this Commission, and the context of the Commission's work. We have serious reservations about the Commission in so far as Executive Branch representation is concerned. . . . We are eager to cooperate but are really concerned that what our participation would do to Executive Branch–Legislative Branch relations and to the confidentiality of Executive Branch discussions."[62]

No sooner had Kissinger finished his sentence than Fenwick piped up. "What if the Executive Branch members were to act as observers, without a vote? They could stay away from the meetings when they believed it necessary to do so. Wouldn't that be okay?," she asked.

"That would be okay if it's okay with the Secretary," said Fascell.

"I'd want to talk to the President," said Kissinger.

Then Kissinger expressed his concern with the mixed commission. "If we have Executive Branch members sitting on the Commission examining other members of the Executive Branch who are appearing as witnesses, we'll get into interdepartmental maneuvering." As he reiterated his disdain and unwillingness to move forward with the composition of the commission, he also pledged his cooperation.

Fascell emphasized that "this Commission . . . is an independent agency. This one is law."

"Did the President sign the bill?" asked Co-Chair Pell who surprisingly had no knowledge of the low-key bill signing two months earlier.

"Yes, he signed it," said Kissinger, expressing his contempt. "There was almost a signing ceremony but shall we say it was with less than full understanding. And I didn't really understand what was happening."[63] This was one of the few instances Kissinger admitted ignorance.

As the group talked in circles about potential obstacles and conflicts, Fenwick reiterated that the executive branch members could serve in an advisory capacity. What they needed to take into consideration was the bill was already signed into law, mandating executive branch participation. Although they discussed amending the law, they concluded that an exchange of letters between the chairman of the commission,

Fascell, and the president would be needed to clearly indicate the conditions and limitations of executive branch membership. In the end they adopted her compromise, but it was Fascell who signed the letter and received credit for finding a viable solution.

In early October, an exchange of letters between Fascell and Ford indicated their agreement of an observer status of the executive branch members to be appointed. Simultaneously, Fascell applied additional pressure by announcing that Senator Walter Mondale, the Democratic vice-presidential candidate, would raise the issue in a televised debate with Republican vice-presidential nominee Bob Dole. That threat got Ford's attention. On the day of the debate Ford appointed three executive branch members to the Commission. He did so with the understanding that these three members were not to partake in any votes nor question any witnesses. Fascell agreed. But, to nullify the fact that the executive representatives were deprived the right to vote, Fascell rarely called for a vote.[64]

———

Fenwick never lost sight of the implementation of her CSCE vision, now law. Once the Helsinki Commission was established and staffed, she dedicated much of her first and second terms toward protecting individuals' civil liberties. Thanks to her, "the Helsinki Final Act humanized the debate so the cold war was not just about missiles, but people," recalled Fenwick legislative aide Bill Canis.[65]

Fenwick constantly questioned witnesses at committee hearings, fervently tried to secure the release of countless dissidents seeking exit visas from countries in violation of the HFA, appealed to world leaders such as Soviet Secretary General Leonid Brezhnev and Romanian dictator Nicolae Ceausescu for the release of imprisoned individuals, and badgered Communist ambassadors to the United States such as Anatoly Dobrynin about the plights of hundreds of individuals brought to her attention. In one instance she dragged Bill Canis with her to personally deliver a letter to the Soviet embassy on Sixteenth Street in Washington, D.C.—later renamed Andrei Sakharov Plaza after the noted Soviet scientist and dissident. Because of Millicent's personal commitment to human rights, Millicent received letters from around the globe documenting human rights violations. These letters became the basis for her appeals.

Monitoring commissions sprouted in Eastern Europe and brought additional cases to Millicent's attention. One of the earliest groups was Orlov's Moscow Helsinki Watch Group. While Fenwick's memory of Orlov was clouded by Lilia's story, he never forgot the ferocious older woman who had perpetually jotted down notes, prompting him to think, initially, that Millicent was the delegation's secretary.

Orlov formed the Moscow Helsinki Watch Group with eight other dissidents to monitor the Soviet Union's compliance with the human rights provisions of the Helsinki Final Act. The group's intent was to document violations and forward them to the governments and citizens of other countries. Within three days of forming the group Orlov was interrogated by Soviet authorities. They officially warned him that his Helsinki Watch Group was illegal and that legal action would be taken if the group's activities continued.

In the United States, the U.S. Helsinki Commission overcame a different kind of resistance. While it survived the hurdle of executive branch appointments, its battles with the administration continued. Kissinger reportedly colluded with Soviet Ambassador Anatoly Dobrynin to have Soviet visas denied to Commission members traveling to Europe to monitor the observance of the Final Act.[66]

The Eastern bloc countries followed the Soviet lead in denying visas for the November trip. As a result, Fenwick and her colleagues ended up going to eighteen Western European nations to monitor compliance with the Helsinki Final Act. The delegation reported that in Western Europe there was virtual agreement that the HFA was already more productive than expected.[67]

Days before the delegation left on their fact-finding mission, Ford was defeated for the presidency by Democratic Georgia Governor Jimmy Carter. Less volatile days for the CSCE were on the horizon. With the election of Jimmy Carter, as president, the Helsinki Commission no longer had to battle an administration reluctant to embrace human rights as a guiding policy. During his Inaugural Address Carter said: "Because we are free, we can never be indifferent to the fate of freedom elsewhere. Our moral sense dictates a clear cut preference for those societies which share with us an abiding respect for individual human rights. We do not seek to intimidate, but it is clear that a world which others can dominate with impunity would be inhospitable to decency and a threat to the well-being of all people."[68]

President Ford repeatedly said, "When I was in the White House, and since, that the Helsinki Final Act was one of my major [foreign policy] accomplishments as president. The U.S. Helsinki Commission was an important follow-up in terms of making sure the Helsinki Accords were implemented. I applaud President Carter for taking over and making sure the legislation was implemented."[69]

By 1977, monitoring groups in the United States and Moscow represented a sampling of efforts aimed at protecting the rights of individuals in the CSCE nations. In Czechoslovakia, more than three hundred people signed Charter 77, a human rights manifesto that sought to protect the rights of individuals in accordance with the Helsinki Final Act. In Poland, a Committee on Workers' Self-Defense (KOR) was established to seek the extension and protection of human rights in Poland. This ultimately led to the Solidarity movement. Activities such as these were praised by foreign policy leaders such as Henry Kissinger who acknowledged, "Visionary and courageous activists like Vaclav Havel and Lech Walesa turned these clauses of the Final Act into rallying cries for resisting totalitarianism in the Communist world and thereby ultimately brought about liberation in Eastern Europe."[70] The Helsinki Final Act had been utilized as a powerful tool to combat human rights violations and as such it rejuvenated hope in Eastern Europeans that they would one day attain freedoms enjoyed in the West.

As part of the Helsinki Accords, two review conferences were planned to monitor the implementation of the Final Act. The first such conference was held in Belgrade, Yugoslavia, in 1977. The members of the Helsinki Commission, including Fenwick, were part of that delegation. Five years later, she was a member of a subsequent delegation that went to Madrid for the second monitoring conference.

In 2001, the U.S. Helsinki Commission on Security and Cooperation in Europe was still in existence—twenty-five years after the Case-Fenwick bill was signed by President Ford. In 1995, the committee was renamed the Organization for Security and Cooperation in Europe (OSCE). The committee had grown in size to twenty-one members—nine from the House, nine from the Senate, and three from the executive branch. Their primary purpose still involved military security; economic and environmental cooperation; and human rights.

---

It had been an uphill battle, but during Fenwick's first term in Congress she was the only freshman to conceptualize legislation enacted by the president. "The Helsinki Commission created a new priority where none would have existed," said Canis. "The Commission kept human rights a priority."[71]

As Madeleine Albright and Albert Friendly noted, "Given the normal delays on the legislative process, especially in handling a proposal initiated by a first-term member of a minority party, the nine-month gestation period of the law that established the Commission was remarkably short. In that time only one hearing was held. No administration witness testified. No roll-call votes in either chamber were required. All that evidence suggests that the initiative was looked on as a minor but timely bit of 'motherhood' law-making."[72] That "motherhood" spawned an international movement in which dissidents had a concrete document to latch onto and monitoring commissions, such as the United States [Helsinki] Commission on Security and Cooperation in Europe, had a mechanism to assess compliance.

The HFA breathed new life into activists abroad and led to a weakening of the hold Communist nations maintained over their people. The individual, which Fenwick fought so desperately to protect, was able to triumph. The HFA, despite controversy, particularly in the United States, became one of many important catalysts that led to the end of the cold war. Within fifteen years of the signing of the Helsinki Accords, Estonia, Latvia, and Lithuania regained their independence; the Soviet satellite countries collapsed; the Soviet Union dissolved; and the Berlin Wall came down at the hands of the people.

In honor of that symbolic occasion Millicent reflected on the challenges and successes of establishing the Helsinki Commission. "It is as though in Eastern Europe a great ice jam is breaking up. Thousands fill the streets of cities where until now people would have been afraid to take part in any such demonstrations. But, we should have known that there is power and danger for the people and for despots in the world," she said. "Pronouncement must be taken seriously. For me, a circle had been completed when, some years after I met Lilia Roitburd in Moscow, her husband was introduced at a meeting in a synagogue in my congressional district—Lev Roitburd—free at last, free at last."[73]

# 13

## *Lacey*

## *Davenport*

The woods are lovely, dark and deep,
But I have promises to keep,
And miles to go before I sleep,
And miles to go before I sleep.

—Robert Frost

Fenwick's long hours and legislative accomplishments were rewarded in 1976 when she defeated Somerset County Freeholder Frank Nero by a two-to-one margin in her first reelection campaign. In her second term, she continued to advocate on behalf of human rights and the full implementation of the HFA. "Either you believe in human rights or you don't," she said. "How can we have relationships with countries or people who do not understand what we care about most strongly?"[1] As a public figure Fenwick was able to draw attention to the plights of Soviet dissidents such as Andrei Sakharov and Anatoly Shcharansky. She appeared on the *Today* show in 1977 with Nataly Shcharansky, Anatoly Shcharansky's wife, to seek his release from the Soviet Union where he was a prisoner of conscience. It was nearly a decade before the Soviets permitted him to emigrate to Israel in 1986. All the while, Fenwick never lost hope, nor did she lose track of the many individuals refused their right to the freedom of movement referred to in basket three of the Helsinki Final Act.

The voters loved her and her passion for her job as a public servant. She returned their affection by working even harder. In 1978, Millicent won reelection against Parsippany–Troy Hills Mayor John Fahy, with more than 70 percent of the vote. "She was an absolute workaholic, often spending eighty to ninety hours a week at the office," said Hollis McLoughlin, her chief of staff.[2] But as much as she savored her work, in

1978 she learned how fragile her job could be. Senator Case, running for a fifth term, received a jolting reality check in the Republican primary. Ambitious thirty-four-year-old Jeff Bell tapped into the conservative base of the GOP, unseating the popular liberal Republican but losing the general election to newcomer Bill Bradley.

For Millicent, better news awaited in Washington. In this, her third term, she finally gained her coveted seat on the House Foreign Affairs Committee. At the same time, she received a résumé from Michael Kraft, Case's top foreign policy aide. With Case's defeat Kraft moved to the Senate Foreign Relations staff. Shortly thereafter, with the Democrats in control and a new chairman of the committee, Kraft was let go, but he wasn't job hunting long. Millicent hired him.

Kraft became one of the senior members on her staff. He was both older and more experienced than the twenty-somethings Fenwick relied on. Prior to working for Case, Kraft was a Reuters reporter assigned to Capitol Hill. "It was kind of funny," said Kraft. "After Watergate and the impeachment, I was a bit burnt out, and I remembered thinking—as I waited for a closed-door meeting of the Intelligence Committee to end so I could grab some members to piece together a story—that it was a heck of a way to spend the summer."[3] Not long after that, Senator Case approached Kraft, whom he knew from his coverage of the Foreign Affairs Committee, with a job offer. Kraft, ready for a change, accepted.

By the time Kraft moved to Fenwick's office, he knew some of her staffers from his work on the Helsinki legislation that Fenwick and Case had pushed through Congress together. Kraft became Millicent's in-house foreign policy adviser, much as he had been with Case. One issue he spearheaded for Fenwick was antiterrorism legislation. Ironically, on September 11, 1979, exactly twenty-two years before the attacks on the World Trade Center and the Pentagon, Fenwick offered an amendment to the Export Administration Act, a particularly complex bill that, through export controls, had implications for the domestic economy, foreign policy, and national security of the United States. "The amendment is intended to close this loophole [that allowed the approval of sales to Libya and Syria of civilian versions of military transport planes and trucks]. Such sales could have major foreign policy implications and if we are to be serious in our efforts to encourage other countries to stop assisting terrorists, these kinds of sales should be made only after full consideration," said Fenwick.[4]

One incident that gave rise to her concern was the Department of Commerce's approval of a license to sell four hundred heavy-duty Oshkosh trucks, generally used for oil, to Libya. That same type of truck was used as a military tank transporter by the United States and Canada. Libya's license was approved because the order did not include armored trucks or other military enhancements. The sale, however, did catch the attention of a State Department staffer who called Kraft and explained his concern that Libya would use these trucks against Egypt.

In another example, the sale of C-130 aircraft—a civilian version of a military cargo plane—to Syria was approved. The civilian version had a larger fuselage, and no doors for paratroopers. Shortly after that sale, members of Congress expressed their concern that the State Department approved the deal. They feared the planes would be used for military purposes. In an attempt to prevent such sales, Kraft and Fenwick drafted an amendment. Export licenses would not be approved for goods and services that could potentially aid terrorist activity or military transports to countries identified by the secretary of state as posing a terrorist threat unless the license went to Congress thirty days before a deal was finalized. Congress would thus have an opportunity to stop the sale. The language of the amendment read: "The Secretary and the Secretary of State shall notify the Committee on Foreign Affairs of the House of Representatives and the Committee on Foreign Relations of the Senate before any license is approved for the export of goods or technology valued at more than $7,000,000 to any country concerning which the Secretary of State has made the following determinations:

(1) Such country has repeatedly provided support for acts of international terrorism.
(2) Such exports would make a significant contribution to the military potential of such country, including its military logistics capability, or would enhance the ability of such country to support acts of international terrorism.[5]

On September 29, 1979, President Carter signed the legislation, Public Law No: 96–72. Provisions in the new law took into consideration third-party sales and transfers, requiring congressional review if the end user was identified as a terrorist country.

One of the first sales impacted by the law was an export of gas turbine engines—afterburners to provide extra speed—to be used in missile frigates, that is, warships, that Italy was building for Iraq. Kraft was tipped off by the White House and shared the information with Fenwick. As a result, Congress stopped delivery after the first two engines were sent, causing the frigate production to be delayed because the Italians had to redesign the ships to accommodate the wider Rolls-Royce engines they had to purchase from Britain in lieu of the American ones. More than a decade later, the Iraqis still had not received the frigates, which Iraq might have used during the Gulf War. Thus, the Fenwick Amendment indirectly "blocked the Iraqis getting these four missile ships that would have given them a strong naval punch," said Kraft.[6] The Export Administration Act of 1979 is now a major diplomatic tool the United States uses against economic-sanctioned countries and is even more crucial in light of the September 11, 2001, terrorist attacks against the United States.

Many of the amendments Fenwick introduced on the House floor were handwritten and spontaneous, causing her staff to scramble. Her amendments generally failed because when other members called to follow up, her staff usually had no knowledge of the amendments. "Thus they were doomed to failure," said Bill Canis.[7] Regardless of the success or lack of success of her amendments, Fenwick had a reputation for her eloquence on the House floor. Unlike many of her colleagues, she wrote her own speeches. Sometimes she shared them with her staff, sometimes she didn't. Occasionally, if she planned to read a statement on the House floor specifically for inclusion in the *Congressional Record*, the staff might write a first draft covering the more technical aspects of the legislation, or amendment, for historical purposes. "She never had a press secretary, so her staff had two jobs for the price of one," said staffer Larry Rosenshein, who met his wife, Katie, when they both worked for Fenwick.[8]

Early on, Millicent's enjoyment of writing, coupled with her desire to keep constituents informed, led to the creation of her congressional district newsletter, *Millicent Fenwick Reports to the Fifth District of New Jersey*. The first issue was released two days after the 94th Congress convened in January of 1975. Wasting no time in tackling issues, she addressed the challenges of the new Congress and the unfinished legislation of the prior session. "We [the new Congress] must find ways of striking a delicate economic balance that will arrest and reverse our downward slide without accelerating the rampant inflation that has eroded the value of our dollars. . . . We of the 94th must complete the work begun during the last two years on national health insurance, tax reform, a national energy policy, no-fault insurance and a host of other important matters, not the least of which is putting more Americans to work. . . . The Administration and we in Congress cannot accomplish alone this shared goal of restoring our nation's economic and moral well-being without the support and cooperation of a concerned and cooperative citizenry."[9]

Kraft was struck by Millicent's writing ability, particularly when compared to other members of Congress. "She had developed an elegant writing style, her sentences and paragraphs flowed well. She came from that generation of people who could write well, with a flow and rhythm, and I assume some of that was tailored at *Vogue*."[10]

As a result of her days at *Vogue*, Millicent understood the job of reporters better than most. Her candor and availability made her a media favorite. Local Bernardsville reporter Sandy Stuart, said, "If anything, Fenwick frequently related more information and detail than necessary to insure that one comprehended the matter at hand."[11] Millicent's power to communicate via the press overflowed from print to radio to television. Even she realized it. "I hope you won't think I'm being immodest, but I have a tremendous impact on television. I don't know why. But the problem is nobody ever remembers what I said. I don't know whether I'm putting things clearly, but apparently the effect is of somebody who cares terribly about whatever she's saying which seems to strike people as a good thing. But then they never can remember what the good thing is."[12] Part of her appeal can be attributed to her novelty as one of the relatively few female members of Congress, as well as to her graceful demeanor.

What was memorable in the minds of many was Fenwick's uncanny similarity to cartoonist Garry Trudeau's lovable Lacey Davenport. Lacey, an elderly female member of Congress, appeared in his *Doonesbury* comic strips and represented the last honest member of Congress. Lacey's vocabulary was punctuated with Millicent's favorite phrases, such as, "my dear."

Davenport's emergence paralleled Fenwick's. The first time well-heeled Lacey appeared in *Doonesbury* was on May 15, 1974, in the midst of Millicent's highly publicized primary against Tom Kean. But then Lacey took a hiatus, appearing in only two strips in 1975, until her reemergence in 1976 as her alter ego was grabbing headlines.

Millicent's staffers immediately recognized their boss in Lacey Davenport. Knowing that Millicent didn't read the comic pages, they left a copy on her desk. The next morning she came into her office, noticed the pages, moved them, and went about reading her mail. When her staff arrived, they anxiously awaited her reaction. Finally, someone went into her office and asked what she thought. Puzzled, she said she thought someone had been sitting at her desk and accidentally left the paper behind. Fenwick didn't realize it was meant for her. "When it first came out Millicent thought it was all about Bella, because Lacey wore a hat," said Canis. "Millicent's reaction was part of her charming naiveté. Everyone else told Millicent it sounded like her."[13] Eventually she, too, couldn't deny the similarities found in Trudeau's Pulitzer Prize–winning comic strip.

"Lacey had a boyfriend from Yale," said Canis, "and that prompted Millicent to tell a story about someone she knew from Yale who was just like the character. . . . It was like Garry Trudeau had a semiconductor chip into Millicent Fenwick's brain."[14] Despite the undeniable similarities between Lacey Davenport and Millicent Fenwick, Garry Trudeau said, "A benign secret that Millicent Fenwick and I shared was the fact that I created the character of Lacey Davenport before I was aware that there was a real-life Congresswoman whom she resembled, and who resembled her. The coincidence pleased us both I think."[15]

"I like Lacey Davenport," said Millicent. "I think she's truthful. She's not self-important. She's not vindictive. Sometimes I can hear the cadence of my own voice in what Lacey says."[16] "We're all comic figures," said Millicent, "and some of us are more comic than others. It [*Doonesbury*] doesn't bother me a bit."[17] Amused by the likeness, Millicent's staff proudly plastered their office walls with Lacey Davenport cartoons.

In 1977, Lacey, like Millicent, was a member of the Committee on Standards of Official Conduct, better known as the Ethics Committee. "No one really likes being on that Ethics Committee," said Fenwick. "But if you're on it and you haven't got the stomach for following leads where they take you, then you should get off."[18] Fenwick and the eleven other committee members had the unenviable task of investigating their peers involved in Koreagate, a scandal in which members of Congress were accused of accepting gifts and bribes from South Korean government officials in exchange for favorable policy decisions.

Not everyone on the Ethics Committee was pleased to see Lacey assigned the same challenge. Rep. Floyd Spence (R-South Carolina) noted that Congress did not "have a PR firm to defend the [Ethics] committee and it's very frustrating to deal with the misconceptions people get from reading something like that cartoonist [Trudeau]."[19]

In 1981, *60 Minutes* aired a flattering profile of Millicent Fenwick aptly titled "Thoroughly Modern Millicent." Morley Safer, the *60 Minutes* correspondent, introduced the segment, saying, "This old-fashioned lady is also a thoroughly modern woman. . . . She is an elegant, literate, dead-honest legislator whose somewhat patrician manner gets on some people's nerves and amuses others. She has often defied the Republican Party line, championing consumer causes, women's rights and civil rights long before they were fashionable."[20] After the story ran, *60 Minutes* was inundated with mail urging Fenwick to run for president, and her national recognition skyrocketed with features in widely read publications such as *People* and *Parade*.

Working for a celebrity politician was sometimes a challenge. "She was a really nutty boss," said Scott Seligman. "Sometimes we learned her position by reading a pinky [carbon copy of her handwritten letters to constituents]."[21] Staff members were a necessary evil. During her first months in office, Millicent often answered the phones herself. When callers asked to speak to one of her staffers about a specific issue, Fenwick would say, "They are too busy. Talk to me."[22]

Her informal management style took some adjusting to. Running the office became the responsibility first of Hollis McLoughlin and then of Larry Rosenshein, her loyal chiefs of staff. They became adept at dealing with the more idiosyncratic aspects of her personality. They also realized that you didn't have conversations with Millicent Fenwick, you listened. But she listened too, particularly to her constituents. Many of the causes she championed in Congress were on behalf of constituents who had been in touch with her about their problems.

David Carter, a constituent whom Fenwick met at a town meeting, told her, "I want to be a trucker but I can't get into the business because of all those interstate commerce regulations."[23] Looking into the matter, Millicent learned that independent owner-operated truckers needed certificates that cost a minimum of $15,000, and they needed to overcome the monopoly larger certified carriers maintained. As a result, there was a booming black market in which certificates were sold for $300,000,[24] making it impossible for independent owner-operated truckers like Carter to break into the business. In June of 1977, Fenwick introduced the Motor Carrier Act of 1977, "which will benefit the consuming public as well as all users of motor carrier services by reforming some of the excessive and outdated regulations of the Interstate Commerce Commission. This legislation," she said, "will stimulate and promote competition in the motor carrier industry, eliminate restrictions requiring wasteful transportation practices, regulate the private sale or transfer of ICC operating certificates and permit the motor carrier industry to adjust to the needs of the consuming public for an efficient and low-cost transportation system."[25] Although the bill did not pass that year, she persisted. In 1979, in testimony before the Senate Commerce Committee she said, "My bill would exempt from the regulation of the Interstate Commerce Commission all food products for human consumption, in the interests of lower food transportation costs and more consistent regulatory policies with regard to our agriculture sector."[26] Fenwick believed that exempting food from regulations would not only lower consumer food prices but would save fuel costs as well. Eventually, her efforts led to the deregulation of the trucking industry.

Alleviating the marriage tax penalty was another cause Fenwick embraced as a result of a constituent. After an op-ed piece appeared in the *Washington Post* entitled "Let's Stop the Tax on Marriage," one woman wrote Fenwick that "she and her husband had married last year and found that they were paying $4,900 *more* in total taxes now than they had when she was single and he was a head of household."[27] Outraged, Fenwick repeatedly submitted legislation, beginning in 1975, to repeal the marriage tax penalty. Again, her thorough research on the matter led her to testify before the Senate Finance Committee's Subcommittee on Taxation and Debt Management. By 1981, Fenwick's bill to eliminate the marriage tax was incorporated into the income tax bill and "eliminated what the Justice Department called the most glaring example of sex discrimination in the U.S. tax code."[28] Ranking GOP Representative Barber Conable of the House Ways and Means Committee said, "Mrs. Fenwick took up the cause of the many taxpayers who had to pay this extra levy . . . [and] with more and more married men and women entering the work force, we should express our gratitude to Mrs. Fenwick for her efforts to reduce the penalty and make our tax laws fairer."[29]

Always the voice of reason, when she learned about the health problems plaguing asbestos workers in her district employed at the Johns-Manville Corporation—an industrial manufacturer specializing in insulation products and fiberglass—Fenwick felt the need to protect them. She repeatedly introduced legislation to establish an asbestos victims compensation fund, but "it was dead on arrival," said Larry Rosenshein. "The trial lawyers opposed it and a powerful attorney made money on the backs of asbestos victims."[30]

If the House was in session, Fenwick was there. "She thought that was her job," said Rosenshein.[31] *Congressional Quarterly* reported that Fenwick had a 99 percent roll-call attendance rate.[32] Although she rarely missed a vote and could not be counted on to vote with her party, she felt a sense of duty to enter into the *Congressional Record* whether she was for or against bills that were voted on in her absence. Virtually the only things that kept her from voting were funerals and congressional trips.[33]

Special-interest groups routinely rate members of Congress, basing the ratings on legislation relating to their particular causes. Fenwick's voting record was often unpredictable. The GOP could not count on her. By 1981, however, she was voting more conservatively. She usually received low scores (averaging 35 percent) from the American Conservative Union, but in 1981 she received a 73 percent favorable rating.[34] Yet she continued to receive high marks from the League of Women Voters (80 percent); the League of Conservation Voters (94 percent); and the National Association for the Advancement of Colored People (91 percent).[35] She received perfect scores from Friends of the Earth and Common Cause.[36]

She consistently drew high marks from women's groups for her pro-choice stance, a position that prompted a flood of letters from right-to-life groups beginning with her election to the state assembly in 1969. She would write back, "I don't think anyone likes the idea of abortion, but I have come to the conclusion that when two reputable groups of citizens feel so strongly about a subject the State should make it possible for each person to follow the guidance of his conscience and his religion."[37] Steadfast about women, not the government, deciding what to do in that situation, she continued to express her opposition to conservative attempts to limit choice in America. "Mr. Chairman," she said to Henry Hyde on the House floor, "I determined never to speak again on this subject, but I cannot stay silent. You do not stop abortions by laws. You merely drive it somewhere else, and this has been proved in country after country. You are not going to stop it." She was protesting an amendment that would prohibit federal funds from being used for abortions unless the life of the mother was endangered if the fetus was carried to term.[38]

"I think I bewildered her," said Hyde. "She couldn't understand how I could be pro-life. She would ask rhetorical questions like, 'How could you?' but that didn't interfere with our friendship. We became friends even though we had different philosophies about issues," he said. "We used to exchange quotations. One she taught me was: 'We proud men pompously compete for nameless grades, while some fondling of fate forges his way into immortality.' I think that was a Wendell Phillips quote. She was always tossing these literary gems off and I was always eagerly listening."[39]

Active on agriculture issues as well, Fenwick voted against subsidies that would raise consumer prices—a 50-cent increase on the price of a ten-pound bag of sugar was unacceptable by her standards. Legislation she supported included the establishment of an Agricultural Land Review Commission to protect agricultural land from being used for nonagricultural purposes. She also weighed in on debates concerning the price of milk and a minimum 80 percent of parity dairy price support level. Viewing the legislation from the vantage of a consumer and a former dairy farmer Fenwick said, "I think it [the Federal price program] is probably necessary. I was a milk farmer. I used to produce 4 percent butterfat, 10,000 bacteria count, certified milk under the laws of the State of New Jersey, so I know something about it. But I do think as good as the Federal support program might be, the freedom of individual producers to sell within his own State at whatever he thinks is proper should not constitute a criminal act or a misdemeanor or any other kind of an offense. I wish our Federal support program would say we support it under those conditions. Maybe next year."[40]

Upset by congressional pay raises, Fenwick said, "I had been trained in Trenton, where you cannot benefit from something you vote for, so I tried to get them [the U.S. government] not to pay me the raise. They wouldn't do that, so every month I had to return the money to the Treasury, because we had been elected in November and we voted this in February and it took effect in March. I mean it was outrageous."[41] Not many of her peers agreed. On at least one occasion she took to the House floor and denounced the congressional pay raise. "She thought it was terrible and advocated for a pay cut," said Hyde. "The gallery applauded, but I was immediately offended. I wondered why people whose bank account reached into the millions advocated for a cut in my pay? She took great offense to my remarks and she came over and took a swipe at my hand. As soon as that happened the press gathered and Millicent realized it was becoming a bigger thing than either of us wanted it to be. And she said to me, 'I am not leaving until you give me a hug.' And so I gave the gentlewoman a hug," remembered Hyde.[42]

Beginning in her first term, Fenwick returned $2,625 to the U.S. Treasury, representing the salary increase passed after her election. Then, in 1978, Congress voted itself another raise, increasing congressional salaries from $44,000 to $57,500. The *New York Times* reported that Fenwick wrote a check for the difference, $12,900, and sent it to the U.S. Treasury.[43] In reality, she usually reimbursed the government quarterly and in response always received a letter from the clerk of the U.S. House of Representatives acknowledging receipt of her "gift to the United States Treasury."[44] As reported by Morley Safer: "Since '74, she's returned more than $450,000 to the Treasury in unspent office expenses. She's given back another $35,000 in congressional raises she felt uncomfortable about."[45]

From the moment Fenwick entered Congress she advocated campaign finance reform to an unresponsive chamber. "Do you know that any member of Congress can accept any amount of money from anyone? From a foreign government!" she said. "We've got to change that. . . . And slush funds. Where a Congressman merely pockets any money left over from a campaign. It's shocking!"[46] To support her claims against PAC money she said, "2,551 special interest groups contributed $55.3 million to congressional candidates in 1980 and [by 1982], 3,479 PAC's are estimated to be giving $80 million."[47] She said, "The only strength of our government really basically is if the people have confidence."[48]

She funneled her outrage and introduced legislation to restore justice to the campaign-financing process and to minimize what she considered an unnecessary increase in congressional benefits and pay. "I believe that it is time that we bring full accountability and open procedures to any salary and benefit raise for Congress. Our present system consistently strengthens the public's worst suspicions about the ethical standards of the House," she said. "I am offering two measures that raise the standards that the public so deeply deplores. The first bill would prohibit all automatic salary adjustments for Members of Congress. The second bill would ensure that all Members will be accountable for any increase in financial benefits. Both bills provide for an open, recorded vote and delay the effective date of any increase in salary or financial benefit to the next Congress, requiring Members to face re-election before receiving additional compensation."[49] As might have been expected, she garnered little support.

As a result of Fenwick's individual stands and unpredictable party allegiance, not everyone was a Fenwick fan. "Petty people enjoyed ridiculing and criticizing her," said Representative Tom Lantos (D-California). "Millicent was fully aware that people ridiculed her and she could not care less. They did not like her lack of partisanship nor did they like her pipe-smoking. . . . Those who liked Millicent viewed her pipe-smoking as an attribute to her independence and was an added twist to their love for her, others viewed it as a physical manifestation of her absurdity. The more intelligent, the more sophisticated, the more serious, the more thoughtful, the more well informed the member of Congress, the higher regard they had for her. Millicent was the quintessential public servant . . . always arrived early . . . so unconventional . . . so untypical."[50]

In 1980, seventy-year-old Millicent Fenwick ran against a twenty-six-year-old lawyer, Kieran Pillion Jr. "He said I won't bring up the issue of age unless she does," recalled Fenwick.[51] The amicable duo capped their campaign spending at $22,500. This time Millicent captured nearly 80 percent of the vote, her biggest victory yet. Among the freshmen in Congress that year was Tom Lantos, a Holocaust survivor. "When I first came to Congress there were two friends that Annette [his wife] and I made right away—Al Gore and Millicent Fenwick," he said.[52] Fenwick and Lantos met through Gore's Futures Caucus, but their friendship blossomed through serving together on the Foreign Affairs Committee.

By 1981, war was about to break out between Israel and Lebanon, and Lantos was very concerned about it. "I spent the night discussing this with my wife, and I concluded [that] . . . I was going to go to Israel the next day to talk to the Israeli leadership," he said. Because he was a Democrat he felt he should not go alone, and he wanted a Republican to come. He decided to ask Fenwick. The next morning he found her on the House floor. He walked up to her, and said, "'Millicent, listen to me carefully. There is a very serious possibility of war breaking out and we can try and prevent it. . . . I am leaving this afternoon and I want you to go home, pack what you need, and come with me.' And she looked at me as if this was an invitation to coffee in the afternoon in a restaurant and she said, 'Tom, do you really think this is important?' I said, 'Yes.' And, she said, 'I'll go home and pack my suitcase.'"[53]

So the freshman member and the idiosyncratic member flew to Israel. First they saw Foreign Minister Yitzhak Shamir, and then they saw Prime Minister Menachem Begin. Begin's office was two flights up in an old stone building. It was very hot as they climbed the stairs, and Fenwick asked Lantos to pause because she had a pacemaker and needed to rest. "I did not know until that moment that she had a pacemaker," said Lantos. Once they climbed the stairs, they had a "terrific meeting with Begin. . . . In the end we did not succeed [in preventing the war], but we did make our points."[54]

After the meetings, Lantos bought Millicent a huge umbrella to provide her with some shade from the hundred-plus degree heat. As they walked along the streets of Jerusalem, Lantos said something about all the changes in Israel, and Fenwick said, "I wouldn't know." It was her first trip to Israel. Learning that, Lantos showed her the sights. They went to the Wailing Wall, Temple Mount, and the Dome of the Rock. Between the meetings, sight seeing, and excruciating heat, Millicent was not well. Afterward, Lantos felt guilty for not realizing how fragile her health was and asking her to come on the trip. "I should not have asked her, but in the end we were both glad we went. I don't want to be overly dramatic, but she literally put her life on the line [to go] . . . she was unbelievably thin. No other member would have done it," said Lantos.[55]

Lantos admired Fenwick so much that, he said, "when I disagreed with her I felt unclean and immediately would go home and take a shower because on those very rare occasions when I voted the other way, I knew I was wrong because she always voted on principle."[56]

# 14

## *Seeking*

## *the Senate*

The 1982 elections have become a watershed for women candidates in New Jersey, thanks to Rep. Millicent Fenwick of Bernardsville. Whether or not she wins the Republican primary for the U.S. Senate on June 8, Mrs. Fenwick has become the first woman candidate whose strong presence has dictated political strategy in both parties during a campaign.

—Joseph F. Sullivan, *New York Times,* May 23, 1982

In 1981, Democrats dominated New Jersey's political scene. They held not only the governorship but also the majority in the state legislature. When new congressional boundaries needed to be drawn, based on the 1980 census, it was the Democrats who were in control. As a result of the census data, New Jersey was losing a congressional seat. Instead of fifteen congressional districts there would be fourteen. *The Almanac of American Politics* reported, "New Jersey deserves the award for the least aesthetically pleasing redistricting plan of 1981–82. It is, plain and simple, a Democratic gerrymandering, passed by the Democratic legislature in the last days of Brendan Byrne's governorship."[1] Once the new boundaries were drawn, Republicans lost two seats, one in Bergen County and the other in Somerset County. The latter was Millicent's congressional district. Parts of her district and the districts of two other Republicans, Matt Rinaldo and Jim Courter, were absorbed into the redrawn Fifth, Seventh, and Twelfth Districts. Much of Fenwick's old Fifth District, including Bernardsville, was now part of the Twelfth District, as was Rinaldo's hometown, Union. Although Rinaldo and Fenwick lived in the new Twelfth District, neither sought office there. Instead, Rinaldo ran in the Seventh District, which encompassed much of his constituency. Fenwick, on the other hand, decided to run for the Senate, leaving Courter to wage a successful primary campaign against Rodney Frelinghuysen, the son of Peter Frelinghuysen who had represented Fenwick's congressional district for twenty-two years before resigning in 1974. Rodney Frelinghuysen was elected to Congress in 1994. Prior to his election to Congress, he had been a member of the New Jersey assembly, and before that he served as a Morris County freeholder.

In 1982, New Jersey had an open Senate seat because of the resignation of Democrat Harrison Williams. After twenty-three years in the Senate and three terms in the House, Williams left office with a marred reputation. He had been convicted of bribery charges related to an FBI investigation, later known as Abscam, which led to the indictment of seven members of Congress. Williams's resignation in March of 1982 caused a flood of hopeful candidates to emerge and provided an opportunity for Governor Tom Kean to appoint someone to finish Williams's term, which ended that November. Two months earlier Fenwick had declared her Senate candidacy, and some had speculated that Kean would appoint her to fill the vacant seat. "I would love to be appointed," Millicent said. "It'd mean the governor thought I'd be a good candidate. . . . Whatever he decide[s] is okay with me," she said. "No hard feelings. I'm not counting on it."[2] That was good, because Kean appointed investment banker Nicholas Brady, a Republican who later became U.S. treasury secretary under President George H. W. Bush. "Kean chose Brady," said Hollis McLoughlin, who worked for Brady when he was in the Senate, "because both Millicent Fenwick and Jeff Bell had supported his gubernatorial campaign. Kean decided to let the primary determine the Republican candidate; he was above the fray."[3]

From the outset, the redistricting plan concerned Fenwick. "I am truly distressed. . . . It appears that my district will be terribly torn up. To be quite honest with you, I feel shaken. If they would just leave me alone in my beloved Fifth District, I don't think I'd even think about the Senate."[4] But she did, and political strategist John Deardourff encouraged her. Deardourff had managed Kean's successful 1981 gubernatorial campaign. Polls conducted by pollster Bob Teeter field-tested questions about the possibility of Fenwick running for the Senate. The results were favorable. When Deardourff saw her he told her about the poll, hoping she would seriously consider the possibility.

While Fenwick toyed with the idea, she sought guidance from many of her political cohorts. Ray Bateman, a senior member of the state senate and an unsuccessful GOP gubernatorial candidate in 1977, was among those who felt Millicent should not run. He candidly told her that he did not think that becoming a senator would make her more effective than she was as a representative. He noted what many other people thought:

she was widely recognized and one of the few members who was able to make a name for herself among the 435 members of the House of Representatives. With her best interests in mind, Bateman, explained what it was like to run a statewide campaign as opposed to a local campaign. He told her of the physical and emotional toll a statewide contest has on an individual, regardless of age.[5] Yet on Thanksgiving Day in 1981, Millicent, in bed with a cold, wrote in her journal, "I lie here now, 71 years old, wondering endlessly whether or nor to run for the Senate next year. I've never thought I was ambitious, but is it pushing me now? Why not just retire?"[6]

Many others, including Hollis McLoughlin, echoed Bateman's sentiments. Aware of her inner circle's hesitation about her candidacy, Millicent was challenged. She wanted to run, and not just because she thought she could win, but because she felt she could serve the people of New Jersey better in the Senate, which had a Republican majority, than in the House, which did not. She wanted a broader platform to showcase issues such as human rights, social security, and health care. For the first time, she was openly ambitious. She dismissed the advice of those she trusted and plowed forward, announcing her candidacy in January 1982. She did so somewhat blindly, not even calling all of the twenty-one county chairmen for input. At the time of her announcement she had raised no money, unheard of before such a decision, nor had she attended many events outside her district. What prompted her into action was her Republican challenger, Jeffrey Bell, a young, ambitious issue-oriented conservative. Bell had sent ripples through New Jersey politics in the 1978 GOP primary when he defeated four-term Senator Clifford Case. Shocked, Fenwick said, "My God, this is a rough game. Twenty-four years of an unblemished record. . . . To be down here 24 years. . . . Never had we cause to be ashamed of that man. . . . Maybe that's it. Why didn't he campaign harder?"[7]

Bell's 1978 primary win helped pave the way to victory in the general election for his Democratic opponent, political novice Bill Bradley. Bradley defeated Bell in a close contest. It would have been much more difficult for Bradley to unseat incumbent Case than Bell, also a newcomer on the New Jersey political scene. Case and Fenwick were both Rockefeller Republicans. It was by working on Case's campaigns in the 1950s and 1960s that Millicent was first exposed to life on the campaign trail. In 1982, it was time for her to even the score against Bell. She felt that if the GOP was considering the conservative Bell as the nominee, it was headed in the wrong direction. That, combined with the data from Deardourff, propelled her forward.

Bell had worked with Ronald Reagan during his last year as governor of California and had also worked in Reagan's 1976 presidential primary campaign. After Ford secured the 1976 GOP nomination, Bell moved to New Jersey, set on unseating the popular Case, a liberal Republican. Bell, who had lived in New Jersey on and off during his childhood, thought that "New Jersey [was] a good state for someone with very few connections—it was amorphous."[8] He felt the parties were not that powerful and that an insurgent could emerge victorious. Bell's plan worked in 1978, startling the state in the process. He won the primary by tapping into the conservative base of the GOP and focusing on the economy. When he lost the general election to Bradley, Bell had every intention of running again in 1982.

Bell focused his campaign against Fenwick around economic issues, much as he had done against Case. In 1982, the U.S. economy was struggling, unemployment was reaching double digits, and interest rates were out of control, causing an economic downturn in New Jersey and the rest of the country. Bell advocated supply-side economics—tax cuts, particularly among the wealthy, which would lead to increased spending and jumpstart the economy.

To offset Fenwick's popularity, Bell sought to align himself with his former boss, Ronald Reagan, who had been elected to the presidency two years earlier in 1980. Bell said, "You don't try to compete with the charm of somebody like [Fenwick]." Instead, he ran radio ads that painted her as a liberal who "would be Reagan's greatest Republican opponent in the Senate." This was a drastically different tactic than Millicent had faced in her amicable congressional races. Responding to Bell's attack ads she said, "I've never been in a thing like this. It takes your breath away. I'm not as mild a person as I would like to be, but you might as well not get down in the mud."[9]

To counter Bell's five-week advertising campaign, Fenwick was forced to spend close to $500,000 dollars of her own money to air her message in the expensive New York and Philadelphia media markets. Bell spent $2 million in his effort to secure the nomination. "I had comparison attacks that tried to paint her as a moderate liberal. That was in contrast to my campaign against Case," said Bell. "Fenwick was willing to give ground on issues . . . which made it harder to set her up as a protagonist because, nominally, she was in favor of a number of the issues [like Reagan's tax cut] I was in favor of. Case was not."[10]

Bell, an issue activist, had aligned himself with Reaganomics. No amount of planning could have helped him overcome the faltering economy. "I had four years to strategize," said Bell. "I was known as an early advocate of Reaganomics. My main identity was as an issue activist in supply-side economics. That brand of economics was seen as a complete failure in 1982. The country was in a recession, unemployment shot up to 11 percent . . . the economy knocked down my strategy, which was identifying myself with Reaganomics, which in 1982 was putting people out of work."[11]

Bell was an effective campaigner, and as primary day approached, the race was too close to call. Fenwick received some help from her colleagues in Washington, fifty-three of whom endorsed her. "Endorsements themselves are hardly the stuff of headlines in Washington," said Representative Olympia Snowe (R-Maine). "But never in my experience have so many members of Congress come together for a pre-primary endorsement of a candidate. The reason for this unusual display of support can be summed up in two words: Millicent Fenwick."[12]

In the end, Bell was unable to overcome the combination of a weak economy and a strong personality. As Bell said, "If it had been a personality contest it would be hopeless. . . . No one could hold a candle to her personality because you wouldn't have a prayer against her."[13] On primary day, Fenwick maintained her unblemished election record. "The Millicent magic was just too much," said Bell.[14] "It was a heck of a challenge, enjoyable in certain ways, exasperating in others—especially the outcome. She was a character, she was very hard to dislike. She was very competitive in her own way. She wanted to win very badly, the anomaly we've been talking about is why she didn't put more money in the campaign because my impression was she badly wanted to win," he noted later.[15] Unfortunately, Clifford Case did not live to see Millicent's victory over Bell; he died three months before the primary.

---

While Fenwick focused on the GOP primary, her Democratic opponent survived a crowded field of nine Democrats vying for the vacant Senate seat. One contestant was Barbara Boggs Sigmund, a Mercer County freeholder, daughter of Representatives Lindy Boggs and Hale Boggs and sister of TV news commentator Cokie Roberts. Sigmund was persuaded to abandon her House campaign and enter the Senate primary because the Democrats thought Sigmund would offset Millicent's appeal by neutralizing the gender issue. What the Democrats didn't realize was that while some of the nine candidates had a strong political base, only Frank Lautenberg had a thick wallet. Democratic fund-raising was more difficult in New Jersey following Senator Williams's Abscam conviction and Jim Florio's narrow 1981 gubernatorial loss to Kean, making Lautenberg's ability and willingness to spend his own money more appealing.

Lautenberg, born and raised in New Jersey, the son of immigrant Jews, was a self-proclaimed success story. In 1952, he joined Automatic Data Processing (ADP), a payroll processing company founded in 1949. ADP flourished primarily by processing payrolls. At the time of the Senate race, ADP dominated the market and processed paychecks for one out of every fourteen nongovernment workers nationwide.[16] Lautenberg helped build ADP from a company of five people to one that employed fifteen thousand. By 1982, ADP was a multimillion-dollar company and Lautenberg was extremely wealthy, with an estimated worth of $14 million. When he entered the Democratic primary he was the chief executive officer of ADP. He was married, had four children, and lived in Montclair in Essex County. Because he was a political newcomer he was viewed as a long shot. Although this race was his introduction into politics as a candidate he was no stranger to the political process. In 1972, he managed to secure a place on Richard Nixon's so-called enemies list when he contributed $90,000 to George McGovern's presidential campaign and served on his campaign finance committee.[17]

Lautenberg, a major donor to Jewish causes, was national chairman of the United Jewish Appeal, a nonprofit organization committed to improving the quality of Jewish life worldwide. His philanthropic efforts gained him political leverage and recognition. In 1978, Governor Brendan Byrne appointed Lautenberg to the Port Authority of New York and New Jersey Commission. That appointment was as close as he had come to elected office. With no races under his belt he had little party support in the primary.

To win the Democratic primary Lautenberg knew he had to achieve name recognition and link it to his political stances on major issues. He accomplished this in part by purchasing a full-page ad strategically placed in the New Jersey section of the Sunday edition of the *New York Times* ten days before the primary. The banner headline was clear: "For New Jersey, the economy *is* the issue." What followed was an open letter to the voters of New Jersey in which Lautenberg introduced himself and his issues. His message was clear. He understood the economy and how to provide jobs for the state. The ad defined what became the major campaign issue—jobs.

Just as Bell made the economy an issue in the Republican race, Lautenberg did the same in the Democratic contest. Lautenberg highlighted his success at ADP and the company's four thousand New Jersey employees. His business skills, team of experts, and money helped promote his name. By the time of the June primary, Lautenberg had secured endorsements from Democratic leaders in Essex, Middlesex, and Passaic counties. Because of his high visibility and no-holds-barred campaign style, he represented a hurdle the rest of the field had to overcome. Many of his challengers berated him as a politically inexperienced millionaire trying to buy his way into the political system, but Lautenberg was proud of his success. He felt he had earned his millions, and the right to spend them at his discretion.

New Jersey was unique in that the state provided matching funds to candidates who raised more than $50,000 in private contributions. This was one reason that Lautenberg found himself in such a crowded primary field. What made him stand out among the pack was his ample budget. He spent close to $2 million on his primary campaign, with more than $1 million coming from his personal bank account. It paid off. On primary day, Lautenberg received 37 percent of the vote, edging out former Representative Andrew Maguire of Ridgewood (who had been elected to Congress in 1974 and won two more reelections before being voted out of office in 1980), who had 33 percent, and Joseph LeFante of Bayonne, who had 30 percent. Barbara Boggs Sigmund finished fourth. The other five candidates lagged in the distance.

After Lautenberg survived the first round of his political quest he found himself in a battle that the *New York Times* characterized as Lacey Davenport versus Horatio Alger. Lautenberg had to overcome Fenwick's name recognition and undeniable charm. One analyst said "running against her [Fenwick] is like trying to debate Katharine Hepburn." Early indications showed Fenwick ahead in the polls with a 50 percent to 32 percent lead over Lautenberg and 18 percent of voters undecided.[18] Fenwick was the odds-on favorite to capture the vacant Senate seat.

As Lautenberg gathered support, one of his primary opponents, Barbara Boggs Sigmund, began stumping for him on television. "New Jersey needs in the Senate, someone like Frank Lautenberg who understands the economy, who can promote New Jersey, someone who can bring new industry to New Jersey and someone who could put hundreds of thousands of jobless New Jerseyans back to work," said Sigmund. "Contrast this with . . . Millicent Fenwick who has opposed both the Meadowlands Sports Complex and the resort development in Atlantic City.[19]

Lautenberg was not afraid to go on the offensive against "the pipe-smoking grandmother." He was quick to point out Fenwick's eccentric nature, and she was quick to highlight his lack of a political record. As this dogfight moved into the fall it attracted national attention. A snapshot of the race was captured by reporter Brit Hume of ABC *World News Tonight*. "There is nobody like her in American politics, a genteel, proper, elderly, and elegant lady who goes around calling everybody 'Dear.' She also smokes a pipe and while she may look as if she belongs in a Mercedes, her own car is a battered old Chevy. She inspired the character Lacey Davenport in the *Doonesbury* cartoon strip, which has added much to her celebrity," said Hume. "New Jersey seems crazy about Millicent Fenwick and the polls now say she is eighteen points ahead in her race for the Senate after four terms in the House. The recession has hit this industrial state hard and Mrs. Fenwick has largely backed the Reagan economic program. Indeed, the President said, on a widely publicized recent visit here, that he and Fenwick stand shoulder to shoulder. Her

Democratic opponent, self-made millionaire and political newcomer Frank Lautenberg, is campaigning with heavy labor support on one issue, jobs, and he's spending more than two and a half million dollars, much of it his own, to make himself known."[20]

With each campaign appearance, Lautenberg emphasized jobs and his ability to deliver them. His campaign manager, Tim Ridley, put it best when he said, "We had been talking about jobs for four weeks. Before the unemployment figure came out [10% unemployment for the first time since the 1930s], about 30% of the people said jobs was the most important issue. After the figure was released, it was up to 50% [in our polls]."[21] Fenwick only aided Lautenberg by conceding that employment was the number-one issue. "It reminded voters of the shortcomings of the President's economic programs without mentioning the accomplishments. Since Fenwick's concern over jobs was not accompanied by a convincing program to deal with unemployment, Lautenberg's argument that he was the candidate better qualified to deal with this problem was made more believable," said Steven Salmore, Fenwick's pollster.[22]

With jobs solidified as the leading campaign issue, Lautenberg went on the attack. He brought up Fenwick's voting record on unemployment and linked her votes to a loss of 80,000 jobs in the state. He portrayed himself as a provider of jobs and cast her as someone who had curbed employment. Fenwick poorly defended her voting record and admitted that she was not an economist. She said she could only "pray" for Reaganomics to work and forwarded few proposals to alleviate unemployment.[23] Lautenberg knew her weaknesses and her inability to combat such highly charged accusations.

Without political experience, Lautenberg focused on his business expertise. In 1982, unemployment reached its highest level in forty-two years, and the zealous media coverage caused many to fear for their own job security. In this economically insecure environment, Lautenberg appealed to voters because he underscored the importance of job creation. At the same time, newspapers portrayed Millicent as a personality rather than a politician. They concentrated on her patrician background and pipe-smoking than on her political stances. Although Fenwick had both personality and substance, the press was captivated by the former and chose to ignore the latter. For example, a *Wall Street Journal* article opened with, "Millicent Fenwick, the front-running Republican Senate candidate, is rallying against using tax dollars for so many public-works projects," and continued by explaining she was from a "superaffluent" community that had more "polo ponies than poor people." Before focusing on the issue at hand, the article digressed to Millicent's persona. "Millicent Fenwick may be unique in American politics. She is a 72-year-old, pipe-smoking patrician who wears a heart pacemaker and rarely works less than 12 hours a day. She is fashionably feisty and eminently quotable. She is the authentic model for Lacey Davenport, the colorful dowager and member of Congress in satirist Garry Trudeau's comic strip 'Doonesbury.' . . . Politicians and voters agree her appeal is extraordinary. 'She's a character . . . a once-in-a-lifetime sort of candidate,' suggests Bill McDowell, the GOP chairman in populous Bergen County. Janet Spiller, a household-products distributor in Edison, enthusiastically volunteers: 'She doesn't pull any punches. People are just intrigued by her.'"[24]

To help get her message out, Fenwick published a collection of her verbal and written commentary. The idea came from Robin Reynolds, a Harper & Row editor.[25] Conceived before Millicent decided to run for the Senate, the publication was well timed and well titled. *Speaking Up*, published in 1982, was Fenwick's first book since her 1948 *Vogue's Book of Etiquette*, and it was vintage Millicent. Her words danced off the pages and presented a vivid picture of her opinions. A reviewer for the *Washington Post Book Review* wrote, "Rarely has so much been endorsed or deplored in so few pages."[26] The book was organized into four categories: "Freedom and Self-Discipline," "The Business of Government," "Congressional Reform—A View from the Inside," and "Foreign Affairs." Norman Cousins, author and longtime editor of the *Saturday Review*, wrote in the foreword, "Millicent Fenwick is a thinking person who believes in the importance of ideas and who seeks to relate the national interest to the human interest. Her book is as much a tribute to the people who make it possible for her to serve the American community as a whole as it is to her own independence of mind and action."[27]

———

Fenwick's independence hindered her campaign. As in the past, she steadfastly refused PAC money because of her moral principles and unwillingness to feel compromised by accepting such funds. When it came to campaign finance reform, Millicent was one politician who practiced what she preached and it affected her campaign. She was at a disadvantage against Lautenberg, who accepted PAC money. Not only was his campaign successful in securing sizable contributions, but his personal campaign war chest was nine million dollars greater than Millicent's. Most of her money was tied up in trust funds for her children, and she was reluctant to spend her liquid assets. Lautenberg was not.

Fenwick had already spent more than she intended just to win the primary and she had no desire to see her campaign costs continue to skyrocket in the general election. She approached Lautenberg about capping their campaign spending at $800,000. He refused. Fenwick made a second offer, raising the figure to $1.7 million dollars. Again she was rebuffed. Lautenberg believed a spending limit would "deprive New Jersey voters of a full, fair, and balanced airing of the issues."[28] In previous contests Millicent had easily secured agreements from her challengers to limit campaign spending. This race was not like the others.

As Lautenberg said, "Because she's a character, Mrs. Fenwick gets all sorts of free publicity. I'm going to spend whatever it takes to catch up."[29] And he did. He spent money on print, radio, and television advertising, but he still lagged in the polls. It was generally believed that Fenwick would join Paula Hawkins (R-Florida) and Nancy Kassenbaum (R-Kansas) as the third woman in the Senate during the 98th Congress.

A few weeks after Fenwick's primary victory, Bailey, Deardourff & Associates, her political consultants, were fired because her advisers thought Deardourff had too many candidates. "[Fenwick] agreed to it, but was not the one who forced the issue," said Hollis McLoughlin.[30] The campaign advisers felt they needed more attention to better counter Lautenberg's verbal attacks, media blitz, and unlimited funds. Nicholas Brady telephoned John Deardourff and fired his firm with no warning. Deardourff had encouraged Fenwick to run for the Senate. It was his firm that guided her to her close primary victory over Bell. Deardourff had met with Hollis McLoughlin, Julius Mastro, and other Fenwick confidants, but not with Brady. The firing itself was symbolic of the conflict within her campaign. Larry Rosenshein, Fenwick's campaign manager, had expressed his disappointment to McLoughlin about the lack of personal attention Deardourff had given Fenwick's campaign, but "I never intended for Deardourff to be fired," said Rosenshein.[31] Without consulting Rosenshein, a decision was made to switch consultants. Deardourff was shocked. "Since our first discussion almost a year ago about your running," wrote Deardourff to Fenwick, "I have done everything I could both to encourage you to make the race and to help insure its success. It seems self-serving to say so, but without our participation in the primary campaign, I believe it would have failed. . . . [This] coupled with the earlier decision to drop Bob Teeter, a prominent Republican pollster . . . I am afraid that your chances for success have been impaired. There is now *no one* associated with the campaign who has had significant successful experience (without outside professional help) in the kind of campaign you face." Despite his bruised feelings he wrote, "There is no campaign anywhere that means more to me than yours." And if anyone doubted that, all they needed to do was read the next two pages in which Deardourff offered his unsolicited advice. He told Fenwick to spend more money; not to get too comfortable with her lead in the polls; match her opponent's media bombardment; and recognize some of the shortcomings of her staff.[32]

Changing political consulting firms midstream was a risky decision, although it was clearly meant to ensure victory. Smith & Harroff were hired to do just that. Partners Jay Smith, a former press secretary to House Minority Leader John Rhodes (R-Arizona), and Mark Harroff, a former press secretary to Representative Peter Frelinghuysen, had a strong local and national reputation. In 1980, they helped Representative Marge Roukema (R-New Jersey) unseat incumbent Andrew Maguire. During the 1982 campaign cycle, Smith & Harroff's clients included Roukema and fellow New Jersey Representative Matt Rinaldo. Nationally they represented John Sununu and John McCain, both of whom won their races for governor of New Hampshire and congressman from Arizona, respectively.

By the time Smith & Harroff took over the campaign it was already mid-July. Mark Harroff, who took the lead, needed to earn the trust of Millicent's staff and to understand the campaign issues, positions, and strategies—a daunting task in a fast-paced campaign. He had less than four months to deliver a win.

Harroff soon realized there was virtually no political director and no political staff. Millicent's campaign staff quickly dismissed attempts to bring in a proven outsider as political director. Harroff found the campaign to be in a disastrous state of disorganization, and his efforts to improve it were largely ignored. Despite the internal strife, Fenwick maintained a two-to-one lead in the polls according to the Eagleton Institute of Politics at Rutgers University.[33]

One area that Harroff set out to improve was the volunteer base. While the campaign had plenty of volunteers eager to help, Harroff felt they were underutilized because the campaign failed to provide the framework for an active volunteer organization. While volunteers aimlessly flitted in and out of Fenwick's headquarters in Warren, none remembered a visit from the candidate. Essentially, volunteers, a critical part of any campaign, went unnoticed. This marked a drastic change from Fenwick's previous campaigns, in which she had been a visible presence. Part of the problem was Fenwick herself. She refused to leave Washington if Congress was in session.

While Fenwick's campaign was in a state of flux, Lautenberg had assembled a top-notch team, including Robert Squier to head the media campaign. Squier understood the unique disposition of New Jersey's multimedia market. In 1982, New Jersey was one of only two states that did not have its own television station. New Jerseyans relied on media outlets in New York City and Philadelphia for their evening news. As a result, coverage of New Jersey races often took a back seat to campaigns in those cities. Since nightly news coverage was limited, New Jersey candidates had to spend money to get on television. New York was one of the costliest advertising markets in the country, but that did not deter the Lautenberg campaign, which embarked on a well-planned advertising blitz that deluged the New York and Philadelphia airwaves.

Lautenberg's first round of ads presented his humble background and business success. Negativity was the core of his second round. Fenwick was portrayed as "anti-jobs" because she opposed the Meadowlands sports complex and casino gambling, both of which would create in-state jobs. The ads showed a clip of Millicent saying, "I'm beginning to think industries should go to Ohio or Nevada."[34]

Meanwhile, Fenwick was unwilling to spend the kind of money needed in this high-octane political environment. Larry Rosenshein and Hollis McLoughlin tried to impress upon her the importance of advertising as Lautenberg's third wave hit the air. These ads chastised Fenwick for her votes "against" social security and student loans and "flip-flops" on a nuclear freeze and the balanced budget amendment. Lautenberg even attacked her as anti-black, anti-gay, anti-women, and anti-environment. These negative, and inaccurate ads saturated and impacted the voting public. Squier explained his strategy: "We learned early on that a few attacks on her simply were not believed. Her image was too strong; people rejected what we were saying . . . so we produced an inordinate amount of negative commercials on a variety of issues, and even paid commercial rates to get them aired."[35] The negative ads succeeded in creating public doubt about Fenwick and forced her to go on the defensive. Plans for Fenwick ads changed from a positive perspective promoting her accomplishments to a defensive tone countering Lautenberg's attacks.

Fenwick herself exacerbated the situation. When questioned about Lautenberg's charges that she was essentially a racist, Fenwick responded, "The people of New Jersey know my record." But they did not. Her retort resulted in a useless sound bite and a missed opportunity to highlight her work in Newark, tenure on the U.S. Commission of Civil Rights, and her lifetime membership in the NAACP. In another interview, a reporter asked her what her greatest accomplishment was and she said, "The Bernardsville swimming pool." Lautenberg's response was, "If that was her greatest accomplishment, vote for me."[36]

Lautenberg's campaign strategy was to promote himself while discounting Fenwick's credibility. "We ran a fairly hard-hitting campaign against Millicent," said Lautenberg. "She thought the Senate seat was her domain, and she thought I was an unpleasant guy who had no rights to the seat. Millicent had an air of grandeur and station about her. She could easily be described as a blue-blood, elegant in her demeanor."[37]

By the time the campaign reached the home stretch Lautenberg had found a way to effectively question Fenwick's character without making himself look as if he were attacking a lovable grandmother. He subtly introduced her quirky habits and repackaged them: a vote for Fenwick would be a vote for personality, a vote for him would be a vote for substance. Millicent's political celebrity and charm were being used against her. That Lautenberg had overcome Fenwick's celebrity status and name recognition was evident when the pair sparred during their five debates. Fenwick found herself with a formidable challenger and orator. "I sometimes wondered if she knew my name," said Lautenberg.[38] He alluded to her age whenever he could. By 1982, the creamy skin of Fenwick's youth had turned into a well-chiseled face. Despite her prominent wrinkles, Millicent still had an elegant air. Lautenberg, relentless in using her age against her, used Fenwick's creased face as ammunition in his campaign. Poor-quality pictures that accentuated her sagging skin permeated the print and television markets. "In campaigns there are few barriers," said Lautenberg. "The last thing I wanted to do was assault her, but I thought it was important to remind the voters of age because to develop standing [in the Senate], starting out in your seventies, it would be harder to garner seniority and ranking positions."[39]

With Lautenberg's tactics and the poor economy hovering over the country, the Fenwick campaign had a crucial decision to make. Should President Ronald Reagan make a public appearance on Millicent's behalf? Reaganomics was not working, and the campaign was concerned about the president's impact on the independent swing voters Fenwick usually attracted. After weighing the decision, they decided to invite him. They hoped "that the president's tremendous personal appeal, coupled with signs of an improving economy, [would] help more than hurt."[40]

On September 17, 1982, President Reagan's helicopter landed on the Flemington Fairgrounds in central New Jersey. The president had a busy day in the state, presiding over a naturalization ceremony, meeting with Republican state chairmen from eleven states, the District of Columbia, and the Virgin Islands, and attending a Fenwick fund-raiser before speaking at an Italian American festival. He had a hard act to follow—Millicent, who charmed the crowd in her fluent Italian. But Reagan was equally charming. He shared anecdotes with the crowd before addressing more serious matters such as the economy. Presenting an uplifting picture, the president said, "With the help of New Jersey leaders like Millicent Fenwick . . . we brought down inflation, the deadliest tax of all. It was 12.4 percent. A great many people aren't aware [of] that today, and since January, it's only been 5.4 percent. . . . Leading economic indicators, which forecast future economic activity, have been up for four months in a row." In Reagan's speech he announced that the Department of Housing and Urban Development had approved Section 8 funding for 125 units of elderly housing in New Jersey. "And if you don't elect her [Fenwick] Senator, we'll take it away," said the President amid laughter from the crowd.[41] Although the pair differed on issues such as the Equal Rights

Amendment, abortion, and gun control, they both shared a common political goal, for the U.S. Senate to maintain its narrow Republican majority.

When Congress was not in session, Fenwick continued to rely on what she knew best, personal appearances. Few could match her ease in a public forum, but Lautenberg did. Before one of their debates Fenwick's campaign manager, Larry Rosenshein, suggested to her that she might want to dress down, perhaps not wear her pearls. "These pearls were given to me by my sister and I am *not* taking them off," she responded.[42] Nor did she change her persona. As staffer John Schmidt drove her to a debate at a local high school, he saw a crowd of protesters at the entrance. He told Millicent he was going to drive around back, but she insisted on being dropped off at the front where she was met by an antagonistic crowd of Lautenberg and NOW supporters.[43] Although Fenwick was pro-choice, NOW did not support her. "We regret that we cannot support Millicent Fenwick," said Christine Carmody-Arey, NOW's New Jersey coordinator. "I am an affirmative action person, and I want to see more women in the House and Senate. But we insist on qualified people who have a record that we can support. Unfortunately, Millicent Fenwick fails to meet our criteria."[44] That response enraged pro-choice Republicans and independents. Even a pro-life Republican like Henry Hyde was surprised. "Millicent should have been a female senator, she was a feminist dream but NOW endorsed her opponent because they thought a Democrat could do more for them than a woman. That indicated the shallowness of NOW, because if anyone deserved their support, it was her. I don't know if it embittered her [Fenwick] toward them, but it should have," said Hyde.[45] But Representative Pat Schroeder noted another reason for NOW's opposition to Fenwick: "NOW didn't support her because . . . [they] wanted Democratic control of the Senate and chairmanships."[46] Governor Christine Todd Whitman was more blunt: "I think those organizations are really Democratic . . . they've proven that over time in the selectiveness that they've supported women's candidates. I mean they will always argue that you are not pro-choice enough, but you put them against some of the male candidates they've supported with a D [Democrat] after their name, and they're not as pure as they make themselves out to be. [Fenwick] was frustrated by that."[47]

As Fenwick got out of the car to debate Lautenberg, she tried unsuccessfully to engage the protesters in meaningful dialogue. "She could never walk by someone opposed to her without making a point," said Rosenshein.[48] By the time she went inside she was frazzled. Fenwick staffers believed her opponent had orchestrated the protesters' appearance, knowing Millicent would not ignore them.

During the campaign, while Lautenberg was meeting and greeting voters, Fenwick was often in Washington. Her literal commitment to her public service was rare among politicians, particularly in an election year when members of the House and Senate abandon Washington to campaign in their home districts or on behalf of their colleagues. Although involved in an increasingly tight race, Fenwick fulfilled her commitment to serving the Fifth District. She often rearranged her campaign schedule to accommodate the House voting schedule. Because she served in New Jersey, an already flooded news market, her dedication on the Hill went largely unnoticed, as did the lesson learned from Senator Case's 1978 upset loss in the primary to Bell, after which Case was criticized for spending too much time in Washington. Fenwick's unwillingness to leave Washington to campaign underscored why some of her colleagues had advised her against the Senate race. They understood that her stubbornness would limit her time on the campaign trail. This, combined with her reluctance to take PAC money, provided a challenge for the Fenwick camp.

Lautenberg didn't have that problem. He mobilized every resource he could think of: money, media, volunteers, and transportation. To appear on the nightly news in the New York and Philadelphia markets, Lautenberg scheduled events in the northern and southern parts of the state on the same day. He often rented helicopters to transport him from one end of the state to the other. When Fenwick's campaign team confronted her with this idea she failed to recognize its value and rejected it as another wasteful use of money. One of the few times that she acquiesced was when she flew in a helicopter from Atlantic City to East Rutherford to attend a fund-raising event at a Meadowlands hotel, where Henry Kissinger appeared on her behalf. I have been "an unabashed fan since we met in 1972," said Kissinger. "On one or two occasions, she has disagreed with me, but not even Millicent can be right 100 percent of the time."[49] Other powerbrokers who hosted fund-raisers on her behalf were then Vice-President George H. W. Bush, Senator Howard Baker, and former President Gerald Ford.

It was weeks before election day and Fenwick had not yet seemed to acknowledge the differences between running a statewide campaign and a congressional-district race. Her three congressional reelections were easily won, the last with a resounding 78 percent of the vote. With statistics like that it is easy to understand why she emphasized her work in Congress rather than trying to reshape the election around issues that exemplified her strengths, not Lautenberg's. She believed the people of New Jersey knew her, and her record, well enough that she did not have to spend an exorbitant amount of money to counter Lautenberg's negative advertising. She still hesitated to spend her own money or raise funds. She relied on her celebrity status, heightened by the *60 Minutes* profile a year earlier, not realizing that her name recognition was limited to northern and central New Jersey. Polls showed she was virtually unknown in the southern part of the state; thus, Lautenberg's saturation of the Philadelphia market had added impact. Southern Jersey did not know his competition. A week before the election, Fenwick's lead had diminished from a comfortable 18 points to a 3- to 5-point margin.[50]

The narrowed gap could have been attributed, in part, to Lautenberg's ties to organized labor. After the 1980 election of President Ronald Reagan, the labor movement was determined to get blue-collar workers back to the voting booth to elect Democrats to counter the Republican White House. In the last three weeks of the campaign, New Jersey labor groups mailed half a million pieces of campaign literature per week supporting Lautenberg.

The stark contrasts in campaign strategy between Fenwick and Lautenberg could not have been more visible than on election day. While thousands of Lautenberg supporters canvassed the state, the Fenwick staff closed down more than half of its telephone banks at midday because "We had called our people enough."[51]

On election day, Fenwick, still the frontrunner, but with a tighter margin than expected, was optimistic. As the election results poured in, Millicent and her supporters gathered at Bernardsville's Olde Mill Inn. Initially she had an early lead. But, as more precincts reported, the atmosphere changed. Millicent Fenwick, the widely popular politician, was losing ground. She never caught up. By 11 P.M., she conceded to a jubilant Lautenberg. Fenwick's 48 percent to 52 percent defeat caught everyone, including her, by surprise. The difference was less than 66,000 votes out of nearly 2,000,000 cast.[52]

The Lautenberg campaign succeeded because it defined the campaign issues, hired experienced political operatives, had virtually unlimited funding, utilized the media effectively, and mobilized volunteers. After three terms, at the age of seventy-six, Lautenberg retired in 2000. His successor, Jon Corzine, a Wall Street mogul, commanded headlines by winning his first election in much the same way as Lautenberg did. Corzine spent his own fortune, an estimated $60 million compared to Lautenberg's $6 million eighteen years earlier.

At seventy-two, Fenwick had suffered her first electoral defeat. Her loss stunned many and was widely thought to be a protest vote against Reagan and his supply-side economics. Voters later admitted they wanted to send a message to the White House, but never imagined it would cost Millicent the election. Hollis McLoughlin, Fenwick's chief of staff, said, "Thomas Jefferson could not get elected in the twentieth century."[53] Fenwick was as gracious in defeat as she had been in victory. She told her supporters, "It has been a wonderful battle but we lost. I've just got to admit it and take it in good spirits and go on to work for the good of the state."[54] Fenwick spent the next forty-eight hours in a daze. "I thought this [the loss] is absolutely ridiculous, it's impossible. But then, I felt, well the good Lord knows best. . . . Maybe I would have been too old by that time to be really useful. Six years, it would have been. . . . Well, I did my best," she said.[55]

# 15

## *A Little*

## *Bit Useful*

If I can stop one Heart from breaking
I shall not live in vain
If I can ease one Life the Aching
Or cool one pain

Or help one fainting Robin
Unto his Nest again
I shall not live in Vain.

—Emily Dickinson

Once the reality of her Senate loss set in, Millicent found herself with several opportunities to consider. Offers included teaching at a university, joining the lecture circuit, being a television commentator, and publishing her memoirs. Although Millicent had writing aspirations that predated her *Vogue* years, she did not seriously consider penning her memoirs. She was content with her book *Speaking Up,* which had been published in 1982. Mark Harroff, her political consultant, encouraged her to consider a syndicated column or a radio commentary program, "It would enable you to have your 'bully pulpit'—and many Americans want to be assured that you will continue to be a voice for them."[1] Although she had been voted out of office, Millicent still received both public praise and a great deal of mail delivered to her Bernardsville doorstep. A magazine called *50 Plus* named Fenwick its "Woman of the Year" in 1982, stating, "She literally put her political future up for grabs. . . . Although she may find her first political defeat personally disappointing . . . whatever the future holds for her, Mrs. Fenwick has proven that age and sex need not be barriers to political progress."[2] Fenwick herself was surprised by all the speculation and praise. "I don't understand it," she said. "A woman 72 years old. Defeated. . . . You'd think that would be it, wouldn't you?"[3] But, it wasn't.

A month after Fenwick's Senate loss, more than seventy-five of her congressional colleagues signed a letter to the president urging "the appointment of Millicent Fenwick as senior permanent U.S. Representative to the United Nations Human Rights Commission . . . [her] eight years of experience in the U.S. House of Representatives have made obvious her unceasing commitment to insuring protection of human rights internationally."[4] Among those who signed the letter were Republicans Lynn Martin, Bob Michel, Trent Lott, Henry Hyde, Jim Jeffords, and Olympia Snowe. Even before Fenwick's loss, the House Foreign Affairs Committee had suggested she be considered for the post of assistant secretary of state for human rights at the State Department. That position went to thirty-four-year-old Harvard lawyer Elliott Abrams, who, at the time, was President Reagan's assistant secretary of state for international organization affairs. In his new position, Abrams served as the State Department representative to the Helsinki Commission that Fenwick had been instrumental in creating. Ironically, in 1991, Elliott Abrams pleaded guilty to charges that he had lied while testifying before Congress about the U.S. government's knowledge and involvement in the Iran-Contra affair. In 1992, President George H. W. Bush pardoned him; in 2001, President George W. Bush appointed him special assistant to the president and senior director for democracy, human rights, and international operations at the National Security Council.

Additional support for Fenwick to continue her public service through a presidential appointment came from a variety of individuals, including former Senator Nicholas Brady and former Representative Barber Conable, then serving as president of the World Bank. Brady wrote to Michael Deaver, Reagan's deputy chief of staff, recommending Millicent for an ambassadorial post in Italy, France, or Spain. "I plan to mention Millicent's availability to George Shultz [secretary of state], as I feel the President's cause and this country's interest would be well served by her participation."[5] Conable concurred, noting, "I do not see how she [Fenwick] could fail to be a substantial asset for our Party at a time when the Democrats are so obviously concentrating on the 'gender gap.'"[6]

The Republican administration needed little prompting. Not long after the election, White House staffers asked Fenwick if she would be willing to work for the Reagan administration. "Well, I hadn't thought of that," said Millicent, "but if I could be useful, I would be happy to."[7] She filled out the requisite paperwork—leaving the position title blank— and waited.

Nine months after Fenwick's loss in the Senate race, President Reagan, speaking before the Republican Women's Leadership Forum, said "I'm still disappointed that Millicent Fenwick didn't make it to the Senate, and I regret that some who supposedly are women's advocates didn't support that distinguished legislator. Indeed, in last year's election, it was apparent that some who talk the loudest in behalf of women's equality only extend their advocacy to women candidates if they're Democrats."[8]

Two months earlier he had offered Fenwick a job as permanent representative to the United Nations Food and Agriculture Organization (FAO) headquartered in Rome, but within three days he upgraded the position. "Reagan, in trouble with women's groups who view his administration as antifeminist, boosted the rank to ambassador [to FAO]," reported one newspaper.[9] Officially, a spokesperson for the State Department said that the importance of the position warranted a higher level of representation.[10] At the same time, Reagan also upgraded the title of the permanent representative to the Vatican to ambassador. Previously, the permanent representatives of the FAO and the Vatican worked out of and reported to the American embassy in Rome. Now they were independent. With Fenwick's appointment came the establishment of the U.S. Mission to the United Nations Agencies for Food and Agriculture (FODAG).

---

Nominated to the post in June of 1983, Fenwick was unanimously confirmed by the Senate Foreign Relations Committee in what the press reported as a love fest, with members from both parties praising the nominee. One character witness, Representative Stephen Solarz (D-New York), made the hearing an unprecedented bipartisan endorsement. "I must tell you that I come here entirely unsolicited. I am neither a representative from Mrs. Fenwick's State nor a member of her political party," said Solarz. "She is what I would characterize as an idealist without illusions. She recognizes the need for a higher purpose in the affairs of men and women, yet recognizes that in the world in which we live, compromises have to be made from time to time in order to achieve progress. . . . There is none for whom I developed greater respect or more admiration or affection than Millicent Fenwick."[11] With the approval of the Senate Foreign Relations Committee, Millicent's nomination was forwarded to the U.S. Senate, but Congress recessed before voting on her nomination. Not one to wait, Millicent flew to Rome in August to familiarize herself with the job before the Senate confirmed her in September to succeed Roger Sorenson, the brother of Theodore Sorenson, former special counsel to President John F. Kennedy.

In 1983, UNFAO had more than 150 member nations. It had been established in 1945 "to raise levels of nutrition and standards of living, to secure improvements in the efficiency of the production and distribution of all food and agricultural products, to better the condition of rural populations and thus contribute to an expanding world economy."[12] Its dual purpose was to reduce world hunger and malnutrition and to improve agricultural production. The position appealed to Fenwick's desire to help others. As ambassador, she was responsible for representing the American position to the United Nations' Food and Agriculture Organization (FAO), the World Food Council (WFC), and the World Food Program (WFP). A fourth food agency, the International Fund for Agricultural Development (IFAD), was the only UN food agency with which the U.S. representative was not officially affiliated, because the official U.S. representative to IFAD was the head of the Agency for International Development (AID).

Before Fenwick assumed her post she sought guidance from retired Senator George McGovern, who had been the Democratic presidential nominee in 1972. "She called me," said McGovern, "because she knew of my interest in fighting hunger and she asked me a number of questions. She said she wanted her time in Rome to count for something. She wanted to get into the nitty-gritty and asked about what I learned from the Food for Peace days [McGovern headed the agency during John F. Kennedy's Administration]. Her questions were always good and relevant and she left no doubt that she wanted to be effective."[13] Fifteen years after McGovern helped educate Fenwick about the issues she would face in Rome, he was appointed to the same post. Both Fenwick and McGovern assumed the rank of ambassador to the FAO, but the title was not bestowed on all representatives.

The significance of Fenwick's rank as the first U.S. ambassador to the FAO did not go unnoticed. The FAO representatives in Rome viewed the upgraded title as signaling a stronger commitment by the United States to the food agencies. The early 1980s were a tumultuous period for the United Nations because the United States pulled out of the United Nations Educational, Scientific, and Cultural Organization (UNESCO), charging that it was poorly managed and prompting other UN agencies to fear the withdrawal of U.S. funding from their programs.

By the mid-1980s the FAO was the largest specialized UN agency. It concentrated on sustaining and maintaining agriculture, forestry, fisheries, and rural development, primarily through technical assistance programs, global information sharing, data collection, and research. One goal was to encourage developing countries to rely upon their own resources to foster food production.[14] Because of growing populations, due in part to medical advances and longer life expectancies, the world food situation was getting worse, not better. Fenwick advocated self-sufficiency in cultivating land and family planning as essential parts of the solution, but she noted, "Family planning must be voluntary. We cannot encourage plans that destroy people in their religious beliefs or their holding to personal principles."[15]

————————

Somerset County, Fenwick's home base and congressional district, had more than 400 farms in 1982.[16] During World War I, her father served as the chairman of the United States Food Administration for Somerset County, and he, like Millicent, was concerned with food production. Two decades after her appointment, the state was still a leader in a number of areas. "Farmers in the Garden State produce more than 100 different kinds of fruits and vegetables. . . . Nationally, New Jersey is one of the top ten producers of cranberries, blueberries, peaches, asparagus, bell peppers, spinach, lettuce, cucumbers, sweet corn, tomatoes, snap beans, cabbage, escarole/endive and eggplant."[17]

"I was really best prepared [for the job]," said Fenwick, "by being a farmer myself some years ago, a dairy farmer and chicken farmer. And working for consumers . . . that was invaluable. Of course, Congress was a very good experience, too, the whole Foreign Affairs Committee, listening to the arguments about the agricultural bills. . . . There's no substitute for it in my books. I think it all helped. But no special courses or anything."[18]

From the moment she arrived in Rome, she had a social network of people she met over the years during her many visits to see her Italian brother-in-law, Ghino, and his second wife, Ginevra Pasolini. Ghino had died two years before Millicent moved to Rome, but she remained close to Ginevra and her siblings.[19] Fenwick still arrived at the office early and stayed late; some of Millicent's colleagues saw a woman consumed by work. The fact that she had a life beyond the office seemed improbable to them.[20] But she did. Among Millicent's social circle were many Italian aristocrats. One friend, Princess Sciarra, a short and energetic woman who headed Elizabeth Arden in Rome, had been Mary's friend, and she and Millicent remained close.[21] Princess Sciarra had a wide circle of friends and had a castle in Ravenna, north of Rome, where Millicent sometimes retreated on weekends.

In the summer of 1984, Millicent's grandson, Jonathan Reckford, was introduced to her social milieu. After graduating from the University of North Carolina at Chapel Hill, Jonathan backpacked through Europe, visiting his grandmother twice that summer. On his first visit, Fenwick told him they were going to spend a long weekend in the country. "It was something out of a movie," said Jonathan. "As we drove I could see a castle in the distance, from half an hour away. It did not look modern at all. Half of it looked ruined . . . the exterior walls looked like they had been that way since the tenth century." What Jonathan didn't realize was that the castle was their destination. Waiting for them upon their arrival were Princess Sciarra and Countess Flavia Desadaria Pasolini Dall'Onda, another friend. "It was the most relaxed I ever saw grandma," said Jonathan. "This was her, with her friends. She was high-spirited and relaxed. It was nice to see her feeling so completely at home, and to see her with her friends, whom she had known for forty years."[22]

The contrast for Jonathan was remarkable. One day he was backpacking and the next day he found himself spending a weekend at a picturesque castle. It was like stepping into a fairytale. "The castle was outstanding. It had some modern conveniences, including an elevator and a pool on the terrace." On the ground level was a chapel where the villagers came to worship on Sundays. The castle itself was surrounded by farmland, with the village of Ravenna at the bottom. "All these women [Princess Sciarra, Countess Desadaria], were down to earth . . . not affected at all, unlike the movie star paparazzi types," said Jonathan. "It was fun to soak it all in. That trip is my favorite memory of grandma, such a once-in-a-lifetime experience."[23]

Also included in Millicent's social circle was Fey Pirzio-Biroli, granddaughter of Alfred von Tirpitz, the founder of the imperial fleet of Kaiser Wilhelm II, and daughter of the German ambassador to Rome, Ulrich von Hassell. In 1938, von Hassell's disdain for Nazism led to his dismissal as ambassador and return to Germany. Six years later, he was involved in an unsuccessful plot to assassinate Hitler. That failed attempt resulted in von Hassell's execution and the imprisonment of his kin, including Fey.[24] Her story of survival no doubt intrigued Millicent.

Another friend was Iris Origo, an Anglo-American writer who had married into Italian nobility. Origo was best known for her book *War in Val d'Orcia: An Italian War Diary, 1943–1944*, in which she recounted her efforts and those of her husband to aid refugees and political prisoners at their Tuscany farm during World War II.

As ambassador, Millicent was provided with a limousine and an Italian driver, Arnaldo Deisori. Deisori was a legend among Fenwick's predecessors and successors. "There were a couple of ambassadors that preceded me," said McGovern, "who told me, 'Don't let Arnaldo go,' because he was so valuable. He could do everything from making arrangements to see the Pope to picking up dry cleaning. . . . He knew Italy and the Italian people and the history. . . . He was a great storyteller and one of the most remarkable people I've ever encountered."[25] Millicent, too, was fond of Deisori. Deisori had been working for the American embassy for decades, and his noted passengers included President John F. Kennedy and Clare Boothe Luce. Deisori, protective of Millicent, usually could be seen trailing a few paces behind her, carrying her large satchel. Unlike other drivers, Deisori did not wait in the car for his passenger;

instead he accompanied her inside the UNFAO building. By virtue of Fenwick's personality and age, she was able to get special passes for Deisori to accompany her to meetings. Some ambassadors protested. They wanted their drivers to have the same access. But, as one UNFAO employee said, "It was very difficult to say no to any request by Millicent Fenwick."[26]

As much as Millicent liked Arnaldo, she detested the lavish car he drove her around in, so she replaced it with a Ford. For security purposes it was outfitted with bulletproof glass. "I'm not going to drive up in a 25-foot Cadillac when I am accredited to an organization that is trying to feed the hungry," she said. "There's something very inappropriate about that."[27]

Because of the tight security required for American diplomats worldwide and the potential threat of the Red Brigades and other terrorist cells, Millicent was assigned an armed bodyguard in addition to the car and driver. "She didn't have much faith in him [the bodyguard]," said her grandson Jonathan. "He had a gun, and that worried her."[28] The security measures frustrated Millicent, who was officially prohibited from riding in a cab or a friend's car. "If I weren't working so hard, it would drive me crazy. I can't go out weekends to social events or to see a movie or museum without costing the taxpayers overtime for the car and driver," she said.[29]

———

As the U.S. ambassador to the U.N. Food and Agriculture Organization it was Fenwick's responsibility to represent American policy. As in Congress, her remarks were punctuated with passion. She waxed eloquent about the plight of farmers in third world countries and the need to advance harvesting and food production. The only problem was, what she said did not always reflect official Washington, but she thought it did. "I'm always perfectly clear," said Fenwick. "This is my government's position. Then I say, 'And now I have a few personal words to add,' . . . a little more colorful than the words my government may have written down for me to recite."[30] Staff members from the U.S. Department of Agriculture, the State Department, and other federal agencies that worked closely on FAO issues often drafted Washington's policy positions for Fenwick. But she rarely referred to the drafts, preferring to speak spontaneously instead. Because her impromptu remarks did not always accurately reflect the United States' position, American officials discreetly worked the hallways to clarify the U.S. stance with FAO representatives.

Although Washington bureaucrats were frustrated by Millicent's style, international dignitaries were charmed by her. They felt privileged to work with the American grand dame whose reputation for honesty and integrity preceded her arrival in Rome. Because the American post was upgraded from permanent representative to ambassador, many mistakenly believed that Millicent was a close personal friend of President Reagan, a belief that gave her even more power in the eyes of her associates overseas.[31]

In fact, in 1980, Fenwick had chaired George H. W. Bush's presidential campaign in New Jersey. Reagan did not receive her support until he defeated Bush in the primary. Her last term in Congress coincided with Reagan's first term as president. "I've become very fond of Mr. Reagan," she said. "He rather reminds me of myself. . . . There is always a human being in it for Mr. Reagan. That is exactly the way I am."[32]

————

Considerably older than most of her colleagues, and again noticed for her elegant style, Millicent said, "I keep my clothes neat and tidy and—believe it or not—the garments I wore . . . abroad were clothes that I had bought in Rome 30 years ago. Some of my clothes were older than my colleagues."[33] Yet, as one UNFAO staffer observed, "her age was an asset."[34]

In Rome, the U.S. Mission included between ten and twelve people from the State Department, USDA, and USAID. When Fenwick arrived she set a clear tone. "From now on every cable that goes out I'll have to see," she told the staff, "and it will go out with my approval and signature." She observed, "I think it was quite a shock. I don't think it was terribly happily received, but it's worked very well. I have a wonderful staff, and I've always had very, very fine cooperation."[35] Some staff needed time to adjust, however, to Fenwick's Capitol Hill mentality and work ethic. Fenwick's style had not changed, she was still a demanding boss, and not everyone adapted to her style. Her secretary, a foreign service employee, left and was replaced by Erin O'Shea, who had previously worked as a personal assistant to John D. Rockefeller and to Alan Keyes, ambassador to the U.S. mission at the United Nations headquarters in New York. O'Shea easily adjusted to Fenwick's work style and quickly earned her trust. Unwittingly, Fenwick served as a matchmaker for O'Shea, who met her future husband, Jim Ross, at the U.S. mission in Rome, where Ross was the agricultural attaché to FODAG.

Fenwick put in twelve-hour days and did extensive research to become knowledgeable about UNFAO issues. "The work is hard, in a way, long conference and committee hours, receptions, dinners, and so much to learn," wrote Millicent to her goddaughter Susan Powers. "There is always the hope—and sometimes the illusion—of being useful. That is what makes it worth doing."[36]

Although Fenwick made it a point to be knowledgeable about UNFAO issues, she was also aware of her staff's expertise. She let them present their own information at UNFAO meetings and conferences because, as she said, she felt like an "overloaded circuit. . . . Trying to make sure that none of these confidential cables were mentioned in places and times they shouldn't be."[37] Only once, in the spring of 1986, did she cable Washington about the mounting pressures of the job. "The whole process swells beyond the simple practical necessities and the bureaucracies that grow out of that process . . . impose an ever increasing cost on the state. . . . I will have been here three years in August and I feel I have been useful. But if I recommend cutting other positions, I feel I must start with my own."[38] In a cable, Secretary of State George Shultz responded, "I appreciated the courage and consideration of your offer to step down as our Ambassador to FAO. . . . However, I would not consider for a moment asking the President to let you go. You are doing a superb job for the nation. It is [a] false economy to save a few dollars while losing the services of the very best people in the top jobs."[39]

Millicent Fenwick was the first woman in the forty-year history of the food agencies to represent the United States. In this environment, age and gender worked to her advantage. She instantaneously commanded respect from her peers, and she felt age gave her a license to be unusually candid. Feeling no added pressure to prove herself, she said, "I don't have to prove that women can function, because that's been done over and over. We had a wonderfully able woman in London, Ann Armstrong from Texas . . . so there's no question that on the international scene women have proved themselves."[40]

"I don't think there is any doubt that she made a difference," said Ambassador McGovern. "She improved the morale, the energy level and got it [FODAG] functioning more vigorously through her example. . . . I think that's what happens when you have an enthusiastic person. It is very infectious, my guess is she did that with every organization."[41]

Fenwick worked diligently on the issues that mattered most to her, such as self-sufficiency. On trips to underdeveloped countries, she concluded that neither technological nor agricultural breakthroughs would alleviate hunger because the underlying problem was political as well as agrarian. "Believe it or not, people in these underdeveloped areas need simple organization more than anything else," she said. "They need to convene, inventory their resources and apply intelligence to their efforts in order to produce more food. They need to be shown how to get their act together."[42]

Even while concentrating on agricultural issues, Fenwick kept an eye on human rights abuses. Always candid, she voiced her concern about the Ethiopian famine, and in particular "the cruelty of the government of Ethiopia, which she [said] is using donated food as 'bait' to force a relocation program on its starving people . . . [and she highlighted the fact that] Ethiopian soldiers killed four villagers for 'refusing to get on a truck.'"[43] Africa was of particular interest to her, and she spoke about the continent's needs at every opportunity, whether it was to her colleagues, friends, or grandchildren. She was frustrated by the global bureaucracy that advocated throwing money at problems, and in particular, buying modern machinery for underdeveloped nations. She would have preferred funding for seeds, not industrial machines.[44]

While Fenwick was friendly with many of the representatives from the UNFAO member nations, she viewed the relationships as official friendships rather than personal ones. She didn't entertain often, although she occasionally held receptions at her modest but tasteful apartment. When former congressional colleagues, such as Stephen Solarz and Tom Lantos, visited Rome, U.S. Ambassador to Italy Max Rabb would invite Millicent to the embassy for a reception, lunch, or dinner. One of the more opulent occasions was a star-studded gathering hosted by Ambassador Rabb and his wife, Ruth, for Nancy Reagan. While the First Lady was in Rome, Millicent spent some time with her and visited a local church. "Millicent had a presence about her. She was a dying breed—tough and feminine and confident. She moved around easily among all classes of people, comfortable with everyone," said Erin Ross.[45]

During Fenwick's tenure, Edward Saouma of Lebanon was the powerful head of the UNFAO. He held degrees in agricultural chemistry and agronomy and served as director general for three terms, from 1976 to 1994, but his affiliation with the UNFAO dated to 1961, when he served as a delegate. Fenwick and Saouma had a fairly good relationship, and Saouma gave her more time than he gave most of the other representatives.[46] Like Millicent, he could be charming. But "his charm was a bit more calculated . . . to serve his own purposes, but she was no fool," said Jim Ross.[47]

In the fall of 1986, Millicent enjoyed a visit with her daughter, Mary, who had been diagnosed with leukemia. Mother and daughter, while not always close, had come to respect each other. Fenwick, demanding by nature, was not easy to please. Mary succeeded where Millicent failed—at motherhood. The fact that Mary and Ken Reckford had five children always puzzled Millicent. She would have preferred it if Mary sought a career outside the home.[48] But by the time Mary went to Rome, they had put their differences behind them.

Some thought the workaholic Fenwick would never retire, but in early 1987, with her health declining and her daughter battling leukemia, Millicent decided the time had come. "I want to retire," she admitted. "I ran for my first election for the board of education in Bernardsville—I think it was over 50 years ago."[49] At seventy-seven, she was finally ready to retreat to the country—much as she thought when she retired from *Vogue* thirty-five years earlier. She was ready to return to the safe harbor Bernardsville provided. "I think what I have done here is useful," said Millicent.[50]

# 16

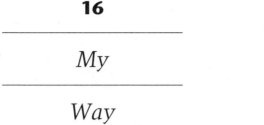

*My*

*Way*

Do justly, love mercy, and walk humbly with thy God.

—Micah 6:8

In March 1987, Millicent Fenwick returned from Rome to her beloved Bernardsville. "I'm back where I belong—where my political career began, where my roots are deeply planted, where I love the townspeople—and here I intend to stay."[1] Where, exactly, was another matter. Her home was uninhabitable.

Before she went to Rome she had decided to economize. Against the advice of Bernardsville friend David Neill, she had her house sealed with plastic and insulation. Only one area in the back—a kitchen, bedroom, and small sitting room—where a groundskeeper stayed, was left untouched. Everything else, including access points into the main part of the house, was literally closed. Millicent had the heat and water turned off while she lived abroad. Her rationale was that she did not want to be wasteful by heating an empty home.

David Neill, who ran his family's local oil business, pleaded with her not to board up the house. He explained to her that it would cost approximately $2,000 to keep the home heated at 50 to 55 degrees while she was in Italy. Fenwick was steadfast about her decision. It wasn't about money, it was about being wasteful. "It's sticking in my head that she spent $2,500 with us," said Neill, and "she spent another couple thousand dollars with the plumber, to drain and winterize the house. . . . She spent probably between $5,000 and $6,000 because she figured she'd be there [Rome] for two to three years. We tried to tell her it would be cheaper to heat the house but we just argued back and forth and around and around."[2]

"It gets better," recalled Neill, with irony. When she returned from Rome, Fenwick and Neill went to the house. From the outside all looked well, but all was not well inside. The insulation and plastic barriers on the inside doorways, which separated the tiny heated section from the unheated main house, had been removed just prior to her return. "When we finally got into the house it was an absolute nightmare," said Neill. "Some ceilings had fallen down. It was all plaster. The white walls were literally almost black because of the mold and mildew because it was never even opened up in the summer to air out. It was sealed. It stunk from the dampness. The destruction was unbelievable."[3] It was clear she couldn't live there. So, Millicent moved into Cousin Mary's house, behind her own, while Mary was at her Sutton Place home in Manhattan.

Neill was given the task of getting someone to fix the mess. Millicent didn't want just anyone. It needed to be someone who came recommended. Neill found a fellow named Dick Landon who had done a considerable amount of work for Jane Engelhard, the Johnson family (of Johnson & Johnson), and Barbara Neill, David's mother. Based on Landon's list of clients Millicent felt he was trustworthy and told David to move forward.

Arrangements were made for Landon, a Fenwick fan, to survey the damage. With Fenwick and Neill, Landon saw firsthand the amount of repair work needed. "It was a mess, trust me," said Neill. When the trio finished touring the house, they returned to the ground floor, and Millicent had a seat on her couch, temporarily located in the middle of the dining room. She asked Landon what he thought about the damage, and then she asked the big question. "I like to pay my bills promptly," Millicent explained. "Do you have an idea how much this is going to cost?" Uncomfortable, Landon shot a glance to David and said, "Oh, Mrs. Fenwick, it is very difficult." She prompted Landon again. "I just want a rough idea, not exact, I just want some idea of how much this will cost." Wary of his reply, Landon kept saying, "This is a lot of work, a lot of damage Mrs. Fenwick." She said, "Just a number." He replied, "I don't know . . . $60,000 to $75,000." Millicent gasped and grabbed her chest. After she regained her composure, which took some time, she had no choice but to move forward.[4]

Not long afterward, her cousin Mary returned from the city and Millicent moved into the cramped pool cottage in her own backyard. It had a bed, small kitchen, and bathroom, but not much else. She wanted to be nearby in case Landon had questions during the repair work. David Neill pleaded with her to move. Millicent conceded and moved to New York City, where she lived with her friend Mary Dunn, widow of diplomat James Clement Dunn.

In Fenwick's absence, Neill oversaw the renovations. Sheetrock was used to repair the cracked plaster ceilings, but in some places she asked that the workers replaster instead, "which made absolutely no sense . . . [and] was more labor intensive," said Neill. In another instance, Fenwick was adamant about saving the water-stained wallpaper in an upstairs bedroom. There was nothing that could be done to restore the rose-colored wallpaper. Not willing to accept this, Fenwick said, "My dear, now listen. Behind the radiators there is wallpaper, nobody ever looks behind the radiator . . . so can you cut out the wallpaper behind the radiator and put it in the spots that are damaged?" Perplexed, Neill said, "You want to do what?" As implausible as this was, Landon appeased his client. In the end the room had to be repainted because the mold and mildew could not be removed from the wallpaper. Before the massive restoration was completed, Millicent admitted to David that he had been right, and she should have spent the money to keep the heat on.[5] Her stubbornness led to months of work and tens of thousands of dollars in repairs.

Once Millicent was able to move back in, she spent much of her time in the ground-floor parlor. The room was painted in a pale sunshine color; portraits of her Stevens ancestors adorned one wall. The long windows and thirteen-foot French doors let rays of light fill the cheerful room. In the front corner sat two parlor chairs, to the right of which was a fireplace and twin floral-pattern sofas where Millicent, usually draped in a blanket, often read the paper and greeted guests. On the back wall built-in bookshelves revealed her literary taste. Beyond the perimeters of the room she could see the terrace garden and back patio which she enjoyed on warm days. To occupy herself she returned to one of her favorite pastimes, gardening. Most of her outdoor work involved plucking weeds with her bare hands and a butter knife or riding around her fourteen acres on a tractor, cutting grass.

She wasn't back in the United States long before her frailty became evident. "I have what's called peripheral arterial disease," she said with a wince, "but I think the word disease is horrible, so I just say trouble with the artery."[6] That trouble led to arterial bypass surgery on her right leg.

A transcontinental flight from Rome to New Jersey—where she accepted the Pride in New Jersey Award presented by her first congressional primary opponent, Governor Kean—raised Fenwick's awareness about her deteriorating health. "I noticed I got terribly tired in the airport. . . . I had a wheelchair. Now, that is really humiliating." Then she added, almost as an afterthought, "I'd like to reassure my taxpayer friends I paid for that trip. They did not."[7] This was classic Fenwick, fretting over money. Two months later she retired.

Not only was her age catching up with her, but she was also concerned for the welfare of her only daughter, who had been diagnosed with leukemia during Fenwick's senatorial campaign in 1982. Doctors told her she had another three or four years to live. Leukemia, however, proved not to be her only health challenge. In 1985, Mary was diagnosed with breast cancer and, like her mother, had a mastectomy. A period of remission followed, but in the summer of 1987, Mary's health again declined.

By early November Mary's situation was grave. Calls were placed to members of her immediate family. Her five children, ranging in age from nineteen to thirty-one, gathered by her bedside at her North Carolina home. Missing from this ensemble was Millicent. She was planning on making the trip a few days later. She never did. On Thursday morning, November 12, 1987, the day Millicent was to fly to Chapel Hill, her daughter lost her battles with leukemia and cancer. Mary had survived five years after her initial leukemia diagnosis, longer than the doctors predicted.

Her last week was peaceful, spent surrounded by close friends and family. And, although her mother was not present, traces of her were evident in Mary. Like Millicent, Mary insisted on answering the phone despite her weakened condition. Her husband, Ken, put it best when he said, "Mary was always brave. Like her Stevens and Hammond ancestors, she had what her mother, Millicent Fenwick, calls pioneer spirit; and, like her mother she had the courage of her convictions."[8] Although not able to say a final farewell in person, Millicent flew commercially to North Carolina for the funeral. Hugo's son Hughie, a pilot, flew his father and brother, Mark, to Chapel Hill for the services.

---

Around the time of Mary's death, the local Somerset Hills YMCA was in the midst of a fund-raising drive to expand its facilities and build a day care center. Fifteen years earlier, as an assemblywoman, Millicent had been at the groundbreaking ceremony for the very same YMCA. One of the committee members for the current fund-raising campaign was David Neill. He suggested naming the day care center after Millicent. "I always wanted to do something to recognize her many contributions," and, he said, "I'd rather do something while she was still alive rather than the postmortem routine."[9]

Since Fenwick was a longtime advocate for children, a supporter of the local YMCA, and an honorary board member, the idea seemed appropriate and easily received the support of the committee. Committee members not only embraced the idea but thought Fenwick's name being associated with the day care center would help bring in the additional funds needed. A far greater challenge was to gain Millicent's support. Since David Neill had proposed the idea he was given the assignment of getting her blessing. Fearing she would be upset at the recognition, he decided to seek support from her close friends before he broached the subject with her.

Both Mary Stevens Baird and Jane Engelhard agreed that naming the day care center after Millicent Fenwick was a "wonderful idea, absolutely wonderful." With their support David went to see Millicent. "I tried to beat around the bush," said David. "I talked about the YMCA, and their fund-raising efforts for the day care center."[10] And she talked about the Y and how it was one of her pet projects, and that it was local. With that, David told her the committee wanted to name the day care center after her and that Mary Stevens Baird, Jane Engelhard, and the president thought it was a great idea. "She looked at me and said the president of what?' I said, 'The United States. They want to name the day care center after you.' She said, 'They are not going to be able to raise that much money just if they name it after me.' I said, 'That's not it, they just want to pay you back for everything you did. Everyone thinks it's a fabulous idea.'" With such a convincing presentation, Millicent couldn't say no.[11]

Associating the name Millicent Fenwick with the project helped propel it forward and helped secure the half-million dollars needed to build the facility. The day care center would expand its capacity from thirty-six to sixty children, handling infants, toddlers, and preschoolers. The center itself was to have its own entrance, kitchen, bathroom, sick room, office, three classrooms, and playground.

At a fund-raising reception held at the U.S. Golf Association in Bernards Township, former U.S. Secretary of the Treasury C. Douglas Dillon, State Senator Jack Ewing, Congressman Dean Gallo, and State Assemblyman Rodney Frelinghuysen (who succeeded Gallo in Congress in 1994) turned out to support the Millicent Fenwick Day Care Center.

Doing some fund-raising of her own, Millicent approached some well-known, but rarely seen, residents of the Somerset Hills such as King Hassan II of Morocco, who owned a $7.5 million estate on three hundred acres in nearby Peapack-Gladstone. Although Fenwick didn't know the king well, she used her friendship with a Moroccan ambassador to gain Hassan's support. King Hassan quietly donated $100,000. His contribution was not made public until the project was near completion. Like many other local residents, King Hassan sought to maintain a low profile.

Local dignitaries assembled on Saturday, September 10, 1988, for the grand opening of the Millicent Fenwick Day Care Center. The star attendee was Fenwick herself. She was welcomed by members of the community, as well as national and local YMCA officials. It was during the day care dedication that Millicent received her first and only *Doonesbury* original cartoon. Creator Garry Trudeau had donated it originally to be auctioned to raise money for the day care center, but the committee decided to give it to Millicent instead. She was thrilled. The *Doonesbury* panel featured a Lacey Davenport campaign ad that read "Davenport. As indispensable as sensible shoes." On the bottom it said, "Paid for by her chums."[12]

Two months after the dedication of the center, Vice-President George H. W. Bush was elected president, and Millicent could not have been more pleased. Her support of his presidential aspirations dated back to the 1980 election in which Ronald Reagan emerged as the Republican nominee and eventual president.

For health reasons, Fenwick was less active in the 1988 campaign than in earlier presidential campaigns, but her first campaign driver, and former staffer, Roger Bodman, who served as commissioner of labor and later as commissioner of transportation in the Kean administration, was vice-chair of the New Jersey Bush for President campaign. As the *Wall Street Journal* reported in early 1989, after Bush was elected, there was a "*Doonesbury* Redux" in Washington. "Associates of pipe-smoking former New Jersey Rep. Millicent Fenwick fill high Bush administration posts. White House Communications Director David Demerest, Assistant Treasury Secretary Hollis McLoughlin, and Associate Budget Director Bob Grady all worked for Fenwick, who inspired a Doonesbury cartoon character, Lacey Davenport."[13]

Two days after that article appeared in the paper Millicent lost her longtime friend and cousin, Mary Stevens Baird, who died at her Bernardsville home on Sunday, March 5, 1989. Mary once said, "In this country friendship and family ties tend to be more casual, but I do make exception for the Stevens family. I remain objective, but I automatically love all of them. That's true, or I wouldn't say it."[14]

During a lunch meeting in New York prior to Mary's death, Mary, Millicent, and three others gathered to discuss the content of Mary's will. Mary was planning to give one of her Stevens cousins, who lived in a cottage on Mary's property, the land. But Millicent talked Mary out of it. Instead, Mary gave the cousin a lifelong lease on the Baird property. Millicent also talked Mary out of giving her Bernardsville property in trust to the Stevens Institute of Technology. Instead Mary left the land to SIT, not in trust, and the school later sold it rather than preserving it. Mary often deferred to Millicent's judgment.[15]

As Fenwick's health declined and loved ones died, she often talked about the aging process. "You know, you've got to forget yourself. As you get old, it's very interesting, because getting old is a whole new ball game, you know." She often repeated something said to her: "'Getting old is no game for sissies.' I love that, because it acknowledges the truth, which is that it's no fun. Don't talk about golden years to somebody who is old. That's just euphemisms. . . . You have to be a good sport, you have to take things in good spirit, you have to accept what has to be accepted and try to put up with whatever happens to come." Millicent also felt that self-pity was "the most destructive emotion that human beings can suffer." She also believed, "As you get older, memories, of course, are inevitable and they crowd . . . your younger years and your middle years. Forget the old grudges. I mean old, bad feelings, old hurt feelings, old angers, old polemics, forget them. They don't do any good. That's not the way to play the game [of life]."[16]

The aging process did not prevent Millicent from socializing. On one occasion she went to a friend's house to have tea with boxer Mike Tyson and his then-wife, Robin Givens. The young couple was new to the area. One can hardly imagine the conversation between the boxing champion and Millicent, Jane Engelhard, and Cousin Mary—three elderly patricians.

Fenwick was weary as she approached her eightieth birthday. In the preceding six months she had endured three operations to replace her pacemaker. The surgeries left her physically drained, and the antibiotics affected her eyesight, making it more difficult to read the daily paper or the many letters that still poured in. Among her frequent correspondents were "a prisoner in Colorado and another in Illinois, a judge in the state of Washington and a lady from Massachusetts, people who write to me all the time, and I try to answer. Some of them have difficulty dealing with agencies and remember that I was a state consumer affairs director," she said.[17]

A Portuguese couple helped her maintain the house. The husband tended to the outside, the wife to the inside. A licensed practical nurse, Kathleen Cullen, was hired in 1990 to assist her with reading, responding to mail, and any medical needs. Fenwick was still courted by the media, political colleagues, and constituents, and even though she no longer held public office, the public held her in high esteem. With her faculties still intact but her "eyesight so poor that writing and reading [were] almost impossible," Fenwick remained true to her reputation and dictated responses to Cullen.[18] Despite demand, she declined most speaking engagements, not wanting to make commitments she couldn't keep.

In the summer of 1990, still in frail health, Millicent managed to survive premature news of her own death. David Neill was alerted that something was awry when his family received a phone call from the local police asking if they could confirm Millicent's death. Surprised by this disturbing message, David asked if anybody had called Millicent. No one had, for fear of what they might learn. Picking up the phone, David dialed. It was busy. He tried again. Busy. After a third time he decided to drive to her house, up her long, winding tree-lined driveway, nervous about what he would find. He parked his car and rang the doorbell. Maria, Millicent's housekeeper, answered the door and told David that Millicent was around back.

Millicent, sitting in a lounge chair on the patio, was very much alive and chatting on the phone. As David approached, Millicent said to the person on the phone, "Oh, here is a very dear friend of mine who just stopped by to make sure I was still alive." Perplexed, David waited for her to get off the phone. When she hung up she barely had enough time to mention that it had been the White House on the line, and then the phone rang again. "I was there quite awhile," said David. The phone didn't stop ringing. News had filtered from Bernardsville to Trenton and Washington that the popular politician had died. What actually happened was that another Bernardsville resident, Mildred [Millie] Fleming, had died. Someone mistakenly thought it was Millicent Fenwick and the rumor spread like wildfire.

As politicians, friends, family, and reporters called the Fenwick home for a statement they were stunned to hear Millicent's distinctive voice answer, "Fenwick here." Millicent was having an absolute ball at the startled callers' expense. Sometimes she answered the phone more directly, "I'm still here." She was having fun. When one caller told her the flags had been lowered at the Somerset County Courthouse she said sternly, "Well, my dear, you get right down there and put them back up."[19]

On the evening of the day reports of her death had circulated, Millicent, looking rather regal, entertained a couple of local reporters. True to form she sidestepped her purported death with a witty line about waking up from an afternoon nap only to learn she was dead.[20] Then she proceeded to discuss topics that interested her, such as the new tax plan proposed by Governor Jim Florio, abortion, and the nomination of David Souter to the Supreme Court. The reporters were more eager to learn who had called that day, but Millicent let that question linger unanswered. Millicent in retirement was no different from Millicent in politics. She talked about the issues she cared about. She was adept at turning a conversation around. Regardless of whether a specific question was answered, one was always certain to hear an interesting comment. By then even Millicent's eleven grandchildren were familiar with what they referred to as her stock stories, but, said grandson Sam Reckford, "They always sounded wonderfully spontaneous."[21]

One of Fenwick's favorite anecdotes was about being useful. "If the business of government is justice, and I do profoundly believe it is, what is the business of a human being? . . . I think it is to be useful. What other real satisfaction is there that compares to being useful to another human being?" Being useful was something she harped on from the moment Rabbi Chertoff shared with her the quote from the Talmud,

"You will never arrive at the solution, but you're never absolved from the responsibility of trying. Success, you see, is not the measure of a human being. Effort is."[22]

A month after her rumored death, local politicians were gearing up for the season's elections, very much aware that Fenwick was alive and well. State Senator Dick Zimmer tapped Fenwick to chair his congressional campaign, although her poor health prompted Zimmer to cancel a press conference with her. As Zimmer put it, "We feel that she stands for many of the better traditions in politics, and we wanted to have her at the top of the campaign organization. . . . Her tradition is she remembers that the political institutions are supposed to serve people rather than vice versa. And she believes government should be clean, and elected officials should conduct themselves in a manner above reproach."[23]

Another Republican active in the state party and seeking elected office in 1990 was Christine Todd Whitman. Her family was steeped in local, state, and national politics. Her father, Webster Todd, had been chairman of the New Jersey GOP; her grandmother, Kate Schley, was a Republican National Committeewoman from 1933 to1952; her mother, Eleanor Schley Todd, chaired the Republican Club of New Jersey, the New Jersey Federation of Republican Women, and the Republican Women's Club of Somerset Country; and her brother, Webster (Danny) Todd Jr. served in the state assembly and at the U.S. Department of Transportation during the Nixon administration. In fact, it was Danny's acceptance of the transportation job that opened the New Jersey Assembly seat that Fenwick was elected to. Through her involvement in the state party and as committeewoman herself, Fenwick had known the Schley and Todd families for years. So when Christie Whitman, a former Somerset County freeholder, sought advice from Fenwick about her experiences running for the U.S. Senate, Fenwick was happy to oblige.

"We had a wide-ranging discussion on what it meant to be a public servant," said Whitman. "Her perspective [was] being a public servant . . . really is the primary reason to run for office. You know she felt very strongly, as did my family, my parents, that you take one of these jobs— you ask for the public's confidence—because you want to do something for the public and not because you are there to enhance yourself, or your reputation, or add titles. She talked a bit about getting along with the good old boy network in Washington. It was more—Don't be put off by some of the colleagues that you might run into—that you still can do your own thing and you are who you are. The people who are voting for you vote for you, not for the establishment or the hierarchy of the party in Washington. It was just a fun, freewheeling discussion and she was very, very supportive."[24]

Come November, Zimmer won his first of three elections to the

House of Representatives. Christie Whitman narrowly lost the Senate race against incumbent Bill Bradley, but she gained statewide name recognition that aided her successful bid to be New Jersey's first female governor in 1993. She was reelected in 1997.

In the 1970s, Millicent Fenwick predicted that within the next twenty years New Jersey would elect a female governor. When Governor Whitman was told of that prediction [in 2001], she made one of her own: "Well, I think within the next twenty years we'll have a female president, hopefully within the next ten. She [Millicent] made that possible in many ways. She wasn't the only reason, but she certainly changed in New Jersey the attitude toward women and women's position in power and in government."[25]

A year after Millicent survived her rumored death, she received news that her ex-husband had had a heart attack; he had been trying to open a second-floor window and fell to his death. In the years leading up to his death, Hugh could often be seen behind the wheel of a car, although his driver's license had been revoked because he had cataracts and was legally blind. Between marriages he led an adventurous lifestyle, socializing with figures such as Barbara Hutton and Cary Grant.

Except for Hugh's brief appearance at his daughter's wedding in 1954, Millicent never saw him again after their marriage ended. Hugo, however, saw his father a bit more as the years passed. A year before Hugh's death, he called his son, "because he needed a place to stay on his way to Newport and asked if he could stay with me," said Hugo. "I was living in the cottage at the time and I told him I didn't think I could do that because I didn't think my mother would appreciate having him a hundred yards away. He said 'Can you ask her?'" Protecting his mother, Hugo said, "No. She is not well, I can't ask."[26] Thus the trip was cancelled. Some time later Hugo mentioned this to his mother, and much to his surprise her response was fairly indifferent. Millicent told Hugo it wouldn't have bothered her if Hugh had come. From her guarded response, Hugo sensed his mother would like to have seen her former husband one final time.

By 1992, age was taking its toll on Millicent's increasingly feeble body. She had survived appendicitis, breast cancer, a mastectomy, heart problems that led to a pacemaker, and the loss of her siblings, friends, and her daughter. Fenwick's deteriorating eyesight, arterial disease, and emphysema led her to remind visitors that "getting old is not for sissies." Cognizant of her failing health, there were three things Millicent wanted to do before she died: (1) see Jane Engelhard; (2) donate a valuable ring to the Newark Museum; and (3) pay all her bills.

Jane Engelhard was her friend and neighbor with whom she had traveled to the Middle East and India decades earlier. Mrs. Engelhard, by now a wealthy widow, was one of Millicent's closest surviving friends. She divided her time between her Nantucket and Far Hills homes, and Millicent summoned her for a visit. Millicent didn't just want to talk to Jane Engelhard, she wanted to see her. Arriving on Tuesday, September 15, she spent the afternoon reminiscing with Millicent.

The other two things Millicent wanted to accomplish were more practical than personal. After Cousin Mary died, Millicent had inherited an exquisite diamond-and-emerald ring that was given to Mary by Lord William Waldorf Astor, a close friend. Fenwick focused her energies on donating this valuable ring to the Newark Museum, which she had served as a member of their board of trustees. When Fenwick called Sam Miller, the director of the museum, he was on vacation. Fenwick was told he would return on Monday, September 14. She prodded, "Is there any way to reach him sooner?"[27] There was not. Patiently awaiting Miller's return, Millicent called him the day he returned and explained that she wanted to donate the Astor ring. Miller, of course, accepted. Fenwick then asked him to send someone to Bernardsville that day with a dated receipt for the ring because she wanted the donation to be credited as a gift during her life, and not a gift of the estate. He agreed, and Millicent turned over possession of the ring later that day. The museum had the ring appraised soon after, and it was determined to be worth $13,000. The ring was later sold through Sotheby's for $49,000, and the proceeds used to establish a jewelry section at the Newark Museum.[28]

The third task Millicent wanted completed before her death was for all of her checks to clear. She had paid her bills in advance, including her quarterly taxes, to avoid having outstanding checks as death approached. By September 15, she had accomplished what she wanted. Then she did one last thing. At five o'clock that evening Fenwick called a registered nurse to replace Kathleen Cullen, her faithful caregiver for the past two years. This was to foreshadow events to come. Millicent knew that according to New Jersey law only a doctor or a registered nurse could sign a death certificate, and Cullen was a licensed practical nurse, not a registered nurse.

In the predawn hours of Wednesday, September 16, 1992, Millicent Fenwick died quietly in her Bernardsville bedroom. She was survived by her son, eleven grandchildren, three great-grandchildren, thousands of admirers, and the fictional Lacey Davenport, who died six years later, in 1998. In December 1992, Lacey Davenport and another *Doonesbury* character, Joanie Caucus, Lacey's legislative aide, were named by *Working Woman* magazine ideal role models for women.

---

Hugo Fenwick viewed his mother's death as a deal she made with God allowing her to do three things: see Jane, donate the ring, and have all her checks cleared. Ironically, one check had not cleared at the time of her death. It was her quarterly tax payment to the Internal Revenue Service.[29] Believing she had done her best to be useful, she was ready to leave this world. If it is possible to will one's own death, Millicent Fenwick did. "She died much as she lived—her way," said Hugo.[30]

Before Millicent's death, Hugo had discussed with his mother the inscription she wanted on her tombstone. Her first response was, "She tried to be useful." She asked Hugo what he thought. "Perhaps something from the Bible," he said. First she suggested a passage from Isaiah before settling on one from Micah. The words chosen for her epitaph were "Do justly, love mercy, and walk humbly with thy God."[31] It was a fitting testament to her life and beliefs. Moved by that passage much earlier in life—in 1963, she concluded a speech with those same words— she said, "I've written those words [from Micah] in every Bible I've given to my godchildren."[32]

Once the media learned of Fenwick's death, her familiar face was seen on the front page of newspapers around the country and her voice once again resonated from television sets as news clips highlighted her illustrious life. President George H. W. Bush, who was in New Jersey two days after her death, said, "She was deeply principled in politics for all the right reasons, to fulfill a deep burning desire to achieve justice for all people. Her commitment to the underdogs of the world was matched only by her wit."[33] Having known and admired Millicent Fenwick, the President told the Secret Service he wanted to pay his respects in person, and Hugo was alerted about the possible visitor.[34] In the end, however, time did not permit Bush to go to the Fenwick home.

On September 19, friends, family, constituents, and the press gathered at St. Bernard's Episcopal Church to pay homage to Millicent Fenwick—mother, grandmother, great-grandmother, civil rights activist, consumer advocate, legislator, editor, author, model, moralist, friend, and neighbor. Two hundred people crowded into the stone church—which her ancestors had helped pay for a century earlier—and a hundred more gathered outside and listened to the service through loudspeakers. Officiating were the Reverend Fred Baldwin and longtime friend Monsignor John R. Torney, who had supported Millicent's efforts to build the Bernardsville public swimming pool four decades earlier.

One of her grandsons, Jonathan Reckford, spoke on behalf of the grandchildren, charming the audience with his humorous and candid portrayal of the woman they called Grandma:

"Grandma. It doesn't really seem like the right word to describe Millicent Fenwick, yet that's who she's always been to us. Conjure up your image of a 'Grandma.' Perhaps lots of warm fuzzy images come to mind depending on your own experiences. Baking cookies, big smothering hugs, spoiling the grandkids, etc. Forget them all—they just don't apply.

"Grandma wasn't very good with birthdays. She wasn't really the warm fuzzy type. . . . Other people's grandmothers may want them to mind their P's and Q's. Ours really did write the book. Dinner at the 'grown-up table' was good preparation for stressful client meetings years later. She did tell bedtime stories—two of them—to every generation. They were highly moralistic tales, where good things happened to worthy children and terrible outcomes were in store for the irresponsible.

"It wouldn't do justice to Grandma to say a lot of gooey, sentimental things. That sort of thing wasn't really her cup of tea. It was exciting to have a famous grandmother. We basked in the reflected glory of being related to Lacey Davenport and accepted that a cost was having to compete for time and attention with the myriad of very worthy causes with which she was always involved.

"She did things with great style. I once was foolish enough to ask facetiously if the passage of the ERA meant that she would hold doors for me in the near future. She gave me one of those 'looks' and reminded me in no uncertain terms that political and economic rights had nothing to do with social graces. She brought elegance to the most mundane matters and showed that indeed one can fight for change without breaching decorum."[35]

When the service was over, the casket was carried out by six men, all of whom had been selected for the honor by Millicent prior to her death. Bipartisan in life and in death, she named Republicans—Tom Kean, former governor; Jack Ewing, former state senator; and Peter Palmer, Bernardsville mayor—and Democrats—Bill Bradley, U.S. senator, and Peter Rodino, former congressman—as pallbearers. The sixth man was her friend David Neill.

Following the funeral service, mourners gathered at St. Bernard's Cemetery, her final resting place where she joined her sister, Mary, and brother, Ogden who had died during her first congressional term. Tombstones in the cemetery also remember her parents, Mary and Ogden Hammond, but neither was actually buried there. Mary's body was never recovered after the *Lusitania* sank, and Ogden was buried with his parents in St. Paul, Minnesota. After the interment invited guests gathered at Fenwick's Bernardsville home for a reception. Former staffers, pollsters, congressmen, senators, and governors joined family and friends in sharing their favorite Millicent memories.

Later Fenwick's will proved to be a topic of conversation for some, particularly those affiliated with the Stevens Institute of Technology. Millicent left nothing to charity, not even to the college that had been founded by her great-grandfather and on whose board of trustees she had served. One of the few provisions she made was oral. Upon his mother's death, Hugo Fenwick carried out his mother's oral wishes to give her goddaughter, Susan Alexander Powers (Lodge), the treasured pearls that had belonged to Millicent's sister and had become Millicent's trademark. Surprised, but appreciative of the gesture, Susan said, "[Millicent] encouraged me to do everything I did—law school and the pursuit of social justice reform—she was not only a role model for me, but like a second mother."[36]

There is some irony in the fact that Fenwick died in 1992, two months before the November elections that caused 1992 to be popularly dubbed the year of the women in politics. That year forty-eight women were elected to the House (twenty-four were reelected and twenty-four were newcomers), and four women were elected to the Senate, raising the number of women in the Senate from two to six.[37] Despite these gains only 10 percent of members of Congress were women.

If Millicent had lived one more year she would undoubtedly have been pleased to see Christine Todd Whitman sworn in as New Jersey's first female governor. As Governor Whitman said, "She [Millicent] certainly broke a lot of the glass ceiling. . . . Millicent was a role model in the way she approached politics, the way she approached her role and who she was. [She] was willing to be her own person and be eccentric if that's the way she was and the rest sort of be damned. . . . She reaffirmed my natural inclination to think that you could do anything you set out to do. Being a woman wasn't necessarily a detriment. I mean obviously there are going to be differences and there were real down sides to it . . . but that wasn't something that came forefront in my mind. It was the more you looked at the kind of success that Millicent had, and my mother and grandmother [who] were also there breaking barriers for me as well, and role models. You sort of thought you could do anything, and the problem with being a female in the business of politics was secondary. It was not something you wasted a whole lot of time on, and that certainly was Millicent's attitude. She just didn't let that hold her down, and she sent the message that it just wasn't worth thinking about and that was very useful. That was something I felt as well."[38]

---

The contributions that Fenwick made in New Jersey were not soon forgotten. The outpouring of love and support from the community inspired the establishment of a Millicent Fenwick Monument Association, which began with a letter to the editor in the *Bernardsville News* written by local resident Christa O'Conner. She suggested naming the new library after Millicent Fenwick. Helen Walton, another Bernardsville resident, called O'Conner to discuss the idea of memorializing Fenwick by erecting a statue of her. A few months later Walton, the driving force behind the project, received Hugo Fenwick's support. When asked what his mother would think he said, "Publicly, she would say,

'Oh my dear, absolutely not,' but privately, I believe she would be pleased because she would see it as the will of the people."[39]

Walton and a team of volunteers, including O'Conner, raised $80,000 to commission Dana Toomey, a former Bernardsville resident and Walton's childhood dance teacher, to sculpt a near-life-size bronze statue of Millicent Fenwick. It took just thirteen months, and donations from more than 700 contributors nationwide, to raise the money needed. "It really was interesting—the people who decided to give," said Walton. "Almost everybody had a story. She [Millicent] was a person who was so universally admired, even if people disagreed with her . . . which was an amazing feat."[40]

Through grassroots efforts, the Millicent Fenwick Monument Association unified a community to honor one of their own. As Helen Walton said, "I knew I wanted to [commission] a sculpture because people missed her, they wanted to see her, and her spirit."[41] Toomey captured Fenwick's spirit by sculpting Fenwick with her arms reaching out ready to embrace the world of those in need. Those who study the statue closely will notice a slight bulge in Fenwick's left pocket—that's her pipe, cleverly present but out of view.

On a warm and sunny October afternoon in 1995, nearly five hundred people gathered in the heart of Bernardsville for the unveiling of the Millicent Fenwick statue in a small park at the railroad station where Fenwick had often campaigned. Among the many on hand for the dedication ceremony were Governor Whitman, the keynote speaker; Representative Marge Roukema; and Hugo Fenwick. He was there not only as Millicent's son but as Bernardsville's mayor, elected in 1994 and reelected in 1998, continuing the family legacy of public service.

The statue established another first. It was the first outdoor sculpture in New Jersey of a woman, and one of the first in the country. Most of the few female statues nationwide represented mythological figures, not real women.[42] This was one instance where Millicent was memorialized before Eleanor Roosevelt, one of her role models. As Millicent once said, "I admired Mrs. Roosevelt because she was demonstrably sincere in her support of civil rights and took steps to prove it."[43] A statue of Eleanor was included as part of the FDR Memorial in Washington, D.C., a few years after the Millicent Fenwick likeness was erected.

Millicent Fenwick died much as she lived—her way. Appropriately, "My Way," the song so closely associated with Hoboken native Frank Sinatra, was her favorite.[44] Governor Whitman also associated Millicent with the Sinatra tune. "You know, everybody attributes and thinks of Frank Sinatra with 'My Way,' but Millicent Fenwick was really 'My Way.' And she did it with class and style. . . . She showed that a single mother could make it, that you could be independent and balance things, and that women could be very credible policy advocates."[45]

# Notes

## Abbreviations Used in Notes

CAWP  Center for the American Woman and Politics, Eagleton Institute of Politics, Rutgers University, New Brunswick, N.J.

CUOH  Peter Jessup, "Interviews with Rep. Millicent Fenwick," Columbia University Oral History, 1980–1981. Courtesy of Hugh Hammond Fenwick.

FAOH  Robert Miller, "Oral History of Millicent Hammond Fenwick." Women Ambassadors Project. Foreign Affairs Oral History Collection. National Foreign Affairs Training Center of the Department of State, December 1985, Rome, Italy.

FPC  Fenwick Private Collection, Bernardsville, N.J., courtesy of Hugh Hammond Fenwick.

HHF  A series of personal interviews conducted in Bernardsville, N.J., and by telephone by the author with Hugh Hammond Fenwick, April 1992 through December 1994 and March 1999 through January 2002.

MFP  Millicent Fenwick Papers, Special Collections and University Archives, Alexander Library, Rutgers University, New Brunswick, N.J.

NAHC  "Interview with the Honorable Millicent Fenwick, former member of the House of Representatives, from the state of New Jersey," National Association of Home Care, Washington D.C., [1989], courtesy of Hugh Hammond Fenwick.

NARA  National Archives and Records Administration.

## Preface

1. *Current Biography 1977* (New York: H. W. Wilson Company, 1978), 155.
2. Marlene Adler, assistant to Walter Cronkite, confirmed via telephone, 7 September 2000, on his behalf that in the 1970s Cronkite did indeed refer to Millicent Fenwick as the "Conscience of Congress."
3. Paul Goldberg, *The Final Act: The Dramatic, Revealing Story of the Moscow Helsinki Watch Group* (New York: William Morrow, 1988), 60.

## 1  A Gilded Past

1. *Millicent Fenwick: A Lesson in Leadership*, interview with Steve Adubato, Caucus NJ, WNET and United Artists Cable, 1991, videocassette.
2. Jean M. White, "A Debut of Sorts for Freshman Congressmen," *Washington Post*, 29 January 1975.
3. George McGovern, telephone interview by author, 16 January 2002.

4. In 1804, Colonel John Stevens established the Hoboken Company (later the Hoboken Land and Improvement Company) to develop and finance a town site that he had mapped out on a section of his 689 acres. Hoboken was incorporated as a city in 1855. George Long Moller, *The Hoboken of Yesterday,* vol. 2 (Hoboken, N.J.: The Poggi Press, 1966), 10 and 7 respectively.

5. Archibald Douglass Turnbull, *John Stevens: An American Record* (New York: Century, 1928), 8.

6. Ibid., 12–13.

7. Ibid., 22.

8. Ibid., 23.

9. Grace Bayard Stevens Sutton, ed., *Mary Stevens Baird Recollections* (New York: Grace Bayard Stevens Sutton, 1988), 3.

10. John T. Cunningham, *Railroads in New Jersey: The Formative Years* (n.p.: Afton Publishing, 1997), 22.

11. John A. Garraty and Mark C. Carnes, eds., *American National Biography* (New York: Oxford University Press, 1999), 702.

12. George Iles, *Leading American Inventors* (New York: Henry Holt, 1912), 5.

13. Turnbull, *John Stevens,* 274–275.

14. Garraty and Carnes, *American National Biography,* 696.

15. Ibid., 709.

16. Ibid.

17. Moller, *The Hoboken of Yesterday,* vol.1 (Hoboken: The Poggi Press, 1964), 15.

18. Moller, *The Hoboken of Yesterday,* 2:7.

19. Stevens, *Mary Stevens Baird Recollections,* 4.

20. Richard Widdicombe, interview by author, Hoboken, N.J., 9 April 1999.

21. Ibid.

22. "Castle Point," *New York Times* magazine, 18 July 1897.

23. Widdicombe interview.

24. Ibid.

25. John Henry Hammond, *Memories for My Children and Grandchildren* (Minneapolis: Minnesota Historical Society, 1950), 5.

26. "In Memoriam: The Chamber of Commerce Takes Action on the Death of Its Progenitor and Most Active Member," *Superior (Wisconsin) Daily Call,* 2 May 1890.

27. "Estate of Gen. J. H. Hammond," 30 April 1890, Hammond Papers, box 2, Superior Public Library, Superior, Wisconsin. His net worth at the time of death was documented as $560,584.46.

28. Bernardsville History Book Committee, *Among the Blue Hills: Bernardsville . . . A History* (Newark: Johnston Letter Company, 1991), 74.

29. HHF.

30. Ibid.

31. CUOH, 8.

32. Ed Rice, interview by author, Mendham, N.J., 3 December 1999.

33. Ron Brochu, "Court Will Allow Sale of Former Library Property: Proceeds Will Go to Heirs of Ogden H. Hammond," *Daily Telegram,* 20 February 1995.

34. "Hammond Memorial Park Today Officially Presented to the City," *Superior (Wisconsin) Telegram,* 1 July 1912; and "Fitting Tribute Paid to Memory of General Hammond on Occasion of Dedication of New City Park," *Superior (Wisconsin) Telegram,* 2 July 1912.

35. HHF.

36. Widdicombe interview.

## 2 *Battle Cry*

1. Grace Bayard Stevens Sutton, *Mary Stevens Baird Recollections* (New York: Grace Bayard Stevens Sutton, 1988), 114.
2. Ibid.
3. Ibid., 115.
4. Robert D. Ballard with Spencer Dunmore, *Exploring the Lusitania: Probing the Mysteries of the Sinking That Changed History* (New York: Warner Books, 1995), 45.
5. Ibid.
6. Ibid.
7. *New York Times*, 1 May 1915.
8. Des Hickey and Gus Smith, *Seven Days to Disaster: The Sinking of the Lusitania* (Norwalk, Conn.: Easton Press, 1988), 31.
9. A. A. Hoehling and Mary Hoehling, *The Last Voyage of the Lusitania* (New York: Henry Holt and Company, 1956), 43–44.
10. Ogden Hammond Testimony, U.S. District Court for the Southern District of New York, Admiralty Case Files, Case Number A61–169, NARA Northeast Region, New York City, 170.
11. C. L. Droste and W. H. Tantum IV, eds., *The Lusitania Case: Document of the War* (Riverside, Conn.: 7 C's Press, 1972), 158.
12. Thomas A. Bailey and Paul B. Ryan, *The Lusitania Disaster: An Episode in Modern Warfare and Diplomacy* (New York: The Free Press, 1975), 94.
13. Hoehling and Hoehling, *The Last Voyage of the Lusitania*, 66.
14. Ibid., 84.
15. Ballard and Dunmore, *Exploring the Lusitania*, 63.
16. Ogden Hammond to Joseph P. Tumulty, 21 May 1915, microfilm 680–197, NARA, College Park, Maryland.
17. "Ogden H. Hammond Struggled in Vain to Prevent Upsetting," *New York Times*, 10 May 1915; and Droste and Tantum, eds., *The Lusitania Case*, 158 and 161.
18. Ogden Hammond Testimony, NARA, 172.
19. Hammond to Tumulty, 21 May 1915.
20. "Fifty New Yorkers Lost in First Cabin," *New York Times*, 9 May 1915.
21. Bailey and Ryan, *The Lusitania Disaster*, 234.
22. Francis A. March in collaboration with Richard J. Beamish, *History of the World War: An Authentic Narrative of the World's Greatest War* (Chicago: The John C. Winston Company, 1928), 252–253.

## 3 *A Blended Family*

1. HHF.
2. Ibid.
3. Kenneth Reckford, interview by author, Washington, D.C., 30 December 1993.
4. Millicent Fenwick, "In the Days When Summers Seemed Endless," *New York Times*, 14 August 1981.
5. CUOH, 5 February 1980, 4.
6. HHF.
7. Dulany Howland, telephone interview with author, 15 November 1993.
8. HHF, and Erin Ross, telephone interview by author, 16 August 1999.
9. HHF.
10. "Ogden Hammond, Newport Colonist, Former Envoy," *[Newport, R.I.] Daily News*, 30 October 1956.

11. Hammond genealogy, FPC.
12. Des Hickey and Gus Smith, *Seven Days to Disaster: The Sinking of the Lusitania* (Norwalk, Conn.: The Easton Press, 1988), 300.
13. Thomas A. Bailey and Paul B. Ryan, *The Lusitania Disaster: An Episode in Modern Warfare and Diplomacy* (New York: The Free Press, 1975), 273.
14. "The Lusitania," *International Conciliation* (New York: American Association for International Conciliation, November 1918, No. 132), 3–4.
15. Ogden Hammond Testimony, U.S. District Court for the Southern District of New York, Admiralty Case Files, Case Number A61–169, NARA Northeast Region, New York City, 169.
16. Bailey and Ryan, *The Lusitania Disaster*, 304.
17. Ibid., 292.
18. Newspaper clipping [1925], FPC.
19. "Mrs. Hammond Left Million: Will of Woman Lost on Lusitania Filed in New Jersey," *New York Times*, 16 June 1915.
20. HHF.

**4** *Building Character*

1. CUOH, 4 February 1980, 9–10.
2. CUOH, 25 April 1980, 128.
3. Ogden Hammond to Sophia Vernon Hammond, June 1922, FPC.
4. *Charlotte Haxall Noland: 1883–1969* (Richmond, Va.: Whittet and Shepperson, 1971), 36–37.
5. Ibid., 26.
6. CUOH, 18 September 1981, 523.
7. Ibid., 524.
8. *Charlotte Haxall Noland*, 32.
9. *Tally Ho! 1924–1925*, Foxcroft yearbook, 90.
10. *Charlotte Haxall Noland*, 35.
11. *Tally Ho! 1924–1925*, 61.
12. Ibid., 62.
13. CUOH, 527 and 14.
14. CUOH, 525–526.
15. Stanley Osowski, "Thoroughly Marvelous Millicent," *Newark! The Magazine of Metropolitan New Jersey* (Newark: Greater Newark Chamber of Commerce, January 1973), 26.

**5** *Ambassador's Daughter*

1. Letter to Ogden Hammond, [1915], FPC.
2. Ogden Hammond to John McGuinness, 28 March 1917, FPC.
3. [John McGuinness] to James E. Bathgate Jr., 31 August 1917, FPC.
4. Harry E. Barnes, *Report of the Prison Inquiry Commission* (Trenton, N.J.: MacCrellish & Quigley Company, 1917), 1.
5. "New Jersey Man Nominated by President Coolidge to Succeed Moore," *New York World*, 19 December 1925.
6. Walter Edge, *A Jerseyman's Journal: Fifty Years of American Business and Politics* (Princeton, N.J.: Princeton University Press, 1948), 139.
7. Millicent Fenwick, *Speaking Up* (New York: Harper & Row, 1982), 33.
8. Newspaper clipping provided by Walter Hyams & Co., [1925], FPC.
9. Edge, *A Jerseyman's Journal*, 139.

10. HHF.
11. "Hammond May be Appointed to Moore Post: New Jersey Man Mentioned as Next Ambassador to Spain," [*Newark News*], 19 December 1925.
12. Associated Press, "Hammond Made Envoy: Senate Confirms Jerseyman as Ambassador to Spain," *New York Times*, 22 December 1925.
13. Newspaper clippings provided by Walter Hyams & Co., [1925], FPC.
14. "New Jersey Man Nominated."
15. Oliver Nicola to Ogden Hammond, 22 January 1926, FPC.
16. *Chippewa (Wisconsin) Telegram*, [December 1925], FPC.
17. CUOH, 4 February 1980, 32.
18. "Spanish Revolt Crushed, Rivera Declares; Alfonso Balks Plot of Kidnappers," *New York Herald Tribune*, 7 September 1926; and Wilbur Forrest, "King, After All Night Motor Ride, Quells Every Sign of Revolt by Word, as Rest of Spain Yawns in Ignorance of State of Siege," *New York Herald Tribune*, 12 September 1926. Both in Mary Hammond's Scrapbook of Spain, FPC.
19. CUOH, 4 February 1980, 11.
20. Ibid., 8.
21. Ibid., 9.
22. Ibid., 8.
23. FAOH, 4.
24. CUOH, 9–10.
25. Ibid., 10.
26. CUOH, 4 February 1980.
27. Spanish newspaper articles [1926–1927], Mary Stevens Hammond Photograph Album, FPC.
28. Hayden Talbot, "An Interview with His Majesty Don Alfonso XIII— King of Spain" (New York: International Telephone & Telegraph Corporation, 1924), 3. Reprinted from the *New York Sunday American*.
29. CUOH, 13.
30. FAOH, 7, and CUOH, 527.
31. W. French Githens, "Reminiscences of Millicent Fenwick," September 1992, courtesy of G. Dulany Howland.
32. Ibid.
33. Ibid.
34. Ibid.
35. Ibid.
36. Charles Petrie, *King Alfonso XIII and His Age* (London: Chapman & Hall, 1963), 139.
37. HHF.
38. CUOH, 10–11.
39. Githens, "Reminiscences of Millicent Fenwick."
40. CUOH, 14.
41. Ibid., 32.
42. Ibid., 16.
43. "Notables Address Blue Goose Dinner: Herbert Adams Gibbons, Ambassador Hammond and Karl Bickel on Program," *New York Evening Post*, 7 February 1927.
44. CUOH, 25–27.
45. Ibid., 28–31.
46. Helen Worden, "What Society Is Wearing," *New York World*, 1928, FPC.
47. FAOH, 34.
48. CUOH, 38–39.

**6** *Love, Scandal, Marriage*

1. CUOH, 4 February 1980, 40.
2. Ibid., 41.
3. Ibid., 40–41.
4. Ibid., 46.
5. "Banker's Son Dies in Fire That Razes Reeve Schley Home," *New York Times*, 20 April 1931.
6. "Reeve Schley's Son, Fire Victim, Is Buried," *New York Times*, 21 April 1931.
7. Christine Todd Whitman, interview by author, Washington, D.C., 20 December 2001.
8. CUOH, 4 March 1980, 61.
9. "Miss Hammond Weds Count Roberti," *Bernardsville News*, 13 August 1931.
10. Elisabeth Bumiller, "The Wit and Grit of Millicent Fenwick," *Washington Post*, 20 January 1982.
11. HHF.
12. Maureen Fenwick Quinn, interview by author, Bernardsville, N.J., 5 August 1999.
13. Frederick Fenwick to Dean C. M. Greenough, 30 September 1924, courtesy of Harvard University.
14. Bumiller, "The Wit and Grit of Millicent Fenwick."
15. Dean C. M. Greenough to Frederick Fenwick, 2 December 1925, courtesy of Harvard University.
16. CUOH, 4 March 1980, 61.
17. Millicent Fenwick to Amy Schapiro, 26 December 1991.
18. HHF.
19. Ibid.
20. [Cholly Knickerbocker, 1932, *New York American*], FPC.
21. "Miss Hammond Engaged to Wed Hugh Fenwick," *Bernardsville News*, 9 June 1932.
22. "Honeymoon Plane Wrecks as Fenwick Ground-Loop: Neither Flier nor His Bride Is Hurt in Accident in Norristown," [June 1932], FPC.
23. CUOH, 4 February 1980, 47.
24. HHF.
25. Maureen Fenwick Quinn interview.
26. Millicent Fenwick, personal journal, 1 March 1934, FPC.
27. Millicent Fenwick, personal journal, 12 November 1987, FPC. This entry was written shortly after her daughter's death, and Millicent was reminiscing about her daughter's beginning in the world.
28. A series of entries in Millicent Fenwick's personal journal from 28 January 1937 to 12 February 1937 alluded to her pleasure every time her husband visited her in the hospital, even if he stayed only a few minutes. FPC.
29. Millicent Fenwick, personal journal, 31 December 1979. Millicent was reflecting about her marriage decades earlier. FPC.
30. HHF.
31. Annette Lantos, interview by author, Washington, D.C., 19 July 2000.
32. Millicent Fenwick journal, no date [1954], FPC.
33. Roger Bodman, interview by author, Trenton, N.J., 10 April 2000.
34. Gioia Diliberto, "Millicent Fenwick: A Political Maverick Aims to Show That a Woman's Place Is in the House—and the Senate." *People*, 13 September 1982, 60.

## 7 *The* Vogue *Years*

1. Elisabeth Bumiller, "The Wit and Grit of Millicent Fenwick," *Washington Post,* 20 January 1982.
2. Peggy Lamson, *In the Vanguard: Six American Women in Public Life* (Boston: Houghton Mifflin, 1979), 12.
3. *Statistical Abstract of the United States 1938* (Washington, D.C.: U.S. Government Printing Office, 1939).
4. Millicent Fenwick, "The Hand of Esau," [circa 1938], FPC.
5. Lamson, *In the Vanguard,* 11.
6. Elizabeth Nowell to Millicent Fenwick, 4 October 1938, FPC.
7. CUOH, 14 March 1980, 91.
8. Ibid.
9. Ibid., 88–89.
10. Ibid., 89.
11. Lamson, *In the Vanguard,* 11.
12. Carlette Winslow, "In Search of a Good Society," *Suburban Life,* November 1969, 47.
13. Millicent Fenwick to Hugh Fenwick, 24 May 1940, FPC.
14. Hugh Fenwick to Millicent Fenwick, 14 June 1940, FPC.
15. Gioia Diliberto, "Millicent Fenwick: A Political Maverick Aims to Show That a Woman's Place Is in the House—and the Senate," *People,* 13 September 1982, 60.
16. Millicent Fenwick to Hugh Fenwick, [1940], FPC.
17. *Statistical Abstract of the United States 1944–1945, Sixty-Sixth Number* (Washington, D.C.: U.S. Government Printing Office, 1946), 46.
18. HHF.
19. Hugh Fenwick, "The Challenge of Air to American Business Men" (speech presented at The New York Times Hall, New York, 18 June 1942).
20. HHF.
21. Bumiller, "The Wit and Grit of Millicent Fenwick."
22. Millicent Fenwick, "At Vogue," *Vogue,* April 1992, 385.
23. Ibid.
24. Edna Woolman Chase and Ilka Chase, *Always in Vogue* (New York: Doubleday, 1954), 73 and 196.
25. CUOH, 14 March 1980, 93.
26. Connecticut Walker, "Rep. Millicent Fenwick: A Star of the New Congress," *Parade,* 4 May 1975.
27. Caroline Seebohm, *The Man Who Was Vogue: The Life and Times of Condé Nast* (New York: The Viking Press, 1982), 220–221.
28. "Vogue's-Eye View of Flight to South America," *Vogue,* 1 February 1940, 58; and Toni Frissell, personal memoir, courtesy of Sidney Frissell Stafford.
29. Frissell, personal memoir.
30. Ibid.
31. CUOH, 14 March 1980, 99–100.
32. Ibid., 100–101.
33. Ibid., 101.
34. Ibid., 102.
35. Ibid., 123–124.
36. Ibid., 103.
37. Ibid.
38. Ibid.

39. Kenneth J. Reckford, *Mary Stevens Reckford: A Memoir* (Chapel Hill, N.C., 1989), 13–14.
40. CUOH, 25 April 1980, 131.
41. Ibid., 131–132.
42. Ibid., 133.
43. Ibid., 134.
44. Bumiller, "The Wit and Grit of Millicent Fenwick."
45. HHF.
46. Millicent Fenwick, "At Vogue," 385.
47. Lamson, *In the Vanguard*, 12.
48. FAOH, 8.
49. Chase and Chase, *Always in Vogue*, 329–330.
50. CUOH, 14 March 1980, 95–97.
51. Ibid., 97.
52. Seebohm, *The Man Who Was Vogue*, 353.
53. Bumiller, "The Wit and Grit of Millicent Fenwick."
54. CUOH, 25 April 1980, 140–141.
55. Ibid., 141.
56. Seebohm, *The Man Who Was Vogue*, 9.
57. Ibid.
58. Betty Rollin, "We Survive Together," *Parade Magazine*, 8 October 2000, 24.
59. Betty Ford and Chris Chase, *The Times of My Life* (New York: Harper & Row, 1978), 194.
60. CUOH, 25 April 1980, 142.
61. Ibid., 142.
62. Millicent Fenwick, personal letter [to Barbara Williams], 31 January 1979, box 127, MFP.
63. CUOH, 25 March 1980, 145.
64. Millicent Fenwick, "At Vogue," 385.
65. CUOH, 25 April 1980, 144.
66. Ibid., 145.
67. Fenwick, letter to Williams, 31 January 1979.
68. Ibid.
69. Stanley Osowski, "Thoroughly Marvelous Millicent," *Newark! The Magazine of Metropolitan New Jersey*, January 1973, 27.
70. Millicent Fenwick, *Vogue's Book of Etiquette* (New York: Simon and Schuster, 1948), 3, 5, and 8.
71. Ibid.
72. Jean Stafford, "In Congress, New Jersey's Perfect Lady Makes a Tough Campaigner, an Adroit Politician," *Vogue*, June 1975.
73. CUOH, 25 April 1980, 151.
74. Ibid., 152–153.
75. HHF.
76. Legal Agreement between Mary Stevens Baird and Millicent Hammond Fenwick, 17 July 1950, FPC.
77. Jane C. Schoner, [article], *Newark News*, 25 January 1970.

**8** *Retreating to the Country*

1. Bernardsville Board of Education, "Meeting Minutes," 1938.
2. Ogden Hammond to John McGuinness, 1 June 1916, FPC.

3. Stanley Osowski, "Thoroughly Marvelous Millicent," *Newark! The Magazine of Metropolitan New Jersey*, January 1973, 25.
4. CUOH, 4 February 1980, 53.
5. John A. Garraty and Mark C. Carnes, eds., *American National Biography* (New York: Oxford University Press, 1999), 906.
6. Millicent Fenwick, *Speaking Up* (New York: Harper & Row, 1982), 33.
7. Ibid., 33–34.
8. HHF.
9. Karen Foerstel and Herbert N. Foerstel, *Climbing the Hill: Gender Conflict in Congress* (Westport, Conn.: Praeger Publishers, 1996), 16.
10. CUOH, 4 February 1980, 51–52.
11. NAHC, 1.
12. Ibid., 1–4.
13. CUOH, 19 September 1980, 283.
14. Ibid.
15. Millicent Fenwick, journal, 31 December 1969, FPC. She was reminiscing after watching Ella Fitzgerald on a PBS broadcast.
16. HHF.
17. HHF.
18. Kenneth J. Reckford, *Mary Stevens Reckford: A Memoir* (Chapel Hill, N.C., 1989), 37.
19. Ibid., 51.
20. *Report of the Prison Inquiry Commission to Governor Walter E. Edge and the Senate and General Assembly of the State of New Jersey* (Trenton: State of New Jersey, 1918), 3.
21. HHF.
22. HHF.
23. Reckford interview.
24. HHF.
25. 1974 campaign material, n.d. [1974], box 292, MFP.
26. CUOH, 3 July 1980, 257.
27. Father John Torney, interview by author, Somerset, New Jersey, 23 November 1999.
28. CUOH, 3 July 1980, 258.
29. Ibid., 258–259.
30. Ibid., 259.
31. Borough of Bernardsville, "No. 16 Minutes," November 1957 to July 1959.
32. "Your Leadership Manual: A Handbook for National Committeewoman and State Vice-Chairmen of the Republican Party" (Washington, D.C.: Republican National Committee, n.d.), box 297, MFP.
33. Mark Howat, *Record* [magazine supplement], 17 August 1963.
34. Irwin J. Zachar to Millicent Fenwick, 28 October 1960, box 297, MFP.
35. Sophie Glazner to Millicent Fenwick, 22 October 1960, box 297, MFP.
36. Millicent Fenwick to Sophie Glazner, 25 October 1960, box 297, MFP.
37. "Clifford Philip Case [obituary]," *Washington Post*, 9 March 1982.
38. Thomas H. Kean, interview by author, Madison, N.J., 17 August 1993.
39. Rhoda [Lieberman] Denholtz, interview by author, Watchung, N.J., 6 September 2000.
40. Ibid.
41. "Ex-Sen. Case Is Dead at 77; Served 4 Terms," *Newark Star-Ledger*, 7 March 1982.

42. Steve Chambers, "Rabbi Chertoff, Scholar and Activist, Dies at 81," *Newark Star-Ledger*, 27 December 1996.
43. Michael Chertoff, interview by author, Washington, D.C., 10 January 2002.
44. Millicent Fenwick, personal journal, 17 February 1971, FPC; and CUOH, 19 September 1980, 300.
45. CUOH, 19 September 1980, 300.
46. *Blood and History: The Principles of Millicent Fenwick* (Boston: Bogosian Productions, 1989).
47. Millicent Fenwick, [untitled] (speech delivered to Bi-Partisan Conference on Equal Opportunity, Trenton, New Jersey, 19 June 1963. The last sentence of this speech is from the Bible, Micah 6:8, and is the epitaph on her tombstone.
48. Bruce Bahrenburg, "Right Leader on Leave: Mrs. Fenwick Sees Gains from Demonstrations," *Newark News*, 13 October 1963.
49. Millicent Fenwick to Mary Stevens Baird, 2 November 1963, FPC.
50. Millicent Fenwick to Mary Stevens Baird, 10 November 1963, FPC.
51. Millicent Fenwick to Mary Stevens Baird, 15 November 1963, FPC.
52. Ibid.
53. Millicent Fenwick to Mary Stevens Baird, 26 November 1963, FPC.

## 9  Outhouse Millie

1. "Newark Open Meeting, June 29–30, 1966," New Jersey State Advisory Committee to the United States Commission on Civil Rights, Public Housing in the Central Ward, box 296, MFP.
2. Douglas Eldridge, "Invitation to Tenants: Rights Group Seeking Opinions on Central Ward Housing," *Newark Sunday News*, 12 June 1966.
3. Barbara Williams, *Breakthrough: Women in Politics* (New York: Walker, 1979), 99.
4. Barbara Kukla, telephone interview by author, 8 August 2000.
5. Barbara Kukla, "Mary Burch, 95, Newark 'Visionary,'" *Newark Star-Ledger*, 16 August 2001.
6. Bill Payne, interview by author, Newark, 8 September 2000.
7. "Citizen of the Year," *Newark News*, 19 June 1968.
8. Donald Payne, interview by author, Washington, D.C., 18 July 2000.
9. Kukla, "Mary Burch, " and Donald Payne, interview, 18 July 2000.
10. Kenneth Gibson, interview by author, Newark, 1 May 2000.
11. John T. Cunningham, *Newark*, rev. ed. (Newark: New Jersey Historical Society, 1988), 315.
12. HHF.
13. Cunningham, *Newark*, 314.
14. Ibid., 316.
15. "Newark Open Meeting, June 29–30, 1966."
16. Cunningham, *Newark*, 317.
17. Ibid., 322.
18. Ibid., 325.
19. Millicent Fenwick, *Speaking Up* (New York: Harper & Row, 1982), 46.
20. Ibid.
21. Gus Heningburg, interview by author, Newark, 16 May 2000.
22. Ibid.
23. Ibid.
24. Ibid.
25. Associated Press, "Ex-Congresswoman Scared of Backlash: Fenwick Still

Defending Civil Rights," *Morristown (N.J.) Daily Record*, 26 December 1991. Of the fourteen nonwhite apprentices, eleven were black and three were Hispanic.

26. "Probers Told of Bias in Construction Hiring," *Newark Star-Ledger*, 19 March 1970.
27. Connecticut Walker, "Rep. Millicent Fenwick: A Star of the New Congress," *Parade*, 4 May 1975.
28. Judy Bachrach, "Six from the Class of '75 . . . Millicent Fenwick," *Washington Post*, 23 February 1975.
29. James T. Prior, "Profile: Millicent H. Fenwick," *New Jersey Business*, March 1973.
30. Dr. Gershon B. Chertoff to Millicent Fenwick, 3 December 1969, box 292, MFP.
31. Ray Bateman, interview by author, Somerville, N.J., 6 January 1992.
32. John T. McGowan. "Boost for N.J. Women," *Newark News*, 22 March 1970.
33. CUOH, 19 September 1980, 313.
34. Transcript, Conference for Women State Legislators, CAWP, 18–21 May 1972, 162, courtesy of CAWP, Eagleton Institute, Rutgers University.
35. Angelo Baglivo, "Women's Work Law Repeal Up to Cahill," *Newark Evening News*, 2 February 1971.
36. Ibid.
37. Linda Lamendola, "Assembly Panel Finds Kids Need a 'Bill of Rights,'" *Newark Star-Ledger*, 10 May 1971.
38. "Strong Bill on Child Abuse Wins Assembly Approval," *Newark Star-Ledger*, 11 May 1971.
39. FAOH, 14.
40. Ibid.
41. "Charges Fly on State Assembly," *Bernardsville News*, 20 January 1972.
42. Ibid.
43. Millicent Fenwick to John Werring, 17 November 1971, box 292, MFP.
44. Thomas H. Kean, interview by author, Madison, N.J., 17 August 1993.
45. Bateman, interview, 9 January 1992.
46. "Women State Legislators. Report from a Conference for Women in Public Life, May 18–21, 1972, 3, CAWP, and Beth Gillin, "No Taxation without Ms. Representation," *Today: The Philadelphia Inquirer Magazine*, 18 June 1972.
47. Transcript, Conference for Women State Legislators, CAWP, 216.
48. Ibid., 30.
49. Isabelle Shelton, "Battle of Wits," *Washington Star-News*, 29 January 1975.
50. Transcript, Conference for Women State Legislators, 18–21 May 1972, CAWP, 63.
51. Charles J. Garrity and Roger Harris, "Assembly Kills Tax Plan: Governor Acknowledges Defeat, Predicts Soaring Real Estate Levies," *Newark Star-Ledger*, 18 July 1972.
52. Joe Reckford, telephone interview by author, 7 February 2002.
53. Richard W. De Korte to Millicent Fenwick, 23 May 1972, box 292, MFP.
54. Kean, interview, 17 August 1993.
55. Jane Schoener, "[Interview] with a Lady Politician," *Newark News*, 25 January 1970.
56. Angelo Baglivo, "Assembly Passes Measure on Convicts' Voting Rights," *Newark Evening News*, 2 April 1971.
57. Hollis McLoughlin, interview with author, Washington, D.C., 19 March 1992.
58. Robert L. Pierre to Millicent Fenwick, December 1985, FPC.

59. "Flood Plains Bill Signed," *New Jersey Environmental Times,* January 1973, vol. 5, no. 3 (Trenton: New Jersey State Department of Environmental Protection, 1973).
60. Warren Sloat, "Mrs. Fenwick Hailed for Floodplains Bill," *New Brunswick (N.J.) Home News,* 13 December 1972.
61. Leo Carney III, "Cahill Appoints Mrs. Fenwick as Consumer Chief," *Newark Star-Ledger,* 29 November 1972.
62. Stanley Osowski, "Thoroughly Marvelous Millicent," *Newark! The Magazine of Metropolitan New Jersey* (January 1973), 25.
63. Edward J. Gorin, "A Model for Consumers," *Bergen Record,* 29 November 1972.
64. Jeff Laderman, "Fenwick Vows 'Passionate' Concern for Consumer," *Newark Star-Ledger,* 2 January 1973.
65. Ibid., and Janet Bodnar, "She's Passionately Concerned," *New Brunswick (N.J.) Home News,* 5 December 1972.
66. Bodnar, "She's Passionately Concerned."
67. Carney, "Cahill Appoints Mrs. Fenwick."
68. Ceil Kozek, "Consumer Advocate Works to Restore Public's Confidence," *Trenton Daily Times,* 6 March 1973.
69. Kukla, interview, 8 August 2000.
70. CUOH, 19 September 1980, 318.
71. Ibid.
72. Chip Stapleton, "Consumerism Goes to School," *Bridgewater (N.J.) Courier-News,* 28 April 1973.

**10**  *A Geriatric Triumph*

1. *American National Biography* (London: Oxford University Press, 1999), 454.
2. Peggy Lamson, *In the Vanguard: Six American Women in Public Life* (Boston: Houghton Mifflin, 1979), 17.
3. John Davies, telephone interview by author, 2 October 2000.
4. "Wide-Open Race Is Seen for Frelinghuysen's Seat," *New York Times,* 10 March 1974.
5. Joseph F. Sullivan, "GOP Considering Kean for U.S. Race," *New York Times,* 12 March 1974.
6. Thomas H. Kean, *The Politics of Inclusion* (New York: The Free Press, 1988), 131.
7. Lamson, *In the Vanguard,* 19.
8. Millicent Fenwick, "Statement of Candidacy for Fifth Congressional District," 8 April 1974, box 292, MFP.
9. Thomas H. Kean, interview by author, Madison, N.J., 17 August 1993.
10. Ronald Sullivan, "Primary Vote Focuses on 2 Key Races," *New York Times,* 2 June 1974.
11. "Kean Concedes to Mrs. Fenwick," *New York Times,* 21 June 1974.
12. Kean, interview, 17 August 1993.
13. Jack Ewing, interview by author, Bernardsville, N.J., 17 August 1993.
14. Press release, "Fenwick Names Campaign Committee; Kean and Frelinghuysen Agree to Serve," 17 July 1974, box 292, MFP.
15. Roger Bodman, interview by author, Trenton, N.J., 10 April 2000.
16. Ewing, interview, 17 August 1993.
17. Mary Churchill, "A Woman for All Seasons," *New York Times,* 1 December 1974.

18. Lamson, *In the Vanguard*, 21.
19. Karen Foerstel, *Biographical Dictionary of Congressional Women* (Westport, Conn.: Greenwood Press, 1999), 78.
20. Lamson, *In the Vanguard*, 20.
21. Bodman, interview, 10 April 2000.
22. David Neill, interview by author, Bernardsville, N.J., 23 November 1999.
23. Editorial, "New Jersey Endorsements," *New York Times*, 30 October 1974.
24. Lamson, *In the Vanguard*, 19–20.
25. Joseph Sullivan, "Jersey Republicans Lose 4 of 7 Seats in the House," *New York Times*, 6 November 1974.
26. Robert Misseck, "Somerset GOP Credit Fenwick," *Newark Star-Ledger*, 7 November 1974.
27. *Congressional Quarterly*, 9 November 1974 (Washington, D.C.: Congressional Quarterly, Inc., 1974), 3104.
28. Bodman, interview, 10 April 2000.

**11** *The Conscience of Congress*

1. *Congressional Quarterly Weekly Report*, 9 November 1975, 3060.
2. Isabelle Shelton, "Battle of Wits: Millicent Fenwick, a Republican, Puts Down the Men of Capitol Hill," *Washington Star-News*, 29 January 1975.
3. Catherine Rosenshein, interview by author, Montclair, N.J., 23 November 2001.
4. Hollis McLoughlin, interview by author, Washington, D.C., October 1993.
5. Michael Barone, Grant Ujifusa, and Douglas Matthews. *The Almanac of American Politics 1976* (New York: E. P. Dutton, 1976), 537.
6. Corinne (Lindy) Boggs, telephone interview by author, 16 November 2001.
7. Patricia Schroeder, *24 Years of House Work and the Place Is Still a Mess* (Kansas City, Mo.: Andrews McMeel, 1998), 30.
8. Boggs, interview, 16 November 2001.
9. Patricia Schroeder, interview by author, Washington, D.C., 19 December 2001, and Schroeder, *24 Years*, 28–29.
10. Peggy Lamson, *In the Vanguard: Six American Women in Public Life* (Boston: Houghton Mifflin, 1979), 33.
11. Joseph Reckford, telephone interview by author, 3 June 2002.
12. Marge Roukema, interview by author, Washington, D.C., 25 July 2001.
13. Hollis McLoughlin, interview by author, Washington, D.C., 19 March 1992.
14. Connecticut Walker, "Rep. Millicent Fenwick: A Star of the New Congress," *Parade*, 4 May 1975.
15. Sandy Stuart, "Millicent Fenwick—A Personal and Public Life Seem to Be One and the Same," *The Bernardsville News*, 20 May 1982.
16. Sandy Stuart, interview by author, Bernardsville, N.J., 10 January 1992.
17. Judy Bachrach, "Six from the Class of '75 . . . Millicent Fenwick," *Sunday Washington Post*, 23 February 1975.
18. Dennis Teti to J.B. [Jeff Bell], memo, "Fenwick and Abzug—Comparison of Voting Records," 3 May 1982, Box 128a, MFP.
19. Martin Tolchin, "An Odd Couple on Capitol Hill: Daughter of the Bronx and Well-Bred Jersey Lady," *New York Times*, 5 March 1976.
20. Ibid.
21. Lamson, *In the Vanguard*, 25.
22. Ibid.
23. Ibid., 26.

24. Bob Wolthuis to Max L. Friedersdorf, memo, "Viet Nam/Cambodia Congressional Trip," 3 March 1975, John Marsh Files, 1974–1977, box 43, folder Vietnam Congressional Trip 2/75–5/75, Gerald R. Ford Library, Ann Arbor, Mich.

25. President Thieu's speech to the congressional delegation, 1 March 1975, Robert K. Wolthuis Files, box 5, folder Vietnam: Visit by Members of Congress Feb. 1975, Gerald R. Ford Library.

26. Wolthuis to Friedersdorf.

27. President Thieu's speech, 1 March 1975.

28. Memorandum of conversation, 5 March 1975, National Security Adviser, Memorandum of Conversations, 1973–1977, box 9, folder 5 March 1975, Ford, Kissinger, Congressional Vietnam Delegation, Gerald R. Ford Library.

29. Millicent Fenwick, "Military Aid for Vietnam and Cambodia? No," *New York Times,* 21 March 1975.

30. McLoughlin, interview, October 1993.

31. Robert W. Maitlin, "Fenwick Back in Action with Pacemaker Implant," *Newark Star-Ledger,* 1 October 1975.

32. Schroeder, interview, 19 December 2001.

33. Ibid.

34. Reckford, interview, 3 June 2002.

35. Gerald R. Ford, "Statement on the Death of Premier Chou En-lai of the People's Republic of China, 8 January 1976, *Public Papers of the Presidents* (Washington, D.C.: Government Printing Office, 1976), 24–25.

36. Mary Breasted, "China Tour: Warm Talk, Cold Hotels," *New York Times,* 18 January 1976.

37. Ibid.

38. Elisabeth Bumiller, "The Wit & Grit of Millicent Fenwick," *Washington Post,* 20 January 1982.

39. Bill Canis, interview by author, Washington, D.C., 18 May 2001.

40. Bumiller, "Wit & Grit."

41. Bureau of the Census, *Statistical Abstract of the United States* (Washington, D.C.: Government Printing Office, 1979), 425. The median income listed in the text is for 1975 when Elizabeth Ray was on the committee payroll.

42. Marion Clark and Rudy Maxa, "Closed Session Romance on the Hill," *Washington Post,* 23 May 1976.

43. Tom Mathews with Henry W. Hubbard, Anthony Marro, and Jon Lowell, "Capitol Capers," *Newsweek,* 14 June 1976, 18.

44. Walter Kravitz, *Congressional Quarterly's American Congressional Dictionary* (Washington, D.C.: Congressional Quarterly, 1993), 106.

45. CUOH, 15 April 1981, 444.

46. Marlene Adler, assistant to Walter Cronkite, confirmed on his behalf that he did call Millicent Fenwick the "Conscience of Congress," 7 September 2000.

## 12 *Pursuing Human Rights*

1. Raymond Garthoff, *Detente and Confrontation: American-Soviet Relations from Nixon to Reagan,* rev. ed. (Washington, D.C.: Brookings Institution, 1994), 131.

2. William Korey, *Human Rights and the Helsinki Accord: Focus on U.S. Policy* (New York: Foreign Policy Association, 1984), 5.

3. Ibid., 14–15.

4. Garthoff, *Detente and Confrontation,* 611.

5. William Korey, *The Promises We Keep* (New York: St. Martin's Press, 1993), 21–22.
6. President Gerald R. Ford, telephone interview by author, 30 August 2001.
7. Garthoff, *Detente and Confrontation*, 532.
8. Gerald Ford, *A Time to Heal: The Autobiography of Gerald R. Ford* (Norwalk, Conn.: Easton Press, 1987), 301.
9. Gerald R. Ford, "Statement by the President," 25 July 1975, National Security Adviser, National Security Council, Canada, Europe, and Ocean Affairs, box 44, CSCE, 1975 (4) WH, Gerald R. Ford Library, Ann Arbor, Mich.
10. "Meeting with Americans of Eastern European Background to Discuss European Security Conference [outline]," 25 July 1975, box 6, folder: Presidential Meetings with House Members, July 1975, Max L. Friedersdorf Papers, Gerald R. Ford Library.
11. Korey, *Human Rights and the Helsinki Accord*, 16.
12. Ford, *A Time to Heal*, 304–305.
13. Ibid., 305.
14. John J. Maresca, *To Helsinki: The Conference on Security and Cooperation in Europe, 1973–1975*, foreword by William E. Griffith (Durham, N.C.: Duke University Press, 1987), 198.
15. Paul Goldberg, *The Final Act: The Dramatic, Revealing Story of the Moscow Helsinki Watch Group* (New York: William Morrow, 1988), 62.
16. Christopher Wren, telephone interview by author, 6 June 2001.
17. Ibid.
18. Peggy Lamson, *In the Vanguard: Six American Women in Public Life* (Boston: Houghton Mifflin, 1979), 27.
19. Ludmilla Alexeyeva and Paul Goldberg, *The Thaw Generation: Coming of Age in the Post-Stalin Era* (Pittsburgh: University of Pittsburgh Press, 1993), 283.
20. Lamson, *In the Vanguard*, 26–27.
21. Ibid., 27.
22. Yuri Orlov, Grigoriy Podyapolskiy, and Malva Landa, "An Appeal to the United States Congressmen," translated from Russian by Sheila Penner, 11 August 1975, box 181, MFP.
23. Mary Ann Glendon, *A World Made New: Eleanor Roosevelt and the Universal Declaration of Human Rights* (New York: Random House, 2001), 139 and 164.
24. Ibid., 167 and 231.
25. Ibid., xxi and 206.
26. Goldberg, *The Final Act*, 61–62.
27. Lilia Roitburd, conversation with Millicent Fenwick, Moscow, August 1975, translated by Sheila Penner of the Library of Congress, 10 November 1975, box 181, MFP.
28. Paul Goldberg, *The Final Act*, 62; and CUOH, 20 February 1981, 404.
29. CUOH, 20 February 1981, 405.
30. Memo from Arthur A. Hartman to Robert J. McCloskey, Department of State, 11 September 1975, WHCF, subject file FG 430–FG 433, box 216, folder FG 431 CSCE, 8/9/74–6/30/76, Gerald R. Ford Library.
31. Memorandum of conversation, 26 July 1976, Department of State, NSA, NSC Collection, CSCE, 1976 (2) WH folder, box 44, Gerald R. Ford Library.
32. Goldberg, *The Final Act*, 60.
33. Henry Kissinger, *American Foreign Policy*, 3rd ed. (New York: W. W. Norton, 1977), 143.

34. Ibid., 145.
35. Vojtech Mastny, *Helsinki, Human Rights, and European Security* (Durham, N.C.: Duke University Press, 1986), 11.
36. Michael Kraft, telephone interview by author, 22 December 2001.
37. Millicent Fenwick, *Congressional Record*, 23 March, 1976, 7737.
38. "Fenwick Assists in Freeing Russian," press release, 15 March 1976, box 208, MFP.
39. Millicent Fenwick, *Congressional Record*, 23 March 1976, 7737, and "Monitoring Helsinki" [editorial], *Washington Star*, 22 March 1976.
40. CUOH, 20 February 1981, 405.
41. Ibid.
42. *Congressional Record*, 17 May 1976, 14060–14061.
43. Millicent Fenwick, *Congressional Record*, 17 May 1976, 14190.
44. "Congress to Oversee Helsinki Agreement," *Congressional Quarterly*, 29 May 1976, 1409.
45. Korey, *Human Rights and the Helsinki Accord*, 29.
46. Kraft, interview, 22 December 2001.
47. Brent Scowcroft to Max Friedersdorf, White House Memo, 29 May 1976, WHCF–Subject File FG 430–FG 433, box 216, folder FG 431 CSCE 8/7/74 to 6/30/76, Gerald R. Ford Library.
48. Memorandum of Conversation, State Department, 26 July 1976, NSA, NSC Europe, Canada, and Ocean Affairs, box 44, folder CSCE, 1976 (5) WH, Gerald R. Ford Library.
49. President Ford, interview, 30 August 2001.
50. Typed notes, 29 July 1976, Philip Buchen Files: 1974–1977, box 19, folder Helsinki, Gerald R. Ford Library.
51. Michael J. Magner, "Ford Authorizes Panel to Oversee Helsinki Pact," *Newark Star-Ledger*, 4 June 1976.
52. "Ford Visits Great Falls, Assails Reagan Remarks," *Newark Star-Ledger*, 7 June 1976.
53. Ford, *A Time to Heal*, 296.
54. Tanya Melich, *The Republican War Against Women: An Insider's Report from Behind the Lines* (New York: Bantam Books, 1996), 69.
55. White House Communication Agency (WHCA) videotape of NBC coverage of Republican National Convention, 16 August 1976, Gerald R. Ford Library.
56. Betty Ford and Chris Chase, *The Times of My Life* (New York: Harper & Row, 1978), 203.
57. "Fenwick Inspires in Address," *Newark Star-Ledger*, 18 August 1976.
58. Ibid.
59. "Ford Sweeps the Ballots of State Delegates," *Newark Star-Ledger*, 19 August 1976.
60. Lamson, *In the Vanguard*, 29.
61. Memorandum of Conversation, Department of State, 24 August, 1976, National Security Adviser, NSC Europe, Canada, and Ocean Affairs Staff Files, box 45, folder CSCE, 1976 (5) WH, Gerald R. Ford Library.
62. Ibid.
63. Ibid.
64. Korey, *The Promises We Keep*, 30; Gerald R. Ford to Dante Fassell, 2 October 1976, White House Central Files, box 216, Gerald R. Ford Library; and Dante Fassell to Gerald R. Ford, 6 October 1976, National Security Advisor, National Security Council, Canada, Europe, and Ocean Affairs, box 44, CSCE, 1976 (4) WH, Gerald R. Ford Library.

65. Bill Canis, interview by author, Washington, D.C., 16 April 2001.
66. Spencer Oliver, interview with Vajtech Mastny, Washington, D.C., 31 October 1985, cited in Mastny, *Helsinki*, 12.
67. Korey, *Human Rights and the Helsinki Accord*, 30.
68. *Public Papers of the Presidents of the United States: Jimmy Carter Book 1— January 20, 1977–June 24, 1977* (Washington, D.C.: Government Printing Office, 1977), 3.
69. President Ford, interview.
70. Henry Kissinger, *Years of Renewal* (New York: Simon & Schuster, 1999), 639.
71. Canis, interview, 16 April 2001.
72. Madeleine K. Albright and Albert Friendly Jr., "Helsinki and Human Rights," in *The President, the Congress, and Foreign Policy*, ed. Edmund S. Muskie, Kenneth Rush, and Kenneth W. Thompson (Lanham, Md.: University Press of America, 1986), 296.
73. Millicent Fenwick, "The Helsinki Pact," November 1989, courtesy of Bill Canis.

## 13   *Lacey Davenport*

1. Vojtech Mastny, *Helsinki, Human Rights, and European Security: Analysis and Documentation* (Durham: Duke University Press, 1986), 156.
2. Hollis McLoughlin, interview by author, Washington, D.C., 19 March 1992.
3. Michael Kraft, telephone interview by author, 22 December 2001.
4. "House Passes Major Bill Containing Fenwick Anti-Terrorism Amendments," press release, 25 September 1979, box 118, MFP.
5. *Congressional Record*, 11 September 1979, 24040.
6. Kraft, interview.
7. Bill Canis, interview by author, Washington, D.C., 3 April 2001.
8. Larry Rosenshein, interview by author, Upper Montclair, N.J., 23 November 2001.
9. Millicent Fenwick, *Millicent Fenwick Reports to the People of the Fifth District of New Jersey*, 16 January 1975, box 284, MFP.
10. Kraft, interview.
11. Sandy Stuart, interview by author, Bernardsville, N.J., 10 January 1992.
12. Peggy Lamson, *In the Vanguard: Six American Women in Public Life* (Boston: Houghton Mifflin, 1979), 6.
13. Canis, interview.
14. Ibid.
15. Garry Trudeau to Amy Schapiro, 10 August 1993.
16. Peggy Polk, "Ex-Congresswoman Millicent Fenwick Is Still Fighting the Good Fight," *Los Angeles Times*, 1 February 1987.
17. John O. Membrino, "Fenwick Finds 'Lacey' Take-Off 'Jolly,'" *New Brunswick (N.J.) Home News*, 3 July 1977.
18. Lamson, *In the Vanguard*, 31.
19. Membrino, "Fenwick Finds 'Lacey.'"
20. *60 Minutes* transcript, 21 June 1981, 16–17.
21. Scott Seligman, interview by author, Washington, D.C., 30 May 2001.
22. Canis, interview.
23. Lamson, *In the Vanguard*, 6.
24. Ibid.
25. *Congressional Record*, 14 June 1977, 18843.

26. Testimony of the Honorable Millicent Fenwick before the Senate Commerce Committee, 26 June 1979, box 98, MFP.
27. Millicent Fenwick, form letter to members of Congress [Dear Colleague], 7 February 1978, box 127, MFP.
28. "Millicent Fenwick for United State Senate," box 122, MFP.
29. "Top Republican Tax-Writer Acknowledges Fenwick's Leadership in Marriage Tax Relief," press release, 26 January 1982, Rutgers University, Box 122.
30. Rosenshein, interview.
31. Ibid.
32. Cited in "The Roll-Call on Capitol Hill," *New York Times*, 4 January 1978.
33. *Congressional Record*, 16 November 1979, 32864 (personal explanation of Millicent Fenwick stating how she would have voted if she had not been in Cambodia and Thailand on a congressional mission).
34. Associated Press, "Congressional Voting Survey Shows Fenwick More Conservative in 1981," *New Brunswick (N.J.) Home News*, 2 April 1982.
35. Gabriel H. Gluck, "Congressmen Get Report Cards," *Bridgewater (N.J.) Courier-News*, [1982].
36. "Environmentalists Give Fenwick Perfect Rating," press release [1982], box 122, MFP; and "Common Cause Gives Fenwick Perfect Rating," press release, 14 September 1982, box 122, MFP.
37. Millicent Fenwick constituent letter, 13 November 1970, Box 292, MFP.
38. *Congressional Record*, 11 December 1979, 35430.
39. Henry Hyde, telephone interview by author, 17 June 2002.
40. *Congressional Record*, 29 October 1979, 29849.
41. NAHC, 15.
42. Hyde, interview.
43. Edward C. Burks, "Mrs. Fenwick's Day," *New York Times*, 6 March 1977.
44. Series of letters from Edmund Henshaw Jr., Clerk of the U.S. House of Representatives, to Millicent Fenwick, acknowledging her checks to the U.S. Treasury: 26 July 1977; 11 October 1977; 18 January 1978; 18 April 1978; 20 July 1978; 10 January 1979, box 296, MFP.
45. *60 Minutes* transcript, 19.
46. Sophy Burnham, "A Congresswoman Who Cares," *McCall's*, June 1977, 36.
47. United Press International, "Fenwick Raps Special-Interest Contributions," *Atlantic City Press*, 10 November 1982.
48. Lamson, *In the Vanguard*, 5.
49. *Congressional Record*, 23 March 1982, 5239.
50. Tom Lantos, interview by author, Washington, D.C., 19 July 2000.
51. *60 Minutes* transcript.
52. Lantos, interview.
53. Ibid.
54. Ibid.
55. Ibid.
56. Ibid.

**14**  *Seeking the Senate*

1. Michael Barone and Grant Ujifusa, *The Almanac of American Politics 1984* (Washington, D.C.: National Journal, 1983), 726.
2. Carl Schoettler, "Well-Bred Fenwick Eyed for Senate Seat," *Baltimore Evening Sun*, 18 March 1982.
3. Hollis McLoughlin, telephone interview by author, 11 January 2002.

4. Sandra Sugawara, "Redistricting Talk Has Fenwick Talking Senate," *Trenton Times*, 15 September 1981.

5. Ray Bateman, interview by author, Somerville, N.J., 6 January 1992.

6. Millicent Fenwick, journal, 26 November 1981, FPC.

7. "Ex-Sen. Case Is Dead at 77; Served 4 Terms," *Newark Star-Ledger*, 7 March 1982.

8. Jeffrey Bell, telephone interview by author, 15 January 2002.

9. Michael Norman, "Bell-Fenwick Primary Posing Tough Choices," *New York Times*, 28 May 1982.

10. Bell, interview.

11. Ibid.

12. "53 GOP Senators and Congressmen Endorse Fenwick for U.S. Senate" [press release], 3 June 1982, Box 128a, MFP.

13. Bell, interview.

14. Quoted in William E. Geist, "Millicent Fenwick: Marching to Her Own Drum," *New York Times Magazine*, 27 June 1982.

15. Bell, interview.

16. Barone and Ujifusa, *The Almanac of American Politics 1984*, 725.

17. Joseph F. Sullivan, "U.S. Senate Race Tops Jersey Elections," *New York Times*, 31 October 1982.

18. "When a Legend Runs for the Senate," *Newsweek*, [no date] 1982, 38.

19. Barbara Boggs Sigmund, "Editorial Reply," WCBS-TV, 1 October 1982, box 128b, MFP.

20. Brit Hume, "ABC World News Tonight" transcript, 21 October 1982, box 128B, MFP.

21. Mark Harroff, "Analysis of the Electoral Defeat of Hon. Millicent Fenwick," 30 December 1982, 4, FPC.

22. Steven Salmore, "Memo from the Candidate's Pollster: Mrs. Fenwick Stays Home," *New Jersey Reporter*, January 1983, 14.

23. Harroff, "Analysis," 7.

24. Albert R. Hunt, "Millicent Fenwick Is Rich, Feisty, Candid, 72 and Smokes a Pipe," *Wall Street Journal*, 21 May 1982.

25. Lawrence Rosenshein, interview by author, Montclair, N.J., 23 November 2001.

26. James Conaway, "Hype, Hype, Hooray!" (review of *Speaking Up* by Millicent Fenwick), *Washington Post*, 16 May 1982.

27. Norman Cousins, foreword to *Speaking Up*, by Millicent Fenwick (New York: Harper & Row, 1982), xiii.

28. Joseph F. Sullivan, "Root of the Evil Enters Senate Race," *New York Times*, 25 July 1982.

29. Gioia Diliberto, "Millicent Fenwick: A Political Maverick Aims to Show That a Woman's Place Is in the House—and the Senate," *People*, 13 September 1982, 57.

30. McLoughlin interview, 11 January 2002.

31. Rosenshein interview.

32. John Deardourff to Millicent Fenwick, 12 July 1982, FPC.

33. Sullivan, "Root of the Evil."

34. Harroff, "Analysis," 7.

35. Ibid., 13.

36. Rosenshein interview.

37. Frank Lautenberg, interview by author, Washington, D.C., 4 January 2001.

38. Ibid.

39. Ibid.
40. Ward Morehouse III, "Millicent and the Millionaire: Big Bucks, Tough Talk Mean Lively Race," *Christian Science Monitor*, 20 September 1982.
41. Ronald Reagan, "Remarks at the San Gennaro Festival in Flemington, NJ," 17 September 1982, *Public Papers of the U.S. Presidents: Ronald Reagan Book: II—July 3 to December 31, 1982* (Washington, D.C.: U.S. Government Printing Office, 1983), 1180.
42. Rosenshein interview.
43. John Schmidt, interview by author, Chatham, N.J., 3 June 2001.
44. Albert J. Parisi, "New Jersey Journal," *New York Times*, 10 October 1982.
45. Henry Hyde, telephone interview by author, 17 June 2002.
46. Pat Schroeder, interview by author, Washington, D.C., 19 December 2001.
47. Christine Todd Whitman, interview by author, Washington, D.C., 20 December 2001.
48. Rosenshein interview.
49. Gale Scott, "Kissinger: Deaths Won't Block Peace," *Trenton Times*, 25 September 1982.
50. Michael Norman, "Lautenberg Sees Jersey Senate Race as Virtual Tie," *New York Times*, 30 October 1982; and Michael Norman, "Mrs. Fenwick and Lautenberg Meet in Final Debate," *New York Times*, 1 November 1982.
51. Harroff, "Analysis,"19.
52. Arthur K. Lenehan, "Fenwick Can't 'Turn Away' Those in Need," *Newark Star-Ledger*, 13 February 1983; Joseph F. Sullivan, "Jersey Democrat, in First Contest, Upsets Rep. Fenwick for the Senate," *New York Times*, 3 November 1982.
53. Hollis McLoughlin, interview by author, Washington, D.C., 19 March 1992.
54. Sullivan, "Jersey Democrat."
55. Lenehan, "Fenwick Can't."

## 15   *A Little Bit Useful*

1. Mark Harroff to Millicent Fenwick, 3 January 1983, FPC.
2. Donald Robinson, "1982's Top 25 Americans Over 50," *50 Plus*, December 1982, 27.
3. Arthur K. Lenehan, "Fenwick Can't 'Turn Away' Those in Need," *Newark Star-Ledger*, 13 February 1983.
4. Lynn Martin, Bob Michel, Trent Lott, et al., to President Ronald Reagan, 17 December 1982, box 296, MFP.
5. Nicholas F. Brady to Michael K. Deaver, 20 December 1982, box 296, MFP.
6. Barber B. Conable Jr. to President Ronald Reagan, 4 January 1983, box 296, MFP.
7. FAOH, 17.
8. Ronald Reagan, "Remarks at the Republican Women's Leadership Forum in San Diego, California," 26 August 1983, *Public Papers of the President of the United States: Ronald Reagan Book II—July 3 to December 31, 1983* (Washington, D.C.: U.S. Government Printing Office, 1983), 1204.
9. Paul Bedard (State News Service), "No Senate Hearings for Fenwick," *New Brunswick (N.J.) Home News*, 9 July 1983.
10. Ibid.
11. "Statement of Hon. Stephen J. Solarz," *Hearing before the Committee on Foreign Relations United States Senate on the Nomination of Hon. Millicent*

*Fenwick, of New Jersey, for the Rank of Ambassador* (Washington, D.C.: U.S. Government Printing Office,1983), 3–4.

12. "The Basic Text," Food and Agricultural Organization of the United Nations, Volumes I and II, Rome, March 1980, from the Preamble to the FAO Constitution as quoted by Georges Fauriol, "The Food and Agriculture Organization: A Flawed Strategy in the War Against Hunger" (Washington, D.C.: The Heritage Foundation, 1984), 5.

13. George McGovern, telephone interview by author, 16 January 2002.

14. *FAO Fact Sheet* (Rome: United Nations Food and Agriculture Organization, 1999).

15. "Statement of Hon. Millicent Fenwick," *Hearing before the Committee on Foreign Relations United States Senate on the Nomination of Hon. Millicent Fenwick*, 7.

16. U.S. Department of Commerce, Bureau of the Census, *1982 Census of Agriculture: Geographic Area Series Part 30 New Jersey State and County Data* (Washington, D.C.: U.S. Government Printing Office, 1984), 122.

17. State of New Jersey Department of Agriculture, "Overview of New Jersey's Agriculture Industry," http://www.state.nj.us/agriculture/2001.

18. FAOH, 25.

19. HHF.

20. Avram Guroff, interview by author, Washington, D.C., 8 June 1999.

21. HHF.

22. Jonathan Reckford, telephone interview by author, 21 January 2002.

23. Ibid.

24. Fey [von Hassell] Pirzio-Biroli and David Forbes Watt, interview by author, Rome, July 1999; and Fey von Hassell, *Hostage of the Third Reich*, ed. David Forbes Watt (New York: Charles Scribner's Sons, 1989), ix–x.

25. McGovern interview.

26. Giovanni Tedesco, interview by author, Rome, 7 July 1999.

27. Andrew Nagorski, "Millicent Fenwick: A Maverick in Rome," *Newsweek*, 7 November 1983, 14H.

28. Jonathan Reckford interview.

29. Jill Gerston, "Ever-Effervescent Millicent Fenwick," *New Brunswick (N.J.) Home News*, 23 May 1985.

30. FAOH, 20.

31. Miriam Saif, interview by author, Rome, 8 July 1999.

32. Jane Perlez, "New Race Updates Fenwick Style," *New York Times*, 15 January 1982.

33. Ralph Ginzburg, "Fenwick Returns 'Forever' to Where Her 'Roots Are Planted,' " *New York Times*, 15 March 1987.

34. Saif, interview.

35. FAOH, 26.

36. Millicent Fenwick to Susan Powers, 11 December 1983, courtesy of Susan Powers Lodge.

37. FAOH, 28.

38. Millicent Fenwick to George Shultz, 21 April 1986, FPC.

39. George Shultz to Millicent Fenwick, 25 April 1986, FPC.

40. FAOH, 32.

41. McGovern interview.

42. Ginzburg, "Fenwick Returns."

43. "Warning from Abroad," *Newark Star-Ledger*, 30 March 1985.

44. Ibid.

45. Erin Ross, telephone interview by author, 16 August 1999.
46. Saif interview.
47. James Ross, telephone interview by author, 16 August 1999.
48. Kenneth Reckford, interview by author, Washington, D.C., 30 December 1993.
49. Cathy Bugman, "Millicent Fenwick to Resign Post at UN Agency," *Newark Star-Ledger*, 19 December 1986.
50. Ibid.

**16**  *My Way*

1. Ralph Ginzburg, "Fenwick Returns 'Forever' to Where Her 'Roots Are Planted,'" *New York Times*, 15 March, 1987.
2. David Neill, interview by author, Bernardsville, N.J., 23 November 1999.
3. Ibid.
4. Ibid.
5. Ibid.
6. Rudy Larini, "Millicent Fenwick Finds Peace at Home," *Newark Star-Ledger*, 21 June 1987.
7. Ibid.
8. Kenneth J. Reckford, *Mary Stevens Reckford: A Memoir* (Chapel Hill, N.C., 1989), 12–13.
9. Neill interview.
10. Ibid.
11. Ibid.
12. The cartoon original hangs in her Bernardsville home, now the home of Joyce Fenwick, widow of Hugo Fenwick.
13. "*Doonesbury* Redux," *Wall Street Journal*, 3 March 1989.
14. Grace Baird Stevens Sutton, ed., *Mary Stevens Baird Recollections* (New York: Grace Bayard Stevens Sutton, 1988), 119.
15. Richard Widdicombe, interview by author, Hoboken, N.J., 9 April 1999.
16. NAHC, 14.
17. Joan Cook, "At 80, Fenwick Continues to Confront Challenges," *New York Times*, 25 February 1990.
18. Millicent Fenwick to Amy Schapiro, 15 November 1991.
19. Neill interview.
20. Jill Vejnoska and Robin Gaby, "Millicent Fenwick Survives Rumor," *Bridgewater (N.J.) Courier-News*, 7 August 1990.
21. Sam Reckford, interview by author, Short Hills, N.J., November 1993.
22. Larini, "Millicent Fenwick Finds Peace."
23. Bev McCarron, "Fenwick to Head Zimmer Campaign," *Newark Star-Ledger*, 5 September 1990.
24. Christine Todd Whitman, interview by author, Washington, D.C., 20 December 2001.
25. Ibid.
26. HHF.
27. HHF.
28. HHF.
29. HHF.
30. HHF.
31. HHF.
32. Peggy Lamson, *In the Vanguard: Six American Women in Public Life* (Boston: Houghton Mifflin, 1979), 35.

33. "Remarks to AT&T Employees, Basking Ridge, NJ, 18 September 1992," *Public Papers of the Presidents of the United States: George [H.W.] Bush, Book II—August 1, 1992, to January 20, 1993* (Washington, D.C.: U.S. Government Printing Office, 1993), 1591.

34. "Statement on Death of Millicent Fenwick, 16 September 1992," *Public Papers of the Presidents of the United States: George [H.W.] Bush, Book II—August 1, 1992, to January 20, 1993*, 1577; and HHF.

35. Jonathan Reckford, "Grandma" [eulogy], 19 September 1992, courtesy of the Reckford and Fenwick families.

36. Susan Powers Lodge, interview by author, Beverly, Mass., 7 November 2001.

37. John R. Cranford, "The New Class: More Diverse, Less Lawyerly, Younger," *Congressional Quarterly* 50, supplement to no. 44 (7 November 1992): 9.

38. Whitman, interview, 20 December 2001.

39. Quoted in Alison Roth, "Residents Join in Campaign for a Statue of Millicent Fenwick," *New York Times*, 27 November 1994.

40. Helen Walton, telephone interview by author, 8 January 2002.

41. Ibid.

42. Ibid.

43. Millicent Fenwick to Amy Schapiro, 26 December 1991.

44. HHF.

45. Whitman, interview, 20 December 2001.

# Selected

# Bibliography

## Primary Sources

### Archives

Buchen, Philip, Files. Gerald R. Ford Library, Ann Arbor, Mich.
Fenwick, Millicent, Papers. Special Collections and University Archives. Alexander Library, Rutgers University, New Brunswick, N.J.
Fenwick Private Collection. Bernardsville, N.J. Courtesy of Hugh Hammond Fenwick.
Friedersdorf, Max L., Papers. Gerald R. Ford Library, Ann Arbor, Mich.
Hammond, John Henry, Papers. Superior Public Library, Superior, Wis.
National Security Adviser. National Security Council, Canada, Europe, and Ocean Affairs. Gerald R. Ford Library, Ann Arbor, Mich.
White House Central File. Subject File FG 430–FG 433. Gerald R. Ford Library, Ann Arbor, Mich.

### Interviews

Alum, Roland Armando. Interview by author. Hoboken, N.J., 28 November 1999.
Bateman, Raymond. Interview by author. Somerville, N.J., 6 January 1992.
Bell, Jeffrey. Interview by author. Telephone, 15 January 2002.
Bodman, Roger. Interview by author. Trenton, N.J., 10 April 2000.
Boggs, Corinne (Lindy). Interview by author. Telephone, 16 November 2001.
Canis, Bill. Interview by author. Washington, D.C., 3 April 2001.
Chertoff, Michael. Interview by author. Washington, D.C., 10 January 2002.
Cipparulo, Louise. Interview by author. Bernardsville, N.J., 3 December 1999.
Cutting, Mary Pyne. Interview by author. Bedminster, N.J., 1994.
Davies, John O. Interview by author. Telephone, 2 October 2000.
Deisori, Arnaldo. Interview by author. Rome, Italy, 9 July 1999.
Denholtz, Rhoda. Interview by author. Watchung, N.J., 6 September 2000.
Denney, Wayne. Interview by author. Washington, D.C., 30 June 1999.
Ewing, John H. Interview by author. Bernardsville, N.J., 17 August 1993.
Fenwick, Bayard Stevens. Interview by author. Bernardsville, N.J., summer 1993.
Fenwick, Hugh Hammond. Interviews by author. Bernardsville, N.J., 1992–1994 and 1999–2002.
Fenwick, Joyce K. Interview by author. Bernardsville, N.J., 25 August 2001.
Fenwick, Leigh Hammond. Interview by author. Bernardsville, N.J., summer 1993.

Fenwick, Millicent. Interviews by author. Telephone, 29 November 1991 and 7 January 1992.
Fenwick, Sibyl Stevens. Interview by author. Bernardsville, N.J., summer 2001.
Filley, Oliver. Interview by author. Telephone, 24 November 1999.
Forbes Watt, David. Interview by author. Rome, Italy, 7 July 1999.
Ford, Gerald R. Interview by author. Telephone, 30 August 2001.
Frelinghuysen, Rodney. Interview by author. Washington, D.C., 26 July 2001.
Gibson, Kenneth. Interview by author. Newark, N.J., 1 May 2000.
Githens, W. French (Bill), Interview by author. McLean, Va., 11 December 1993.
Gray, Sarah Reckford. Interview by author. Short Hills, N.J., 27 November 1993.
Guroff, Avram (Buzz). Interview by author. Washington, D.C., 8 June 1999.
Heningburg, Gustav. Interviews by author. Newark, N.J., 16 May 2000, and telephone, 14 December 2001.
Howland, G. Dulany. Interview by author. Telephone, 15 November 1993.
Hyde, Henry. Interview by author. Telephone, 17 June 2002.
Kean, Thomas H. Interview by author. Madison, N.J., 17 August 1993.
Kleeman, Katherine. Interview by author. New Brunswick, N.J., 1 June 2001.
Killingsworth, Kay. Interview by author. Rome, Italy, 7 July 1999.
Kraft, Michael. Interview by author. Telephone, 22 December 2001.
Kukla, Barbara. Interview by author. Telephone, 8 August 2000.
Lantos, Annette. Interview by author. Washington, D.C., 18 July 2000.
Lantos, Tom P. Interview by author. Washington, D.C., 18 July 2000.
Lautenberg, Frank. Interview by author. Washington, D.C., 4 January 2001.
Lodge, Susan Powers. Interview by author. Beverly, Mass., 7 November 2001.
Mandel, Ruth B. Interview by author. New Brunswick, N.J., 1 June 2000.
Martindell, Anne Clark. Interview by author. Princeton, N.J., 19 July 1999.
McGovern, George. Interview by author. Telephone, 16 January 2002.
McLoughlin, Hollis. Interviews by author. Washington, D.C., 19 March 1992 and October 1993, and telephone, 7 April 1992 and 11 January 2001.
McNamara, John J. Interview by author. Telephone, 14 July 2001.
Miranda, John. Interview by author. Telephone, 8 June 1999.
Neill, David A. Interview by author. Bernardsville, N.J., 23 November 1999.
Oliver, Sheila. Interview by author. Telephone, 4 August 2000.
Payne, Donald. Interview by author. Washington, D.C., 18 July 2000.
Payne, William. Interview by author. Newark, N.J., 8 September 2000.
Penn, John S. Interview by author. Bedminster, N.J., 25 August 2001.
Perez de Vega, Javier. Interview by author. Rome, Italy, 8 July 1999.
Quinn, Maureen Fenwick. Interview by author. Bernardsville, N.J., 5 August 1999.
Reckford, Jonathan. Interview by author. Telephone, 21 January 2002.
Reckford, Joseph. Interviews by author. Telephone, 7 February 2002 and 3 June 2002.
Reckford, Kenneth. Interview by author. Washington, D.C., 30 December 1993.
Reckford, Samuel. Interview by author. Short Hills, N.J., 27 November 1993.
Rice, Edward. Interview by author. Bernardsville, N.J., 3 December 1999.
Rosenshein, Lawrence. Interview by author. Upper Montclair, N.J., 23 November 2001.
Rosenshein, Catherine Scott. Interview by author. Upper Montclair, N.J., 23 November 2001.
Ross, Erin. Interview by author. Telephone, 16 August 1999.
Ross, James. Interview by author. Telephone, 16 August 1999.
Roukema, Marge. Interview by author. Washington, D.C., 25 July 2001.
Saif, Miriam. Interview by author. Rome, Italy, 8 July 1999.

Schmidt, John. Interview by author. Chatham, N.J., 3 June 2001.
Schroeder, Patricia. Interview by author. Washington, D.C., 19 December 2001.
Seligman, Scott. Interview by author. Washington, D.C., 30 May 2001.
Solarz, Stephen. Interview by author. McLean, Va., 8 April 2001.
Stuart, Sandy. Interviews by author. Bernardsville, N.J., 10 January 1992, and telephone, April 1992.
Tedesco, Giovanni. Interview by author. Rome, Italy, 7 July 1999.
Thackston, Larry. Interview by author. Telephone, 1 June 1999.
Torney, John. Interview by author. Somerset, N.J., 1 December 1999.
Trenner, Richard. Interview by author. Princeton, N.J., 28 April 2000.
von Hassell, Fey [Pirzio-Biroli]. Interview by author. Rome, Italy, 7 July 1999.
Walton, Helen. Interview by author. Telephone, 8 January 2001.
Whitman, Christine Todd. Interview by author. Washington, D.C., 20 December 2001.
Widdicombe, Richard. Interview by author. Hoboken, N.J., 9 April 1999.
Wilmerding, Harold. Interview by author. Mendham, N.J., 25 August 2001.
Wilmerding, Joannah. Interview by author. Mendham, N.J., 25 August 2001.
Wren, Christopher. Interview by author. Telephone, 6 June 2001.
Wyatt, Jane. Interview by author. Telephone, 27 May 1999.

## Oral Histories/Transcripts

Conference for Women State Legislators, convened by the Center for American Women and Politics, May 18–21, 1972. Transcript Courtesy of Ruth B. Mandel, Center for the American Woman and Politics, Eagleton Institute of Politics, Rutgers University, New Brunswick, N.J.
"Interview with the Honorable Millicent Fenwick, former member of the House of Representatives, from the state of New Jersey." National Association of Home Care, Washington D.C., [1989]. Courtesy of Hugh Hammond Fenwick.
Jessup, Peter. "Interviews with Rep. Millicent Fenwick." Columbia University Oral History, 1980–1981. Courtesy of Hugh Hammond Fenwick.
Miller, Robert. "Oral History of Millicent Hammond Fenwick." Women Ambassadors Project. Foreign Affairs Oral History Collection. National Foreign Affairs Training Center of the Department of State, December 1985.

## Published Sources

Abbott, John. *Politics and Poverty: A Critique of the Food and Agriculture Organization of the United Nations.* London: Routledge, 1992.
Abzug, Bella, and Mim Kelber. *Gender Gap: Bella Abzug's Guide to Political Power for American Women.* Boston: Houghton Mifflin, 1984.
Alexeyeva, Ludmilla, and Paul Goldberg. *The Thaw Generation: Coming of Age in the Post-Stalin Era.* Pittsburgh: University of Pittsburgh Press, 1993.
Armour, Robert E. *Superior Wisconsin: A Planned City.* Superior, Wis.: Robert E. Armour/Telegram Commercial Printing Division, 1976.
———. *Superior, Wisconsin 1857–1885.* Superior, Wis.: Robert E. Armour/Silver-Tonsberg Printing, 1994.
Bailey, Thomas A., and Paul B. Ryan. *The Lusitania Disaster: An Episode in Modern Warfare and Diplomacy.* New York: The Free Press, 1975.
Ballard, Robert, and Spencer Dunmore. *Exploring the Lusitania: Probing the Mysteries of the Sinking That Changed History.* New York: Warner Books, 1995.

Barnes, Harry E. *State of New Jersey: Report of the Prison Inquiry Commission. Vol. 2.* Trenton, N.J.: MacCrellish & Quigley Co., Printers, 1917.

Barone, Michael, Grant Ujifusa, and Douglas Matthews. *The Almanac of American Politics 1976.* New York: E. P. Dutton, 1976.

Barone, Michael, and Grant Ujifusa. *The Almanac of American Politics 1982.* Washington, D.C.: Barone & Company, 1982.

———. *The Almanac of American Politics 1984.* Washington, D.C.: National Journal, 1984.

Bernardsville History Book Committee. *Among the Blue Hills . . . Bernardsville . . . A History.* Newark, N.J.: Johnston Letter Company, 1991.

*Blood and History: The Principles of Millicent Fenwick.* Boston: Bogosian Productions [WGBH], 1989. Videocassette.

Bowers, Claude G. *My Mission to Spain: Watching the Rehearsal for World War II.* New York: Simon and Schuster, 1954.

Carroll, Susan J. *Women as Candidates in American Politics.* 2nd ed. Bloomington: Indiana University Press, 1994.

Casey, Robert J., and W.A.S. Douglas. *The Lackawanna Story: The First Hundred Years of the Delaware, Lackawanna and Western Railroad.* New York: McGraw-Hill, 1951.

*Charlotte Haxall Noland 1883–1969.* Richmond, Va.: Whittel and Shepperson/ Foxcroft School, 1971.

Chase, Edna Woolman, and Ilka Chase. *Always in Vogue.* Garden City, N.Y.: Doubleday, 1954.

Cunningham, John T. *Newark.* Rev. ed. Newark, N.J.: New Jersey Historical Society, 1988.

———. *Railroads in New Jersey: The Formative Years.* N.p.: Afton Publishing, 1997.

———. *This Is New Jersey.* 4th ed. New Brunswick, N.J.: Rutgers University Press, 1994.

Droste, C. L., and W. H. Tantum IV, eds. *The Lusitania Case: Documents on the War.* Riverside, Conn.: 7 C's Press,1972.

Edge, Walter Evans. *A Jerseyman's Journal: Fifty Years of American Business and Politics.* Princeton, N.J.: Princeton University Press, 1948.

Elliott, Howard. "The City of Superior: The Northern Pacific Railway and Their Future Growth." Rotary Club of Superior, Superior, Wis., 7 January 1913.

Fauriol, Georges. *The Food and Agriculture Organization: A Flawed Strategy in the War Against Hunger.* Washington, D.C.: The Heritage Foundation, 1984.

Fenwick, Millicent. *Speaking Up.* New York: Harper & Row, 1982.

———.*Vogue's Book of Etiquette: A Complete Guide to Traditional Forms and Modern Usage.* New York: Simon and Schuster, 1948.

Fireside, Bryna J. *Is There a Woman in the House . . . or Senate?* Morton Grove, Ill.: Albert Whitman & Company, 1994.

Flower, Frank A. *The Eye of the North-West.* Milwaukee: King, Fowle & Co., 1890.

Foerstel, Karen. *Biographical Dictionary of Congressional Woman.* Westport, Conn.: Greenwood Press, 1999.

Foerstel, Karen, and Herbert N. Foerstel. *Climbing the Hill: Gender Conflict in Congress.* Westport, Conn.: Praeger Publishers, 1996.

Ford, Betty, and Chris Chase. *The Times of My Life.* New York: Harper & Row, 1978.

Ford, Gerald R. *A Time to Heal: The Autobiography of Gerald R. Ford.* Norwalk, Conn.: Easton Press, 1987.

Garraty John A., and Mark C. Carnes, eds. *American National Biography.* New York: Oxford University Press, 1999.

Garthoff, Raymond L. *Detente and Confrontation: American Soviet Relations from Nixon to Reagan.* Rev. ed. Washington, D.C.: The Brookings Institution, 1994.

Glendon, Mary Ann. *A World Made New: Eleanor Roosevelt and the Universal Declaration of Human Rights.* New York: Random House, 2001.

Goldberg, Paul. *The Final Act: The Dramatic Revealing Story of the Moscow Helsinki Watch Group.* New York: William Morrow, 1988.

Graham, Evelyn. *The Life Story of King Alfonso XIII.* London: Herbert Jenkins Limited, 1930.

———. *The Queen of Spain: An Authorized Life-Story.* London: Hutchinson & Co., 1929.

Hammond, John, and Irving Townsend. *John Hammond on Record.* New York: Ridge Press/Summit Books, 1977.

Hammond, John Henry. *Memories for My Children and Grandchildren.* Minneapolis: Minnesota Historical Society, 1950.

Hickey, Des, and Gus Smith. *Seven Days to Disaster.* Norwalk, Conn.: Easton Press, 1962.

Hoehling, A. A., and Mary Hoehling. *The Last Voyage of the Lusitania.* New York: Henry Holt, 1956.

Iles, George. *Leading American Inventors.* New York: Henry Holt, 1912.

Kean, Thomas H. *The Politics of Inclusion.* New York: The Free Press, 1988.

Kirkpatrick, Jeanne J. *Political Woman.* New York: Basic Books, 1974.

Kissinger, Henry. *Years of Renewal.* New York: Simon & Schuster, 1999.

Korey, William. *Human Rights and the Helsinki Accord: Focus on U.S. Policy.* New York: Foreign Policy Association, 1984.

———. *The Promises We Keep.* New York: St. Martin's Press, 1993.

Lamson, Peggy. *In the Vanguard: Six American Women in Public Life.* Boston: Houghton Mifflin, 1979.

Lane, Wheaton J. *From Indian Trail to Iron Horse: Travel and Transportation in New Jersey 1620–1860.* Princeton, N.J.: Princeton University Press, 1939.

Leebaert, Derek, ed. *European Security: Prospects for the 1980s.* Lexington, Mass.: Lexington Books, 1979.

"The Lusitania." *International Conciliation.* Nos. 122 and 132. New York: American Association for International Conciliation, 1918.

McClure, Sandy. *Christie Whitman—For the People: A Political Biography.* Amherst, N.Y.: Prometheus Books, 1996.

McCormick, Richard, *Experiment in Independence: New Jersey in the Critical Period 1781–1789.* New Brunswick, N.J.: Rutgers University Press, 1950.

McCormick, Richard P., and Katheryne C. McCormick. *Equality Deferred: Women Candidates for the New Jersey Assembly 1920–1993.* New Brunswick, N.J.: Center for the American Woman and Politics, Eagleton Institute of Politics, Rutgers University, 1994.

March, Francis A., in collaboration with Richard J. Beamish. *History of the World War: An Authentic Narrative of the World's Greatest War.* Chicago: John C. Winston, 1928.

Maresca, John J. *To Helsinki: The Conference on Security and Cooperation in Europe 1973–1975.* Durham, N.C.: Duke University Press, 1987.

Mastny, Vojtech. *Helsinki, Human Rights, and European Security.* Durham, N.C.: Duke University Press, 1986.

————. *The Helsinki Process and the Reintegration of Europe, 1986–1991: Analysis and Documentation.* New York: New York University Press, 1992.

Melich, Tanya. *The Republican War Against Women: An Insider's Report from Behind the Lines.* New York: Bantam Books, 1996.

Mershart, Ronald V. *Pioneers of Superior, Wisconsin.* Roseville, Minn.: Park Genealogical Books, 1996.

*Millicent Fenwick: A Lesson in Leadership.* Newark, N.J.: Caucus New Jersey, 1991. Videocassette.

Moller, George Long. *The Hoboken of Yesterday.* 2 vols. Hoboken, N.J.: The Poggi Press, 1964 and 1966.

Petrie, Charles. *King Alfonso XIII and His Age.* London: Chapman & Hall,, 1963.

Reckford, Kenneth. *Mary Stevens Reckford: A Memoir.* Chapel Hill, N.C., 1989.

*Report of the New Jersey State Civil Service Investigation Committee, 1916.* Trenton, N.J.: MacCrellish & Quigley Co., State Printers, 1917.

*Report of the Prison Inquiry Commission to Governor Walter E. Edge and the Senate and General Assembly of the State of New Jersey.* Vol. 1. Trenton, N.J.: [Prison Inquiry Commission], 1 January 1918.

Schroeder, Patricia. *24 Years of House Work . . . and the Place Is Still a Mess: My Life in Politics.* Kansas City, Mo.: Andrews McMeel Publishing, 1998.

Seebohm, Caroline. *The Man Who Was Vogue: The Life and Times of Condé Nast.* New York: Viking, 1982.

Sencourt, Robert. *King Alfonso: A Biography.* London: Faber and Faber, 1942.

Stafford, Sidney Frissell, and George Plimpton. *Toni Frissell Photographs: 1933–1967.* New York: Doubleday, 1994.

Stevens, John. *Observations on Government, including some Animadversions on Mr. Adams's Defence of the Constitutions of Government of the United States of America and on Mr. De Lolme's Constitution of England.* New York: W. Ross, 1787.

Studley, Miriam V., Charles F. Cummings, and Thaddeus J. Krom. *Guide to the Microfilm Edition of the Stevens Family Papers.* Newark, N.J.: New Jersey Historical Society, 1968.

Sutton, Grace Bayard Stevens. *Mary Stevens Baird Recollections.* New York: Grace Bayard Stevens Sutton, 1988.

Talbot, Hayden. *An Interview with the King of Spain, His Majesty Don Alfonso XIII.* New York: International Telephone & Telegraph Corporation, 1924. Reprinted from the *New York Sunday American.*

Talmey, Allene, ed. *People Are Talking about . . . People and Things in Vogue.* Englewood Cliffs, N.J.: Prentice-Hall, 1969.

Thurston, R. H. *The Messrs. Stevens, of Hoboken, as Engineers, Naval Architects and Philanthropists.* Philadelphia: Wm. P. Kildare, 1874.

Turnbull, Archibald Douglas. *John Stevens: An American Record.* New York: Century, 1928.

U.S. Helsinki Watch Committee. *The Moscow Helsinki Monitors: Their Vision, Their Achievement, the Price They Paid. May 12, 1976–May 12, 1986.* U.S. Helsinki Watch Committee, 1986.

von Hassell, Fey [Fey Pirzio-Biroli]. *Hostage of the Third Reich.* Edited by David Forbes Watt. New York: Charles Scribner's Sons, 1989.

Williams, Barbara. *Breakthrough: Women in Politics.* New York: Walker, 1979.

Winfield, Charles H. *Hopoghan Hackingh: Hoboken a Pleasure Resort for Old New York.* New York: The Caxton Press, 1895.

*Women in Congress, 1917–1990.* Washington, D.C.: Government Printing Office, 1991.

*Women State Legislators: Report from a Conference, May 18–21, 1972.* Center for the American Woman and Politics, Eagleton Institute of Politics, Rutgers University. New Brunswick, N.J.: Center for the American Woman and Politics, 1973.

Woods, Harriet. *Stepping Up to Power: The Political Journey of American Women.* Boulder, Colo.: Westview Press, 2000.

# Index

## About the Author

Amy Schapiro is a native New Jerseyan who currently resides in the Washington, D.C., area and works at the U.S. Department of Justice.

AAZ-5119